NEW DIRECTIONS IN GENOCIDE

Genocide studies is a relatively new field of comparative inquiry, but recent years have seen an increasing range of themes and subject-matter being addressed that reflect a variety of features of the field and transformations within it. This edited book brings together established scholars with rising stars and seeks to capture the range of new approaches, theories, and case studies in the field.

The book is divided into three broad sections:

- **Section I** focuses on broad theories of comparative genocide, covering a number of different perspectives.
- **Section II** critically reconsiders core themes of genocide studies and unfolds a range of challenging new directions, including cultural genocide, gender and genocide (as it pertains to both women and men), structural violence, and the novel application of remote-sensing technologies to the detection and study of genocide.
- **Section III** is case-study focused, seeking to place both canonical and little-known cases of genocide in broader comparative perspective. Cases analyzed include genocide in North America, the Nazi Holocaust, the Armenian genocide, and the Sri Lankan genocide.

The combination of cutting-edge scholarship and innovative approaches to familiar subjects makes this essential reading for all students and scholars in the field of genocide studies.

Adam Jones is Associate Professor of Political Science at the University of British Columbia Okanagan in Kelowna, Canada. His recent books include *Genocide: A Comprehensive Introduction* (2nd edition, 2010) and *Gender Inclusive: Essays on Violence, Men, and Feminist International Relations* (2009).

Fresh, critical, and original, these essays highlight the destructive dimensions of modern governmentality and gender orders so often overlooked by conventional genocide studies. They crackle with insight.

A. Dirk Moses, European University Institute, Florence, Italy

A stimulating and sometimes provocative collection which ranges wide across the burgeoning field of genocide research and showcases valuable new contributions to the field.

Martin Shaw, Research Professor, Institut Barcelona d'Estudis Internacionals and Sussex University, and Professorial Fellow in International Relations and Human Rights, University of Roehampton, London, UK

Genocide studies is a fast-moving, interdisciplinary field. Adam Jones's formidable team of scholars not only provides readers with compelling examples of the insights that are driving the field, but skilfully guides them through the maze of competing interpretations.

Dan Stone, Royal Holloway, University of London, UK

NEW DIRECTIONS IN GENOCIDE RESEARCH

Edited by Adam Jones

Routledge
Taylor & Francis Group

LONDON AND NEW YORK

First published 2012 by Routledge
2 Park Square, Milton Park, Abingdon, Oxon, OX14 4RN

Simultaneously published in the USA and Canada
by Routledge
711 Third Avenue, New York, NY 10017

Routledge is an imprint of the Taylor & Francis Group, an informa business

British Library Cataloguing in Publication Data
A catalogue record for this book is available from the British Library

Library of Congress Cataloging in Publication Data
New directions in genocide research / edited by Adam Jones.
p. cm.
Includes bibliographical references and index.
ISBN 978–0-415–49596–7 (alk. paper) — ISBN 978–0–415–49597–4 (alk. paper)
— ISBN 978–0–203–69832–7 (ebk.) 1. Genocide—Research.
2. Genocide—Research—Methodology. 3. Genocide—Case studies.
I. Jones, Adam, 1963–
HV6322.7.N47 2011
304.6'63—dc22
2011015594

ISBN: 978–0–415–49596–7 (hbk)
ISBN: 978–0–415–49597–4 (pbk)
ISBN: 978–0–203–69832–7 (ebk)

Typeset in Adobe Garamond by
Keystroke, Station Road, Codsall, Wolverhampton

MIX
Paper from
responsible sources
FSC   FSC® C004839
www.fsc.org

Printed and bound in Great Britain by
TJ International Ltd, Padstow, Cornwall

CONTENTS

FIGURES

TABLES

NOTES ON THE CONTRIBUTORS

Paula Drumond is Lecturer at the Institute of International Relations at the Pontifical Catholic University of Rio de Janeiro, Brazil. She holds an M.A. in International Relations from the Pontifical Catholic University of Rio de Janeiro (PUC-Rio, 2010). Her research has focused on genocide studies, gender, and international security. Drumond has Bachelor's degrees in Law from the State University of Rio de Janeiro (UERJ, 2006) and in International Relations from the Pontifical Catholic University of Rio de Janeiro (PUC-Rio, 2007). In 2009, she was granted an Outstanding Academic Performance Scholarship from the Rio de Janeiro State Research Foundation (FAPERJ). Email: pdrumond@gmail.com.

Daniel Feierstein holds a Ph.D. in Social Sciences from the University of Buenos Aires, Argentina, where he founded and holds the Chair of Genocide. He is also Director of the Center for Genocide Studies at the National University of Tres de Febrero, Argentina. He is the second Vice President of the International Association for Genocide Scholars (IAGS, 2009–2011), and was a consultant to the United Nations in the preparation of Argentina's National Plan to Combat Discrimination (2004–2006) and National Human Rights Plan (2007–2008). His recent books include *El genocidio como práctica social. Entre el nazismo y la experiencia argentina* (Genocide as a Social Practice. Between Nazism and the Experience of Argentina, 2007, forthcoming in French, English, and German translation); *Terrorismo de estado y genocidio en América Latina* (State Terrorism and Genocide in Latin America, 2009) and *State Violence and Genocide in Latin America* (with Marcia Esparza and Henry Huttenbach) (2010). Email: dfeierstein@untref.edu.ar.

Donna-Lee Frieze, Ph.D., is a Research Fellow at the School of History, Heritage and Society, Deakin University, Melbourne. She is collaborating with a team of historians and museologists on a history of the Melbourne Jewish Holocaust Centre. Her teaching and research areas include genocide studies, film, and philosophy. Email: donna-lee.frieze@deakin.edu.au.

Carol Jean Gallo has a B.F.A. in Film and has held positions at Amnesty International USA, the International Center for Transitional Justice, and the Yale Council on African Studies. She earned her M.S. in Global Affairs from New York University (NYU) and her M.A. in African Studies from Yale. She was a consultant in the UN Department of

Peacekeeping Operations where she advised on disarmament, demobilization and reintegration (DDR) in Darfur. In fall 2011, she began work on her Ph.D. at Cambridge University. Email: carol.gallo42@gmail.com.

Adam Jones, Ph.D. (editor) is the author of *Genocide: A Comprehensive Introduction* (2nd edition, 2010), and author or editor of a dozen other books, including *Gender Inclusive: Essays on Violence, Men, and Feminist International Relations* (2009), *Crimes Against Humanity: A Beginner's Guide* (2008), and *Genocide, War Crimes and the West: History and Complicity*. He is Associate Professor of Political Science at the University of British Columbia Okanagan in Kelowna, Canada, and Executive Director of Gendercide Watch (www.gendercide.org), a web-based educational initiative. He held a postdoctoral fellowship in Yale University's Genocide Studies Program from 2005 to 2007. Jones serves as book review editor of the *Journal of Genocide Research*, sits on the Advisory Board of the International Association of Genocide Scholars (IAGS), and was selected as one of *Fifty Key Thinkers on the Holocaust and Genocide* for the book of that title. Email: adamj_jones@hotmail.com.

Benjamin Lieberman, Ph.D., is Professor of History at Fitchburg State University, USA. He is the author of *Terrible Fate: Ethnic Cleansing in the Making of Modern Europe* (2006). His research focuses on genocide and identity. Email: BLieberman@fitch burgstate.edu.

Benjamin Madley, Ph.D., is an Andrew Mellon Postdoctoral Fellow at Dartmouth College, where he teaches History and Native American Studies. Educated at Yale and Oxford, he studies the United States and Native America but has also written about colonial genocides in Africa, Australia, and Europe, often applying a transnational and comparative approach. Ben's articles include: "California's Yuki Indians: Defining Genocide in Native American History" (*The Western Historical Quarterly*, 2008); "From Terror to Genocide: Britain's Tasmanian Penal Colony and Australia's History Wars" (*Journal of British Studies*, 2008); "From Africa to Auschwitz: How German South West Africa Incubated Ideas and Methods Adopted and Developed by the Nazis in Eastern Europe" (*European History Quarterly*, 2005); and "Patterns of Frontier Genocide, 1803–1910: The Aboriginal Tasmanians, the Yuki of California, and the Herero of Namibia" (*Journal of Genocide Research*, 2004). Ben is currently turning his dissertation, "American Genocide: The California Indian Catastrophe, 1846–1873," into a book. Email: Benjamin.L.Madley@Dartmouth.edu.

Christopher J. Powell, Ph.D., is an Assistant Professor at the University of Manitoba in Winnipeg, Canada. His book *Barbaric Civilization: A Critical Sociology of Genocide* (2011) examines how Western civilization systematically produces genocidal violence. He is also the author of "Four Concepts of Morality," in the *Handbook of the Sociology of Morality* (2010), "The Wound at the Heart of the World," in *Evoking Genocide: Scholars and Activists Describe the Works that Shaped Their Lives* (2009), and "What Do Genocides Kill? A Relational Sociology of Genocide," *Journal of Genocide Research* (2007). Email: chris_powell@umanitoba.ca.

Russell F. Schimmer is a dual-degree J.D.–Ph.D. student at the University of Connecticut (UConn). His Ph.D. research in the Department of Natural Resources and the Environment focuses specifically on geomatics. After graduating from Yale University in 2005, Schimmer worked for three years with the Yale Genocide Studies Program under the direction of Professor Ben Kiernan, documenting genocide activities using spaceborne remote sensing imagery. He has continued this research at UConn. His legal interests are primarily in developing approaches to spaceborne remote sensing evidence obtention and admissibility, and land use management. Schimmer also researches the environmental and social impacts of large-scale mineral-extraction processes, primarily global copper and gold mining. Email: russell. schimmer@siasglobal.com.

David J. Simon is a Lecturer in Political Science at Yale University. His work addresses the Rwandan genocide and its aftermath. He also works on the topic of genocide prevention. He holds a Ph.D. in Political Science from the University of California, Los Angeles. Email: david.simon@yale.edu.

Benita Sumita was a television journalist in India before moving to Sri Lanka as a researcher at the International Centre for Ethnic Studies in Colombo. She later worked at the United Nations Development Programme (UNDP) in New Delhi. She holds an M.Sc. in Violence, Conflict and Development from the School of Oriental and African Studies (SOAS), University of London. Currently, she is doing her doctoral research on rethinking the development and dynamics of international norms, examining the case of the 1998 UN Guiding Principles on Internal Displacement. Email: benitasumita@ gmail.com.

Uğur Ümit Üngör, Ph.D., is Assistant Professor of History at Utrecht University and affiliated with the Centre for War Studies of University College, Dublin and the Center for Holocaust and Genocide Studies in Amsterdam. His main area of interest is the historical sociology of mass violence and nationalism. His most recent publications include *Confiscation and Destruction: The Young Turk Seizure of Armenian Property* (2011), and *The Making of Modern Turkey: Nation and State in Eastern Anatolia, 1913–1950* (2011), which was awarded the 2010 Erasmus Research Prize. Email: ugur_ungor@yahoo.com.

Ernesto Verdeja, Ph.D., is Assistant Professor of Political Science and Peace Studies in the Department of Political Science and Kroc Institute for International Peace Studies at the University of Notre Dame, USA. He is the author of *Unchopping a Tree: Reconciliation in the Aftermath of Political Violence* (2009) and has published articles on justice, reconciliation, and political violence in *Constellations*, *Res Publica*, *Metaphilosophy*, *Contemporary Political Theory*, *The European Journal of Political Theory*, *The Review of Politics*, and *Contemporary Politics*. Verdeja is also a board member of the Institute for the Study of Genocide. Email: Ernesto.Verdeja.1@nd.edu.

Elisa von Joeden-Forgey received her B.A. from Columbia University and her Ph.D. in History from the University of Pennsylvania. Her doctoral thesis, "Nobody's People:

Colonial Subjects, Race Power, and the German State, 1884–1945," was funded by the SSRC-MacArthur Fellowship for International Peace and Security. She is currently working on a project on gender and genocide that develops the idea of "life force atrocities" and examines how this concept can be helpful to the early detection of genocide. Her book on gender and genocide prevention will be published by the University of Pennsylvania Press in 2012. Her work has also appeared (and is forthcoming) in several other journals and collected volumes, including *Hannah Arendt and the Uses of History*, and *The Oxford Handbook of Genocide Studies*. She resides in Philadelphia and teaches genocide, imperialism, human rights, and war in the Department of History at the University of Pennsylvania. Email:elisaforgey@ gmail.com.

Figure 0.1 A sparrow rests in the gun barrel of a tank at the memorial to the Battle of Kursk from the Nazi–Soviet war, Prokhorovka, Russia.

Source: Adam Jones.

Editor's Preface

The present and future of genocide studies

Adam Jones

The publication of this book in 2011 finds the field it surveys – comparative genocide studies – at a stage of unprecedented growth and ferment. Graduate programs in Genocide and Holocaust Studies, courses in the same, journals in the field, conferences and seminars – all have expanded exponentially in the space of two decades. And that is to limit the discussion to the academic aspect. In public debate and policy discourse, genocide has never been so prominent – sometimes almost fetishistically so, reflecting the way in which a concept coined by a still-obscure Polish lawyer many decades ago, enshrined in a tailor-made Convention, has established itself as a touchstone of contemporary human-rights discourse.

The expansion and deepening of the genocide-studies literature, even in very recent years, have been equally breathtaking. Between 2006 and 2010 alone, when the first two editions of my encompassing textbook appeared, a whole range of core texts was published in English: Ben Kiernan's *Blood and Soil*; Jacques Sémelin's *Purify and Destroy*; Daniel Feierstein's *El genocidio como práctica social* [Genocide as a Social Practice]; Martin Shaw's *What Is Genocide?*; Hannibal Travis's *Genocide in the Middle East* (much broader in scope than the title suggests); Christian Gerlach's *Extremely Violent Societies*; and highly ambitious edited collections like Dan Stone's *The Historiography of Genocide* and Dirk Moses's *Empire, Colony, Genocide*.[1] This is only to reckon with the global–historical *magnum opus*: the proliferation of high-quality monographs and edited projects addressing individual and regional cases of genocide is also gratifying.

What explains this outpouring? In large part, the relative youth and freshness of the field. Comparative genocide studies arose from the corpus of Holocaust studies, first with attention to a small number of "canonical" cases alongside the pivotal event of the Jewish

Shoah, then evolving into a kind of canon or "greatest hits" of twentieth-century genocides[2] – Armenia, Cambodia, and finally the Balkans and Rwanda – when the field was overtaken by current events in the early and mid-1990s. Despite this canonical structure, and an often unspoken Holocaust exceptionalism, most of the "founding" texts of genocide studies were more eclectic than is often recognized. Leo Kuper's *Genocide: Its Political Use in the Twentieth Century* (1981), Chalk and Jonassohn's *The History and Sociology of Genocide* (1990), and Totten *et al.*'s *Century of Genocide* (1997, 2008) incorporate a wide range of contemporary examples, like Bangladesh and Burundi (Kuper, Totten *et al.*), as well as ancient and early-modern cases and pay close attention to the destruction of indigenous peoples worldwide (Chalk and Jonassohn).[3]

The field was thus well-equipped from the outset to move in diverse and exploratory directions. And in many ways this reflects the very deepest foundation of comparative genocide studies, one that is only now – with the new generation of genocide scholarship – coming full-circle. Raphael Lemkin, the Polish-Jewish jurist who coined the word "genocide" in 1943 and was the lead player in the drafting of the United Nations Genocide Convention (1948), was himself the paragon of the questing, expansive, cosmopolitan genocide scholar. From his earliest days of hearing his mother, Bella, spin historical narratives to him, Lemkin was struck by the vulnerability of minority groups to destruction by their "own" rulers – and also by the richness of the civilizational contributions that those minorities made. His location in pogrom-ridden eastern Europe (a portion of what was then Poland, today in Belarus), and the suffering of his own family members in anti-Semitic violence, certainly sensitized him to the historic persecution of the Jews; but then, as in his 1944 book, *Axis Rule in Occupied Europe*, his searchlight roved far beyond – around the world and across the millennia.

Axis Rule was the only book Lemkin ever published; it is virtually unread except for the core "Genocide" chapter.[4] He nonetheless wrote voluminously if fragmentarily, and among the most exciting current trends in genocide studies is the "return to Lemkin" exemplified by the work of Dirk Moses, Martin Shaw, and several other luminaries. This consists both of a reexamination of Lemkin's original framing of genocide – far more focused on the destruction of social and cultural bonds among minority groups, and the disappearance of those groups as civilizational entities, than on the physical extermination of their members – and of an intensive investigation into the Lemkin archives, stored at the New York Public Library and the American Jewish Archives in Cincinnati. At the time of writing (mid-2011), for example, a team of Rutgers University graduate students led by Alex Hinton was copying, sifting, and analyzing Lemkin's scholarly writings and correspondence, including the approximately 150 manuscript pages of his own anticipated *magnum opus*, a world history of genocide. What has appeared so far from such investigations, which include a strong antipodean component, suggests the restlessness of Lemkin's mind and the empathy and inclusiveness of his spirit – qualities which have continued to serve as a touchstone for genocide scholars and students.

He was, for example, highly inquisitive about indigenous cultures and civilizations, respectful of them, and acutely aware of the frequency and savagery with which they were targeted for genocide by colonizing and imperialist forces. In this respect, Lemkin anticipated and directly influenced what is probably the single most significant line of investigation in genocide studies since the turn of the millennium. This is the shift from studying genocide as an *exogenous* phenomenon – something that occurs safely *out there*, perpetrated by alien others; a perspective that immunizes the centers of western power and intellectual life against searching analysis – to studying it additionally and perhaps essentially as an *indigenous* phenomenon (one closely associated in the modern period with the rise of the West, and with especially devastating consequences for the indigenous peoples targeted by the West and those influenced by discourses of western modernity).[5] Lemkin had his blind spots, and he was too prone in his last years to be swayed by political considerations in his pronouncements on what was and was not "genocide," the better to advance the cause of the Genocide Convention and try to assuage the concerns of the US government. (The US would not ratify the Convention until 1986, and then only with stated "reservations" to immunize it against application of the Convention to its own African American and indigenous peoples.[6]) Nonetheless, Lemkin's influence has never been stronger than it is today. Not only do several of the chapters in this volume (in the editor's view) draw directly on his framings – Benjamin Lieberman, with his conceptual survey of the field; Benjamin Madley, with his study of the genocide of the Tolowa Indians of Oregon and California; Donna-Lee Frieze, on the cultural dimension of genocide in the Balkans – but the project as a whole seeks to reflect Lemkin's probing approach to studying the crime that he first named.

Deriving both from Lemkin's fertile framework, and from the manifest urgency of the subject-matter, the field of comparative genocide studies has been characterized from the start by an extraordinary *interdisciplinarity* – something this book project was also designed to exemplify. I can indeed not think of another field in the humanities or social sciences which draws in such an omnivorous way on such a wide range of academic and non-academic disciplines. The core early contributions in the field were the work of historians, sociologists, legal theorists, psychologists, political scientists, and moral philosophers. Newer waves of scholarship have added anthropology, indigenous studies, gender studies, and literary and cultural studies to this mix. Flourishing subfields have arisen in all these categories. A spillover to the mathematical and natural sciences is also under way. Statistical investigations of genocide and related mass crimes were prominent from the start, in the work of R.J. Rummel, Barbara Harff, Ted Gurr, and others.[7] They have expanded significantly to include the work of Patrick Ball's Human Rights Data Analysis Group (HRDAG)[8] and others, as well as the highly original remote-sensing research of Russell Schimmer in this volume.

The sense of "all hands on deck" which has prevailed in genocide studies from the outset promotes an unusual openness to the contribution of graduate students, who are often among the freshest and most fertile minds in the field. *New Directions in Genocide Research* combines contributions from longer-established scholars with some truly impressive up-and-comers (Gallo, Madley, Drumond, Schimmer, Sumita). Many of the contributors, moreover, move in other professional circles, and in particular straddle the public policy/advocacy realm – another respect in which the field reflects Lemkin's founding influence, and another way in which it is distinctive. Everyone represented in this book is an engaged scholar and advocate on some level, it seems to me (some more overtly than others, naturally). This remains one of the most nourishing and inspiring features of genocide studies and the anti-genocide struggle *tout court*.

CHARTING *NEW DIRECTIONS*

The vitality of comparative genocide studies comes as something of a surprise when one recognizes that no one quite agrees what genocide *is*. The UN Genocide Convention definition supplies the closest to a consensus; but it is notoriously deficient in its framing (leaving out key victim groups and specific mechanisms of genocide intervention) and ambiguous in its phrasing ("intent to destroy," "as such," "in whole or in part," and so on). The most recent edition of my "comprehensive introduction" to genocide, meanwhile, reproduces *dozens* of definitions of genocide, beginning with Raphael Lemkin's foundational one, and carrying through to the new millennium: the new generation of genocide scholars seems no less immune to the definitional temptation than the previous one.[9]

However one views genocide's "essentially contested" status – whether as the field's Achilles' heel, or (as I do) an opportunity constantly to revisit core assumptions – it is clear that core definitional issues pervade many of the chapters in this volume. The book begins with a section on "Theories," introduced by Benjamin Lieberman's framing discussion, "From Definition to Process: the effects and roots of genocide." Lieberman expresses skepticism about the endless definitional wrangling and the viability of grand theorizing in genocide studies. Shortcomings in the field, he writes,

> create the most serious theoretical and practical problems when it comes to the urgent task of preventing genocide . . . Lessons derived from one or even several cases may provide no help in detecting genocide, let alone halting it – especially if similar outcomes obscure fundamental differences.

Daniel Feierstein's chapter, "The Concept of 'Genocidal Social Practices,'" makes available in English a distillation of the insights contained in his major 2007 work, *El genocidio como práctica social* (see note 1). Influenced by the work of Michel Foucault, Feierstein's study of the sociology of modernity and the Holocaust shows how "modern states managed the move from stigmatization to extermination" of national minorities. His finely-tuned stage-model of genocidal social practice depicts it as "a *technology of power* that aims (1) to destroy social relationships based on autonomy and cooperation . . . and (2) to use the fear of annihilation to establish new models of identity and social relationships among the survivors."

In "Genocidal Moralities: a critique," Christopher J. Powell conducts a similarly wide-ranging theoretical inquiry, this time into the moral foundations of genocide. While the title may seem a misnomer, Powell, making nuanced use of the work of Zygmunt Bauman, contends that insufficient attention has been paid to the moral framework that genocidal regimes and supporters develop and project in order to mobilize and justify the genocidal enterprise. Powell's twofold argument offers a striking purchase both on moral–philosophical constructions of genocide, and on constructions of moral philosophy. The fact that "in some times and places, genocide has been instituted as a moral obligation," demonstrates that genocide is easily "impelled . . . by a sense of *moral duty* and *higher purpose*." Crucially for Powell, though, such a demonstration "should prompt us to take a critical attitude to morality itself – not only to particular kinds of morality, but to morality as an institution."

Questions of "cultural genocide" have attended the genocide debate from its earliest days. Lemkin, as we saw, was especially sensitive to attacks on the cultural foundations of groups, and the absence of a cultural-genocide provision was an especially sore sacrifice for him during the Genocide Convention drafting process. As the Jewish Holocaust was entrenched as the iconic genocide, an aura of physical extermination (indeed total physical extermination) was attached to the concept. Cultural genocide tended to be marginalized to analyses of and by indigenous peoples. But as noted, a fresh engagement with Lemkin's work has revitalized the concept, and Donna-Lee Frieze's chapter exemplifies the trend. Her study of the destruction of the Sarajevo *Vijećnica* (library and archives) in Bosnia-Herzegovina explores the most vivid symbol of the multiculturalism and cosmopolitanism at the heart of the Bosnian and Sarajevan ideal, and its gutting by the forces of nationalist xenophobia.

Cultural and social constructions of group and personal identity lie at the heart of Elisa von Joeden-Forgey's study of "Genocidal Masculinity." With an almost anthropological eye, von Joeden-Forgey turns the focus to the inscription of physical atrocities, specifically "life force atrocities," in genocide and crimes against humanity. Such grisly crimes, she contends, reflect specific constructions of masculinity and femininity – in particular, a "genocidal masculinity [that] disavows the civilian world and its institutions of peacetime, replacing the transcendent and creative power of birth-giving . . . with the transcendent and creative power of killing." The life-force dimension of "ritualized cruelty" which is then directed against females and males alike helps to account for the apparently gratuitous atrocities which have featured so long and so centrally in genocidal assaults.

von Joeden-Forgey's chapter anticipates her two groundbreaking book publications, shortly to appear at the time of writing, which will substantially advance the discussion of gender and genocide. The gender variable arrived relatively late to comparative genocide studies, and in a somewhat unorthodox form – with my own project on *gendercide* (Mary Anne Warren's word), emphasizing the gender-selective massacre of "military-age" males.[10] Paula Drumond's chapter, "Invisible Males: a critical assessment of UN gender mainstreaming policies in the Congolese genocide," draws on this research in the context of the Congolese catastrophe, which appears to have exacted a death toll greater than any conflict since the Second World War. Analyses of sexual violence and "genocidal rape" have tended exclusively to focus on the victimization of women – nowhere more so than in the Democratic Republic of Congo, which has led to an outpouring of feminist critiques and international activism. Drumond looks instead at the context and character of sexual violence against males in the war and genocide(s), and inquires searchingly why United Nations agencies and spokespersons have so consistently failed to incorporate male victims and survivors in their framings and resource allocations.

The remaining chapters in Part 2 address further explorations and reconfigurations in genocide studies. Russell Schimmer's cutting-edge work in the natural sciences, sponsored by Yale's Genocide Studies Program, uses high-resolution images gathered through satellite remote sensing to draw sophisticated conclusions about land use and despoliation, population movement, and destruction of physical infrastructure. Drawing on fascinating findings from Guatemala, Rwanda, and East Timor, Schimmer's chapter – "Tracking Evidence of Genocide through Environmental Change: applying remote sensing to the study of genocide" – explores the implications of these technologies for prosecuting genocidal perpetrators, and predicting and preventing new genocidal outbreaks.

Hovering also at the margins of the discussion since the dawn of genocide studies have been structural and institutional forms of the crime – arguably those recognized under Article 2(c) of the Genocide Convention, with its elegant reference to "deliberately inflicting on the group conditions of life calculated to bring about its physical destruction." Terms such as *poorcide* and *structural genocide* have occasionally been deployed by exponents of Johann Galtung's structural violence school and others. Foundational genocide scholars like Richard Rubenstein (in *The Age of Triage*, which examines how populations were rendered marginal and disposable by messianic modernizing projects) supplied important signposts for later work by, among others, Mike Davis, whose *Late Victorian Holocausts* (2001) is now a classic.[11] So did the anthropologist Nancy Scheper-Hughes with her seminal concept of a "genocidal continuum," composed "of a multitude of 'small wars and invisible genocides'" conducted in ordinary social and institutional settings.[12] My own chapter in this volume, "Genocide and Structural Violence: charting the terrain," moves beyond the question of whether structural forms of violence *can* be considered genocidal, to ask *when* and *on which grounds* they may warrant the designation – and what the implications are for strategies of "humanitarian intervention."

If a "genocidal continuum" exists, then in a sense we are all bystanders to genocidal and proto-genocidal practices. Such a notion suggests the breadth of the "bystander" concept, and the need to examine it according to its own continuum of social position and practice. In "Moral Bystanders and Mass Violence," Ernesto Verdeja conducts such an inquiry, perhaps for the first time in the genocide-studies literature. Teasing out the elements of knowledge, agency, and structure that underpin bystander positioning, he calls for (and provides) a balanced and self-conscious appraisal that does much to flesh out a previously amorphous agent in the genocidal equation.

The final part of *New Directions in Genocide Research* turns to the kind of case-study treatments of genocide that are now proliferating. Such works markedly enrich the wider comparative–theoretical inquiry. But they also stand on their own as models of historical investigation – sometimes the first (or the first contemporary) carried out on their "forgotten" subjects. A kind of Hippocratic Oath of our field, I feel, should be that all victims and survivors of genocide are worthy of attention and recognition. And there is a powerful sense of contribution and vindication in "resuscitating" the many overlooked and under-examined genocidal assaults that have not been entirely lost to history.

The case studies, moreover, return us to many of the definitional and conceptual debates that animate genocide studies. In his meticulous rendering of the experience of the Tolowa Indians of California and Oregon, "When 'The World Was Turned Upside Down,'" Benjamin Madley offers a portrait of a people that experienced a genocidal campaign that was among the most relentless, multifaceted, and destructive ever launched on United States territory. His chapter is a reminder that the catch-all term "indigenous peoples" conceals a tapestry of individual nations and cultures – many of which experienced genocides that exterminated the majority of their members, but many of which have survived to seek redress and restitution today. Madley's emphasis on the intertwining of state authority with state-led militias, vigilantes, and death squads provides a powerful example of the role of non-state agents in genocidal processes, particularly when indigenous populations are targeted by colonizers and conquerors.

One of the unexpected features of Jewish Holocaust studies is that it is thriving today as never in its history. In part, this reflects a kind of boomerang process between studies of the Shoah and comparative genocide research. The three central theoretical reframings of the Shoah in the past twenty years – as a paragon and culmination of European colonialism; as a campaign of Nazi extermination/genocide against one population among others; and as an extermination campaign waged in the "bloodlands" struggled over by Hitler and Stalin – are all comparative in their essence. Can this fertile interaction of case-specific and comparative research be extended to other genocides? Uğur Ümit Üngör's chapter, "Fresh Understandings of the Armenian Genocide: mapping new terrain with old questions," suggests that it can. Üngör brings the comparativist's eye to his tripartite division of the analytical task into macro, meso, and micro levels. He also "suggests new research directions" in this case of genocide, again placing "a particular focus on existing problems in comparative genocide research." Üngör's study, like Madley's, also typifies the *intimacy* of many of these historical portraits: his "micro" recounting of the lives of two Ottoman perpetrators and their families allows the reader to gain valuable – and chilling – insights into their actions during the Armenian genocide.

Why are some cases counted as genocide and some not? With the conceptual contestation (many would say confusion) that pervades the field, it is unsurprising that scholars would disagree whether a particular case qualifies. Unexpected, perhaps, is that some contemporary cases are rarely considered at all, unless it is by members and advocates of afflicted populations. The long-running civil war in Sri Lanka, which came to a brutal and conclusive end in May 2009, is a significant example, explored in depth by Benita Sumita in her chapter on "Sri Lanka and Genocidal Violence: from retrospective to prospective research." Surveying the comparative genocide literature, Sumita locates an excessive emphasis on event-based and political–military understandings of genocide, as well as a persistent failure to examine all actors in a genocidal equation for evidence of mass atrocity – whether as agents, targets, or both. As the subtitle of her chapter suggests, Sumita also stresses a forward-looking perspective, one that distinguishes between academic and legal applications of the genocide framework, and seeks to advance genocide studies in a proactive and preventive way, rather than just retrospectively.

In central respects, whether genocides are recognized as such, and how their dynamics are depicted, reflect guiding (westernized) assumptions that, as Sumita shows, may be poor guides to complex genocidal formations. Very much the same is conveyed in Carol Jean Gallo's critique, "Researching Genocide in Africa: establishing ethnological and historical context." Exploring the gulf between media and popular representations and the deeper patterns revealed by "an ethnological perspective on racial constructions," Gallo shows how crude understandings of genocide in Sudan/Darfur – for example, as a campaign by homogeneous "Arab" villains versus generalized "African" victims – are challenged by studies of the *longue durée* (generally including colonial and precolonial influences) and local–regional "political ecological environments." Her chapter also provides a welcome survey of the anthropological writing on both genocide and Sudan/Darfur.

Work like Gallo's contributes notably to projects of truth, redress, and reconciliation in a post-genocide environment. If well-informed and culturally sensitive analyses of given genocidal formations can be crafted, then more effective and grassroots means might be found to encourage healing in the aftermath – healing that in turn may discourage future genocidal outbreaks. Of all the cases of post-conflict reconciliation, perhaps only South Africa's compares with Rwanda's in the global attention and institutional/scholarly resources accorded to it. David Simon concludes this volume with a perceptive appraisal of "The Challenge of Social Reconciliation in Rwanda: identity, justice, and transformation." Written at an ideal moment – with the perspective afforded by a decade-and-a-half of redress strategies and initiatives; with the storied *gacaca* (hilltop justice) process reaching its conclusion – Simon provides a balanced but generally positive portrait of the paths and pitfalls of reconciliation following the 1994 holocaust of the Tutsis. *Gacaca*, he asserts, has laid "a foundation for transformation . . . by creating a shared experience, providing a forum for discourse, creating an opening for social reintegration, and generating a record of what happened." All of these offer "particular benefit[s]" to given sectors and/or the wider Rwandan society, bolstering an emerging sense of civic citizenship.

Such innovations are among the strategies and approaches that post-genocidal societies devise. Simon's analysis, and those preceding it in this book, remind us that genocide scholars, too, are busy forging their own fresh approaches and "new directions." By volume's end, the reader should have gained a keener appreciation of the range and vigor of that enterprise.

NOTES

1 Ben Kiernan, *Blood and Soil: A World History of Genocide and Extermination from Sparta to Darfur* (New Haven, CT: Yale University Press, 2007); Jacques Sémelin, *Purify and Destroy: The Political Uses of Massacre and Genocide* (New York: Columbia University Press, 2007); Daniel Feierstein, *El genocidio como práctica social. Entre el nazismo y la experiencia argentina* (Buenos Aires: Fondo de Cultura Económica, 2007); Martin Shaw, *What Is Genocide?* (Cambridge: Polity Press, 2007); Hannibal Travis, *Genocide in the Middle East: The Ottoman Empire, Iraq, and Sudan* (Durham, NC: Carolina Academic Press, 2010); Christian Gerlach, *Extremely Violent Societies: Mass Violence in the Twentieth-Century World* (Cambridge: Cambridge University Press, 2010); Dan Stone, ed., *The Historiography of Genocide* (London: Palgrave Macmillan, 2008); A. Dirk Moses, ed., *Empire, Colony, Genocide: Conquest, Occupation, and Subaltern Resistance in World History* (New York: Berghahn Books, 2008).

2 The "greatest hits" term was used by Dirk Moses in his presentation to the conference on "Forgotten Genocides" at Rutgers University, Newark, New Jersey, March 28, 2011.

3 Leo Kuper, *Genocide: Its Political Use in the Twentieth Century* (Harmondsworth: Penguin, 1981); Frank Chalk and Kurt Jonassohn, *The History and Sociology of Genocide* (New Haven, CT: Yale University Press, 1990); Samuel Totten, William S. Parsons, and Israel W. Charny, eds, *A Century of Genocide: Critical Essays and Eyewitness Accounts*, 3rd edn (New York: Routledge, 2008).

4 Raphael Lemkin, *Axis Rule in Occupied Europe: Laws of Occupation, Analysis of Government, Proposals for Redress*, 2nd edn (New York: The Lawbook Exchange, Ltd., 2008 [1944]).

5 One should acknowledge the early probing of the psychological literature on genocide into individuals' capacities and motivations for genocide; but this is inherently "safer" than a

direct socio-political critique. See, for example, Ervin Staub, *The Roots of Evil: The Origins of Genocide and Other Group Violence* (Cambridge: Cambridge University Press, 1989).

6 See John Bart Gerald, "Is the US Really a Signatory to the UN Convention on Genocide?," http://www.serendipity.li/more/genocide.html.

7 R.J. Rummel, *Death by Government* (New Brunswick, NJ: Transaction Publishers, 1994); Barbara Harff and Ted Gurr (recently), "Assessing Country Risks of Genocide and Politicide in 2009," http://www.gpanet.org/webfm_send/76.

8 For an overview of the HRDAG's research in East Timor, see Ann Harrison, "Coders Bare Invasion Death Count," *Wired*, February 9, 2006, http://www.wired.com/science/discoveries/news/2006/02/70196.

9 See the discussion in Adam Jones, *Genocide: A Comprehensive Introduction*, 2nd edn (London: Routledge, 2010), esp. pp. 13–29.

10 Mary Anne Warren, *Gendercide: The Implications of Sex Selection* (Totowa, NJ: Rowman & Allanheld, 1985); Adam Jones, ed., *Gendercide and Genocide* (Nashville, TN: Vanderbilt University Press, 2004).

11 Richard L. Rubenstein, *The Age of Triage: Fear and Hope in an Overcrowded World* (Boston, MA: Beacon Press, 1983); Mike Davis, *Late Victorian Holocausts: El Niño Famines and the Making of the Third World* (New York: Verso, 2001).

12 Nancy Scheper-Hughes, "The Genocidal Continuum: Peace-time Crimes," in Jeannette Marie Mageo, ed., *Power and the Self* (Cambridge: Cambridge University Press, 2002), pp. 29–47.

Acknowledgments

This book has its origins in a seminar series that I built and oversaw in 2006–07, as part of my postdoctoral research in the Yale Genocide Studies Program. The founder and director of that program, Ben Kiernan, immediately saw the appeal of a wide-ranging series that would survey something of the range and dynamism of the genocide-studies field. That attests to Ben's own almost Olympian grasp of genocide in world history and around the world at present, captured in his magisterial *Blood and Soil*. The present collaborative venture would never have occurred without Ben's encouragement and the auspices of the Yale Genocide Studies Program. On a personal level, I thank him as a mentor, and as the person who granted me my critical professional "break" in the field.

This said, the book underwent a number of permutations after it first coalesced among scholars leading seminars in the 2006–07 series. In fact, that is to put it euphemistically: an unusually large component of contributors had to step in to replace dropouts. In the end, I am slightly stunned to realize, only Benjamin Lieberman, Benjamin Madley, Russell Schimmer, and I myself remain from the crowd that originally presented "New Directions" seminars. The call for contributions quickly attracted a new set of commitments which form the backbone of the book – von Joeden-Forgey, Feierstein, Powell, Drumond, Verdeja. Together with this stalwart contingent, however, I must thank the wonderful cohort – Frieze, Üngör, Gallo, Simon, Sumita – who promptly and with good humor stepped in to fill the breach left by some unanticipated withdrawals. Without them and their fresh, dynamic contributions, the book could never have progressed to publication.

The end result is a book that is more challenging and field-expanding than even I had hoped at the outset. The unpredictability of its evolution meant that it became a pleasure to edit and shape only toward the end. But a true pleasure it now is.

At Routledge, the publisher with whom I have worked most closely in recent years, I offer deep thanks to editor Craig Fowlie and editorial assistant Nicola Parkin, for their exemplary grace, patience, and good counsel throughout this years-long process. The typically high standards of copy-editing and production design that Routledge supplies mean that the end result is a book that is visually as well as intellectually engaging. Additional gratitude goes to those who contributed images to this volume, either personally or through Creative Commons databases such as Wikimedia Commons. The new profusion of such copyright-cleared imagery is one of the greatest boons for an editor and authors seeking to leaven their seas of text with eye-catching imagery.

I and all contributors welcome correspondence from readers at the email addresses supplied in the biographical notes.

Adam Jones
Kelowna, Canada
June 2011

PART 1 THEORIES

Figure 1.1 Commemorative plaque outside the home in Warsaw, Poland, where Raphael Lemkin lived during the 1930s. Lemkin invented the term "genocide" and helped to draft the UN Genocide Convention.

Source: Courtesy Joseph Kolker/Flickr.

CHAPTER 1

From Definition to Process

The effects and roots of genocide

Benjamin Lieberman

No other branch of history or field of inquiry centered on historical events is so dependent on a definition as genocide studies. Studies of war, politics, wealth and poverty, society, culture, men and women, and a host of other topics have all given rise to detailed analysis of terms and definitions; but no other field depends for its very existence upon the invention and definition of a single term. Extermination, mass killings, and massacres were all well known long before the creation of the term "genocide," but there was no field of historical study devoted to examining and comparing such massacres and killings from different historical epochs. Histories, whether of the Roman Empire, the Mongols, the Pennsylvania frontier, or the French Revolution, often discussed killings or massacres, but there was no field of history dedicated to massacres or mass killing as such.

Genocide studies only became possible with the search by the legal scholar Raphael Lemkin for a single concept "to encompass the phenomenon of existential killing."[1] In the interwar period, Lemkin began to investigate past instances of mass killing, but he did so without a unifying term to describe his research. Only during the Second World War did he coin the word "genocide" to capture the meaning of a phenomenon that he had already noted. Many other concepts of historical analysis, including race, nation, class, and gender, cause intense debates over proper definition, but none of them was invented by a scholar seeking to describe something already perceived. Multiple books, volumes of scholarly journals, seminars, conferences, and encyclopedias debate the terms "nation" or "nationalism," for example, but neither nation nor nationalism were defined on their very first appearance on the historical stage.

Lemkin logically sought to define the term he had invented. Genocide, he explained, meant "the destruction of a nation or an ethnic group." Specifically, he referred to "a coordinated plan of different actions aiming at the destruction of essential foundations of the life of national groups, with the aim of annihilating the groups themselves."[2] Within a few years, the newly-created United Nations had anchored the crime of genocide in international law in the 1948 UN Convention on the Prevention and Punishment of the Crime of Genocide. The Genocide Convention defined genocide as a set of acts "committed with intent to destroy, in whole or in part, a national, ethnical, racial or religious group as such." The short list of five acts began with the most obvious, "killing members of the group," but also included the infliction of severe physical and mental harm, along with "conditions of life calculated" to destroy the group, impeding the reproduction of the group, and transferring children of the group.

As research into genocide proliferated from the 1980s onward, debate over the term's definition also intensified. A host of authors elaborated on the UN definition, many offering their own amended definitions. This lengthy and often fruitful discussion cannot be recapitulated here. In general, scholars focused on the flaws of either an overly elastic or an overly restrictive definition. The list of protected groups under the Genocide Convention struck some observers as too narrow: was there no room for the destruction of political groups? To take just one such critique, Totten and Parsons "believe that both political and social groups should be included in any definition of genocide."[3] A revised definition could also include groups defined by sexual identity and gender, though some elements of the original UN Convention cover some targeting according to gender (such as the prevention of births), and international case law developed by such tribunals as the ICTY (International Criminal Tribunal for the former Yugoslavia) has refined and added detail to our understanding of this aspect.[4]

A definition-driven analysis of genocide creates a common strategy for research. Whatever their methodology or approach, genocide scholars typically begin with a definition. They next identify a sample of cases that meets that definition, then describe and analyze the diverse cases, and conclude by tracing similarities among those case studies.

Individually and collectively, comparative works on genocide have advanced knowledge of violence and victimization; but their shared approach also creates deep and well-worn paths that obscure key conceptual problems and occlude new directions for inquiry. Such definition-driven research tends toward predictable conclusions. We learn that perpetrators dehumanize victims; that genocide may be motivated by hatred of targeted groups; that the effort to destroy a race in whole or in part often reveals intense racism; that perpetrators – when they can – use the instruments of state power to achieve their ends; that genocide in modern states displays key features of modernity, while genocide in the ancient or early modern world does not. None of these conclusions is wrong, though some may be incomplete; but they tend repeatedly to confirm the original hypotheses. At the same time, definition-driven research has spawned practices and assumptions that at the very least require greater scrutiny. These include issues of sampling, historical approach, images of perpetrators and victims, and methods for preventing genocide. Above all, genocide research assumes that genocide as an outcome lends unity to the field, without actually investigating how such a starting point might shape conclusions, or demonstrating that shared outcomes mean that genocide is a single phenomenon.

SAMPLING AND BOUNDARIES

Definition-driven genocide research typically confronts sampling problems. From the start, most discussions of genocide have recognized that genocide existed long before the term was invented and defined. Describing the concept in his 1944 book *Axis Rule in Occupied Europe*, Lemkin called genocide a "new word . . . to denote an old practice in its modern development." The United Nations Convention of 1948 similarly stressed the antiquity of genocide, stating "that at all periods of history genocide has inflicted great losses on humanity." In other words, genocide predates the invention and definition of the crime of genocide by centuries if not millennia, and the field of genocide studies by and large takes this as a given. Even works that focus on the twentieth century make this point, as Eric Weitz does in observing that "Genocides have occurred since the earliest recorded history" – though he suggests they became more deadly during the last century.[5] The debate over whether the Holocaust was unique seldom leads to the extremist and counterfactual position that genocide has only occurred once. Historians – and for that matter, poets, playwrights, and novelists – have long known and lamented that history is full of dreadful instances of massive killing. This means that any comparative analysis of genocide confronts an immense diversity of examples drawn from different time periods, geographical locations, and cultures, employing different techniques in widely varied political and social settings. The writer who chooses to compare any other subject of historical inquiry from ancient Rome to modern Europe, Latin America, Asia, and Africa would confront an extraordinary task; but this is exactly what historians of genocide undertake, if they choose to see the destruction of Carthage as genocide, and expand the analysis to the Holocaust along with mass violence in Guatemala, Cambodia, Rwanda, and Darfur, to take only some of the many examples.

Facing this bewildering array of potential cases and examples, some studies of genocide seek to reduce the sample set. The most common approach is to take a particular time period, such as the twentieth century, or to concentrate on only the most important examples. Only a few enterprising works attempt a comprehensive approach. Either approach shapes likely conclusions. The more expansive the sample in geographical space and historical time, the harder it is to find a convincing common theme or thread. Interpretations of genocide based on broad samples run the risk of isolating the peripheral or highlighting the very general. Two of the most impressive recent comprehensive histories, Ben Kiernan's *Blood and Soil* and Mark Levene's *Genocide in the Age of the Nation State*, highlight these challenges. Kiernan considers four major themes, including "the preoccupation of perpetrators with race, antiquity, agriculture and expansion."[6] But factors that prove significant in one case of genocide, such as a cult of antiquity, may have little obvious connection to mass killing in another instance. Where did such a cult rank among all the important causes of the Armenian genocide, for example? And a desire for agricultural land would hardly explain why Nazis targeted *Jews* for extermination in areas of Eastern Europe where, for the most part, they were proportionally less likely to be landowners than other ethnic and religious groups. Levene, for his part, notes the development of "what we think of as the specific phenomenon of genocide primarily through the historical transformation of human societies worldwide as a politically and economically interacting and universal system of modern – mostly nation – states."[7] The point is a reasonable one: a territorially-bounded state that represents a single nation may endanger populations within those borders that do not belong to the state's chosen nation. But the connection to genocide is still notably indirect. Many such states exist, but only a small minority of such states carries out genocide.

The use of a narrower sample, on the other hand, introduces risks of another kind. Isolating a small number of cases creates a hierarchy of genocide, with those deemed essential at the top. While he mentions other cases, Manus Midlarsky in *The Killing Trap*, for example, focuses on the Holocaust, the Armenian genocide, and the Rwandan genocide, on the grounds that these three cases "meet the criteria of state-sponsored systematic mass murder of a targeted ethnoreligious group and of non-combatant status of the victims."[8] Presumably, any broadly authoritative study of comparative genocide would include these cases. But such sampling brings with it a danger of circular logic. The principles used to select the essential cases of genocide will most likely turn up in whatever conclusions are drawn about the core common factors, causes, and effects of genocide. If state sponsorship of mass killing is a key criterion for selecting the sample, we would expect the analysis to confirm the importance of such state sponsorship. The criteria for selection derived from "essential" cases also lead to the exclusion of cases that are widely recognized as genocide. Thus, Midlarsky excludes the mass killing of Herero in German Southwest Africa "because of the absence of state policy authorizing genocide, and the status of virtually all Herero including women and older children at least as combat associates," though he does refer to "genocidal behavior."[9] Stressing such criteria lends a veneer of science to the decision to leave out the Herero case, but the criteria chosen seem almost arbitrary, given the actual effects of the assault on the Herero. If criteria derived from a total of three "essential" cases can so easily produce such results, then perhaps the criteria themselves require revision, or alternatively should be derived from a larger sample; but even a larger sample would still likely betray a circular logic.

Another approach to comparative genocide potentially avoids some of the problems of arbitrary sampling by focusing on genocide within a given time period – most often the twentieth century. Such studies still rely on examples chosen according to a particular definition, but at least they offer a common rationale for inclusion. More than one study has referred to the twentieth century as a "century of genocide." However, even with this chronological focus, surveys of twentieth-century genocide share the same difficulty in locating common factors for killings carried out in extremely varied settings. If one identifies the twentieth century with genocide, it is hardly surprising to discover that powerful modern states are responsible for genocide. The conclusion is plausible; but is this a real finding, or again the result of initial assumptions shaping conclusions? Take the case of Rwanda, cited in all comparative studies of twentieth-century genocide written after 1994. It is possible to find elements of modernity in the Rwandan events: killers rifled through official records of identity to sort out Tutsis from Hutus and find victims, though they sometimes killed Hutus as well as Tutsis, and propagandists employed the modern technology of hate radio to whip up animosity. At the same time, how many of the authors who stress the modernity of killing in Rwanda would have cited the country, one of the poorest and least-developed in the world, as emblematic of modernity prior to the genocide of 1994? Does a society only become modern after it has suffered genocide?

The labeling of the twentieth century as a "century of genocide" confronts a particularly vexing issue when it identifies genocide in the cases of mass killing and death in the Soviet Union. Genocide studies, as many observers have noted, sprang from research into the

Holocaust. From the start, contemporaries wondered how a society such as Germany, widely regarded as one of the most advanced in the world, could have given rise to such carnage. The Dresden diarist Victor Klemperer agonized over this question before he even knew of the existence of the Holocaust as a program of mass extermination. Klemperer identified strongly with German culture. "I am German and am waiting for the Germans to come back," he wrote in his diary on May 30, 1942.[10] One example, of course, does not a trend make, but contemporaries soon also drew comparisons between massive human rights abuses in the two most powerful dictatorships of the day: Nazi Germany and Stalin's Soviet Union. The coupling of these two dictatorships lent a powerful impetus to the notion of mass murder as a crime committed by modern states. Continuing discussion of this point gave rise to efforts to calculate killings by governments, and sometimes to polemical arguments about which side was worse.[11] But when the issue is genocide, it is not universally accepted that the Soviet Union was guilty. Stalin was responsible for immense suffering and loss of life in regions such as Ukraine, but it can also be argued that terrorist social engineering and the desire for economic transformation led to massive loss of life without a killing campaign that first and foremost targeted groups for destruction.[12] The concept of the twentieth century as a paradigm for genocide rests, in part, on applying the definition to a case where genocidal intent remains at issue.

Whatever their sampling strategy, studies of comparative genocide, whether inclusive or exclusive, also generally suffer from a tendency to establish historical boundaries that artificially demarcate genocide from other events. This is a structural problem; it does not reflect any lack of diligence by scholars who typically devote extraordinary effort to researching diverse societies. The danger of erecting artificial historical boundaries is most obvious with an exclusive approach: concern for defending the definition of genocide may lead in the most extreme cases to a decision to avoid actually doing history. Genocide scholars frequently explain their rationale for exclusion, but definition-driven history will still likely stop short of fully investigating cases deemed to lie outside the definitional boundary.

Even the most inclusive sampling, however, suffers from the tendency to establish artificial historical boundaries. Inclusive approaches consider cases of genocide from highly diverse regions and historical periods, on the grounds that they share a common identity as genocide. But a common or shared identification as genocide does not preclude a much greater similarity between a given case of genocide and other examples lying outside even a broad sample. Mark Levene raises this issue with reference to the destruction of Herero, which, owing to German responsibility, could be seen as evidence of a trend that would later culminate with the Holocaust. Levene points out:

> The problem is that what the Germans were doing in Africa . . . has close parallels with British actions in the same regional context a few years earlier, American ones almost simultaneously in the Philippines, or for that matter Dutch ones in a far-flung corner of their East Indies colonies at that precise moment. These other exterminatory assaults . . . are more immediately and obviously relatable to the fate of the Herero than anything to do with the Holocaust.[13]

The close similarities between some cases of genocide and other violent events deemed to lie outside almost any sample raise the highly unsettling possibility that genocide, by itself, may not provide an important nexus of similarity between two or more episodes of mass violence. To raise this problem is not to deny that genocide occurs: tragically, it is all too real, and the disastrous outcome is mass slaughter in many societies. By and large, however, the field of genocide studies has not addressed the question of whether shared outcomes necessarily indicate core similarities or demonstrate important connections between different societies. Such connections may exist, but to a large extent they have been assumed rather than demonstrated or explained. Suppose, for example, that a particular study of genocide identified Stalin's policies in Ukraine and England's conquest and occupation of Ireland as genocidal. Both arguments are plausible, without being universally accepted; but would that assessment necessarily demonstrate any important similarity in causes, policies, and goals between those two cases, or would the similarity in outcomes amount to no more than a dreadful coincidence?

LAW AND FINAL OUTCOMES

Given these uncertainties, it is tempting to return to the starting point for genocide in international law to unify the field of genocide studies, but this strategy may prove to be misplaced. Genocide was defined very quickly as a crime: the 1948 Genocide Convention is a Convention on the Prevention and Punishment of the *Crime* of Genocide. This legal definition is crucial for persecution and prevention of genocide. In the convention's very first article, the "Contracting Parties confirm that genocide . . . is a crime under international law which they undertake to prevent and to punish." But such a concept, defined for a legal purpose, neglects many of the factors critical to the historical or anthropological study of genocide. The legal definition focuses on an end result: the destruction "in whole or in part" of particular groups, rather than on what genocide *is* in terms of causes and goals. Following this path, the field of genocide studies considers first and foremost final outcomes, rather than historical processes and conflicts. Unity comes only from the final product. But while this may serve as the ultimate criterion for legal prosecution, history does not consist only of ultimate acts. A violent conflict with nearly all the ingredients of genocide could easily escape notice if it does not produce genocide in the end, while genocide research may seek to discover similarities between fundamentally different historical cases that share only an outcome.

Likewise, genocide requires that the destruction target particular groups. This distinguishes genocide quite sharply from many other crimes. A host of factors determines the level of culpability and punishment for crimes such as murder, for example; but murder is murder, regardless of the identity of the victim. Genocide is a form of mass murder or mass destruction, but mass murder and mass destruction are not necessarily genocide, unless the victims are attacked as members of a particular group. The very list of groups whose destruction amounts to genocide stems from intellectual, social, cultural, political, and scientific trends separate from the end result of destruction in whole or in part. Possible omissions from the original list of groups in the UN Convention revealed both political disputes and divisions during the onset of the Cold War. Other omissions have become more apparent with the continued development of human rights and civil rights movements. Debate about the list is not simply a matter of arriving at a better definition. Rather, the goals of perpetrators in targeting particular groups indicate how groups are imagined and constructed during particular historical epochs (see also Daniel Feierstein's Chapter 2 in this volume). A campaign to purify a nation by eliminating its supposed racial enemies, for example, would have been unimaginable in many periods when race was not a salient category of identity.

GENOCIDE AND GENOCIDES

The field of genocide studies treats genocide as a single outcome, but the cumulative body of knowledge compiled through research into genocide runs counter to this understanding. Genocide is many things. Genocide is a violent means to achieve purity within a given imagined community or nation. The Holocaust in Germany and the Cambodian genocide targeted groups of victims who had previously viewed themselves, respectively, as Germans and Khmer. Though obviously aware of pre-existing anti-Semitism, German Jews found their plight shocking and inexplicable, because they had generally identified themselves as Germans. Nazi Germany carried out wars of imperial expansion, but casting Jews out of the German nation and deporting the Jews from Frankfurt, Berlin and other cities and towns advanced no imperial goals. In Cambodia, the Khmer Rouge targeted ethnic minorities such as Vietnamese, but they also sought to purify the Khmer people through violence by destroying those Khmer allegedly corrupted by foreign ways.

In the early stages of the development of an imagined community such as a nation, genocide is also a method to forge or build that community or nation. Turkey provides an important example. The Armenian Genocide and the simultaneous destruction of Assyrian Christians within core areas of the shell of the Ottoman Empire sped the formation of a Turkish nation within what would soon become a Turkish nation-state. When Young Turk radicals defined Armenians as lying outside the boundaries of the Turkish people, they were not casting Armenians out of any nation that most Armenians had ever belonged to. Armenians could and did express shock at the vanishing diversity of Ottoman life, but there were few, if any, exact Armenian counterparts to Victor Klemperer: what Armenian during the First World War would have echoed Klemperer's shock at being driven out of the nation? Klemperer had regarded himself as German, but few, if any, Armenians saw themselves as Turks. In the last years of the Ottoman Empire, genocide and related violence functioned as methods for founding and defining a nation; but in Germany the nation already existed. This distinction helps to explain why coming to terms with the past has proven so much more difficult in Turkey than in Germany. In Turkey, to even discuss the Armenian Genocide, is to risk calling into question founding national myths.[14]

Genocidal policies are also a type of violent social engineering. These cases can diverge from the UN definition in that they often focus on destroying class or political enemies, neither of which constitutes a protected group under the Genocide Convention of 1948. Such goals can merge with campaigns of racial or national purification. Thus, the Khmer Rouge in Cambodia sought to create a pure Khmer racial identity through killing, while also targeting urban dwellers and anyone with a bourgeois background as "new people" who had to be converted into "base people." Persecution in the Soviet Union also revealed ethnic targeting, but on the whole the Soviet Union did not seek to impose racial, ethnic, or national purity.

Genocide is also a strategy through which expanding societies and imperial powers remake the maps of newly-incorporated frontier and border areas. It functions as a violent instrument for transforming the human landscape. Almost any large human landscape, as well as many smaller ones, is composed of a mix of different identities – these can include languages, religions, and ethnic groups. The human landscape has changed throughout history, often as a result of causes over which humans in previous eras had no control, such as global cooling and warming before the onset of large-scale anthropogenic climate change. Unintended effects of human actions, such as the transporting of new religions along routes originally blazed for commerce, have likewise altered the map of human identities. But states and societies have also deliberately remade the human landscape, or carried out what some scholars have seen as a kind of "gardening" directed toward cultivating, moving, altering, and sometimes eradicating "fields" of people.[15] Genocide is hardly the only such method; colonization or transplanting populations can also tilt the demographic balance against a particular identity to the point where its very existence becomes endangered. But killing off an unwanted population constitutes an especially violent form of human landscaping.

The Nazi war of extermination aimed, for example, to remake the map of identities throughout Central and Eastern Europe. This genocidal project paradoxically permanently altered the identity of many towns, cities, and regions, without meeting the Nazi vision of establishing a new racial order. The Holocaust eradicated the Jewish presence across wide swathes of Europe, but Hitler and Himmler did not aim only to eliminate an unwanted population. They also wished to place a German imprint on lands all the way toward the eastern frontiers of Europe, and in this goal they failed. Himmler envisioned breaking and destroying nations on a grand scale through a combination of racial sifting, ethnic cleansing, forced labor, and assimilation of those elements of the local population found to be of good racial stock. He intended to destroy unwanted populations in whole, though the means did not always correspond to those later described in the Genocide Convention; but even some of Himmler's own colleagues doubted the feasibility of his plans, and the German defeat in the Second World War doomed this vision of remaking Eastern Europe into a German or Aryan realm.

Genocidal remaking of the human landscape can also serve economic goals within particular regions. Expanding settler societies in North America and Australia coveted particular areas rich in resources, grazing lands, timber, or gold fields and targeted indigenous residents of these areas for destruction. The most extreme result was total eradication, often described as the fate of the indigenous population of Tasmania, though Ann Curthoys describes a more complex process of destruction.[16] Other areas of Australia and of the United States, such as California, saw campaigns of destruction as settler societies seized control of regions rich in natural resources.

For conquering armies, genocide can also demonstrate power with the aim of cowing and controlling subject peoples. Whether or not Carthage was the first genocide,[17] or simply a major early genocide, Rome did not seek to destroy all conquered peoples. The goal of complete destruction was rare, but not unknown. Thus, Julius Caesar sent his troops to destroy the Germanic tribe of the Eburons after they had attacked a Roman legion.[18] Warlords and rulers of the Central Asian steppes also engaged in genocidal massacres, without seeking any larger goal of creating racial or national purity. To resist a conqueror such as Tamerlane was to risk the very real possibility of complete destruction, but neither Tamerlane nor Mongol warlords and rulers sought to destroy all, or even most, conquered peoples.

The extensive research into genocide thus shows genocide to be many things. It may involve purifying or creating nations, reengineering societies, remaking borderlands, ensuring control of resources, and preventing uprisings by newly conquered subject peoples. The list itself is not definitive – some genocides might be grouped together, and others could be eliminated or added to the list. What few could do, however, except those operating under the narrowest and most exclusive possible definition, is produce a list of genocides closely linked by anything more than final outcomes.

Observing the variation among cases of genocide, scholars of genocide have searched for classes or categories of genocide. The collection edited by Robert Gellately and Ben Kiernan, *The Specter of Genocide*, discusses genocide and modernity, indigenous people and colonial issues, the era of the world wars, and genocide and mass murder since 1945. Mark Levene has so far described "the Meaning of Genocide" and "the Rise of the West and the Coming of Genocide," and will add volumes on "Europe in the Era of Ultimate Genocide," and "the Cold War and Genocide." William Rubinstein divides his cases into "Pre-Modern Societies," "the Colonial Age," "the Age of Totalitarianism," and "the Era of Ethnic Cleansing and Third World Dictators." Ben Kiernan's magisterial study employs the categories of early imperial expansion, settler colonialism, and twentieth-century genocides. Benjamin Valentino, who focuses on mass killing, or "the intentional killing of a massive number of non-combatants," divides his cases into "Communist Mass Killings," "Ethnic Mass Killings," and "Counter-guerrilla Mass Killings."[19] Creating such systems of categories, however, does not necessarily establish a common form of genocide. Collectively, these exercises indicate that varied perpetrators have destroyed different types of groups at different times for different reasons. These and other studies divide examples by time and place, but neither chronology nor space establishes that a single motive or type of perpetrator drove genocidal killing in a particular time and place. For some authors, genocide can be located in European imperial expansion; but it was not only Europeans who carried out genocide. There are also cases where indigenous rebellions against colonial power took "a genocidal form."[20]

PERPETRATORS AND VICTIMS

The sheer variety of genocides calls into question common assumptions about perpetrators and victims. The United Nations Genocide Convention itself leaves the category of perpetrator open, stipulating punishment for those committing genocide "whether they are constitutionally responsible rulers, public officials or private individuals." This makes sense from a legal perspective: laws against murder do not detail a particular type of culprit, and neither should a law against the destruction of groups. Research into genocide has paradoxically underscored the variety of perpetrators while also identifying an ideal type of perpetrator. Driven by examples such as the Holocaust, and the Rwandan and Armenian genocides, discussion of genocide tends to focus on states as the ultimate perpetrators. At the same time, researchers have also scrutinized the role of ordinary people in committing and carrying out genocide, and supporting or profiting from it. We have learned of grassroots support for and participation in geno-cide, at the same time as researchers have also asserted that genocide is a crime carried out by small groups. Benjamin Valentino, for example, argues that "the impetus for mass killing usually originates from a relatively small group of powerful political and military leaders." The actual "violence itself is typically performed by a relatively small group of people, usually members of military or paramilitary organizations."[21] Militaries and paramilitary organizations have carried out mass murder during genocide, but the shift in focus from a small band of leaders to the actual killers reopens the question about the breadth of support for killing: militaries can be mass organizations, and paramilitary bands can operate far from state control. Even in powerful states, actual killers may not be highly trained elites. Few if any books on the Holocaust have been more widely read or influential than Christopher Browning's *Ordinary Men*.[22]

The paradigm of a "century of genocide" depicts genocide as a crime not just of states, but of a very particular kind of state: namely the powerful, modern, bureau-cratic state. "To write about genocides in the twentieth century," Weitz states, "means grappling, of necessity, with the two very large and powerful dictatorial systems of twentieth-century Europe, Nazi Germany and the Stalinist Soviet Union."[23] Midlarsky stresses the connection between such state power and the means to kill: "State-generated genocidal policies put at the disposal of the perpetrators the tools of modern mass killing."[24] The murderous power available to such a modern state cannot be overlooked, but to focus only or even chiefly on such an idealized perpetrator overlooks the actual complexity of perpetrators. The image of the powerful modern state implies a highly unified apparatus with vast powers to command: a cadre of highly educated leaders and functionaries; an elaborate, well-organized bureaucracy; scientific specialists; and the latest technology. But how many of these elements are really essential to genocide? Mark Mazower accepts the modernity of the Holocaust, but adds that "Most other states that have perpetrated acts of mass violence over the past century were less efficient, differently organized, and motivated by different sets of beliefs and strategies."[25] Among twentieth-century genocides, the Armenian case would seem to require a great deal of scholarly pushing and shoving to conform to the idealized theoretical image of the powerful modern state. The Young Turks' leaders certainly saw themselves as new men who wished to modernize an empire they viewed as decrepit; but their government was also new, embattled, and by some measures divided. A powerful modern state is also hard to find in cases of genocide in expanding settler societies where some of the most extreme violence took place on frontiers far from the centers of government power.

Genocide research has also struggled to describe victims. The UN Genocide Convention says little about the victims beyond stating that genocide involves the destruc-tion of groups. Much of the subsequent discussion and debate surrounding the UN Convention has called for opening up the definition by adding to the list of groups beyond "national, ethnical, racial or religious" groups, but in other ways genocide research has created a much more sharply delineated and even narrow image of the typical target of genocide. Victims are depicted as non-combatant civilians and as guiltless of aggression. Chalk and Jonassohn, for example, refer to "one-sided mass killing."[26]

These images are certainly true of most victims, and in many cases of genocide. This has rarely been so powerfully and tragically conveyed as in Serge Klarsfeld's collection of photographs of 2,500 French children deported to death camps.[27] Or, as Primo Levi wrote of the selection for death of Jews on arriving at Auschwitz:

> This is the reason why three-year-old Emilia died: the historical necessity of killing the children of Jews was self-demonstrative to the Germans. Emilia, daughter of Aldo Levi of Milan, was a curious, ambitious, cheerful, intelligent child; her parents had succeeded in washing her during the journey in the packed car in a tub with tepid water which the degenerate German engineer had allowed them to draw from the engine that was dragging us all to death.[28]

Genocide studies have made clear how perpetrators perceived such non-combatant civilian victims, even children, as threats, but what often remains unexplored is the relationship of targeted populations to combatants.[29] The reasons for such omissions are obvious. Blameless victims should never be blamed, but discussion of genocide as a response to a real, as opposed to a perceived, threat can very quickly introduce topics that feature prominently in works that deny genocide. Today, even deniers of the Armenian genocide generally concede that Armenians suffered immense hardships during the First World War. They cast that suffering, though, as part of generalized wartime misery, produced by a clash in which Ottoman forces faced off against both enemy powers and Armenian guerillas.[30] Marginalizing the issue of the relationship between combatants and non-combatants, however, has obscured an understanding of varied forms of genocide. Midlarsky identifies the Holocaust and the Armenian and Rwandan genocides as central examples "because they meet the criteria of state-sponsored systematic mass murder of a targeted ethnoreligious group and of non-combatant status of the victims."[31] But while the victims themselves were non-combatants, the non-existent nature of the threat Nazi Germany faced from Jews was quite different from the threat that Hutu militants faced from Tutsi exiles, who would very soon and comprehensively drive them from power.

In other cases, victim populations may themselves merge into the ranks of combatants. Genocide as a strategy of terror to demonstrate the futility of resistance has targeted both combatants and non-combatants. Perpetrators of genocide in settler societies frequently attacked both warriors and those who did not bear arms. At times, genocide even singles out combatants for destruction, though this is most obvious once combatants have been disarmed, as with the killing of prisoners-of-war and so-called "partisans" during the German war of extermination on the Eastern Front in the Second World War.

OLD ASSUMPTIONS, NEW DIRECTIONS, AND GENOCIDE PREVENTION

As a field that began with an invented term, genocide studies can ill afford to dispense with definitions. But a definition so critical for law proves less effective in detecting historical connections. The problem lies less with any particular definition of genocide than with how definitions shape research. A host of amendments and revisions to the definition of genocide have been suggested, but the cottage industry of defining genocide better is unlikely, by itself, to resolve the sampling problems and artificial boundaries created by definition-driven research into genocide. Nor would any amended legal definition likely demonstrate that all forms of genocide share anything other than a common outcome.

Definition-driven research has both created an impressive body of scholarship and generated questionable, sometimes unstated, assumptions. For a start, the sampling process usually begins with core cases – those thought best to fit a given definition. From such a selection of core cases, it is easy to assume that these central examples provide key clues for analyzing other cases, but the assumption remains unproven. Genocide research developed first and foremost on a base created by research into the Holocaust. The Holocaust therefore did serve as a historical core for the field. Indeed, the Holocaust is central to the field of genocide studies: Holocaust texts are core documents in the field of genocide studies, and the Holocaust was a core experience of modernity. However, it does not follow that research based on the Holocaust, or on the Holocaust and other such core cases, necessarily provides the most useful guide for analyzing all other possible cases of genocide.

Now that genocide research has vastly increased our knowledge of mass violence, researchers can also examine the assumption that a common outcome proves that cases of genocide share other key features. Of the many elements found in models of genocide from notions of typical perpetrators to genocidal ideologies, which are actually fundamental to all or even most cases of genocide?

By overlooking examples that fall just short of genocide, definition-driven research may also miss conflicts that escalate to the point of genocide. Research into the Spanish conquest of the Americas, for example, probably does not furnish full proof of Spanish genocide in most continental regions of the Americas, but reaction to Spanish rule sometimes took a genocidal form. French colonial rule in Haiti may also not meet many definitions of genocide, but a genocidal campaign against French settlers revealed the animosity and hatred built up under the oppressive colonial regime.[32] Escalating conflict in more recent times has also led to genocidal violence in numerous areas beset by civil wars such as Bosnia.

Current shortcomings in genocide studies create the most serious theoretical and practical problems when it comes to the urgent task of preventing genocide. As a single dreadful outcome marked by mass graves, killing fields, and trails of death, genocide can only lead us to demand: "never again." But identifying similar outcomes provides little practical guidance for reaching that goal. Lessons derived from one or even several cases may provide no help in detecting genocide, let alone halting it – especially if similar outcomes obscure fundamental differences. One obvious problem is that the conditions said to lead to genocide generally do not. Genocide studies can give the impression that genocide is commonplace. But while even one case of genocide is too many, human societies have also developed mechanisms to curb the scale and extent of killing.[33] Where modern societies developed laws of war, other human societies created mechanisms such as hostage-taking that similarly restrained the level of killing and destruction of groups. If we confine ourselves only to key cases from the last century, we will still find false positives: powerful states presiding over modern means of killing that nonetheless did not engage in genocide. Amnesty International, Human Rights Watch, and other international human rights organizations have over many years catalogued and documented abuses by a host of such regimes, many of them abhorrent but not genocidal.

Conversely, the assumption that a single genocidal type leads to a single outcome would miss genuine cases of genocide. Madeleine Albright and William Cohen observed that "genocide fuels instability – usually in weak, undemocratic, corrupt states. It is in these states that we find terrorist recruitment and training, human trafficking and civil strife."[34] At first glance, such states do not seem strikingly similar to Nazi Germany. After the fact, proponents of the modernist school of genocide could presumably fit almost any regime into a model of powerful, state-driven genocide. But would such an approach really help us to detect another Darfur in advance?

NOTES

1   Henry R. Huttenbach, "From the Editor: Lemkin Redux: In Quest of a Word," *Journal of Genocide Research*, 7: 5 (December 2005), pp. 443–444; and Tanya Elder, "What you See Before your Eyes: Documenting Raphael Lemkin's Life by Exploring his Archival Papers, 1900–1959," *Journal of Genocide Research*, 7: 5 (December 2005), pp. 473–475.

2   See *Prevent Genocide International*, http://www.preventgenocide.org/lemkin/AxisRule 1944-1.htm.

3   Samuel Totten and William S. Parsons, "Introduction," in S. Totten, W.S. Parsons, and I.W. Charny, eds, *A Century of Genocide: Critical Essays and Eyewitness Accounts*, 3rd edn (New York: Routledge, 2009), p. 3.

4   Adam Jones, ed., *Gendercide and Genocide* (Nashville, TN: Vanderbilt University Press, 2004).

5   See *Prevent Genocide International*, http://www.preventgenocide.org/lemkin/AxisRule 1944-1.htm; and Eric D. Weitz, *A Century of Genocide* (Princeton, NJ: Princeton University Press, 2003), p. 8.

6   Ben Kiernan, *Blood and Soil: A World History of Genocide and Extermination* (New Haven, CT: Yale University Press, 2006), p. 605.

7   Mark Levene, *Genocide in the Age of the Nation State, Vol. 1: The Meaning of Genocide* (London: I.B. Tauris, 2005), p. 205.

8   Manus I. Midlarsky, *The Killing Trap: Genocide in the Twentieth Century* (New York: Cambridge University Press, 2005), p. 34.

9   Ibid., p. 33.

10 Victor Klemperer, *I Will Bear Witness 1942–1945: A Diary of the Nazi Years*, trans. Martin Chalmers (New York: Random House, 2001), p. 63.

11 R.J. Rummel, *Death by Government* (New Brunswick, NJ: Transaction Publishers, 1994); and Stéphane Courtois, Nicolas Werth, Jean-Louis Panné, Andrzej Paczkowski, Karel Bartosek, and Jean-Louis Margolin, *The Black Book of Communism: Crimes, Terror, Repression*, trans. Jonathan Murphy and Mark Kramer (Cambridge, MA: Harvard University Press, 1999).

12 The concept of genocide, so central to discussion of Nazi Germany, is not always employed in works on terror in the Soviet Union. See, for example, J. Arch Getty and Roberta Thompson Manning, eds, *Stalinist Terror: New Perspectives* (New York: Cambridge University Press, 1993).

13 Levene, *Genocide in the Age of the Nation State*, p. 19.

14 Taner Akçam, *A Shameful Act: The Armenian Genocide and the Question of Turkish Responsibility*, trans. Paul Bessemer (New York: Metropolitan Books, 2006).

15 Amir Weiner, ed., *Landscaping the Human Garden: Twentieth-century Population Management in a Comparative Framework* (Stanford, CA: Stanford University Press, 2003).

16 Ann Curthoys, "Genocide in Tasmania: The History of an Idea," in A. Dirk Moses, ed., *Empire, Colony, Genocide: Conquest, Occupation, and Subaltern Resistance in World History* (New York: Berghahn Books, 2008), pp. 229–252.

17 Ben Kiernan, "The First Genocide: Carthage, 146 BC," *Diogenes*, 51: 3 (2004), pp. 27–39.

18 Daniel Chirot and Clark R. McCauley, *Why Not Kill Them All?: The Logic and Prevention of Mass Political Murder* (Princeton, NJ: Princeton University Press, 2006), p. 24.

19 Robert Gellately and Ben Kiernan, eds, *The Specter of Genocide: Mass Murder in Historical Perspective* (New York: Cambridge University Press, 2003); Levene, *Genocide in the Age of the Nation State*; William D. Rubinstein, *Genocide: A History* (New York: Pearson Longman, 2004); Kiernan, *Blood and Soil*; and Benjamin Valentino, *Final Solutions: Genocide and Mass Killing in the Twentieth Century* (Ithaca, NY: Cornell University Press, 2004).

20 Adam Jones, *Genocide: A Comprehensive Introduction* (London: Routledge, 2006), p. 29; and Nicholas A. Robins and Adam Jones, eds, *Genocides by the Oppressed: Subaltern Genocide in Theory and Practice* (Bloomington, IN: Indiana University Press, 2009).

21 Valentino, *Final Solutions*, pp. 2–3.

22 Christopher R. Browning, *Ordinary Men: Reserve Police Battalion 101 and the Final Solution in Poland* (New York: HarperCollins, 1992).

23 Weitz, *A Century of Genocide*, p. 10.

24 Midlarsky, *The Killing Trap*, p. 34.

25 Mark Mazower, "Violence and the State in the Twentieth Century," *American Historical Review*, 107: 4 (October 2002), p. 1160.

26 Frank Chalk and Kurt Jonassohn, *The History and Sociology of Genocide: Analyses and Case Studies* (New Haven, CT: Yale University Press, 1990), p. 23.

27 Serge Klarsfeld, *French Children of the Holocaust: A Memorial*, ed. Susan Cohen, Howard M. Epstein, and Serge Klarsfeld; trans. Glorianne Depondt and Howard M. Epstein (New York: New York University Press, 1996).

28 Primo Levi, *Survival in Auschwitz: The Nazi Assault on Humanity*, trans. Stuart Woolf (New York: Simon and Schuster, 1996), p. 20.

29 Omer Bartov, "Defining Enemies, Making Victims: Germans, Jews, and the Holocaust," *American Historical Review*, 103: 3 (1998), pp. 771–816.

30 Justin McCarthy, *Death and Exile: The Ethnic Cleansing of Ottoman Muslims, 1821–1922* (Princeton, NJ: Darwin Press, 1995).

31 Midlarsky, *The Killing Trap*, p. 34.

32 Philippe Girard, "Caribbean Genocide: Racial War in Haiti, 1802–1804," *Patterns of Prejudice*, 39: 2 (2005), pp. 144–167.

33 Chirot and McCauley, *Why Not Kill Them All?*

34 Madeleine K. Albright and William S. Cohen, "Never Again, for Real," *The New York Times*, 20 December 2008.

Figure 2.1 "The Wandering Jew." European anti-Semitic image of unknown (French?) origin.

CHAPTER 2

The Concept of "Genocidal Social Practices"

Daniel Feierstein

> What I am is not important,
> whether I live or die –
> It is the same for me,
> the same for you.
> What we do is important.
> This is what I have learnt.
> It is not what we are
> but what we do.
>
> James Fenton, *Children in Exile*[1]

The annihilation of populations is an age-old phenomenon. The destruction of Troy by the Greeks, the razing of Carthage by the Romans, and the military incursions of the Mongols under Genghis Khan are just a few examples that can be found in any history book. Genocide, on the other hand, is a distinctly modern concept. The term was first coined by the Polish-Jewish legal scholar Raphael Lemkin in the 1940s, and a legal definition of genocide was not incorporated into international law until 1948, following the programs of mass murder carried out by the Nazis during World War II. These included the extermination of such diverse groups as the Jewish and Gypsy populations of Europe, ethnic Poles and Russians, political opponents, children and adults with disabilities, homosexuals, and religious groups like Jehovah's Witnesses.

The first question that we need to address, then, is whether genocide is simply a new name for an old practice, or whether it refers to something qualitatively different from earlier mass annihilation processes. The model of genocide presented in this chapter points to a distinctly modern phenomenon, first appearing in the nineteenth century, although rooted in the early modern period (circa AD 1500 to 1800). The forced exodus of large numbers of Jews and Muslims from Spain in 1492, and the subsequent persecution of those who converted to Catholicism in order to escape expulsion, is perhaps the earliest precursor of modern genocide (together with the European witch-hunts). The distinguishing features of genocide are the ways in which annihilation is typically legitimized and implemented, as well as its consequences, not only for the targeted groups but for perpetrators, witnesses, and society as a whole.[2]

My contention is that modern genocides constitute a deliberate attempt to change survivors' identities by modifying relationships within a given society.[3] This is what sets genocide apart from earlier annihilation processes involving civilian populations, as well as other contemporary processes of destruction. The fact that genocide has proved one of the most effective tools for bringing about such changes – equaled only by revolutionary processes – suggests that modern genocide is not simply a spontaneous occurrence that reappears when historical circumstances are conducive to it. Rather, it is a process that starts long before, and ends long after, the actual physical annihilation of the victims – even though the exact moment at which any social practice commences or ceases to play a role in the "workings" of a society is always uncertain. It is important to bear this in mind if we are to develop effective early warning systems to prevent new instances of genocide.

GENOCIDE AS A SOCIAL PRACTICE

Almost half a century separates the drafting of the Convention on the Prevention and Punishment of the Crime of Genocide, adopted on December 9, 1948, and the sentences handed down by the international criminal tribunals for the former Yugoslavia and Rwanda in the second half of the 1990s. Since this time and subsequently, debates have raged among sociologists and historians over definitions that would allow for empirical research, suggesting that the concept of genocide remains an "essentially contested" one. Reviewing the various legal, sociological, and historical definitions of genocide, Bjørnlund *et al.* found that the fundamental point of agreement was "the systematic annihilation of a population group as such"; the three main points of disagreement concerned the question of "intent," the nature of the groups encompassed by these definitions, and the importance of actual physical annihilation – whether total or partial – as an element of genocide.[4]

Significantly, nearly all of these definitions take Article II of the 1948 Genocide Convention as their starting point. As Martin Shaw (2007) points out:

> The study of genocide has generally been framed by legal and historical, rather than sociological perspectives. Law provided the impetus to the definition of the crime, through the pioneering efforts of Raphael Lemkin and the drafters of the United Nations Convention; it has continued to provide much of the drive towards recognition of recent genocides, in the work of the international criminal tribunals for former Yugoslavia and Rwanda.[5]

In a sense, this predominantly legal approach is unfortunate. Legal definitions tend to be narrowly focused, rooted in specific historical contexts, and difficult to modify. Law requires unambiguous categories, as well as clear and convincing evidence in order to reach a judgment of guilty or not guilty. The categories of protected groups established by the 1948 Genocide Convention – in particular, its list of protected groups – were the result of political compromise, not of legal philosophy. It was the opposition of the Soviet Union, Great Britain, and South Africa to earlier drafts of the Convention that produced the current definition of "genocide" in Article II, and one can argue that the limitation of designated groups to "national, ethnical, racial, and religious" ones constituted a violation of the elementary principle of equality before the law, protecting some groups and not others. If the legal framing of genocide is ever to move beyond its 1948 roots, it will need to include this principle, as well as incorporate the customary law that has emerged from the history of relations between human communities. In other words, a legal definition of genocide – beyond what has been achieved so far in international law – needs to be based on the concept of genocide in its widest sense, namely, *the implementation of a massive and systematic plan intended to destroy all or part of a human group as such*. In this sense, modern genocide is no different from the mass *annihilation of populations* by the Ancient Greeks, Romans, or Mongols.

In contrast, the concept of genocide as a social practice allows historians and sociologists to adopt a broader, more flexible approach to problems of causality and responsibility, as well as to distinguish genocide from other social processes of mass destruction that have occurred at different periods of history, such as high death rates among certain segments of the population as the result of economic policies, or the more or less intentional destruction of the environment.

What, then, is a social practice? In a paper describing law from a sociological point of view, the Australian legal scholar Suzette Barnaby writes:

> A social practice can be defined as a social grouping or social institution whose members are committed to a common or overall purpose. They give effect to this common purpose through a shared set of beliefs and actions which have developed out of the traditions of the practice. New practice members are inducted into the practice and socialised in the culture and shared understandings of the practice by other members. The social practice is both legitimised by and subject to the authority of an organisational structure.[6]

It is precisely organization, training, practice, legitimation and consensus that distinguish genocide as a social practice from other, more spontaneous or less intentional, acts of killing and mass destruction. Also, because a social practice consists of shared beliefs and understandings as well as shared actions, a genocidal social practice may be one that contributes directly or indirectly to the commission or attempted commission of genocide, including symbolic representations and discourses that promote or justify genocide.

Moreover, it is clear from this definition that social practices are ongoing and under permanent construction. In many instances, the appropriateness of the term "genocide" has been questioned, on the grounds that the process has not proceeded far enough to warrant a designation as full-blown genocide. But when does genocide actually begin?

At what point can we say that the term is legitimately applied? Adopting the concept of genocidal social practices allows us to address a thorny methodological issue in the social sciences, namely that of *periodization*. Moreover, because social practices are constructions, and are therefore open to deconstruction, academic study should be able to contribute to policies aimed at preventing and resisting genocide.

Bearing this in mind, then, I define a genocidal social practice as a *technology of power* – that is, a way of managing people as a group – that aims (1) to destroy social relationships based on autonomy and cooperation by annihilating a significant part of the population (significant either in terms of numbers or in terms of practices); and (2) to use the fear of annihilation to establish new models of identity and social relationships among the survivors. Unlike what occurs in war, the disappearance of the victims forces the survivors to deny their own identity – an identity created from a synthesis of being and doing – while a way of life that once defined a specific form of identity is suppressed.[7]

GENOCIDE AND THE REFORMULATION OF SOCIAL RELATIONS

In his studies of children's rule games, the Swiss psychologist and philosopher Jean Piaget distinguished three broad stages of moral and social development related to children's awareness of rules. The first was *pre-moral judgment*, in which rules are not understood (up to the age of 4 or 5 years). The second was *morality of constraint* or "heteronomous morality," in which children accept the rules and authority of adults as permanent and inflexible (from 5 to 10 years old). A third stage was *morality of cooperation*, or "autonomous morality," wherein rules are mutually agreed, and can be changed by mutual consent (from the age of 10). At this autonomous stage, children's thinking is no longer constrained by authority, and children can discern new solutions to problems – what Piaget refers to as the construction of knowledge, as opposed to its social transmission.

Piaget believed that a true sense of justice emerges only through "constructive" cooperation with peers:

> Thus adult authority, although perhaps it constitutes a necessary moment in the moral evolution of the child, is not in itself sufficient to create a sense of justice. This can develop only through the progress made by cooperation and mutual respect – cooperation between children to begin with, and then between child and adult as the child approaches adolescence and comes, secretly at least, to consider himself as the adult's equal.[8]

He also claimed that a morality of cooperation was necessary for what he termed "reciprocity" – that is, for evaluating "in-groups" and "others" as being of equal worth, despite one's own in-group attachment – and for an equitable distribution of wealth and resources in society:

> In conclusion, then, we find in the domain of justice, as in the other two domains already dealt with, that opposition of two moralities to which we have so often drawn the reader's attention. The ethics of authority, which is that of duty and obedience, leads, in the domain of justice, to the confusion of what is just with the content of

established law and to the acceptance of expiatory punishment. The ethics of mutual respect, which is that of good (as opposed to duty), and of autonomy, leads, in the domain of justice, to the development of equality, which is the idea at the bottom of distributive justice and of reciprocity.[9]

Not surprisingly, critics have claimed that the games of marbles on which Piaget based his theory of moral development do not represent children's whole perception of morality. Piaget's theory has also been criticized for assuming moral universals, whereas moral and social development in non-Western cultures may differ from those of the children that Piaget and his collaborators studied. Nevertheless, in sociological terms, the emergence of cooperative relations of reciprocity and solidarity obviously depends on members of a given society being able to perceive others as equals.

On the other hand, as Robert Paul Wolff has pointed out, "Insofar as a man fulfills his obligation to make himself the author of his decisions, he will resist the state's claim to have authority over him."[10] For this reason, history provides numerous examples of attempts to block and dismantle nascent relations of cooperation by stigmatizing non-conformists as "Others." Stigmatization works through binary oppositions, such as believer/heretic, civilized/primitive, normal/pathological, in which one pole always dominates. The binary logic of imperialism, in which white/civilized/moral/teacher/colonizer (and so on) is collectively opposed to black/uncivilized/immoral/pupil/colonized (and so on), is just one example of how "negative Otherness" is applied and extended.[11] This process disempowers and alienates the "Othered" from their experience by forcing them to identify with stereotypes, as described in Frantz Fanon's classic study of racism and colonization.[12]

How, then, have modern states managed the move from stigmatization to extermination? Michel Foucault argues that one of the key technologies of power of the modern nation state is *biopower*. According to Foucault, biopower emerged in the mid-eighteenth century with the aim of defending the life and health of populations; it is exercised at the collective level through regulatory control, and at the individual level through discipline and punishment.[13] For example, the state might use prenatal programs to increase birth rates ("the biopolitics of the population") and, at the same time, punish "deviants" who engage in non-reproductive sex ("the anatomo-politics of the human body"). Foucault claims that in a modern, normalizing society, these two levels are essentially complementary.

According to Foucault:

If genocide is indeed the dream of modern power, this is not because of the recent return to the ancient right [of monarchs] to kill; it is because power is situated and exercised at the level of life, the species, the race, and the large-scale phenomena of the population.[14]

However – and this cannot be stressed too strongly – in any discussion about definitions, the political purposes of extermination must remain hidden. As Foucault explains:

In the biopower system, in other words, killing or the imperative to kill is acceptable only if it results not in a victory over political adversaries, but in the elimination of the biological threat to and the improvement of the species or race.[15]

In this sense, genocidal social practices not only attempt to destroy individuals as subjects "for themselves" by alienating them from their experience, but also to strip them of control over their own bodies. The choice of victims and the methods used in genocidal social practices are always political, and are meant to eliminate all forms of physical autonomy in subjects with a history of self-determination.

TOWARD AN ATTEMPT AT PERIODIZATION

In the following sections, I argue that a sociological understanding of genocide as a social practice needs to take into account three interconnected processes: the construction, destruction, and reorganization of social relations. Accordingly, the periodization that I propose is broader than that suggested by Gregory Stanton in his "Eight Stages of Genocide," which begins with the classification of groups into "us and them," and ends with the attempts of the perpetrators to block investigations of the crimes.[16]

What I present here is a six-stage process, beginning at the moment that a group of individuals with an autonomous social identity is negatively constructed as "Other," and continuing until its symbolic extermination in the minds of the survivors, which may happen *after* the physical acts of extermination themselves, and rob the survivors of the possibility of being subjects "for themselves." Not all the stages described are strictly sequential. In practice, there is often considerable overlap between the different stages, although each of those on the path to mass murder constitutes a necessary step in the process.

The model emphasizes the negative ways in which the state brands those who think or behave differently in such diverse areas as sexuality, politics, religion, and the workplace, but also the fact that the extermination of those groups that lie outside the "norm" is a clear message to the population that no deviation from the "norm" will be tolerated. The ruthless efficiency of state punishment, reinforced by official rhetoric and allowing no exceptions, is designed to make the standardization of society seem inevitable.

Although most of the examples included below are drawn from the Nazi Holocaust (as they are most likely to be familiar to the reader), the model is intended as a tool for understanding many other social practices of genocide, such as those in Indonesia, Latin America under the National Security Doctrine, Cambodia, or the former Yugoslavia, to mention just a few. In other cases, like those of Rwanda or Sudan, some of the stages described may require further adjustments.

Stage one: stigmatization: the construction of "negative otherness"

The first step in destroying previously cooperative relations within or between social groups is *stigmatization*. In order to construct the "negative Other" as a distinctive social category, those in power draw on symbols in the collective imagination, build new myths, and reinforce latent prejudices. Two groups are thus created: the majority ("us") and a minority ("them") that do not wish to be like everyone else – and therefore do not *deserve* to be.

Various religious, ethnic, national, political, or social groups have been branded as "abnormal" or "inferior" in accordance with political needs at different periods in history. These groups have included non-Catholic Christians, such as the Cathars; Armenians, Syrians and Greeks under the Ottoman Empire; kulaks in the Soviet Union; Jews and Gypsies under the Nazis; Communists in Indonesia; the urban population in Cambodia; and Bosniaks in the former Yugoslavia, to name just a few. In the contemporary Western world, the targets of state discrimination are sexual minorities, prostitutes, immigrants, Muslims and the poor, among others.

Violence at this first stage is verbal and symbolic. The categories of thought and perception created will later lend legitimacy to the need for extermination, but it is too early to speak in such terms. Those in power still *tolerate* the stigmatized group, but consistently draw attention to it and problematize it. The "solution" to the problem – genocide – will come later.

Stage two: harassment

This stage marks a qualitative leap from symbolic to physical violence. In general, it advances more quickly in times of crisis, as the anxiety and latent violence resulting from current deprivations and uncertainty about the future can be directed against those who insist on maintaining a separate identity, or flouting norms that others have accepted. Typically, the stigmatized group is accused of causing the crisis by corrupting public morals, undermining national unity or conspiring with foreign agents in ways that would not normally stand the test of common sense.

Harassment is characterized by two types of simultaneous and complementary actions: bullying and disenfranchisement. First, radicals or "shock troops" carry out sporadic attacks, claiming that their "tolerance" is exhausted and calling for "firm action." These attacks achieve several goals simultaneously. They deepen the process of stigmatization; they test society's readiness to "buy into" physical violence; and they provide an excuse to recruit and organize a repressive apparatus to "manage" the situation. The authorities use the breakdown of law and order created by these "spontaneous" acts of aggression to justify authoritarian and repressive policies, and to strengthen the "legitimate" security forces. Often, the victims are so intimidated by these ongoing and seemingly indiscriminate acts of aggression that they are ready to move to the relative safety of a ghetto. Segregation is precisely what happens at Stage Three (see below), and generally marks the point of no return toward extermination, the fifth stage.

Second, the authorities gradually deprive the stigmatized group of its civil rights. This begins with restrictions on property and marriage, as well as on practicing certain professions and customs (for example the Nazi prohibition on *kashrut*, or kosher slaughtering), and ends in the loss of citizenship. These measures increase support for the regime by "normal" citizens, who are able to buy the out-group's property and businesses at bargain prices and gain access to better jobs and positions, while limiting the number of unclassifiable children of mixed marriages. At the same time, they reduce the out-group's freedom of speech, freedom of movement, and potential for development.

At this stage, policies are aimed at forcing the out-group to leave, rather than killing it outright. Those who cannot flee into exile are subject to social exclusion. This exclusion marks a much more important step toward extermination than exile, because isolating the victimized people within the "normalized" society does not resolve the dispute between same and different, but simply creates a need in the minds of the authorities to find a "final solution."[17]

Even though extermination remains a seemingly remote possibility, this is also the point at which recruitment and training of the future perpetrators begin. Just as a regular army requires an officer corps to develop strategy and tactics, as well as to train and discipline the troops and lead them on the battlefield, a genocidal army requires an organizational structure to provide ideological indoctrination and training in kidnapping; tactics to subjugate and dehumanize the victims; torture to extract information; and finally the murder – without moral qualms or physical revulsion – of unarmed civilians.

Stage three: isolation

At this stage, the focus shifts to social and territorial planning. This stage has taken different forms at different moments in modern history, but the goal is always the same: to demarcate a separate social, geographical, economic, political, cultural, and even ideological space for those who are "different," and at the same time to sever their social ties with the rest of society. The ghetto, in the original sense of a restricted area within a European medieval city in which Jews were required to live, has traditionally been the most highly developed form of segregation. Other less sophisticated "ghettoes" have served these same functions at different times and for different populations.

Apart from breaking all ties between the population to be exterminated and the outside world, this stage, too, achieves several objectives simultaneously. First, it makes it easier for the genocidal forces to identify the victims and, at the same time, to hide the process of harassment and extermination from the public, which would likely condemn outright murder committed in full view. Second, confiscated housing and property are transferred to the in-group, again strengthening support for the regime. In fact, most "ordinary" citizens in Nazi Germany felt uncomfortable witnessing the public degradation of the Jews. Although they had internalized the official discourse to the point of considering the victims to be responsible for the violence, they approved of and, in some cases, petitioned the authorities for the removal of Jews to ghettoes on "humanitarian" grounds.

After a period of prolonged harassment, the victimized population often looks forward to, and even demands, relocation in a ghetto. For example, much of the Jewish community saw the Nazi ghettoes as a relief from daily aggression. They did not understand that their removal from society marked a qualitative leap toward their own annihilation:[18]

> The Jews began to yearn for only one thing: to escape from the world of the gentiles and shut themselves within four walls where the enemy could not get at them. It was rumored that all the Jews were soon to be enclosed in a ghetto. Some were afraid; others saw this as their salvation.[19]

However, other Jews were clearer about the meaning of this stage in the overall process:

> The ghetto was not a way to achieve Jewish autonomy, as many thought, but an instrument with which to kill first our souls and then our bodies. The ghetto was destined to destroy our people, to completely erase it from the face of the earth . . . In this way, they were killing the soul of our people, stripping them of the essential logic of common sense. With this system they corrupted the healthier impulses of an organized community. I assured them that the same thing would happen in Bialystok, because if not, the Germans would not have deployed there the ghetto, the police or the Judenrat [Jewish Council]. The Germans did not seek to help but to harm the Jews.[20]

Stage four: policies of systematic weakening

At this stage the perpetrators set priorities. They distinguish between those that *must* be exterminated, and those that *may* be exterminated, depending on the political and social circumstances and the perpetrators' capacity to kill. Once the victims have been isolated from the rest of society, the perpetrators typically implement a series of measures aimed at weakening them systematically. These consist of strategies of both *physical* destruction through overcrowding, malnutrition, epidemics, lack of health care, torture, and sporadic killings; and *psychological* destruction, manifested in humiliation, abuse, the harassment or killing of family members, attempts to undermine solidarity through collective punishment, encouraging collaboration in the categorization and classification of prisoners, and peer denunciation and peer abuse.

The main goal at this stage is to select those who *must* be exterminated. Some are murdered; others die of hunger or disease; yet others *adapt* by identifying with the behavior and ideology of their victimizers. This phenomenon, similar to the Stockholm Syndrome studied in hostage situations, is mentioned by many genocide survivors. It leads not only to the psychological destruction of the individual, but to that of the group, as these individuals are coerced to behave aggressively toward the "so-called unfit."[21]

Once the victims have been systematically weakened, and with the necessary political consensus and technical facilities in place, the process may proceed to the next stage: extermination. If not, the cycle will begin again. Subcategories of "Others" will be established for harassment; and the perpetrators will further degrade their prisoners (whether they still reside in a ghetto or have been transferred to a concentration camp) by making them turn against each other. Primo Levi, an Auschwitz survivor, describes how this was accomplished by the Nazis, using the *kapo* system:

> If one offers a position of privilege to a few individuals in a state of slavery, exacting in exchange the betrayal of natural solidarity with their comrades, there will certainly be someone who will accept. He will be withdrawn from the common law and will become untouchable; the more power that he is given, the more he will be consequently hateful and hated. When he is given command of a group of unfortunates, with the right of life or death over them, he will be cruel and tyrannical, because he will understand that if he is not sufficiently so, someone else, judged more suitable,

will take over his post. Moreover, his capacity for hatred, unfulfilled in the direction of the oppressor, will double back, beyond all reason, on the oppressed; and he will only be satisfied when he has unloaded onto his underlings the injury received from above.[22]

It is not easy to understand why the victims of the Nazi genocide – or of any other genocide, for that matter – did not resist more actively. But these populations have generally been defeated long before they reach the stage of physical annihilation. What is remarkable is that in such extreme circumstances, there are always individuals that attempt to resist – often placing their own lives, along with those of their own children and other family members, at risk.

Stage five: extermination

The extermination stage is characterized by the physical disappearance of those who once embodied certain types of social relations. The Nazi Holocaust marks a qualitative transformation of this stage, not only at the level of technology, but also at a political and symbolic level. Even during the death marches of the Armenian population in 1915, a personal relationship existed between the Armenians and their Turkish guards. In contrast, the industrialization of death by the Third Reich rendered the relationship between victims and perpetrators *anonymous*, as well as dissolving individual moral responsibility by breaking the process into a succession of separate stages. The production line started with the organization of trains and the deportation of the victims to the extermination camps of Auschwitz-Birkenau, Belzec, Chelmno, Majdanek, Sobibor, or Treblinka, and ended with the victims' bodies being burned and their remains ground to dust. With the gas chambers, the perpetrators did not even have to watch their victims die. This depersonalized form of murder has since been copied in other genocidal processes.

This systematic, impersonal, and tremendously efficient ability to make entire populations disappear in a relatively short period of time also marks a new stage in the exercise of power by dominant classes. The perpetrators have demonstrated to the rest of society the consequences of aspiring to autonomous control over one's own body. The new sovereign power is no longer characterized by the spectacular staging of small-scale public executions (as in earlier centuries), but by a new technology of power which, as Foucault points out, fuses the ancient sovereign right to kill with the biopolitical management of life.[23]

Stage six: symbolic enactment[24]

Genocidal social practices do not end in the physical annihilation of the victims, but rather in the symbolic ways that this trauma is represented. If the overarching purpose of genocide is to transform social relationships within a given society, it is not sufficient to kill those who think or behave differently. The types of social relationships that these people embodied (or potentially embodied) must be replaced either with traditional in-group models of relating or, more commonly, with new ways of relating. However, not all representations of the facts contribute to this transition.

For example, those who hold official remembrance ceremonies, whether out of goodwill or in the belief that they can exorcise genocide merely by invoking its name, often stress the need to "remember the victims." However, the most effective form of symbolic genocide is not oblivion, which ignores the disappearance of a way of life as if it had never disappeared, but does not preclude its reappearance. In Foucauldian terms, we need to shift our focus from what the social practices of genocide set out to *destroy* (a culture, a national group, a political tendency), to what they were intended to *create* (usually, a new society). This supplies the key for how genocide can and should be remembered, or reappropriated. To accomplish this, we need to problematize the "*assimilation structures*" or levels of understanding at which various post-genocidal societies tend to narrate events, and which separate genocide from the social order that produced it. They do so not by denying the facts, but by distorting their meaning.[25]

THE DENIAL OF THE IDENTITY OF VICTIMS

The victims of genocidal social practices are deliberately and repeatedly homogenized as "innocent." The dominant discourse at the moment of the implementation of genocide tends to depict victims as culpable in innumerable ways, transforming them into the agents responsible for the majority of social evils. Paradoxically, however, once the genocide has been accomplished, *and to the extent that the social consensus on which the perpetrators depended has eroded*, the hegemonic gaze may move toward an emphasis on the "innocence" of the victims, proceeding hand-in-hand with the demonization of the perpetrators and their consignment to the realm of "irrationality." In some societies, this process is accelerated by military defeat (as with the Nazis in Germany or the Hutu extremists in Rwanda), or by political defeat (as with the military dictatorships of Latin America). In other cases, the process occurs more slowly, as in Turkey or Indonesia. And in still other situations, when a consensus remains as to the legitimacy of the genocide in the society in which it occurred, the process of "constructing innocence" may take generations or even centuries – as with the annihilation of the indigenous populations of the modern states of the Americas.

However it occurs, this mode of constructing "innocent" victims ends up being even more effective than blaming them for their own destruction. It dilutes genocide as it appears to condemn it. It meshes easily with the image of mad, perverse, pathological and evil murderers that emerges from the ways the perpetrators themselves legitimize genocide. Of course, I am not suggesting that the victims deserve their fate. Rather, I am saying that we need to look more carefully at the discourses justifying the persecution, exclusion, and extermination of different victims.

The "hegemonic gaze" may also be located outside the genocidal society itself, affecting how onlookers evaluate the genocidal process. Consider again the case of Nazi Germany as viewed by contemporary members of the societies that combined to defeat it. The Nazis invented the myth of Aryan superiority to differentiate themselves from other groups (ethnic, religious, political, social, national, sexual, or otherwise). Using a biological metaphor, the Nazis stigmatized people belonging to these groups as "degenerates" who had corrupted the race or the *Volk* community.[26] However, something similar occurs in the way that Nazi Germany has been demonized in discourse since. This relies upon a binary structure of the type described earlier, one that contrasts "irrationality" and "absolute evil" with "innocence." The metaphysical category of absolute evil distracts attention from our everyday experience, leaving us safe from the distress that might be caused by examining the genocidal potential latent in every modern society, and all its members.

The question of innocence and absolute evil has been a classic mode of comprehending the Nazi experience. Most writers on Nazism take it for granted that the Jews were annihilated simply because they were Jews. However, if one examines carefully the populations exterminated by the Nazis, it is clear that the Jews played a central role in this process, precisely because being Jewish (from the perspective of the Central and Eastern European regimes of the 1930s) meant *more* than just a question of having three Jewish grandparents. The stigmatizing of certain groups was connected (more or less accurately) with their subversive potential or inability to adapt to a given social order. It should be remembered that most Jews in the 1930s saw themselves as "international" (which does not mean that they were involved in international conspiracies, as the Nazis alleged), and so were unconvinced by nationalist ideologies.

It is surprising to note the extent to which certain political, religious, and moral tendencies of Jewish collectivities in Central and Eastern Europe in the nineteenth and early twentieth centuries – in particular, in the area which the Jews called the "Pale of Settlement" – have been neglected or forgotten in scholarly analysis. A powerful symbol of this is the massive Jewish participation in numerous oppositional and contestatory movements (whether revolutionary or reformist), from the Spartacists to the communists, anarchists, Bundists (the Jewish Workers Party), and socialists, in Germany, Poland, Russia, Ukraine, and Lithuania. These include such specific cases as the "Jewish soviet" in Hungary under the Béla Kun government, the Jewish socialist prime minister Léon Blum in France, and the vital Jewish participation at the leadership level of various Russian and Polish revolutionary movements. The most important dimension, however, is not Jews' numerically large participation in such contestatory movements, but their link with a deeper, more global element, linked to the scant support which Jewish nationalism (Zionism) and non-Jewish European nationalisms generated among Jewish populations, up to the appearance of the Nazis on the scene. Owing to the persecutions suffered by Jews in Russia, Poland, and Lithuania, owing to their marginalization in Germany and France, Jewish communities continued to view themselves as "diasporic" in nature, founded on multiple identities, capable of transcending their Jewish cultural component; their assimilation within the national territories they inhabited, whether German, Polish, Russian, or French; their greater or lesser religious convictions (many Jewish groups were atheists, others were reformists, others orthodox, but all considered themselves Jewish beyond their specific religious or non-religious identification); and their political identity (which was highly varied, though in general forsaking a nationalist tendency for a diverse range of internationalist and diasporic currents of thought).

This is not to suggest that all Jews shared in this process of self-identification. Some, such as those of the Netherlands, were much more assimilated into the national identities of their countries. But these were the exceptions in the world of European Jewry during the first half of the twentieth century. In general, Jews stood apart from the wider patterns of European nationalism in this period. Only by understanding this tendency can we hope to comprehend the key elements of European Jewish identity, and the role these played in fueling the paranoid delirium of the Nazis with respect to the supposed "risks" that Jews posed to "Western European identity." The Jews obviously did not represent a threat of the kind depicted by the Nazis, but their predominant adoption of a multiple identity – their recognition of the multiplicity, complexity, and dynamism of identity formation – *did* pose a challenge to the narrow nationalisms then prevailing in Europe. This could only prove problematic and "subversive" for a model of identity, such as that of the Nazis, which sought to subordinate all such identifications to those of the organic *Volk* of a distinct national territory. In a philosophical sense, Jewish identity was constructed "in time," while modern European identities were constructed "in space."

It is this distinction that allows us to perceive Hitler not only as an alienated figure, but as an extreme expression of a hegemonic political tendency in modern Europe. This perspective also allows us to understand the complicity of diverse European regimes in the annihilation of the Jews, their failure to react, their refusal to accept Jewish refugees in their territories, among other elements that have generally remained unexplained or been relegated to a banal analysis of the greater or lesser "political will" of the diverse governments in question.[27]

Similarly, scattered groups of Gypsies who refused to adopt German as their mother tongue, to water down their centuries-old culture, or to accept the notion of private property, were lumped together with those who refused to accept sexual norms. In fact, any group that maintained a certain level of social self-determination became a political target for the stifling heteronomy imposed by the Nazis. To recover the identity of the victims, and preserve their memory and history, it is essential for us to understand why they were exterminated. Far from justifying their fate, this understanding is intended to reinstate the victims as social subjects.

Bettelheim touched on this controversial issue with his questioning of the Frank family as a worldwide symbol of the Holocaust. It is not that he did not respect their suffering. Rather, he felt that choosing the Franks as a symbol made it harder to understand the genocidal process. In Bruno Bettelheim's words:

> I believe that the worldwide acclaim given [Anne Frank's] story cannot be explained unless we recognize in it our wish to forget the gas chambers and our effort to do so by glorifying the ability to retreat into an extremely private world . . . What we miss is the importance of accepting the gas chambers as facts, so they can never again be allowed to exist. If all men are basically good . . . then, really, we can all continue with our daily lives and forget Auschwitz.[28]

According to Bettelheim, the Frank family became a symbol of the Holocaust not only because they did not try to escape or to fight back, but because they were a "civilized family," an "assimilated" family in this case that was not very different from other non-Jewish families in Europe. They continued to live in their own private world until their last day together. We might also add that the Franks were Dutch Jews, living in a Nazi-occupied territory rather than in Germany. Certainly, the Franks were victims of the Nazis; the point is that the use that has been made of their story does not help us to understand what the Nazis hated about the Jews to the point of wanting to kill them all.

On the other hand, the attention that has been given to the story of the Frank family seems to suggest that the internment in concentration camps of German antifascist Jews – members of the Communist Bund, Zionists, and even Orthodox Jews – was somehow more understandable, and perhaps "almost" justifiable. After all, they were political enemies; they were not murdered simply for being Jewish. The problem is that if we condemn the Holocaust for selecting the "wrong" victims, or because the Nazis over-estimated the subversive potential of Judaism and failed to understand the multiple and contradictory nature of Central European Jewish identity in the first half of the twentieth century, we perversely end up legitimizing the logic of genocide. We also miss the point that Central European Jews were murdered precisely for what they did, and not for what they failed to do.

THE TRANSFERENCE OF GUILT

A more subtle form of symbolic genocide is the transfer of guilt through scapegoating and self-scapegoating. Through a perverse psychological mechanism, those victims who actively oppose a genocidal regime – that is, those who are "less innocent" – are blamed or blame themselves for the deaths of those who are "more innocent." In this way, a chain of responsibility is forged that assigns varying degrees of guilt and innocence to the victims of genocide, while the actual perpetrators are regarded as a mere force of nature, meting out the punishment sought by the "guilty."

The Vilna ghetto established by the Nazis in the Lithuanian capital of Vilnius provides a clear example of transfer of responsibility. In 1943, the Judenrat agreed to hand over Yitzhak Wittenberg, the leader of Jewish armed resistance, to the Gestapo. In a speech delivered in the main square, Jacob Gens, the head of the ghetto, accused the Resistance of provoking the Nazis into liquidating the ghetto, and turned the population against them. Finally, Wittenberg himself made the decision to give himself up.[29]

If there is one lesson to be learned from the Vilna ghetto, it is that appeasement does not work. Later that same year, the whole of the ghetto was liquidated, and the only people who survived were the Resistance forces who fled to the surrounding forests. For the victims, appeasement was a way to buy time and avoid collective punishments; but for the perpetrators, it was simply a predictable result of the strategy of systematic weakening described earlier, allowing them time to solve the technical problems of implementing a "final solution." Appeasement brings no peace but the peace of the cemetery, where even the names of the dead have been erased.

HORROR AND PARALYSIS

In post-genocidal democracies, symbolic annihilation of the victims through the discourses of "innocence" and "metaphysical evil" is reinforced by the morbid fascination of the media and popular historians with the details of the crimes themselves. We are inundated with blow-by-blow accounts of suffering, descriptions of torture and execution, and other horrific testimonies, together with an abundance of spine-chilling photographs. None of these contributes much to an understanding of why the victims were killed. On the contrary, it simply perpetuates a sense of terror and paralysis throughout society. "Memory for the victims" is turned into a sort of horror show.

Similarly, the use of genocide as a political symbol in post-genocidal democracies is not linked to silence and oblivion. If the Armenian genocide continues to be a political taboo in modern Turkey, Western democracies have replaced the strategy of "taboo" with an excess of empty political declarations that avoid the question of the identity of the victims or the true beneficiaries of genocide, and so continue to make restorative justice impossible. In many post-genocidal societies, those who make a genuine effort to confront this injustice may end up being tortured or murdered. But even when the threat of physical violence is no longer present, a network of symbolic and discursive processes continues to imprison jurists, historians, and sociologists – and even poets – within its invisible walls, limiting what can be thought and said about genocide.

REFORMULATING SOCIAL RELATIONS: A STRUGGLE FOR IDENTITY

The six stages of modern genocide described above form a cycle, the central aim of which is to transform the society in which genocide takes place by destroying a way of life embodied by a particular group, and thus reorganizing social relations within the rest of society. The disappearance of the memory of the victims brought about by symbolic enactment – that is, by the enactment of genocide through discursive and other symbolic means – is an attempt to close the cycle. Not only do the victims no longer exist, but they allegedly "never existed" – or, if we know that they existed, we are no longer able to grasp how they lived or why they died. Otherwise the cycle might begin again.

What happens, then, to a society that remains silent while people are beaten in the streets and disappear? What happens to a society in which some denounce their neighbors, while others steal their jobs or businesses, their homes or other assets? All these forms of what might be called "moral participation" in genocide must inevitably lead to a blurring of moral distinctions, an inability to distinguish between right and wrong, or fair and unfair. This is true not only for those who live in a time of genocide, but for subsequent generations as well.

At the same time, the trauma produced in the population by a genocidal process, and internalized as a way of relating to others mediated by terror, may manifest itself in diverse ways. One of these is survivor guilt among those who have lost relatives, friends, or colleagues. Another is the inability to assert oneself in family or social relationships or to find a group identity, found in psychotherapy patients' storylines such as these:

> I am a Nazi, and if I express my anger, I will destroy in a most sadistic manner the lives of those who have frustrated me; in order to keep this a secret, I need to smile all the time.

> I believe that my father was an SS officer, and the fact that he is my love-object has to be hidden, so I should repeat acts to deny my Germanness.[30]

The transgenerational nature of guilt and denial among members of the "in-group" is visible in the way that young ethnic German psychoanalysts, even today, are afraid to explore patients' Nazi-related family histories.[31] The attempt by the perpetrators to create a "strong" homogeneous society through terror also destroys the in-group, to a greater or lesser extent – both morally and psychologically.

Moreover, post-genocidal societies that are unable to recognize and mourn the processes in which they have participated remain vulnerable to the repetition of authoritarian modes of political problem-solving. In Argentina, the expression "You don't exist" was first created by the repressors in the secret detention centers of the 1970s and filtered into the teenage slang of the 1980s and 1990s as a colloquial form of contempt.[32] But if genocide is not directed solely at the material victims of the annihilation process, one must ask: What happens to a society when it is full of people who participated in mass annihilation, preserved its silence, or seized its fruits – the properties of the victims? Is it the case that a small betrayal of human values in the course of one's work, the breaking of a strike, an act of aggression in the street, or an anonymous denunciation can be viewed as comparable to such a moral participation in genocide, whether through active consent or tolerance of inaction?

Perhaps observing the past in terms of the present, as Tzvetan Todorov has recommended, requires us to look at the present with greater mistrust.[33] Without knowing who the victims of genocide were and why they were annihilated, we hardly know who we are ourselves, and why we live as we do.

NOTES

1 Cited at the beginning of the *Revised and Updated Report on the Question of the Prevention and Punishment of the Crime of Genocide*, UN Doc. E/CN.4/Sub.2/1985/6 – also known as the "Whitaker Report," after its author, Benjamin Whitaker.

2 The Kingdom of Spain, founded by Ferdinand and Isabella in 1492, was not only Europe's first modern proto-state. Its Catholic confessionality excluded Jews and Muslims both physically and symbolically, despite centuries of social integration. In the same year, 1492, Columbus reached the Americas, and soon after debates began about whether the newly discovered peoples of the Americas were human or not.

   Perhaps an earlier starting point for our model is the *Malleus Maleficarum* (The Hammer of Witches), published in Germany in 1487. Originally applied to female freethinkers and other outsiders, the methods outlined in this handbook for witch-hunters and Inquisitors were used by the Inquisition over the centuries in the proto-modern stigmatization, harassment, and destruction of people and social relations.

3 Lemkin wrote: "Genocide has two phases: one, destruction of the national pattern of the oppressed group; the other, the imposition of the national pattern of the oppressor." Raphael Lemkin, *Axis Rule in Occupied Europe: Laws of Occupation, Analysis of Government, Proposals for Redress* (Clark, NJ: The Lawbook Exchange Ltd., 2005), p. 79.

4 Matthias Bjørnlund, Eric Markusen, and Martin Mennecke, "What is Genocide? A Search for Common Ground Between the Legal and Non-Legal Definitions," in Daniel Feierstein, ed., *Genocidio: la administración de la muerte en la modernidad* (Buenos Aires: EDUNTREF, 2005), pp. 17–48. This work was submitted in English at the First International Conference on "Analysis of the Social Practices of Genocide," at the Faculty of Law, University of Buenos Aires, 11–15 November, 2003.

5 Martin Shaw, "War and Genocide: A Sociological Approach," in *Online Encyclopedia of Mass Violence*. Available at: www.massviolence.org/Article?id_article=45.

6 Suzette Barnaby, "Legal Ethics for the Real World: A Model for Engaging First Year Law Students," *Queensland University of Technology Law and Justice Journal*, 4: 2 (2004). Available at: http://www.austlii.edu.au/au/journals/QUTLJJ/2004/16.html.

7 Although I have used the term "genocidal social practices" more or less intuitively in earlier writings (for example *Cinco estudios sobre genocidio*, Buenos Aires: Acervo Cultural Editores, 1997), I first became aware of its potential for systematic explanation after speaking to survivors of the Argentine genocide. As Marx says about social relations, and Piaget says about awareness: "he doesn't know it but he does it." It was these survivors who made me *know* it. For an account in Spanish of what I have called "reorganizing genocide," see Daniel Feierstein, *El genocidio como práctica social* (Buenos Aires: Fondo de Cultura Económica, 2007).

8 Jean Piaget, *The Moral Judgment of the Child* (Glencoe, IL: The Free Press, 1948), p. 319.

9 Ibid., p. 324.

10 Robert Paul Wolff, *In Defense of Anarchism* (Berkeley, CA: University of California Press, 1998), p. 19.

11 See Bill Ashcroft, Gareth Griffiths, and Helen Tiffin, *Key Concepts in Postcolonial Studies* (London: Routledge, 2003).

12 See Frantz Fanon, *Black Skin, White Mask* (New York: Grove Press, 1967).

13 Michel Foucault, *Society Must Be Defended: Lectures at the Collège de France, 1975–1976* (London: Penguin, 2004), pp. 15–16.

14 Michel Foucault, *The History of Sexuality, Vol. 1: The Will to Knowledge* (London: Penguin, 1998), p. 137.

15 Foucault, *Society Must Be Defended*, p. 256.

16 Gregory Stanton, "The 8 Stages of Genocide." Available at: www.genocidewatch.org/eightstages.htm.

17 Discussions of why the Nazis moved from a policy of forcing Jews to emigrate to one of extermination often assume that the earlier policies failed, as if the Nazis' only goal were to separate the "different" from the "same." One wonders, however, if migration actually solves the problems of eradicating certain social relations (autonomy, solidarity, and critical thinking), or if it is just an intermediate step toward genocide. What would have happened if the policy of expelling Jews from Germany had succeeded? Would it have been enough to expel stigmatized groups, as the Inquisition had done in Spain? Or did death play a central role in this new technology of power in constructing power relations? Could the Nazis have broken down social relations within the German state – let alone within the Reich or across the whole of Europe – without the use of terror involving mass annihilation? See, for example, Christopher Browning, *The Path to Genocide* (Cambridge: Cambridge University Press, 1992). For the role of the term "Nazi terror" in Nazi genocidal social practices, see Eric. A. Johnson's *Nazi Terror: The Gestapo, Jews and Ordinary Germans* (New York: Basic Books, 1999). For a discussion of the role of terror in Argentina, see the early work of Juan Corradi: "The Mode of Destruction: Terror in Argentina," *Telos*, 54 (1982–1983), pp. 61–76; *A veinte años del golpe. Con memoria democrática* (Rosario: Homo Sapiens, 1996); and Juan Corradi, Patricia Weiss Fagen, and Manuel Antonio Garretón, *Fear at the Edge: State Terror and Resistance in Latin America* (Berkeley, CA: University of California Press, 1992).

18 In general, this is how isolation is perceived in the logic of the ghetto. The perception was similar in the first proto-Jewish ghetto in the city of Venice from 1515.

19 Jaika Grossman, *La resistencia clandestina* (Buenos Aires: Ed. Milá, 1990), p. 30.

20 Ibid., p. 83.

21 See Bruno Bettelheim, "Individual and Mass Behavior in Extreme Situations," *Journal of Abnormal and Social Psychology*, 38 (1943), pp. 417–452.

22 Primo Levi, *If This is a Man* (London: Abacus, 1987), p. 97.

23 Foucault, *Society Must Be Defended*, Chapter 11.

24 For a more extended account of what I understand by this concept, see my *Cinco estudios sobre genocidio*, and *Seis estudios sobre genocidio. Análisis de relaciones sociales: otredad, exclusión, exterminio* (Buenos Aires: EUDEBA, 2000).

25 For an account of assimilation structures, see the work of Jean Piaget and Rolando García, *Psicogénesis e historia de la ciencia* (México: Siglo XXI, 1982).

26 The Nazis also applied "re-education" policies for "undisciplined workers" and even for some political dissidents and those accused of "crimes of opinion" (who were sent to labor camps or concentration camps). On the other hand, Jews, Gypsies, homosexuals, the "anti-social," "Bolsheviks," and Russian political prisoners were considered "racially degenerate," and thus irredeemable, with definitely no place in the new German society. Members of these groups were at first shot publicly and/or secretly, and later annihilated in mass extermination camps.

27 For a historical analysis of the political, cultural, and identity aspects of Jews in the Pale of Settlement during the interwar period, see Ezra Mendelsohn, *The Jews of East Central Europe between the World Wars* (Bloomington, IN: Indiana University Press, 1987). For a perspective that emphasizes the political character of Jewish identity during this time, and its links to the Nazi logic of destruction, see Arno Mayer, *Why Did the Heavens Not Darken? The "Final Solution" in History* (New York: Pantheon Books, 1990). For a perspective more centered in Jewish identity as multiple identity, see Zygmunt Bauman, *Modernity and the Holocaust* (Cambridge: Polity Press, 1989).

28 Bruno Bettelheim, "The Ignored Lesson of Anne Frank," in Sandra Solotaroff-Enzer, ed., *Anne Frank: Reflections on Her Life and Legacy* (Urbana, IL: University of Illinois Press, 2000), pp. 186–190.

29 For a detailed analysis of the Vilna ghetto, see my article, "The Dilemma of Wittenberg: Reflections on Tactics and Ethics," *Shofar: Journal of Jewish Studies*, 20: 2 (Winter 2002), pp. 61–68.

30 Vamik Volkan, Gabriele Ast, and William F. Greer, Jr., *The Third Reich in the Unconscious: Transgenerational Transmission and Its Consequences* (New York: Brunner-Routledge, 2002), p. 40.

31 Ibid., p. 160.

32 For a detailed account of the effects of the Argentine genocide on language, see Marguerite Feitlowitz, *A Lexicon of Terror: Argentina and the Legacies of Torture* (New York: Oxford University Press, 1998).

33 Tzvetan Todorov, *Los abusos de la memoria* (Barcelona: Paidós, 2000).

Figure 3.1 Émile Durkheim
(1858–1917).

Source: Unknown.

Figure 3.2 Zygmunt Bauman
(1925–).

Source: Courtesy Emanuele
Scotti/Flickr.

CHAPTER 3

Genocidal Moralities

A critique

Christopher J. Powell

INTRODUCTION

This chapter uses Émile Durkheim's conception of morality to advance a new theoretical concept for the empirical investigation of genocides: genocidal moralities. Genocidal moralities are emergent social structures within which shared practices of approval and disapproval work to positively sanction genocidal action and negatively sanction resistance to or non-participation in genocide. Genocidal moralities can share familiar features of more pedestrian moralities, including: framing of action as duty or obligation pursued for its own sake; orientation to the achievement of a perceived supra-individual good and the promotion of social solidarity; and the integration of individuals into an organic whole through knowledge of the dynamics of that entity and their relation to it. The existence of genocidal moralities helps to explain the quasi-voluntary, self-directed aspects of individuals' participation in genocide, especially at the grassroots level of genocidal violence.

To conceive of the possibility of genocidal moralities, it is necessary to frame morality not as a transcendent metaphysical essence, but as a particular kind of social institution, and to investigate the historical relationship between that institution and genocide. I will argue that the relationship between genocide and morality so conceived has not always been negative. In some times and places, morality has made a positive contribution to enabling and facilitating genocide, and to denial or triumphalism about it by the perpetrators after the fact. In such situations, genocide has been *moralized*. The moralizing of genocide means that, for genocide to take place, it is not always the case that people's moral sensibilities must simply be neutralized or overpowered. Sometimes individuals' moral dispositions are activated and strengthened through their involvement in genocide. This is important to understanding genocide, and it also prompts us to revise our understanding of morality. When genocide has occurred or is occurring, social scientists trying to explain its occurrence should ask, among their other questions, how local moral norms were enlisted, and how they were modified or redirected or reconstructed, to contribute to genocide. More radically, the occasional complicity of morality in genocide implies that morality is not always opposed to the most extreme negations of human life. Morality cannot reliably protect us from becoming perpetrators of atrocity.

In the 1980s and early 1990s, when few sociologists were writing about genocide, those who did so issued a challenge: genocide should be investigated sociologically, not only for its own sake, but for what it tells us about normal social institutions. "No stream of sociology or major theorist since 1945 has considered genocide focally, either to explain genocide or to consider its implications for theories of the state, of development, and of community and society".[1]

Sociologists since then have taken up this challenge, examining the implications of genocide for our understanding of state power, of liberal democracy, and of gender.[2] Much of this work has come from the framework of analytic conflict theory, which emphasizes interests and power in the analysis of social structures. This work de-emphasizes morality as an empirical phenomenon and explanatory category. The concept of "morality" has been more often a feature of functionalist thought that analyzes society as an integrated whole, unified by shared moral norms. But between thinking of morality as the dominant organizing force of society and conceptualizing it as an epiphenomenon of political and economic interests, there lies a third position: one that treats morality as consequential in its own right, but ambivalent and contested. In other words, morality can be analyzed as an emergent social structure, with its own inner imperatives and effects on social action. It does not always and automatically tend to produce social solidarity – much less inclusion, tolerance, or human dignity – and is not usually defined by consensus. From one social setting to another, and within any given social setting, morality can take multiple forms. Some of these may oppose genocide, while others may facilitate it.

My argument, briefly, is as follows: (1) in some times and places, genocide has been instituted as a moral obligation, so that individuals have been impelled to genocide not only by hatred, or greed, or obedience, or fear, but by a sense of *moral duty* and *higher purpose*, as service to something outside of and greater than themselves; and (2) that this historical fact should prompt us to take a critical attitude to morality itself – not only to particular kinds of morality, but to morality as an institution.

The argument unfolds in three stages. In the first and longest section, I provide a theoretical discussion of morality as it has been conceptualized by sociologists. My aim here is to explain what is involved in treating morality as an empirical object of study: as something that we can examine to discern how it operates. In the second part, I offer a historical discussion of how particular genocides have been moralized. In the conclusion, I briefly consider where the notion of genocidal moralities leaves us in terms of our attitude toward morality as a social practice.

PART 1: THE SOCIOLOGY OF MORALITY

Bauman and Arendt

Zygmunt Bauman's *Modernity and the Holocaust*[3] was an important step forward in genocide scholarship. The predominant tendencies in the field at the time Bauman's work appeared were either to explain genocide in terms of the breakdown of social norms, or to explain each particular genocide in terms of factors unique to the society that produced it. In contrast to both of these tendencies, Bauman sought to show how the Holocaust was produced by norms and institutions that are general to modern society.

Bauman's argument highlighted two particular forms of modern rationality. The first was scientific rationality, which in the nineteenth century took the cultural practices of hating and despising those who are different from us (what Bauman calls "heterophobia"), and gave them a new currency in the form of biological racism. The second was bureaucratic rationality, which allowed the state to mobilize and coordinate human action on an unprecedented scale and with unprecedented efficiency, while at the same time distancing social actors from the human and moral consequences of their actions. Bauman argued that the Holocaust was not a throwback to some atavistic evil lurking "in the hearts of men"; it actually expressed that most modernist of aspirations, the impulse to improve society through planning and deliberate action. What went wrong was not that the modern project broke down, but that it was granted unchecked power: "When the modernist dream is embraced by an absolute power able to monopolize modern vehicles of rational action, and when that power attains freedom from effective social control, genocide follows. A modern genocide – like the Holocaust."[4]

Central to this argument is the observation that modern institutions, especially bureaucratic rationality, work to distance individuals from the consequences of their actions, and to separate action from the demands of conscience. People participate in genocide not by stoning their neighbors to death in a furious mob action, but by flipping switches, redirecting rail traffic, or filling out requisition forms for truck parts. Bauman was not the first to arrive at this insight; rather, he drew upon Raul Hilberg's ground-breaking historical work, *The Destruction of the European Jews*.[5] But distinctive to Bauman's argument was his joining of this analysis to a critique of modernity, and in particular to a critique of the sociological tradition grounded in the work of Émile Durkheim.

According to Bauman, Durkheim, and the sociological tradition that follows him, have treated society as the source of all morality: as always and everywhere a moralizing influence on essentially amoral individuals. Bauman argued that his own analysis of the Holocaust refuted the Durkheimian position: in the Holocaust, modern society was a source of immorality. Discourses of scientific racism and techniques of social distancing worked specifically to nullify people's moral qualms about participating in mass murder. The Holocaust happened because of the social production of immorality.

The terms in which Bauman frames the problem echo the ones used by Hannah Arendt in *Eichmann in Jerusalem*.[6] Adolf Eichmann was a senior Nazi bureaucrat who oversaw the deportation of Jews to ghettoes and concentration camps in occupied Eastern Europe. After the war, he went into hiding in Argentina, was seized there by Israeli Mossad agents in 1960, and was tried, convicted, and executed in Jerusalem in

1961–1962. As reported by Arendt, Eichmann's testimony at his trial indicated clearly that he did not have strong anti-Semitic feelings, and that his involvement in the Jewish extermination campaign was driven by obedience and a sense of duty, rather than hatred. In fact, Eichmann claimed that news of the Final Solution demoralized and angered him, because he had hoped to be able to secure some existence for Jews outside the borders of the Third Reich. Arendt understood Eichmann's continued involvement in the Final Solution as an expression of moral cowardice and blind submission to authority. For both Arendt and Bauman, the institutional structures of the Nazi state worked to silence the human conscience. From this thesis, Bauman infers that Durkheim was wrong: society is not the ultimate source of morality; human nature is. Society is at best ambivalent. Sometimes it contributes to morality, and sometimes it detracts from it.

Against essentialism

Bauman opened up the possibility for sociological explanations of genocide that treated it as a systemic product of normal social institutions. Although Leo Kuper had theorized genocide as a specific product of the political tensions found in all modern states, other genocide scholars persisted in reading genocide as symptomatic of a breakdown of society.[7] Bauman's analysis rebutted the crude functionalism that treats society as always tending toward greater integration and mutual complementarity of its parts.

On these grounds, Bauman called for a new sociology of morality that recognized the capacity of society to negate individuals' impulses toward compassion and common human feeling. However, his project had its own built-in limitations. Where Durkheimian functionalism might be considered to have uncritically treated society as the foundation of all that is good, Bauman found his own timeless foundation for the good: the human individual:

> The socially enforced moral systems are communally based and promoted – and hence in a pluralist, heterogeneous world, irreparably relative. *This relativism, however, does not apply to the human "ability to tell right from wrong."* Such an ability must be grounded in something other than the *conscience collective* of society. Every given society faces such an ability ready formed, much as it faces human biological constitution, physiological needs, or psychological drives. And it does with such ability what it admits of doing with those other stubborn realities: it tries to suppress it, or harness it to its own ends, or channel it in a direction it considers useful or harmless. *The process of socialization consists in the manipulation of moral capacity* – not in its production. And the moral capacity that is manipulated entails not only certain principles which later become a passive object of social processing; it includes as well the ability to resist, escape and survive the processing, so that at the end of the day the authority and the responsibility for moral choices rest where they resided at the start: with the human person.[8]

In a word, Bauman's position is *essentialist*. He assumes that the terms "morally right" and "morally wrong" have a truth-value that is irreducible to their status as social constructions, and that human beings have an innate capacity to identify this moral truth. Bauman cites Levinas in support of the contention that the essence of morality, its "pristine source," is "human responsibility for the other."[9] And this essence does not just exist passively: it is expressed as a definite natural tendency in human beings, which must be negated by society to make genocide possible:

> The Holocaust could be accomplished only on the condition of neutralizing the impact of primeval moral drives, of isolating the machinery of murder from the sphere where such drives arise and apply, of rendering such drives marginal or altogether irrelevant to the task.[10]

But while it is appealing to believe that human beings have an essential responsibility for each other, and while it may be productive to argue that we *ought* to practice such a responsibility, assuming that we always already *have* such a responsibility is a sociological error. Bauman's position rests on an empirical and historical claim: that there is a natural human ability to tell right from wrong, and that this ability has definite consequences which tend in a particular direction (a telos). Unless this "ability to tell right from wrong" has a telos, then Bauman's claim lacks substance. An anti-essentialist could take the view that humans have an innate propensity to make moral distinctions, akin to our innate propensity to learn language, but that the content of these distinctions, like the specific language that we will learn, is entirely supplied by socialization. This is not Bauman's position. He wants to hold individuals morally responsible for doing something that he believes is evil, even when they are socialized by state, church, family, and public opinion to believe that their actions are good. For this attribution of responsibility to make sense, it must still be possible to say, in accusation, "you ought to have known better." Essentialism presumes that the essence in question somehow acts as a causal force in human history. Always and everywhere, the essence pushes events toward one particular destination, in opposition to other forces that push them in other directions. Thus, moral essentialism of any kind involves a very large claim about human history. The fact that it accords with a certain common sense should not blind us to the fact that it is an enormous claim, amounting to a presumed law of nature. If there is such a universal tendency in all human beings toward a particular form of moral good, this ought to be visible as exerting a differential effect on the historical development of societies.

Immediately, one faces the question: how can a *universal* differential effect be isolated? If all human beings possess an innate propensity to make particular moral judgments, how can social scientists frame a natural experiment that will allow us to differentiate between the presence and absence of such a propensity? This is not impossible in principle. Natural scientists do, after all, identify universal constants in the physical universe. However, it is easier to identify a constant when it expresses an inviolable relation, such as the relationship between the mass of two bodies, the distance between them, and the gravitational attraction they exert on each other. By contrast, the "sense of right and wrong" that Bauman proposes *is* violated quite frequently. Indeed, his concern is precisely that modern society overrides it too much of the time.[11] So it must be a very *weak* causal force. Isolating the effect of a weak but universal causal force in the complex system that is society is a formidable task. Yet Bauman wants the sociology of morality to proceed as if this verification had already been demonstrated.

Gabriel Abend observes that a sociology of morality must choose between assuming that universal moral essences exist, and therefore that they exert a definite causal influence on social development; or proceeding as if they had no such causal influence and, therefore, as if they did not exist.[12] Either option involves the risk of error. However, Abend points out that the harm done by mistakenly assuming the presence of moral essences is greater than that done by mistakenly assuming their absence. If we assume that moral truth does not exist, when in fact it does, we have left out something important from the analysis. "Still," says Abend, "our analysis of social institutions, culture, language, and so on, would be correct. At least we would have gotten this part of the story right."[13] If we assume that moral truth exists when it does not, the consequences are "much more serious":

> Given the epistemic values supported by the scientific ethos, it is preferable to give a true account that misses part of the story rather than to affirm that x is true when in fact x is false. All other things being equal, theory T1 – which fails to endorse the true statement p – is to be chosen over theory T2 – which makes the false statement not-p.[14]

This is because it is easier to add a missing element to an explanation than to untangle, from a complex theory, a thread of explanation that turns out to depend on something fictitious.

The question of essences in sociological explanation has been considered in an instructive way by sociologists of scientific knowledge. Prior to the emergence of its Strong Programme, the sociology of knowledge treated knowledge considered to be scientifically "correct" differently from that considered scientifically false.[15] Belief in true explanations was considered to be caused by the fact that they were true, combined with the propensity of human reason to perceive the truth through rigorous systematic study. Only false beliefs could be explained by social factors such as language, ideology, or power relations. The sociology of knowledge was therefore merely a "sociology of error." One flaw in this approach was that the causal factors included in sociologists' explanations of what people considered to be true depended crucially on what the sociologists themselves considered to be true. Sociological explanation thereby became an extension of the sociologist's own prejudices about truth. The Strong Programme's remedy for this was the principle of symmetry: both true and false knowledge-claims had to be explicable in the same sociological terms. This meant that sociologists had to remain agnostic about the truth of those knowledge-claims, and construct their explanations in a way that did not depend on the truth or falsity of those claims.

Bauman's argument exemplifies an asymmetrical sociology of morality, proposing sociological explanations for behavior that the author condemns, and falling back on "primeval moral drives" to explain behavior that the author condones. This procedure lends itself to treating personal or culturally specific moral standards as if they were laws of nature. To implement a symmetrical understanding of morality and its relation to genocide, it helps to return, with a critical eye, to Durkheim.

Durkheim

Durkheim conceptualized morality as a *social fact*, and insisted that "the first and most basic rule" of sociological method "is *to consider social facts as things*."[16] What did he mean by this?

To begin with, Durkheim's method presumes scientific naturalism.[17] Every object that science attempts to explain must exist entirely within the natural universe; scientists have no business commenting on metaphysical universals. Sociology, as a science, treats social phenomena in terms of natural facts. To steer sociology away from reliance on psychological explanations, Durkheim proposed a special kind of natural fact that would serve as the object and the vehicle of sociological explanation: the social fact.

> A social fact is any way of acting, whether fixed or not, capable of exerting over the individual an external constraint; or: which is general over the whole of a given society whilst having an existence of its own, independent of its individual manifestations.[18]

In contemporary terms, we would say that a social fact is an *emergent structure*. Loosely speaking, emergence refers to the quality of "the whole being greater than the sum of its parts," or "much coming from little."[19] More rigorously, it can refer to "the arising of novel and coherent structures, patterns, and properties during the process of self-organization in complex systems."[20] In Durkheim's theory, social facts exist outside individuals and constrain them, because they have dynamic properties that emerge from and exceed the properties of individual human action. Social facts are irreducible to individual human beings, in the same way that a human body is irreducible to the individual cells that compose it, or a living organism is irreducible to the nonliving chemical compounds from which it is formed.[21] The state, the Catholic Church, the rules of baseball, table manners, fashion, economic markets, currents of popular opinion – all of these are examples of structures that Durkheim would consider social facts.

To treat morality sociologically, Durkheim treats it as a social fact. That is, it is a way of acting that exists independently of its individual manifestations, is general throughout society, and constrains individuals from outside themselves. What distinguishes morality from other social facts? Durkheim proposes that social facts must be defined, not in terms of how people experience them subjectively, but with reference to external, objective criteria that can be empirically verified. To do otherwise is to risk the kind of ethnocentric error that I have described above:

> Garofalo takes for the *genus* what is only the species or merely a simple variation . . . The same error of method causes certain observers to deny to savages any kind of morality. They start from the idea that our morality is *the* morality. But it is either clearly unknown among primitive peoples or exists only in a rudimentary state, so that this definition is an arbitrary one.[22]

To avoid this error, we must examine morality not in terms of how people *think*, but of how they *act*. From this perspective Durkheim discerns a rule for uniformly defining moral phenomena:

To decide whether a precept is a moral one or not we must investigate whether it presents the external mark of morality. This mark consists of a widespread, repressive sanction, that is to say a condemnation by public opinion which consists of avenging any violation of the precept. Whenever we are confronted with a fact that presents this characteristic we have no right to deny its moral character, for this is proof that it is of the same nature as other moral facts.[23]

The presence of *sanction* provides Durkheim with a clear and consistent formal standard for deciding whether a phenomenon is moral.[24] He argues that the external property of a social fact is causally linked to its inner nature,[25] so that whenever we find a rule of conduct that is sanctioned, no matter how much it may offend our own sensibilities, this outward characteristic is a sure sign that the inner constitution of this way of acting, its structural nature, will be similar to other ways of acting that we are more accustomed to calling "moral."

This, then, is Durkheim's formal definition of the phenomenon of morality as a kind of social fact. Proceeding from this conception, Durkheim elaborates what he perceives to be the substance of morality in modern societies; that is, societies characterized by a complex division of labor. Contemporary morality has three elements, Durkheim argues: authority, impersonality, and autonomy.[26] To begin with, rules of behavior are considered "moral" to the extent that they are obeyed not merely out of practical utility, but for their own sake, as an obligation or duty. Thus, the first element of morality is that it is *authoritative*.[27] Second, moral rules are those that pursue a greater good beyond merely individual gain. Since, in Durkheim's view, the good of another or even of many others is only an instance of individual gain, it follows that the good that morality seeks must pertain to some supra-individual entity. Within the natural universe, there is one such entity to which individuals belong: society, understood as an objectively existing ensemble of social facts, having a life of its own irreducible to that of the individuals who constitute it:

> Moral goals, then, are those the object of which is society. To act morally is to act in terms of the collective interest . . . Above and beyond me as a conscious being, above and beyond those sentient beings who are other individual human beings, there is nothing else save that sentient being that is society. By this I mean anything that is a human group, the family as well as the nation, and humanity, at least to the extent that they constitute societies.[28]

Third and finally, the morality proper to complex modern societies is one that fosters the autonomy of the individual. However, this is a circumscribed autonomy, bounded by the individual's irreducible dependence on society. This dependence only increases as individuals grow more different from one another – that is to say, more individual. This process, in turn, reflects the increasing complexity of the division of labor. This complexity demands a transition from the blind obedience that characterizes older forms of morality; individuals must possess knowledge of their relation to the organic life of the whole:

> What prompts the faithful to see that the world is good in principle because it is the world of a good being, we can establish a posteriori to the extent that science permits

us to establish rationally what faith postulates a priori. Such conformity does not amount to passive resignation but to enlightened allegiance. Conforming to the order of things because one is sure that it is everything it ought to be is not submitting to a constraint.[29]

These three elements distinguish the morality that Durkheim thought was naturally evolving in modern societies. It was, he believed, the morality best suited to the integration and development of society under the conditions in which it existed, and therefore the form of morality that scientific reason decreed valid.

Whereas Durkheim's formal definition of moral phenomena is generic enough to allow for robust cross-cultural comparisons, his attempt to specify the morality common to modern societies bears the marks of its author's subjective position. Its conception of morality as authoritative and abstract rules bears strong masculine and patriarchal overtones. The assumption of the mutual complementarity of the institutions of society and the integrative character of the division of labor articulates a comfortably middle-class perception of the world. However, as I will show below, it is a robust enough conception to generate consistent but counterintuitive findings. If the actions of the perpetrators of genocide can, in some cases, be shown to be consistent with Durkheim's conception of morality, then his work will have enabled us to frame a new kind of object for empirical investigation: genocidal moralities.

PART 2: GENOCIDAL MORALITIES

In what follows, wherever I use the terms "moral" or "morality," I refer always to the particular kind of social fact defined above, and actions that are consistent with the imperatives of that fact. That is, I use the word "moral" in the same descriptive sense as one uses the word "legal" or "customary": to designate conformity with a particular kind of socially established norm. At no point do I invoke a transcendental or universal standard of morality. *And when I write that some way of acting is moral, I am in no way indicating my approval of it.*

At least three cases of genocidal action have satisfied Durkheim's definition of moral phenomena. These are: the Nazi Holocaust, the Turkish genocide of the Armenians, and the genocides of the First Peoples of North America.

The Nazi Holocaust

Can genocide be an authoritative obligation, a duty carried out for its own sake and not as a means to some personal end? Can this obligation be articulated in terms of an individual autonomy that is defined through knowledge of one's relation to the life of the whole? In *The Nazi Conscience,* historian Claudia Koonz shows that it has been.

While a core of fanatics in the Nazi party were motivated by anti-Semitic hatred, persuading the majority of Germans to support the Nazi agenda meant appealing to their sense of virtue. To do this, the Nazis formulated a value-system with four principal features, three of which were common to other Western societies. First, the life of the people, or *Volk*, was understood to resemble that of an organism, "marked by stages of birth, growth, expansion, decline, and death."[30] This organic life required individuals to "put collective need ahead of individual greed," to ensure the health of the community. Second, values were conceived as relative to the nature and environment of the community in which they evolved. But whereas cultural anthropologists like Franz Boas used moral relativism to argue for humanistic tolerance, the Nazis asserted that a person's *Volk*, and not humanity as a whole, was the ultimate object of morality. Third, aggression against undesirable populations in conquered lands was justified as having ample precedent – in American attitudes toward Native peoples, for example. Fourth, and distinct to Germany at the time, the government was accorded "the right to annul the legal protections of assimilated citizens on the basis of what the government defined as their ethnicity."[31] Even this was not unprecedented; but the Nazis pushed the envelope of persecution by defining ethnicity and exclusion in terms that "bore no physical or cultural markers."[32] Overall, the Nazis' successful effort to present themselves as bearers of a lofty ethical standard must be appreciated if we are to understand how the Final Solution became possible.

From 1923 onwards, and particularly from 1933 to 1939, Hitler learned to minimize anti-Semitic references in his public speeches.[33] After 1933, the undisciplined anti-Semitic violence of the brown-shirted Stormtroopers (SA) was superseded by the educated, disciplined ethnic fundamentalism of the SS (the *Schutzstaffel*, or "protective squadron").[34] In schools and universities, in youth programs and family education seminars, in newspapers and civil society organizations, the Nazis cultivated an idealistic and self-sacrificing sense of love for and duty toward the German *Volk*.[35] Scientists set to work formulating strict racial categorizations, and although they persistently met with failure, the idea of the *Volk* as a natural, biological unit of human community gained widespread legitimacy through discourses that mentioned Jews only tangentially, and usually in moderated tones. Through a lively and participatory public discourse, the Nazis established a conceptual framework that naturalized Jewish exclusion from citizenship and moral obligation by situating that exclusion within a larger framework that defined positive ideals and aspirations for individuals and the nation.

It is this fearsome accomplishment that explains the response of a former Hitler Youth member, Alfons Heck, who in 1940 watched the Gestapo take away his best friend, Heinz, and all the Jews in his village. "He did not say to himself, 'How terrible they are arresting Jews.' Having absorbed knowledge about the 'Jewish menace,' he said, 'what a misfortune Heinz is Jewish.' As an adult he recalled, 'I accepted deportation as just.'"[36] It also explains, I think, the self-defensive claim of Adolf Eichmann that he was only "following orders." Prosecution evidence at his trial showed that Eichmann did more than follow the orders he was given: he acted creatively and proactively in the spirit of those directives. In accordance with the time-honored Western practice of defining morality in opposition to merely animal sentiments, the Nazi leadership exhorted its agents to stifle any "animal pity" they might feel for the victims of genocide.[37] Eichmann, the good Nazi, overcame his animal pity; he did his duty.

Turkey

To what I have written above, one might object that Durkheim understood morality as conducive to social solidarity, and to the preservation of the integrity of the social body. It is clear that the Nazis had their own conception of the organic integrity of the social body, one to which Jews and other foreign elements were parasitic or pathological, and so in need of expulsion. Nevertheless, one might argue on functionalist grounds that the Nazi morality was not a true morality, because it was falsified by its maladaptive evolutionary outcome: that is, the defeat of the Third Reich in the Second World War, and the subsequent occupation and division of the German nation. Two other examples suggest that this is not the inevitable fate of nations that perpetrate genocide.

During the First World War, the "Young Turk" government of what was still formally the Ottoman Empire systematically eliminated most of the Armenian population of the country through a combination of massacre and deportation. Indeed, deportation by forced march of women and children through barren deserts and mountain passes functioned as a form of massacre. The Armenian genocide claimed over 800,000 lives, perhaps as many as 1.5 million.[38]

One of the ideological proponents of the genocide was a sociologist named Ziya Gökalp. Gökalp has been called "the father of Turkish nationalism" and is regarded by many as "the pre-eminent Turkish thinker of the century"; he was also a dominant figure in Turkish sociology.[39] He used the ideas of Comte, Spencer, and Durkheim concerning the organic unity of society to justify an "ultra-nationalist perspective which left no room for individual liberties and initiative."[40] In particular, he borrowed Durkheim's ideas about social solidarity, moral unity, the division of labor, and corporatist political structures to argue that the removal of Armenians from the Ottoman Empire was necessary to create "a society consisting of people who speak the same language, have had the same education and are united in their religious and aesthetic ideals – in short those who have a common culture and religion."[41] These ideas resonated with the agenda of the Young Turk government, and they expressed what that government hoped to achieve by its decision to obliterate the Armenian community by a combination of massacre and forced expulsion.

Although the Nazi genocide did succeed in its monstrous objective of all but obliterating Jewry as a sociocultural force in Western and Central Europe, the military defeat of the Axis powers meant that it could not fulfill its ultimate function of consolidating the moral basis for the German empire. Unlike Hitler's, however, the Turkish genocide succeeded. Through murder, expulsion, and forced conversion, a pre-war Armenian population estimated to be between 1.6 and 2.1 million was reduced to a tiny vestige surviving only in Constantinople.[42] The net effect was to obliterate the Armenian cultural presence within the Ottoman Empire. This obliteration averted continued European intervention into Turkish affairs over the Armenian Question, and removed an ethnic barrier between Ottoman Turks and Turkic peoples of the Caucasus and Transcaspia.[43] The multicultural and cosmopolitan Ottoman Empire, which had been dissolving over the previous several decades, was reincarnated as the modern, ethnically based nation-state of Turkey. Melson observes that "the Turkish revolution initiated by the CUP [Committee of Union and Progress] was successful in creating a new Turkey, but it also came close to destroying an ancient people in the process."[44] It is more precise, however, to observe that the latter was a means to the former. The Turkish state continues to deny that a genocide took place; discussion of any genocide against Armenians is prohibited by law, and Turkey threatens repercussions against other states or even foreign individuals who recognize the genocide. The Turkish solidarity that Gökalp dreamed of survives to this day.

North America

Finally, citizens of colonial states may consider the moralization of genocide in our own history. To this end, we should pause to review the meaning of the term "genocide." For many North Americans, it has come to mean the physical extermination of a group of people, or to be vaguely synonymous with mass murder. This interpretation coheres with the strongly individualistic orientation of Anglo-American political and legal culture. But the term has a broader and, I think, more robust meaning, supplied by the person who coined it.

The word "genocide" was invented by the Polish legal scholar and activist, Raphael Lemkin, and first disseminated in his 1944 book *Axis Rule in Occupied Europe*. Lemkin made a lifetime study of genocide, both in contemporary Europe and historically. Lemkin was convinced that the different nations of the world each made a unique contribution to the collective human heritage, and was concerned to provide for nations a right to life, parallel to the right to life of individuals. He was concerned with nations as Durkheim conceived them, as supra-individual social facts, and his conception of genocide reflects this:

> By "genocide" we mean the destruction of a nation or of an ethnic group . . . Generally speaking, genocide does not necessarily mean the immediate destruction of a nation, except when accomplished by mass killings of all members of a nation. It is intended rather to signify a coordinated plan of different actions aiming at the destruction of essential foundations of the life of national groups, with the aim of annihilating the groups themselves. The objectives of such a plan would be disintegration of the political and social institutions, of culture, language, national feelings, religion, and the economic existence of national groups, and the destruction of the personal security, liberty, health, dignity, and even the lives of the individuals belonging to such groups. Genocide is directed against the national group as an entity, and the actions involved are directed against individuals, not in their individual capacity, but as members of the national group.[45]

Lemkin identified three "methods and techniques" of genocide. They are: physical, including massacre, starvation, and exposure; biological, including separation of families and sterilization; and cultural, including destruction of cultural symbols, leaders, and sites, and prohibition of cultural activities or codes of behavior. These are not different *types* of genocide, but different *methods* by which genocide is achieved. The object of genocide, what defined it for Lemkin, is the destruction of a culture as an organically integrated social fact.[46]

As David Stannard's account makes clear, the expansion into the Americas of Europe's civilization, its manners, its social and political institutions, involved the systematic destruction of the indigenous societies encountered by the colonizers, beyond the devastation caused by alien pathogens.[47] The means of genocide have varied by circumstance, and have included not only outright mass slaughter but also dispossession, enslavement, forced migration, the prohibition of traditional religious and cultural practices, the destruction of cultural monuments, the proscription of indigenous languages, confinement to marginal living conditions, and the large-scale abduction of children.[48] Within Canada, genocide has been implemented most overtly through the Indian Residential School system, operated by several Christian churches and funded first by the British and then by the Canadian state, from the mid-eighteenth century through to 1996.[49] Through the operation of this system, Native children were forcibly seized from their parents and raised in an environment that stigmatized every trace of Native culture, working to produce children entirely assimilated to White settler culture. This process clearly satisfies the definition of genocide established in the 1948 United Nations Convention on the Prevention and Punishment of the Crime of Genocide, which includes among genocide's strategies, "forcibly transferring children of the group to another group."[50] It is no coincidence that physical, sexual, and psychological abuse of Native children was endemic throughout the IRS system, and that many thousands of Native children died while in Residential Schools from preventable diseases and injuries. Native authors have also argued that other practices, not intrinsically genocidal, have operated genocidally in the context of a Canadian colonialism – for example: the appropriation and commodification of Native land;[51] the manipulation of legal definitions of Native status using blood quantum rules and sexist discrimination;[52] and welfare and development policies that impose absolute poverty on reserve populations[53] – inasmuch as that colonialism has aimed consistently to construct a White Canada with no space for Native societies.[54]

Has genocide against indigenous peoples been morally valorized in settler societies? On this question, it would be a mistake to treat morality as a homogeneous whole defined only by its most visible characteristics. The apologies to victims, attempts at compensation, and retroactive assumption of responsibility, as well as the guilty silence and denial by those who have refused to take responsibility, express only one tendency in settler morality – one whose public predominance has emerged only recently, in response to ongoing struggles for recognition by the surviving First Peoples. The historical accounts I have cited above demonstrate that perpetrators of colonial genocide quite frequently acted in the conviction of serving a higher, supra-individual purpose, out of a sense of duty to the Crown or to God or to Western civilization, and in autonomous ways informed by a perception of their relation to the social whole. That their actions were positively sanctioned by widespread public opinion is abundantly evident.

Sven Lindqvist has chronicled the prevalence and public respectability of "scientific" racism during the era of European colonialism. He argues that "one of the fundamental ideas of the nineteenth century was that there are races, peoples, nations and tribes that are in the process of dying out"; by the lifetime of Adolf Hitler, "the air he and all other Western people in his childhood breathed was soaked in the conviction that imperialism is a biologically necessary process, which, according to the laws of nature, leads to the inevitable destruction of the lower races."[55] In this context, cultural annihilation of the sort practiced in Indian Residential Schools can be understood as the most tolerant end of a racist continuum, the other end of which was forcible extermination, and the middle ground of which depicted the extinction of the inferior races as merely inevitable. In this context, Henry Morton Stanley was fêted in Europe for having slaughtered his way through the Congo Basin;[56] evolutionary biologists and anthropologists theorized the extinction of "lower races" as a consequence of the fact that "the lower a race was, the more land it needed to live off of";[57] and the sociologist Herbert Spencer, chief progenitor before Durkheim of functionalist sociology and the organic view of society, argued for genocide as a natural and necessary extension of the evolution of human societies:

> The forces which are working out the great scheme of perfect happiness, taking no account of incidental suffering, exterminate such sections of mankind as stand in their way . . . Be he human or be he brute – the hindrance must be got rid of.[58]

Nor did these attitudes simply fade away in the twentieth century. In 1992, on the 500th anniversary of the discovery of Christopher Columbus by the indigenous peoples of the Caribbean, Western settler societies celebrated their origin myth, while several European nations competed for the right to claim Columbus for themselves. Indigenous peoples, on the other hand, memorialized 500 years of conquest, dispossession, and genocide; their celebration was for the fact of their own survival. A few White authors contributed to the task of calling Western civilization to a critical self-awareness: notably the American historian David Stannard, in *American Holocaust*, and Canadian author Ronald Wright in *Stolen Continents*.[59] But these efforts were met with preemptively prepared apologies for colonialism. For example, historian James Axtell, in his 1992 book *Beyond 1492: Encounters in Colonial North America*, argued against too stern a moral condemnation of colonial genocides:

> To condemn every aggressive military, religious, or economic action in the past is to question some of the fundaments of Western society, past *and present*. If everything associated with mercantilism, capitalism, evangelical religion, and armed force is beyond the moral pale, we may find it difficult, if not impossible, to approach our past – or the histories of most of the world's culture – with the requisite empathy, understanding, and disinterestedness.[60]

From his column in the left-wing US periodical *The Nation*, the prominent English-American social commentator Christopher Hitchens, who has demanded that Henry Kissinger be tried as a war criminal, was even more dismissive of the historical suffering of First Nations: "It does happen to be the way that history is made, and to complain about it is as empty as complaint about climatic, geological or tectonic shift."[61] These are the terms in which a German historian might have spoken, on the centenary of the commencement of the Final Solution, if the Nazis had won *their* war of imperial conquest.

CONCLUSION

If we define morality idealistically, in terms of what it ought to be or what we wish it to be, then we can always deny morality's role in the commission of atrocity. If we assume that universal morality exists and exerts an influence on human action, then we must explain genocide in terms of the negation of that influence. But these strategies, comforting as they may be, do not help us to understand why genocide happens. And that understanding is surely a precondition to preventing it. As Ugandan political scientist Mahmood Mamdani has observed:

> One could go on narrating atrocity stories ad infinitum, and indeed some have. The point of such an exercise may be to show how base human nature can be, or it may be, I fear, more self-serving: to show how base is the nature of some humans, usually some others, not us . . . Violence cannot be allowed to speak for itself, for violence is not its own meaning. To be made thinkable, it needs to be *historicized*.[62]

If we define morality in formal terms, as a kind of social structure, admitting that the contents of that structure may vary historically, then we can perceive that morality is ambivalent – sometimes a force preventing genocide, sometimes part of the ensemble of forces that make genocide happen. Where genocide takes place, it is not simply that morality is negated, but that anti-genocidal moralities are negated and supplanted by genocidal moralities.

This conclusion should not really surprise us. When the resources of a society are mobilized toward some project, new social norms are produced. People's sense of idealism, of service to a higher purpose, is a powerful motivator. The direction that morality takes is not guaranteed by some intrinsic essence, nor by the logic of functional teleology.

Sadly, it comes as no surprise that morality cannot always protect us from becoming victims of genocide. What is more deeply troubling, however, is the thought that morality cannot always protect us from becoming its perpetrators. This invites a range of questions for future investigation: Under what conditions does morality develop in ways that facilitate genocidal violence? How do genocidal moralities emerge? How may they be recognized? Most importantly, by what means might they be undone?

NOTES

1 Helen Fein, *Genocide: A Sociological Perspective* (London: Sage, 1993), p. 32.
2 Patricia Marchak, *Reigns of Terror* (Montreal: McGill-Queen's University Press, 2003); Michael Mann, *The Dark Side of Democracy: Explaining Ethnic Cleansing* (Cambridge: Cambridge University Press, 2005); Adam Jones, ed., *Gendercide and Genocide* (Nashville, TN: Vanderbilt University Press, 2004).
3 Zygmunt Bauman, *Modernity and the Holocaust* (Ithaca, NY: Cornell University Press, 1991).
4 Ibid., pp. 93–94.
5 Raul Hilberg, *The Destruction of the European Jews*, 3rd edn (New Haven, CT: Yale University Press, 2003).

6 Hannah Arendt, *Eichmann in Jerusalem: A Report on the Banality of Evil*, revised and enlarged edn (New York: Penguin Books, 1994).

7 Leo Kuper, *Genocide: Its Political Use in the Twentieth Century* (New Haven, CT: Yale University Press, 1981); Frank Robert Chalk and Kurt Jonassohn, *The History and Sociology of Genocide: Analyses and Case Studies* (New Haven, CT: Yale University Press, 1990).

8 Bauman, *Modernity and the Holocaust*, p. 178.

9 Ibid., p. 199.

10 Ibid., p. 188.

11 Ibid., p. 199.

12 Gabriel Abend, "Two Main Problems in the Sociology of Morality," *Theory and Society*, 37: 2 (2008), pp. 87–125.

13 Ibid., p. 111.

14 Ibid., p. 112.

15 David Bloor, "The Strong Programme in the Sociology of Knowledge," in Bloor, *Knowledge and Social Imagery* (London: Routledge and Kegan Paul, 1976), pp. 1–19.

16 Émile Durkheim, "The Rules of Sociological Method," in Steven Lukes, ed., *Durkheim: The Rules of Sociological Method and Selected Texts on Sociology and Its Method* (New York: The Free Press, 1982), p. 60.

17 Ibid., pp. 236–240.

18 Ibid., p. 59.

19 John H. Holland, *Emergence: From Chaos to Order* (Reading, MA: Addison-Wesley, 1998), p. 2.

20 J. Goldstein, "Emergence as a Construct: History and Issues," *Emergence: A Journal of Complexity Issues in Organizations and Management*, 1: 1 (1999), p. 49.

21 Durkheim, "The Rules of Sociological Method," pp. 38–40.

22 Ibid., p. 79.

23 Ibid., pp. 79–80.

24 Émile Durkheim, *The Division of Labour in Society* (New York: The Free Press, 1984), pp. 14–15; Durkheim, *Professional Ethics and Civic Morals* (London: Routledge, 1992), p. 2; Durkheim, *Selected Writings*, trans. Anthony Giddens (Cambridge: Cambridge University Press, 1972), p. 96; Durkheim, *Moral Education*, trans. Everett K. Wilson and Herman Schnurer (Mineola, NY: Dover Publications, 2002), pp. 24–25, 55.

25 Durkheim, "The Rules of Sociological Method," p. 81.

26 Durkheim, *Moral Education*, esp. pp. 29, 33–35, 57–59, 78–79, 120.

27 Ibid., pp. 29, 33–35.

28 Ibid., pp. 59–60.

29 Ibid., p. 115.

30 Claudia Koonz, *The Nazi Conscience* (Cambridge, MA: Belknap Press, 2003), p. 6.

31 Ibid., p. 8.

32 Ibid.

33 Ibid., pp. 21, 25–29, 36–38, 100.

34 Ibid., pp. 237–241.

35 Ibid., pp. 131ff, 90ff.

36 Ibid., p. 5.

37 Arendt, *Eichmann in Jerusalem*, p. 150.

38 Vahakn N. Dadrian, *The History of the Armenian Genocide: Ethnic Conflict from the Balkans to Anatolia to the Caucasus*, 3rd, revised edn (Providence, RI: Berghahn Books, 1997), p. 225; Samuel Totten, Paul Robert Bartrop, and Steven Leonard Jacobs, *Dictionary of Genocide*, Vol. 1 (Westport, CT: Greenwood Publishing Group, 2008), p. 19.

39 Robert Melson, *Revolution and Genocide: On the Origins of the Armenian Genocide and the Holocaust* (Chicago, IL: University of Chicago Press, 1992), p. 164; David Norman Smith, "Ziya Gökalp and Émile Durkheim: Sociology as an Apology for Chauvinism?," *Durkheimian Studies/Etudes durkheimiennes*, 1 (1995), p. 46.

40 Smith, "Ziya Gökalp," p. 48.

41   Ibid., pp. 47–49; Erol Kahveci, "Durkheim's Sociology in Turkey," *Durkheimian Studies/Etudes durkheimiennes*, 1 (1995), pp. 52–55; Melson, *Revolution and Genocide*, p. 164; Uriel Heyd, *Foundations of Turkish Nationalism* (London: Luzac, 1950), p. 63.

42   Melson, *Revolution and Genocide*, p. 146; Rouben Adalian, "The Armenian Genocide, 1915–1923," in Michael N. Dobkowski and Isidor Wallimann, eds, *Genocide in Our Time: An Annotated Bibliography with Analytical Introductions* (Ann Arbor, MI: Pierian Press, 1992), p. 86.

43   Richard G. Hovannisian, "The Historical Dimension of the Armenian Question, 1878–1923," in Frank Robert Chalk and Kurt Jonassohn, *The History and Sociology of Genocide: Analyses and Case Studies* (New Haven, CT: Yale University Press, 1990), p. 260.

44   Melson, *Revolution and Genocide*, p. 170.

45   Raphael Lemkin, *Axis Rule in Occupied Europe: Laws of Occupation, Analysis of Government, Proposals for Redress*, Publication of the Carnegie Endowment for International Peace, Division of International Law, Washington (Washington, DC: Carnegie Endowment for International Peace, 1944), p. 79.

46   Elsewhere (Christopher Powell, "What Do Genocides Kill? A Relational Conception of Genocide," *Journal of Genocide Research*, 9: 4, (2007), pp. 527–547, I critique the limitations of this objectivist conception of genocide, and propose instead a relational conception of genocide. In particular, Lemkin's account of nations as organic communities carries primordialist and even racist overtones that are dispelled when identity is conceived as a relational social process. I conceptualize genocide as "an identity-difference relation of violent obliteration." Martin Shaw, in his *What is Genocide?*, conceptualizes genocide differently again, as "action in which armed power organizations treat civilian social groups as enemies and aim to destroy their real or putative social power, by means of killing, violence, and coercion against individuals whom they regard as members of the groups" (Martin Shaw, *What Is Genocide?*, Cambridge: Polity Press, 2007, p. 154). Shaw's conceptualization usefully draws attention to the political functions of genocide, but only negatively; my concern is to draw out not only what genocide destroys but what it creates.

47   David E. Stannard, *American Holocaust: The Conquest of the New World* (Oxford: Oxford University Press, 1992).

48   Ward Churchill, *A Little Matter of Genocide: Holocaust and Denial in the Americas, 1492 to the Present* (San Francisco, CA: City Lights, 1998), pp. 151–156.

49   Agnes Grant, *No End of Grief: Indian Residential Schools in Canada* (Winnipeg, MB: Pemmican Publications, 1996).

50   Chalk and Jonassohn, *History and Sociology of Genocide*, p. 44.

51   Robert Davis and Mark Zannis, *The Genocide Machine in Canada* (Montréal: Black Rose Books, 1973); Rex Weyler, *Blood of the Land: The Government and Corporate War against First Nations*, revised edn (Philadelphia, PA: New Society Publishers, 1992).

52   Bonita Lawrence, *"Real" Indians and Others: Mixed-Blood Urban Native Peoples and Indigenous Nationhood* (Vancouver, BC: UBC Press, 2004).

53   Hugh Shewell, *"Enough to Keep Them Alive": Indian Welfare in Canada, 1873–1965* (Toronto, ON: University of Toronto Press, 2004).

54   John Boyko, "Chapter Six: Native Canadians 1867–1991, Attempted Cultural Genocide," in Boyko, *The Last Steps to Freedom: The Evolution of Canadian Racism* (Winnipeg, MB: Watson & Dwyer Publishing, 1995), pp. 186–222; Daniel N. Paul, *We Were Not the Savages: Collision between European and Native American Civilizations*, 3rd edn (Halifax, NS: Fernwood Publishing, 2006); David Maybury-Lewis, "Genocide against Indigenous Peoples," in Alexander Laban Hinton, ed., *Annihilating Difference: The Anthropology of Genocide* (Berkeley, CA: University of California Press, 2002).

55   Sven Lindqvist, *"Exterminate All the Brutes": One Man's Odyssey into the Heart of Darkness and the Origins of European Genocide* (New York: The New Press, 1996), pp. 140, 141.

56   Ibid., pp. 36–41.

57   Ibid.

58 Ibid., p. 8. See also Patrick Brantlinger, *Dark Vanishings: Discourse on the Extinction of Primitive Races, 1800–1930* (Ithaca, NY: Cornell University Press, 2003).
59 Stannard, *American Holocaust*; Ronald Wright, *Stolen Continents: The Americas through Indian Eyes since 1492* (Boston, MA: Houghton Mifflin, 1992).
60 James Axtell, *Beyond 1492: Encounters in Colonial North America* (New York: Oxford University Press, 1992), p. 232.
61 Christopher Hitchens, "Minority Report," *The Nation*, October 19, 1992, p. 422.
62 Mahmood Mamdani, *When Victims Become Killers: Colonialism, Nativism, and the Genocide in Rwanda* (Princeton, NJ: Princeton University Press, 2001), pp. 228–229.

Figure 4.1   The *Vijećnica* in Sarajevo, Bosnia and Herzegovina, 2008.

Source: Donna-Lee Frieze.

CHAPTER 4

The Destruction of Sarajevo's *Vijećnica*

A case of genocidal cultural destruction?[1]

Donna-Lee Frieze

INTRODUCTION

During the attack on Sarajevo between 1992 and 1995, approximately 12,000 occupants of the city were killed, and about 50,000 were injured.[2] The city was relentlessly bombarded from the surrounding hills over four long years: as the Bosnian Serb military commander Ratko Mladić said, "They can't sleep, so we drive them out of their minds."[3] This is the staggering way in which the citizens of Sarajevo had to live, and die; it is also, as Cornelia Sorabji suggests, the legacy of the lives of these people. Part of this legacy includes the intended destruction of memory and culture, typified in the obliteration of the *Vijećnica* (the Serbo-Croatian name for the Sarajevo city hall). This chapter details the assault on the *Vijećnica*, and explores whether this and similar acts of cultural desecration are linked to intentional group harm and thus merit a framing of genocide. To this end, I explore the concept of "cultural genocide" as it evolved in the thinking and writings of Raphael Lemkin, inventor of the concept of genocide; how it figured in the framing of the United Nations Convention on the Prevention and Punishment of the Crime of Genocide (the Genocide Convention) of 1948; and what significance it has held in prosecutions in the recent era of *ad hoc* tribunals, notably that for the former Yugoslavia.

András Riedlmayer – who testified in July 2003 as an expert witness at the trial of Slobodan Milošević[4] – points out that the history of a country is revealed in its buildings.[5] In the case of Sarajevo, the proximity of churches to synagogues and mosques demonstrates powerfully the city's history of cultural heritage and religious tolerance, and reflects the multicultural life of its citizens.

The *Vijećnica* was built in 1896 during the Austro-Hungarian rule over Sarajevo. It was purposely designed by the Viennese architect, Karl Wittek, to stand "near the first Islamic religious structures built in the fifteenth century."[6] After the Second World War, the *Vijećnica* became the national library of Bosnia and Herzegovina, housing works from destroyed libraries from the First World War, including Croatian, Russian colonial, and German libraries. It later incorporated works from the Muslim, Croatian, and Serbian cultural societies. In 1949, it came to house the archives and holdings of the library of the University of Sarajevo,[7] reflecting Sarajevo's culturally and intellectually diverse society.

The *Vijećnica* was specifically and repeatedly attacked on August 25–27, 1992. No other buildings in the vicinity were targeted on those nights, and the only other areas to be hit were the streets surrounding the building – a tactic to ensure that the fire department could not gain access to quench the flames.[8] The intent to destroy the cultural landscape was explicit. The burning of the *Vijećnica* was possibly the "largest single incident of deliberate book-burning in modern history."[9] The attack came from Serbian forces in the surrounding hills of Sarajevo, using incendiary shells and targeting the domed roof, so that the inferno flared in the skies for days. Kemal Bakaršić, the former chief librarian from the National Museum of Bosnia and Herzegovina, wrote: "Catching a page you could feel its heat, and for a moment read a fragment of text in a strange kind of black and grey negative, until, as the heat dissipated, the page melted to dust in your hand."[10]

The *Vijećnica* "contained three million items including rare books and manuscripts, maps, recordings and one million volumes . . . [depicting] the languages of . . . Bosnia." Some archives were irreplaceable, such as "625 Bosnian periodicals" dating from the nineteenth century, and precious incunabula.[11] Ninety percent of the 1.5 to 2 million items in the archives and holdings were destroyed,[12] including 6,000 rare manuscripts[13] and the only copy of the library's catalogue. In addition, the assault destroyed irreplaceable death, birth and marriage records that documented individuals' heritage, history, and lineage.[14] According to one witness, prior to the attack, staff at the *Vijećnica* had repeatedly requested unused atomic bomb shelters to store the library's treasures, but the authorities ignored their petitions.[15]

Of course, the *Vijećnica* was not the only building or archive destroyed during the siege. Many mosques, libraries, cultural buildings, Jewish and Muslim cemeteries and monuments of worship were deliberately obliterated in acts of fanatical nationalism. The Oriental Institute, said to house "the largest collection of Islamic, Jewish and Ottoman documents in southeastern Europe," was also desecrated, as were the Bosnian National Museum and National Archives of Herzegovina, the Academy of Music, the library at the University of Mostar, the National Gallery, and 1,000 mosques all over Bosnia and Herzegovina, in an attempt to "annihilate all Islamic cultural institutions."[16]

Significance of the destruction

The metaphor of book burning resonated deeply with the people of Sarajevo. One of the many firefighters to risk his life trying to save the library commented that he was putting his life in danger because "they are burning a part of me."[17] For others, the act of cultural destruction, but in particular book burning, aims at the annihilation of group identification, or to "erase our remembrance of who we are."[18] What is clear is that many Sarajevans intimately experienced a cataclysmic rupture of their groups' tangible and intangible cultural legacy. As James Raven writes, "Libraries can be national, institutional or familial treasures in which the guardianship offered by the library is a crucial feature."[19] In this respect, libraries, which includes their holdings and their communal, intellectual, and spatial arenas, are linked to groups' identity. The burning of the volumes and the destruction of the physical space are more than Stephen Schwartz's description of "an act of vandalism."[20]

The library's volumes also vividly exemplified the multi-ethnic coexistence at the heart of many Sarajevans' collective identity. They were, as Riedlmayer points out, proof of the "historical roots" of Muslims, Catholics, and Jews in Bosnia and Herzegovina.[21] A witness to the inferno, the intrepid journalist Robert Fisk, wrote: "Sifting through the ashes, I found a scorched filing cabinet entirely filled with reference cards to books in Esperanto. Could there have been a more moving indication, among the embers, of Sarajevo's desire to speak across frontiers?"[22]

Among the holdings destroyed by the Serbs were many precious and rare Serbian texts. As Riedlmayer argues, the short-term aim of the destruction of tangible and intangible cultural elements was part of a campaign of intimidation. But it also reflected a complex kind of self-destruction.[23] In attempting to erase the ethnic memory of the Catholic, Muslim, and Jewish populations, the Serbs crippled their own Bosnian heritage, destroying the Serbian literature that filled the high shelves of the library. Sanja Zgonjanin argues that the Serbs committed "cultural suicide" by destroying part of their own culture, an "ironic" aspect of the assault.[24] But there was a logic to this: the narrative of multicultural intricacies contradicted the rhetoric of extreme nationalism proclaimed by the perpetrators. Destroying it was a kind of confirmation of the allegedly "age-old" ethnic hatreds to which the perpetrators subscribed.[25] A similar strategy prevailed in the Serb destruction of churches, mosques, and bridges.[26] For Schwartz, it was not the history of Muslims in Bosnia and Herzegovina that the Serbs targeted, but rather the proof of coexistence: the "evidence that Serbs had once held property alongside Muslims."[27] The *Vijećnica* housed works that dated back to the Ottoman and Habsburg eras, verifying that "its inhabitants of whatever background [were] able not simply to live next to but also with each other."[28] In mid-1993, the director of the library stated that the Bosnian Serb Forces "knew that if they wanted to destroy this multi-ethnic society, they would have to destroy the library."[29]

Additionally, as the University of Sarajevo library, the *Vijećnica* was loved for more than its tangible qualities, including the building and its contents. As Ferida Duraković explains: "This was the place to exchange opinions . . . where everything began for me as a poet."[30] The *Vijećnica* was a meeting ground for intellectuals, promoting a sense of cultural community that forms the core of a group. As historians from Bosnia and Herzegovina have written, destroying such archives demonstrates a "murder of memory" that encompasses not only the collective ethnic memory and heritage of a group, but also its intellectual life.[31]

CULTURAL DESTRUCTION: LEGAL PRECEDENTS

Although the protection of such intangible qualities has a short history, the international legal safeguard of tangible cultural heritage dates back to the 1800s. There are no distinct laws that specifically mandate prosecution for destroying archives and libraries, but a range of codes and conventions do exist for the protection of such property.[32] The 1863 Lieber Code,[33] adopted in the United States during the Civil War, was arguably the first law explicitly to protect cultural institutions. Others included the 1874 Brussels Declaration;[34] the 1992 UNESCO Memory of the World Programme, which aimed "at preservation and dissemination of valuable archive holdings and library collections worldwide";[35] and the 1977 Protocols added to the 1949 Geneva Conventions, prohibiting hostility toward the spiritual and cultural heritage of people.[36] None of the international declarations and conventions has, however, proved to be effective in prosecuting the perpetrators of such acts of destruction.[37]

The 1954 Hague Convention for the Protection of Cultural Property in the Event of Armed Conflict is considered the key legal document protecting cultural property in an armed conflict, due to its broad inclusion of cultural objects and its recognition of internationalism. Prosecution, however, is rare: as Zgonjanin notes, after the destruction of cultural property, many communities focus on rebuilding efforts rather than pursuing perpetrators.[38] It is likely that this convention was born from the destruction of cultural property during the Holocaust, and it may have also arisen from heated discussions in the United Nations, outlined below, regarding cultural destruction in the lead-up to the ratification of the Genocide Convention.[39]

It is worth noting that an individual was first prosecuted for mass confiscation of cultural property and destruction of cultural heritage in the Nuremberg trials.[40] The Nuremberg Tribunal's reference to "attacks and appropriation of cultural property" did not, however, treat attacks on cultural property as singular or atypical, or linked to an intent to destroy a human collectivity.[41] As such, the "destruction and appropriation of property"[42] is considered a war crime, but legally speaking, not a crime of genocide per the Genocide Convention. Present as an advisor to the United States Chief Prosecutor at the court of the International Military Tribunal at Nuremberg, however, was Raphael Lemkin, inventor of the concept of genocide. And for Lemkin, such acts of cultural destruction had long been central to his evolving understanding of crimes of "vandalism" and "barbarity," climaxing in the concept of "genocide" which he had first unveiled a year before the Nuremberg trials began, and which would become the basis for an international convention only four years later.

LEMKIN AND THE CONCEPT OF GENOCIDAL CULTURAL DESTRUCTION

From an early age, Lemkin was outraged by the "colossal paradox" that while domestic law punished attempts to destroy individuals, there was no equivalent legislation to outlaw the destruction of human groups.[43] Influenced by historical case studies of genocide and those that occurred during his lifetime (such as the Armenian genocide and the attempted obliteration of the Assyrians in Iraq in 1933), Lemkin was further energized to establish an international treaty against group destruction when Hitler became Chancellor of Germany in January 1933. Lemkin submitted a draft law to the Fifth International Conference for the Unification of Penal Law in Madrid in 1933 that detailed two distinct actions: "Acts of Barbarity and Acts of Vandalism." The first described bodily harm to a specific group, while the second Lemkin described as the "malicious destruction of works of art and culture."[44] This demonstrates that Lemkin's early thoughts on genocide were concerned with the cultural destruction of groups as an essential component of genocide. However, as the majority of Lemkin's work has remained unpublished, little is known about his subsequent thinking, which evolved into his concept of genocide. This chapter uses Lemkin's archival papers to demonstrate that genocidal cultural destruction remained a vital component of his thinking, both before and after the adoption of the 1948 Genocide Convention. Indeed, until the end of his life in 1959 – including eleven long years after the convention's adoption – Lemkin continued to advocate the importance of cultural destruction as an integral element of genocide.

According to Zgonjanin, the purpose of all cultural destruction is "to erase ethnic, religious, and cultural memories and therefore to undermine or eliminate groups' identities and existence."[45] For Lemkin, however, not *all* cases of cultural destruction could be deemed genocidal. The *intention* to obliterate a particular group's culture was only genocidal when its aim was "to erase ethnic, religious, and cultural memories and therefore to undermine or eliminate groups' identities and existence."[46] Lemkin noted (precisely when is uncertain, given that many of his archival papers are undated) that "cultural genocide is the most important part of the Convention,"[47] because it underpinned the intentionality of serious bodily, mental, or biological harm to a group outlawed in Article II of the Genocide Convention. For Lemkin, intentional and forceful religious conversions, as well as the transfer of children banned by Article II (e) of the convention, in particular, amounted to genocide of group culture.[48] He wrote: "Cultural genocide need not necessarily involve the substitution of new culture traits . . . but may maliciously undermine the victim group to render its members more defenseless in the face of physical destruction."[49] Again, Lemkin inserts the word "maliciously" to underscore the purposeful nature of the crime.

In his later years, Lemkin clearly distinguished between "the gradual changes a culture may undergo" – what he called "cultural diffusion" (or assimilation of culture) – and cultural genocidal destruction, a point also raised by the objectors to the addition of cultural groups, in the Genocide Convention at the cultural genocide debate at the United Nations in 1948 (examined further below). Embracing the notion of assimilated cultures, Lemkin argued that without such diffusion, "the culture becomes static." Even though some cultures may disappear through such an assimilation process, cultural diffusion clearly, for Lemkin, did not equate to genocide; it was rather "relatively gradual and spontaneous." This cultural assimilation contrasted with absorptions of culture that were abrupt, and in Lemkin's words "implie[d] complete and violent change." This mode, which consisted of calculated attacks on culture and memory, is what Lemkin described as "surgical operations on cultures and deliberate assassination of civilizations," tantamount to genocide.[50] It was, above all, the "pre-meditated goal" of the perpetrators which linked the concept of cultural genocide to genocidal intent.[51]

Lemkin relied on the disciplines of sociology and, in particular, anthropology to explain and understand the significance of cultural genocidal destruction. The mingling of cultures in close proximity was, for him, a sign of hope for civilization.[52] He called both for respect for cultural relativity, and for tolerance of the universal values of basic human rights. His handwritten notes suggest that this hope for worldwide acceptance of cultural diversity and universality is possibly contradictory and therefore problematic.[53]

As we will see in detail below, however, while vestiges of his emphasis on cultural genocide are evident in the Genocide Convention, Lemkin failed to persuade the drafters of the convention explicitly to incorporate cultural destruction as a form of genocide. Long after the convention was ratified, however, he was still appealing fervently for culture as a component of genocide to be understood as an essential element of the crime. In a mid-1950s interview for Italian radio, Lemkin declared:

> Genocide is a very atrocious crime. It destroys nations, races and religious groups and deprives the world of [o]riginal contributions of the particular peoples. World culture is like a concerto to which every nation contributes through its own culture, bringing in its own tone and cultural aroma. Genocide has followed the history of mankind like an ominous shadow. It has destroyed lives and cultures, it has brutalized so many times entire generations, it has deprived the world of sensitivities and human love. Now the United Nations has decided to do away with this shadow and to secure the international world for life and culture.[54]

There are two aspects to Lemkin's arguments concerning cultural genocide. One is that cultural destruction can be an intrinsic element of genocide through its connection to the sociological aspect of the crime. The other is that the outlawing of genocide is essential for the preservation of humanity's cultural element. He wrote in 1957 that genocide "has caused irretrievable losses because culture by its very nature can be neither restored nor duplicated."[55] As Nicholas Adams observes in relation to the cultural sites across Bosnia and Herzegovina, for example, the destruction was predominantly targeted toward "the places where people gather to live out their collective life."[56] As Lemkin understood, there is no "collective life" when tangible and intangible aspects of a group's culture are decimated.[57]

In the lead-up to the adoption of the Genocide Convention by the United Nations, Lemkin frantically attempted to convince delegates that the inclusion of the cultural component of genocide had a preventative aspect to it. In a September 1948 letter to the Chairman of the Genocide Committee, James Rosenberg, Lemkin pointed to the Venezuelan delegate's argument that cultural destruction could act as a prelude to intended physical destruction. Lemkin highlighted the examples of the "mass destruction of synagogues by Hitler in 1938 . . . and the mass destruction of the Christian Armenian Churches prior to the extermination of a million Armenians." He wrote: "Burning books is not the same as burning bodies, but when one intervenes in time against mass destruction of churches and books one arrives just in time to prevent the burning of bodies."[58] By October 1948, the delegates had voted and voiced their final opinions on the inclusion of cultural destruction in a convention on genocide. Lemkin's arguments regarding cultural destruction as a preventative tool for physical destruction were unrealized, but his understanding of the correlation between cultural destruction and intended physical and biological destruction remains pertinent.

Cultural destruction and the UN Genocide Convention

Why and how did the concept of cultural genocidal destruction, which was central to the earliest framings of the Genocide Convention, come to be excluded from that same legal instrument? The following brief account analyzes the reasons for and against the exclusion of cultural destruction as an act enumerated in the convention.

The Genocide Convention was the product of two separate drafts, evaluated and combined by different committees. Illuminating debates on the issue of cultural destruction occurred between April and May 1948 on the second draft, in the Ad Hoc Committee on Genocide, which defined cultural genocide (covered in Article III) as:

> any deliberate act committed with the intent to destroy the language, religion, or culture of a national, racial or religious group on grounds of national or racial origin or religious belief [,] such as:
>
> 1 prohibiting the use of the language of the group in daily intercourse or in schools, or the printing and circulation of publications in the language of the group;
> 2 destroying, or preventing the use of, libraries, museums, schools, historical monuments, places of worship or other cultural institutions and objects of the group.[59]

Representatives of seven nation-states decided upon the fate of cultural destruction as an element of genocide in this Assembly: the United States, the USSR, Lebanon, China, France, Poland, and Venezuela.[60] Despite the objections from some nation-states, the Assembly decided on April 5, 1948, by six votes to one, to retain the concept of cultural destruction.[61]

Later, in October 1948, the Assembly deliberated for three hours over the inclusion of Article III in the convention. During the discussions, Sardar Bahadur Khan from Pakistan reasoned that the cultural destruction of a group could not be separated from physical or biological destruction; and, further, that the defining characteristics of a group were embedded in the crime's cultural composition and expression:

> Cultural genocide represented the end, whereas physical genocide was merely the means. The chief motive of genocide was blind rage to destroy the ideas, the values and the very soul of a national, racial or religious group, rather than its physical existence.[62]

However, some delegates maintained that including cultural genocidal destruction in the convention might restrict the number of countries willing to ratify it. Accordingly, Khan suggested that sub-paragraph 1 of Article III should be deleted, as such a provision broadened the concept of genocide; but he declared that sub-paragraph 2 was essential, "otherwise, the convention would only partially achieve its aim."[63] Responding to complaints that the definition of cultural genocide was equivocal and ambiguous,[64] Venezuelan member Pérez Perozo, the Syrian delegate Tarazi, José Correa from Ecuador, and Wahid Raafat from Egypt also agreed that Article III should be made less vague in order to win support from the delegates.[65]

One of the more rigorous arguments was that of Iranian delegate Djalal Abdoh. He asked whether, under the convention, *all* cultures should be preserved, even barbaric ones. How would a government "determine the concrete elements of a group's religion and culture?" The Union of South Africa questioned the tolerance of, for instance, cannibalism.[66]

Sture Petren of Sweden stated that the protection of cultural destruction belonged with an instrument on minority rights, and asked whether "the fact that Sweden had converted the Lapps to Christianity might not lay her open to the accusation that she had committed an act of cultural genocide."[67] Against cultural genocide as a minority rights issue, Khan and Tsien Tai from China reasoned that if cultural destruction were included only in the Universal Declaration of Human Rights (as the Canadian and Indian delegates proposed), the Genocide Convention would be reduced to a rhetorical statement, rather than a foundation for international jurisprudence; it would therefore lack moral authority.[68] Alexander Morozov from the USSR offered a similar argument with a different theoretical underpinning: the right to life, security, and liberty enshrined in the Universal Declaration of Human Rights "might be interpreted as ensuring . . . protection against any act of physical genocide; yet no one disputed the need for a convention on physical genocide."[69] Likewise, some delegates opposed to the inclusion of cultural genocide maintained that there was no need for an international legal document on genocide, as provisions for such crimes were already enacted in national or domestic legislation.[70] Perozo, however, contended that many civilized nation-states penalized most of the acts specified in the draft convention.[71]

Certain nation-states contended that a genocide convention equating cultural genocidal destruction (in other words, a "less hideous crime") with intentional physical and biological destruction would broaden the interpretation of the crime and "might give rise to abuses by reason of the vagueness" of the concept.[72] Many states thus established a hierarchy of genocidal acts, asserting that physical and biological genocide were more heinous than cultural genocide, and that this lesser act should be confined to debates over minority rights – as if somehow the protection of minorities was an insignificant issue, and safeguarding the culture of majorities mattered little.[73] Ernest Gross from the United States described the concept of cultural genocidal destruction as excessively "far-reaching," and similarly Georges Kaeckenbeek, representing Belgium, understood Article III to be an "indefinite extension" of genocide.[74] Bahadur Khan, however, insisted that this was an archetypal "western" response grounded in "materialistic philosophies" that accorded insufficient weight to spiritual values,[75] while Venezuela's Perozo pointed out that the term "destruction" in the convention was not limited to physical destruction alone: extinguishing the traits or spirit of the group was another way to "deprive the group of its existence."[76] Perozo also argued that these "less spectacular crimes" of genocide must not be disregarded,[77] while Ecuador's Correa maintained that the outcome and consequences of cultural, physical, and biological genocidal destruction were indistinguishable.[78] Morozov of the USSR pointed to the recent Nuremberg verdicts, which had demonstrated that cultural destruction in Czechoslovakia, Luxembourg and Poland during the Nazi era constituted a form of destruction of particular groups.[79]

Some members of the Committee equated cultural assimilation with cultural genocide, a point explicitly raised and distinguished by Lemkin (see above).[80] However, the Belorussian Soviet Socialist Republic representative clarified, as Lemkin had, the difference between assimilation of cultures and the Genocide Convention's concern with "actions aiming at the *destruction* of the language, religion or culture of a group for reasons of national, racial or religious hatred."[81] Gilberto Amado from Brazil, a long-time ally of Lemkin's, nevertheless queried the homogeneity issues of cultural assimilation, whereby a nation-state justifiably amalgamates cultures.[82]

Presaging the ICTY's legal opinion regarding cultural genocidal destruction in the 1990s (see below), and more recent arguments among scholars focusing on the prevention of genocide, Correa illuminated the concept of cultural genocidal destruction in relation to the prevention of physical and biological genocide:

> If attacks against the culture of a group remained unpunished for the want of appropriate provisions in the convention, that would facilitate the perpetration of physical genocide, in which such attacks normally culminated. It should not be forgotten that the chief object of the convention was the prevention of genocide.[83]

Correa's arguments likewise reflected Lemkin's thoughts on the pertinence of cultural destruction, which perhaps made sense in light of their strong rapport.[84] The Czechoslovakian representative referred to the cultural properties of a group as "its distinctive and permanent characteristics," a theory Lemkin also shared.[85]

Ultimately, cultural destruction was excluded as a crime under the Genocide Convention by a vote of 25 to 16, with four abstentions (see note 86 for the list of nation-states).[86] Interestingly, the country where Lemkin lived for his first 39 years, Poland, voted to include cultural genocide, whereas his adopted country, the United States, voted against. Arguably, the votes demonstrate a general rejection of the concept by the western democracies, perhaps reflecting their fear that it would be used to assail them for their treatment of indigenous peoples. On the other hand, countries that had suffered from intentional cultural destruction alongside physical destruction came out strongly in favor of Article III's inclusion.[87] The result was that cultural genocide virtually vanished from the international law of genocide, until its resurrection in a somewhat different guise in the 1990s. It is to this ambiguous reformulation of the concept that I now turn.

CULTURAL DESTRUCTION AND GENOCIDAL INTENT

Despite the intense and thought-provoking debates in the United Nations in the 1940s, the destruction of culture as a crime of genocide has gone unrecognized. It has, however, been acknowledged by some scholars and other observers, spawning new words such as "urbicide" and "warchitecture"[88] – terms used, in particular, to describe the cultural destruction that took place in Bosnia and Herzegovina during the 1990s. Despite the absence of specific legal sanctions for "cultural genocide," cultural destruction did seep into legal framings and processes as well. As Riedlmayer notes:

> There is a clear connection between the targeting of a given group for persecution or destruction . . . and the systematic destruction of its heritage (based on the

association of that heritage with the targeted group). Judges . . . have begun to recognize this link and have taken such evidence into consideration in their rulings on the gravest of charges.[89]

Most notably, the relevance of the concept of cultural genocidal destruction moved to the fore with the advent of the two United Nations *ad hoc* tribunals for the former Yugoslavia and Rwanda.[90] In a historic precedent, the International Criminal Tribunal for the former Yugoslavia (ICTY), prosecuted persons for the destruction of libraries, albeit not as a crime of genocide.[91] The Trial Chamber understood, if not the significance of the destruction of the *Vijećnica*, then at the very least, the connection between "evidence of intent to destroy" and some acts of cultural desecration in the Bosnian region. This is emblematic of a broader understanding in contemporary international law referenced by John Quigley, who notes that international legal bodies have increasingly recognized that if any of the acts in Article II of the Genocide Convention is alleged, "the destruction of cultural objectives may provide evidence that such acts were done with intent to destroy the group."[92] In the 2004 case against Radislav Krstić (Chief of Staff of the Bosnian Serb Army), for example, the Trial Chamber of the ICTY pointed out:

> that where there is physical or biological destruction there are often simultaneous attacks on the cultural and religious property and symbols of the targeted group as well, attacks which may legitimately be considered as evidence of an intent to physically destroy the group. In this case, the Trial Chamber will thus take into account as evidence of intent to destroy the group the deliberate destruction of mosques and houses belonging to members of the group.[93]

CULTURAL DESTRUCTION AND GENOCIDAL INTENT: REEVALUATING THE *VIJEĆNICA*

There are numerous examples – indeed, thousands in recorded history – of acts of cultural destruction. More ancient instances include the Mongols' sacking of Baghdad and its great libraries in 1258; the Spanish burning of the Aztec and Mayan codices after the Conquest; and the more general devastation of indigenous cultures and languages worldwide. A twentieth-century western example was the destruction of the Catholic University of Louvain in Belgium by German forces, first on August 25, 1914 (coincidentally, the same date as the burning of the *Vijećnica* in 1992),[94] and again, after its reconstruction, by the German army during the Second World War.[95]

In my view, however, not all such instances of cultural destruction can or should be considered genocidal. In the case of the Catholic University, for example, the Germans – unlike the Serbs in relation to the Bosniaks in 1992, and their destruction of the *Vijećnica* – were not perpetrating physical or biological genocide against Belgian Catholics. To take another example, the fire that caused the destruction of the Bucharest University Library during the revolution of December 1989[96] was not genocidal, because it was not linked to a campaign of intentional destruction of a designated group. It is this aspect – whether the act of cultural destruction bears a genocidal intent, whether it serves as a precursor to physical or biological genocide – that must be decisive in rendering a verdict of cultural genocidal desecration.

Let us consider this element of intent in the case of the *Vijećnica*. As noted earlier, many cultural and religious monuments and buildings were desecrated all over Bosnia and Herzegovina. But the destruction of the *Vijećnica* was an especially meaningful event, involving as it did the obliteration of approximately 150,000 rare books[97] – meaningful not only for the Bosnians who acknowledge its pronounced historical and cultural significance, but for the instigator of the devastation, who understood the profound violation it represented.

A genocidal intent was manifest in the Serb campaign which included – vitally – the *Vijećnica*'s destruction. Speaking in April 1992, Serb Democratic Party Vice President Nikola Koljević made his intent to destroy clear: he said that the Bosnian Serb nationalists "should start in Sarajevo and that work on [i.e. destruction of] boundaries of 'national communities' should start immediately,"[98] meaning that Sarajevo would be divided into ethnic territories. Speaking four months before the burning of the *Vijećnica*, Koljević's intentions were overt.[99] And it was he who, in the end, ordered the bombing of the *Vijećnica*, and "signed the directive ordering Radko Mladic to shell" and destroy it.[100] This organized desecration of the *Vijećnica* had "logical" conclusions: to "maliciously undermine" (see Lemkin's framing, above) all non-Serbian Sarajevans, and to weaken the cornerstones of their cultural identity.

As such, given that this cultural desecration was accompanied by the genocidal targeting of non-Serbs, we can discern a clear and quite traditional genocidal intent. However, there is another aspect of the *Vijećnica*'s destruction which renders the action even more complex and portentous.

Koljević was a highly cultivated man who, as an academic, actually *capitalized* on the scholarly offerings of the *Vijećnica*. He was, as Raymond Bonner points out, a "Shakespearean scholar who ... lectured at numerous American universities ... notably, Stanford and Berkeley," and was often chosen as a spokesperson for the Bosnian Serbian position due to his eloquent English and his apparent moderate ideology.[101] According to a 1992 report, Koljević was one of the Balkans' most esteemed Shakespearian academics.[102]

Why would this Professor of literature order and desire such destruction? According to Janine di Giovanni, Koljević was

> a scholar who loved books, who placed a high premium on intelligence, who believed that words could liberate a human being, [then] had raised his hand and one million books ... were burnt to a crisp. The library was a symbol of Sarajevo's multi-ethnic tradition – something that he had come to hate more than anything.[103]

It was not the Austrian-Hungarian building *per se* that evoked this hatred, but as Matthew Battles points out, its contents, specifically its rare Ottoman collections.[104] Nor was it incongruous that a professor of literature should mastermind the bombing of books. The Minister of Health of the Republika Srpska told the Bosnian Serb Assembly in May 1992 that he was "for the destruction of Kosova Hospital so that the enemy has nowhere to go for medical help,"[105] and there are numerous examples in Rwanda, and precedents in the Holocaust and in Cambodia, in which elites or intellectuals abused their knowledge and exploited their skills for genocidal purposes.

In a broader sense, given his commitment to the pursuit of knowledge, Koljević's action seems to have been *self*-destructive, both on a personal level and with regard to his ethnic community. Indeed, it is notable that Koljević finally killed himself, on January 16, 1995. Perhaps, then, the shelling of the *Vijećnica*, with its Serbian treasures, was also an act of so-called "auto-genocide." This problematic term was coined by a French journalist, Jean Lacouture, in relation to Cambodians supposedly committing acts of self-destruction during the 1970s.[106] Lacouture implied that the acts committed in Cambodia were not genocide: how can acts be considered as such when the perpetrators intend self-destruction? Although the term is riddled with conceptual difficulties, its finer points beg the question: what happens when a group intentionally attempts to destroy itself, its history and its culture? As established, Koljević's intentions to destroy all Sarajevans through the destruction of the library are arguably clear. However, is the crime still genocide when the perpetrators' intent is to destroy themselves? There is no stipulation in the Genocide Convention which states that perpetrators cannot obliterate themselves. Surely, this is the existential difficulty (apart from the ethical component) of genocide: when the Nazis destroyed the German Jews, the Hutu annihilated the Tutsi, the Turks intentionally destroyed the Armenians, and the Khmer Rouge maimed and tortured the Cambodians, they were all destroying and transforming their societies and cultures. The perpetrators' illusion is that they believed they were somehow "cleansing" themselves as well.

CONCLUSION

In this chapter I began by describing the devastation of cultural destruction in the Bosnian genocide, with a focus on Sarajevo's most significant cultural monument, which symbolized the intellectual and multi-ethnic nature of the region. The core arguments focused on the problematic inclusion or exclusion of cultural destruction in the concept of genocide, and demonstrated that rather than being a relatively recent addition to scholarly arguments, the concept has historical precedents that date back to the discussions of the 1940s in the newly formed United Nations. Despite the vote to exclude the notion of culture from the Genocide Convention, Lemkin continued to argue for its place in the conceptual understanding of genocide long after the ratification of the Convention in 1951. By returning to his archival writings, scholars of genocide studies may appreciate the centrality of culture in Lemkin's thinking on genocide.

As I have argued, not all forms of cultural destruction are genocidal. However, where there is a link, the aspect of the *intent* underlying the crime must be closely analyzed. The case of Koljević highlights the fact that the destruction of certain cultural institutions can be a sign of an intention to destroy a particular group, physically, biologically, and/or psychologically; and that cultural destruction is in some instances not equivalent to genocide, but is inherent within genocide, regardless of the so-called "self-destructive" arguments of "auto-genocide".

It is heartening that despite the exclusion of explicit mention of cultural destruction in the Genocide Convention, the ICTY came to recognize that cultural destruction may provide a clue to intentional physical, biological, or mental group harm, thus illuminating the preventive aspect of the crime. Although the concept of cultural destruction has historically been linked to war crimes and crimes against humanity, the perpetrators' deliberate destruction of the *Vijećnica*, with the concomitant intent of physical and biological destruction of an out-group, shows that in some cases, and this case in particular, cultural destruction is fundamental to the core acts of genocide. As international criminal law is beginning to absorb Lemkin's understanding of the crime, it is time to return to Lemkin's nuanced concepts in order to deepen, rather than broaden, our understanding of genocide.

NOTES

1 A shorter version of this chapter was presented at the International Association of Genocide Scholars conference at George Mason University, Washington, DC, in 2009. Many thanks to my colleagues who presented with me on this panel on cultural genocidal destruction: Peter Balakian, Jutta Lindert, and Armen Marsoobian. I also express gratitude to various members of the audience for their helpful comments and especially to Adam Jones and Pam Maclean for their insightful readings and comments.

2 András J. Riedlmayer, "Crimes of War, Crimes of Peace: Destruction of Libraries During and After the Balkan Wars of the 1990s," *Library Trends*, 56: 1 (Summer 2007), p. 110.

3 Ratko Mladić, quoted in Cornelia Sorabji, "Managing Memories in Post-War Sarajevo: Individuals, Bad Memories, and New Wars," *Journal of the Royal Anthropological Institute*, 12: 1 (March 2006), p. 5.

4 András Riedlmayer, "Sarajevo Library's Destruction," *American Libraries*, 35: 10 (November 2004), pp. 30–31.

5 András Riedlmayer, "From the Ashes: The Past and Future of Bosnia's Cultural Heritage," in Maya Shatzmiller, ed., *Islam and Bosnia: Conflict Resolution and Foreign Policy in Multi-Ethnic States* (Montreal: McGill-Queen's University Press, 2002), p. 5.

6 Robert J. Donia, *Sarajevo: A Biography* (Ann Arbor, MI: The University of Michigan Press, 2006), p. 72.

7 Tatjana Lorkovic, "National Library in Sarajevo Destroyed: Collections, Archives Go Up in Flames," *American Libraries*, 23: 9 (October 1992), p. 736. See also Munevera Zećo and William B. Tomljanovich, "The National and University Library of Bosnia and Herzegovina During the Current War," *Library Quarterly*, 66: 3 (July 1996), p. 294.

8 Zećo and Tomljanovich, "The National and University Library," p. 297.

9 Riedlmayer, "From the Ashes," p. 111.

10 Kemal Bakaršić, "The Libraries of Sarajevo and the Book that Saved Our Lives," *The New Combat*, (Autumn 1994), http://www.newcombat.net/article_thelibraries.html.

11 Burton Bollag, "Rebuilding Bosnia's Library," *The Chronicle of Higher Education*, 41: 18 (January 1995), p. A35. The first books printed before the 1500s are known as "incunabula."

12 Leonard Kniffel, "National Library of Bosnia: To Restore or Memorialize?" *American Libraries*, 27: 2 (February 1996), p. 17. See also Sanja Zgonjanin, "The Prosecution of War Crimes for the Destruction of Libraries and Archives During Times of Armed Conflict," *Libraries and Culture*, 40: 2 (Spring 2005), p. 135, and András Riedlmayer, "Crimes of War," p. 110. Zgonjanin and Riedlmayer estimate that 90 percent of the library's holdings were destroyed. Riedlmayer, the expert on the library, estimates that 1.5 million volumes were in the library before it was destroyed. See András Riedlmayer, "Libraries Are Not for Burning: International Librarianship and the Recovery of the Destroyed Heritage of Bosnia and Herzegovina," in *61st IFLA General Conference – Conference Proceedings – August 20–25, 1995*, http://archive.ifla.org/IV/ifla61/61-riea.htm. Robert Donia estimates that 2 million volumes were in the library and Tatjana Lorkovic and Tara Wigley estimate

3 million volumes. See Robert Donia, "Archives and Cultural Memory Under Fire: Destruction and the Post-war Nationalist Transformation," presentation to the 15th International Congress on Archives, Vienna, 2004, http://www.arhivsa.ba/ica2004/robert.htm; Tatjana Lorkovic, "National Library," p. 736, and Tara Wigley, "Shelled Out: The National Library of Bosnia and Herzegovina is Being Ruined by Politics," *The Bookseller* (August 24, 2007), p. 16.

13 Wigley, "Shelled Out," p. 16.
14 Zećo and Tomljanovich, "The National and University Library," p. 296.
15 Elma Softić, *Sarajevo Days, Sarajevo Nights*, trans. Nadia Conić (Toronto, ON: Key Porter Books, 1995), p. 73.
16 Zećo and Tomljanovich, "The National and University Library," p. 296; Bollag, "Rebuilding Bosnia's Library," p. A35; and Riedlmayer, "From the Ashes," p. 99. According to Riedlmayer, the Oriental Institute lost 5,263 volumes in "Arabic, Persian, Hebrew and *adzamijski* (Bosnian Slavic written in Arabic script)," among many other manuscripts from the Ottoman era. See Riedlmayer in Matthew Battles, *Library: An Unquiet History* (New York: W.W. Norton & Company), pp. 187–188.
17 Kenan Slinić, quoted in Riedlmayer, "Crimes of War," p. 112.
18 Bakaršić, "The Libraries of Sarajevo."
19 James Raven, "Introduction: The Resonances of Loss," in James Raven, ed., *Lost Libraries: The Destruction of Great Book Collections since Antiquity* (Basingstoke: Palgrave Macmillan, 2004), p. 28.
20 Moreover, books became a symbol of destruction and survival during the siege of Sarajevo. When the Serbs cut off water, food supplies, and fuel, burning books was often the only means that Sarajevans had to cook food. See Stephen Schwartz, "Beyond 'Ancient Hatreds'," *Policy Review*, 97 (October–November 1999), p. 41.
21 Riedlmayer, "Libraries Are Not for Burning."
22 Robert Fisk, "The Myths of Sarajevo," *The Independent*, September 26, 1992, p. 25.
23 Riedlmayer, "Libraries Are Not for Burning."
24 Zgonjanin, "The Prosecution of War Crimes," p. 136.
25 Riedlmayer, quoted in Battles, *Library*, p. 189.
26 Roger Boyes, "This is Cultural Genocide," *The Times*, August 28, 1992, p. 12.
27 Schwartz, "Beyond 'Ancient Hatreds'," p. 42.
28 Jeffrey Spurr, quoted in Battles, *Library*, p. 188.
29 Enes Kujundžić, in Bollag, "Rebuilding Bosnia's Library," p. A35.
30 Ferida Duraković, quoted in Christopher Merrill, "Burning of Library Mourned," *Worchester Telegram & Gazette*, January 21, 1996, p. A1.
31 Bollag, "Rebuilding Bosnia's Library," p. A37 and Hans van der Hoeven, in Zgonjanin, "The Prosecution of War Crimes," p. 128.
32 Zgonjanin, "The Prosecution of War Crimes," p. 128.
33 The Lieber Code, formally entitled "Instructions for the Government of Armies of the United States in the Field," states in Section II, Article 35 that,

> Classical works of art, libraries, scientific collections, or precious instruments, such as astronomical telescopes, as well as hospitals, must be secured against all avoidable injury, even when they are contained in fortified places whilst besieged or bombarded.
> See International Committee of the Red Cross (ICRC), http://www.icrc.org/ihl.nsf/FULL/110?OpenDocument.

34 The Brussels Declaration (formally known as the "Project of an International Declaration Concerning the Laws and Customs of War") comprises laws and customs of war initiated by Russia. Article 8 states:

> The property of municipalities, that of institutions dedicated to religion, charity and education, the arts and sciences even when State property, shall be treated as private property. All seizure or destruction of, or wilful damage to, institutions of this character, historic monuments, works of art and science should be made the subject of legal proceedings by the competent authorities.
> (See ICRC, http://www.icrc.org/ihl.nsf/FULL/135?OpenDocument)

35 UNESCO, "Memory of the World: Programme Background," http://portal.unesco.org/ci/en/ev.php-URL_ID=23929&URL_DO=DO_TOPIC&URL_SECTION=201.html.

36 See Article 53, ICRC, http://www.icrc.org/ihl.nsf/7c4d08d9b287a42141256739003e636b/f6c8b9fee14a77fdc125641e0052b079. Also see Peter Maass, "Cultural Property and Historical Monuments," in Roy Gutman and David Rieff, eds, *Crimes of War: What the Public Should Know* (New York: W.W. Norton & Company, 1999), p. 112.

37 See Riedlmayer, "Libraries Are Not for Burning"; Ken Gewertz, "Librarians Riedlmayer and Spurr Honored for Work in Sarajevo," *The Harvard University Gazette*, October 31, 1996, http://www.news.harvard.edu/gazette/1996/10.31/LibrariansRiedl.html; and Zgonjanin, "The Prosecution of War Crimes," pp. 129–130.

38 Zgonjanin, "The Prosecution of War Crimes," p. 129. For the Hague Convention, see UNESCO, http://portal.unesco.org/culture/en/ev.php-URL_ID=35744&URL_DO=DO_TOPIC&URL_SECTION=201.html. In 2009, under the Obama administration, the USA became the 123rd state to ratify the Convention. See Antiquities Watch, http://antiquitieswatch.wordpress.com/2009/03/30/us-ratifies-1954-hague-convention/.

39 For an overview of the number of libraries and museums destroyed during the Second World War and the Holocaust throughout Europe, but in Poland in particular, see Raven, "Introduction," pp. 1–40.

40 See Maass, "Cultural Property," p. 112.

41 Riedlmayer, "Crimes of War," p. 126.

42 International Criminal Court, "Elements of the Crime, ICC-ASP/1/3 (part II-B)," War Crimes, Article 8 (2) (a) (iv), http://www.icc-cpi.int/Menus/ICC/Legal+Texts+and+Tools/Official+Journal/Elements+of+Crimes.htm.

43 "The Man who Abolished Future Eichmanns," New York Public Library, *Raphael Lemkin Papers*, Reel 4, Box 4, Folder 3, "Notes."

44 Raphael Lemkin, *Axis Rule in Occupied Europe: Laws of Occupation, Analysis of Government, Proposals for Redress* (Clark, NJ: The Law Book Exchange, Ltd., 2005), p. 91.

45 Zgonjanin, "The Prosecution of War Crimes," p. 128.

46 Ibid.

47 Raphael Lemkin, "Explanatory Note on Cultural Genocide," American Jewish Historical Society, *Raphael Lemkin Collection*, call P154, Box 6, Folder 5, "Notes and Drafts, Misc. n.d."

48 Article II (e) reads: "Forcibly transferring children of the group to another group." See United Nations, *Convention on the Prevention and Punishment of the Crime of Genocide. Adopted by the General Assembly of the United Nations on 9 December 1948*, http://treaties.un.org/doc/Publication/UNTS/Volume%2078/volume-78-I-1021-English.pdf.

49 Raphael Lemkin, "Diffusion Versus Cultural Genocide," New York Public Library, *Raphael Lemkin Papers*, Reel 3, Box 2, Folder 3, "Writings – Genocide. Genocide as Soc./Psycho/Anthro/Econ. Impact on Culture. Genocide as Sexually Approved Behavior."

50 Raphael Lemkin, "B. Importance of the Project for: 7. The Study of Cultural Changes and Losses," New York Public Library, *Raphael Lemkin Papers*, Reel 3, Box 2, Folder 1, "Writings – Genocide. Outlines and Description of the Project."

51 Raphael Lemkin, "Diffusion Versus Cultural Genocide."

52 Lemkin also writes: "the diversity of nations, [and] religious groups . . . is essential to civilization because every one of these groups has a mission to fulfil and a contribution to make in terms of culture." See Raphael Lemkin, "Totally Unofficial," New York Public Library, *Raphael Lemkin Papers*, Reel 2, Box 1, Folder 36, "Autobiography."

53 Raphael Lemkin, "Diffusion Versus Cultural Genocide" and "The Doctrine of Hope," New York Public Library, *Raphael Lemkin Papers*, Reel 3, Box 2, Folder 3, "Writings – Genocide. Genocide as Soc./Psycho/Anthro/Econ. Impact on Culture. Genocide as Sexually Approved Behavior."

54 Raphael Lemkin in "Interview on the Genocide Convention for Italy," New York Public Library, *Raphael Lemkin Papers,* Reel 1, Box 1, Folder 2, "General Correspondence, 1954–1959."

55 Raphael Lemkin, "Description of the Project: Part A. Scope of the Project," New York Public Library, *Raphael Lemkin Papers*, Reel 3, Box 2, Folder 1, "Writings – Genocide. Outlines and Description of the Project."

56 Nicholas Adams, cited in Martin Coward, "Community as Heterogeneous Ensemble: Mostar and Multiculturalism," *Alternatives*, 27 (2002), p. 31.

57 Nicholas Adams notes the axiomatic point that people are more important than buildings, "but the survival of architecture and urban life are important to the survival of people." Adams, cited in Coward, "Community as Heterogeneous Ensemble," p. 32.

58 Raphael Lemkin, "Letter to James Rosenberg, September 31, 1948," American Jewish Historical Society, *Raphael Lemkin Collection*, call P154, Box 1, Folder 19, "Correspondence 1948."

59 United Nations Economic and Social Council, "Report of the Committee and Draft Convention Drawn up by the Committee/Ad Hoc Committee on Genocide (Dr. Karim Azkoul – Rapporteur)," Document symbol E/794, May 1948, p. 18.

60 John Maktos (the United States), Platon Morozov (the USSR), Karim Azkoul (Lebanon), Lin Mousheng (China), Pierre Ordonneau (France), Aleksander Rudzinski (Poland), Victor Pérez Perozo (Venezuela). See United Nations Economic and Social Council, "Report of the Committee," p. 3.

61 Ibid., p. 18.

62 United Nations General Assembly, "Eighty-Third Meeting, Held at Palais de Chaillot, Paris, on Monday, 25 October 1948: [6th Committee, General Assembly, 3rd Session]," Document symbol A/C.6/SR.83, October 1948, p. 193.

63 United Nations General Assembly, "Eighty-Third Meeting," p. 195.

64 See reports from delegates Federspiel from Denmark, Goytisolo from Peru and de Beus from the Netherlands. United Nations General Assembly, "Eighty-Third Meeting," pp. 198, 202 and 203.

65 United Nations General Assembly, "Eighty-Third Meeting," pp. 197, 199 and 200.

66 Ibid., pp. 201, 202.

67 Ibid., p. 197.

68 Ibid., pp. 194, 198, 199, and 201.

69 Ibid., p. 205.

70 See, for instance, delegate Kaeckenbeeck from Belgium. United Nations General Assembly, "Eighty-Third Meeting," p. 204.

71 Ibid., p. 196.

72 Ibid., p. 194. See reports from the delegates from Egypt, Iran and the Netherlands, pp. 199, 200, and 203.

73 The United States, for instance, declared that genocide "should be confined to those barbarous acts directed against individuals which form the basic concept of public opinion on this subject . . . [cultural genocide] should appropriately be dealt with in connection with the protection of minorities." United Nations Economic and Social Council, "Report of the Committee," p. 18.

74 United Nations General Assembly, "Eighty-Third Meeting," pp. 203 and 204.

75 Ibid., p. 194.

76 Ibid., p. 196.

77 Ibid., p. 195.

78 Ibid., p. 203.

79 Ibid., p. 205.

80 Ibid., p. 194.

81 Ibid., p. 202. Emphasis added.

82 Ibid., p. 197. In his autobiography, Lemkin alludes to a good relationship with Ambassador Amado who wrote that Lemkin is a "generous fanatic but we like his ideas and we will support him." See Raphael Lemkin, "Totally Unofficial," New York Public Library, *Raphael Lemkin Papers*, Reel 2, Box 1, Folder 38, "Autobiography: Summaries and Outlines."

83 United Nations General Assembly, "Eighty-Third Meeting," pp. 203–204.

84 After the adoption of the Genocide Convention by the United Nations in 1948, Lemkin lobbied for ratification, but before 1950, had support from only three continents, but not South America. Lemkin turned to his friend from Ecuador who helped speed the process. See Raphael Lemkin, "Totally Unofficial," New York Public Library, *Raphael Lemkin Papers*, Reel 2, Box 1, Folder 38, "Autobiography: Summaries and Outlines."

85 United Nations General Assembly, "Eighty-Third Meeting," p. 205.

86 Those in favor of the *exclusion* of cultural destruction comprised: Australia, Belgium, Bolivia, Brazil, Canada, Chile, Denmark, Dominican Republic, France, Greece, India, Iran, Liberia, Luxembourg, the Netherlands, New Zealand, Norway, Panama, Peru, Siam, Sweden, Turkey, Union of South Africa, United Kingdom, and the United States. Those against the exclusion were: Belorussian Soviet Socialist Republic, China, Czechoslovakia, Ecuador, Egypt, Ethiopia, Lebanon, Mexico, Pakistan, the Philippines, Poland, Saudi Arabia, Syria, Ukrainian Soviet Socialist Republic, the USSR, and Yugoslavia. Thirteen delegates were absent and four nation-states – Afghanistan, Argentina, Cuba, and Venezuela – abstained. See United Nations General Assembly, "Eighty-Third Meeting," p. 206.

87 The delegate from the Byelorussian Soviet Socialist Republic stated that "his country, and others . . . had suffered from such persecutions, which were aimed at the destruction of cultural institutions and which had always accompanied acts of physical genocide." See United Nations Gerneral Assembly, "Eighty-Third Meeting," p. 202.

88 Andrew Herscher, "Warchitecture Theory," *Journal of Architectural Education*, 61: 3 (February 2008), pp. 35, 37.

89 Riedlmayer, "Crimes of War," pp. 127–128.

90 The International Tribunal for the Prosecution of Persons Responsible for Serious Violations of International Humanitarian Law Committed in the Territory of the former Yugoslavia since 1991 (ICTY) and the International Criminal Tribunal for Rwanda (ICTR).

91 Riedlmayer, "Sarajevo Library's Destruction," p. 30.

92 John Quigley, *The Genocide Convention: An International Law Analysis* (Aldershot: Ashgate, 2006), p. 105. Similarly, Eric Markusen and Martin Mennecke argue that systematic cultural destruction can "serve as circumstantial evidence of Serb desire to destroy Muslims as a group; hence, of genocidal intent." See Eric Markusen and Martin Mennecke, "Genocide in Bosnia and Herzegovina," *Human Rights Review*, 5: 4 (July–September 2004), p. 74.

93 Judgment, *Prosecutor v. Kristic*, Trial Chamber, August 2, 2001, p. 203.

94 UNESCO, "Lost Memory – Libraries and Archives Destroyed in the Twentieth Century," http://www.unesco.org/webworld/mdm/administ/en/detruit.html.

95 Bollag, "Rebuilding Bosnia's Library," p. A37.

96 Raven, "Introduction," p. 5.

97 Battles, *Library*, p. 188.

98 Nikola Koljević, in Donia, *Sarajevo*, p. 288.

99 Also speaking in April 1992, Koljević is reported to have said: "Work on the map should begin in Sarajevo . . . Sarajevo should be portioned, and then we would go further. We think that this would be the best step toward peace in Bosnia and Herzegovina." See Koljević in Charles Sudetic, "Intense Fighting in Sarajevo Threatens U.S. Aid Flights," *The New York Times*, April 18, 1992, p. 14.

100 Battles, *Library*, p. 187.

101 Raymond Bonner, "Rising Bosnian Serb Leader Offers Accord Rare Praise," *The New York Times*, November 26, 1995, p. 22A. See also "Bosnia Serb Official Dies From Self-Inflicted Shot," *The New York Times*, January 26, 1997, p. 19.

102 The report was written before the destruction of the *Vijećnica*. See John F. Burns, "Another Hope is Dashed in Sarajevo, as Serbs Shatter Airport Truce," *The New York Times*, June 27, 1992, p. 15.

103 Janine di Giovanni, "The Cleanser," *The Guardian*, March 1, 1997.

104 Battles, *Library*, p. 186.

105 Dragan Kalinić quoted in Donia, *Sarajevo*, p. 315.
106 Adam LeBor, "City Life – Sarajevo – Heritage Reduced to Ashes as Serbs Tried to Wipe Muslims from History," *The Independent*, August 21, 2000, p. 15. Jean Lacouture first used the term "auto-genocide" in "The Bloodiest Revolution," *The New York Review of Books*, March 31, 1977. See also Jörg Menzel, "Justice Delayed Or Too Late for Justice? The Khmer Rouge Tribunal and the Cambodian 'Genocide' 1975–79," *Journal of Genocide Research*, 9: 2 (June 2007), p. 231, n. 63.

Figure 5.1 "Russian atrocities in Livonia in XVI century (using women for archery target practice)." Anonymous woodcut published by Dariusz Kupisz, Psków, in 1581–1582.

Source: Wikimedia Commons.

CHAPTER 5

Genocidal Masculinity

Elisa von Joeden-Forgey

> For me it became a pleasure to kill. The first time, it's to please the government. After that, I developed a taste for it. I hunted and caught and killed with real enthusiasm. It was work, but work that I enjoyed. It wasn't like working for the government. It was like doing your own true job – like working for myself. I was very, very excited when I killed. I remember each killing. Yes, I woke every morning excited to go into the bush. It was the hunt – the human hunt.
>
> (Jean Girumuhatse, as told to Philip Gourevitch, 2008[1])

The testimony of Jean Girumuhatse exemplifies one of the most puzzling aspects of the crime of genocide – that the specific type of killing involved can be the source of great pleasure for the killers. As recent studies have shown, this pleasure cannot be explained by abnormal psychology, since most perpetrators resemble one another in their basic ordinariness. This pleasure is also hard to explain with reference to evolutionary psychology and situational factors alone, although these help us to understand how genocidal processes get off the ground and become institutionalized. Jean Girumuhatse, and scores of other *génocidaires* in Rwanda and elsewhere, press against the limits of our explanatory capacities, our ability to create an analytical order from the chaos of the crime. This is because *génocidaires* create what Dan Stone has called "ecstatic communities" engaged in "transgressive violence," and the social sciences offer few clues as to how we might interpret this.[2] Stone notes that:

> This momentary participation in legitimized killing takes place in heightened emotional conditions, akin to sustained orgasm, which recall the sexual licence of the

festival (and which in turn are recalled by the mass rapes that occurred during the Bosnian war and the ferocious sexual mutilations that characterized the Rwandan genocide).[3]

Girumuhatse, in fact, explicitly suggests something quite similar. After likening the killing in Rwanda to a hunt, he told Gourevitch that "the genocide was like a festival. At day's end, or any time there was an occasion, we took a cow from the Tutsis, and slaughtered it and grilled it and drank beer. There were no limits anymore. It was a festival. We celebrated."[4]

Girumuhatse seems to be speaking a certain truth in his interview with Gourevitch. He had served eleven years in prison for his crimes, and had completed the *gacaca* process. He had also made the required tour of apology to his neighbors whose family members he had killed. The fact that he would boast of the excitement and pleasure he felt during the killing poses the possibility that some people genuinely enjoy genocidal killing, and do not feel an internal compunction to rationalize, cognitively dissociate, or entirely reframe what they were doing, in order to salvage an image of themselves as worthwhile human beings.[5] Naturally, Girumuhatse's bravado might itself be a way of cognitively dissociating himself from what he did, since it certainly separates his experience from the depth and the enormity of the suffering that he caused, and continues to cause, in his village. But even if this is the case, there is no reason to believe that he did not truly feel the excitement he described.

According to Gourevitch, Girumuhatse admits to killing eleven men. But some of his surviving victims estimate the number to be much higher – as many as seventy people. Girumuhatse had significant power over the course of the genocide in his village, because he was "the leader of a band of *génocidaires* who manned the roadblock in front of his house, and he said he was responsible for the killings there."[6] It is unlikely that his enthusiasm for killing was shared by the majority of the perpetrators in Rwanda, most of whom were caught up in the maelstrom of the process, and made decisions based on situational factors that have little to do with the pleasures of killing. In fact, most studies of ordinary perpetrators in Rwanda and elsewhere suggest that it is such situational factors, especially fear, social pressure, and the promise of personal enrichment, that best explain the majority of ordinary men's participation in mass murder.[7] These perpetrators pursue killing in relatively mechanical ways, in contrast to the significant but smaller group of perpetrators who are highly creative in their cruelties, and who demonstrate a deep commitment to their task. In this chapter, I limit my discussion to this latter group, who exist both at the planning and implementation levels. This includes ideologues like Adolf Hitler, Talat Pasha, and Pol Pot, as well as members of militias who are either specifically trained in genocidal killing, such as the SS and the *interahamwe*, or who volunteer themselves for the task, such as Arkan's Tigers in Bosnia-Herzegovina. These men, and occasionally women, constitute the core of the criminal enterprise, without which genocidal fantasies would remain safely confined in the myopic world of the destructive imagination.

One clue to understanding the pleasure in killing experienced by some *génocidaires* is the fact that the "hunt" of genocide, to use Girumuhatse's word, is clearly a gendered event. It is gendered both in the sense that the killers often see themselves in highly gendered ways, and in the sense that the process of killing frequently unfolds along starkly gendered lines.[8] In this chapter, I will argue that the crime of genocide is tied to the exertion of a specifically genocidal concept of masculine power on the world – a phenomenon I am here calling "genocidal masculinity." Genocidal masculinity emerges historically within patriarchal systems, and is aimed at replacing patriarchy as a governing gender ideology. It is a form of male domination that both rejects the old patriarchy and embraces an expression of power based on killing rather than life-giving. It results from the perceived marginalization of an individual man or group of men from the patriarchal order and the institutions of transcendence monopolized by it. Even in power, genocidal masculinity is a defensive form of masculinity that is self-consciously revolutionary – directed at the old order and interested in creating a new world. In fact, in direct response to this marginalization, genocidal masculinity disavows the civilian world and its institutions of peacetime, replacing the transcendent and creative power of birth-giving – which patriarchal systems claim for men through the institution of the family – with the transcendent and creative power of killing. Both in the pronouncements of the architects and propagandists, and in the actions of the killers, genocidal masculinity is articulated in terms of ritualized cruelty, which becomes the new definitional characteristic of "real men." In genocidal masculinist ideologies and practices, giving birth *becomes* killing, inasmuch as human material is valued only insofar as it furthers the killing machine. As such, genocidal masculinity is one answer to a specifically male existential drama, which revolves around the need to establish a direct link to those generative powers that exhibit themselves in, through, and with women and their bodies. If patriarchy allows men to claim access to and control over these powers as heads of households, genocidal masculinity denies the transcendence of the reproductive realm altogether, claiming this status instead for its particular brand of destruction.

Analyzing genocide – its ideologies and practices – through the concept of genocidal masculinity can serve several purposes. It helps us understand the passion and intimate identification many perpetrators feel for the crimes they are committing. This, in turn, helps explain the real and very particular tendency for genocidal violence to spread beyond the target group. It opens up new directions for historical scholarship on the origins of genocidal ideologies. It can help us explain the shared meaning system that informs both the ideological fantasies of the architects of genocide and the real-world experience of the ground-level perpetrators, in cases where there is no clearly shared ideological commitment or experience of indoctrination. It offers clues to how genocide catches on, spreads, and occasionally appears to become an end in itself. And it sheds light on the close association between genocidal agendas, the types of atrocities that characterize the crime, and the sense of collective and individual selfhood experienced by perpetrators at different levels of the hierarchy. Perhaps most importantly, genocidal masculinity emphasizes the very specific nature of the crime: how it differs from war and other cases of mass slaughter, and the stakes involved in maintaining these distinctions.

MEN AND GENOCIDE

Genocidal masculinity is not a notion that has received much attention in the scholarship on genocide. We routinely write about perpetrators without noting explicitly that the vast majority are men, which is especially the case as one advances up the chain of command. Instead of engaging with the maleness of the majority of the perpetrators as a puzzle, scholarship on genocide has pursued three overlapping approaches to the fact. One approach is simply to assume the fact of male domination in the crime, and use the lives and experiences of men to discuss the deeper truths of what is believed to be a shared *human* nature.[9] Another approach is to note in passing the preponderance of men among the perpetrators, but to leave this factor relatively unexplained, or explained as the natural consequence either of male biology or of men's dominance in the societies committing the murder.[10] A final approach, which has appeared very recently, is to deny the fact that there is any significant relationship between men and genocide, explaining it away with reference to men's historical domination of the military, pointing to women's participation in genocide as evidence that there is an equal capacity in each sex to commit genocide and using gender-inclusive prose to make this point.[11] While the research on gender and violence is far too underdeveloped to assess the relative merits of these approaches, it bears noting that the correlation between men and the impetus for genocide needs to be investigated by social scientists as a subject in its own right.

Despite the fact of women's engagement in the perpetration of genocide, it is important to problematize genocide as a crime committed predominantly by men. As Joane Nagel pointed out over a decade ago, so many major historical processes that we tend to view and describe in gender-neutral terms are in fact masculinist projects. Referring to the titles of some seminal books in political theory, such as *Political Man* and *Why Men Rebel*, she writes that "perhaps the projects described in these titles – state power, citizenship, nationalism, militarism, revolution, political violence, dictatorship, and democracy – are all best understood as masculinist projects, involving masculine institutions, masculine processes and masculine activities."[12] By this, she does not intend to make an essentialist argument, but rather to call attention to the fact that men tend to be the primary decision-makers in major political projects, and that these projects tend to draw upon, reaffirm, and transform ideologies of masculinity. War is, of course, the classic example of this, but state-building, nationalism, imperialism, revolution, decolonization, and even trade unionism also have been inspired by masculinist imagery, constructed around male agendas, and largely controlled by men. In arguing that genocide is a masculinist project, I want to make a similar point. While the origin of genocide may lie in those dark characteristics of the human psychology and the human soul that are shared between men and women, the crime is expressed through the prism of a specific definition of maleness, and is therefore a masculinist crime.

This chapter will be an initial foray into the potential for scholarship on genocidal masculinity to yield insights of use to the field as a whole. Due to its necessarily rudimentary nature, it will no doubt raise more questions than it answers, but it is my hope that it can act as a spark for new research. My approach is meant to challenge both the literature that naturalizes the relationship between men and genocidal violence, and the literature that underestimates the importance of this relationship. By reinserting the question of gender identity into the discussion of violence and genocide, I do not intend to engage essentialist arguments for or against women's propensity to commit mass violence on equal levels with men. But I do believe that the interrogation of gender identity can help us understand genocide as a crime associated with masculinity, while also leaving room for the presence of women as perpetrators and "partners," to use John Roth's formulation.[13]

GENOCIDAL MASCULINITY AND PATRIARCHY

In line with recent research in the field of masculinity studies, I define masculinity as the social construction of male identity that conceptualizes manhood relationally, in opposition to other forms of masculinity, femininity, and a perceived "women's sphere" of reproductive power. R.W. Connell, in his path-breaking work in the field, defined masculinity as "simultaneously a place in gender relations, the practices through which men and women engage that place in gender, and the effects of these practices in bodily experience, personality and culture."[14] Masculinity is produced as a result of the attempt to identify differences between the sexes, and to create meaning and hierarchies from this difference. It evolves historically and therefore is connected to the historical experiences of men in a world characterized by the almost universal existence of patriarchy. Unlike hegemonic forms of masculinity, which support the patriarchal status quo, genocidal masculinity is an identity of resistance and protest, similar to the constructions of manhood that inform revolutionary activity. It is therefore one of many options available to men who, for a vast variety of reasons, feel they cannot find a comfortable space within hegemonic forms of masculinity and the patriarchal systems that they sustain.

Of course, masculinity is not a single thing. Current scholarship speaks of the subject in the plural, as a matter of "masculinities." In any given society, multiple masculinities coexist, often in tension and often beneath a hegemonic form, which is itself subject to change.[15] In other words, masculinity is not inherent in biological sex. Rather,

> [It is] terrifyingly fragile because it does not really exist in the sense we are led to think it exists, that is, as a biological reality . . . It exists in ideology; it exists in scripted behavior; it exists within "gendered" relationships.[16]

So masculinity is something that requires performance to make it real. It is also something that can be taken up by women as well as men – Judith Halberstam speaks of a "female masculinity" that is more than the simple imitation of men.[17] Another way to look at this is that masculinities serve three purposes at once: (1) they define what male-born people should be, and in that way are meant to operate in a sex-specific manner; (2) they set public preference for modes of behavior and identification that are linked to values historically associated with men (including virility, physical prowess, control, hardness, transcendence); and (3) they set out social, economic, and political agendas that may or may not explicitly engage gendered themes. Genocidal masculinity expresses itself in all three dimensions. It prescribes the preferred behavior of men, seeks to define public values, and informs policy agendas. Unlike the taken-for-granted forms of masculinity that are part of the gender hegemony of a specific period in time, genocidal masculinity is *mobilized* masculinity, masculinity that has become translated into a more or less articulated ideology.

Key to the construction of any form of masculinity is what Connell calls the "reproductive arena," since it is in the physical reproduction of the human species that men and women play clearly different roles. Without this crucial distinction, it is hard to imagine the emergence of the often rigid and fetishized binary gender world in which we all live. Cultures assign complex meanings to this distinction, and allocate tasks accordingly. While women's centrality to human regeneration is fairly clear-cut, inasmuch as their bodies carry new human beings inside them, men play a much less direct and obvious role. The feminist philosopher and trained midwife Mary O'Brien has gone as far as to characterize men's relationship to reproduction as a case of alienated labor, which men must seek to mediate via social institutions like the patriarchal family.[18] Whatever the case, it seems evident that human beings place a premium on having access to the mysterious generative forces that account for the existences of all of us. Human societies construct themselves with reference to this mystery and its actualization in family and household units, and ideas about proper gender roles, masculinity and femininity, tend to grow from it.

In most societies in the world, reproduction is socially organized around the model of the patriarchal (and usually patrilineal) family, which frequently involves the legal or economic dependence of women and children on male heads of households, the male domination of public institutions, the allocation of high-status social roles and tasks to elite senior males, and the primacy of the father's name and lineage in bestowing identity on offspring. Patriarchal institutions are rarely total, and they are always contested. Thus, I speak of *patriarchal models*, those abiding abstractions that cultures define as icons of proper family life and the key to social peace and harmony. Because patriarchy is a vertical system of allocating power that relies on the subordination of some men to other men, usually the heads of large and prosperous households, I prefer to distinguish patriarchy from the more general concept of male domination. Male domination refers to the power that men in general have over women, regardless of their own status in the patriarchy. A man excluded from the main circuits of power in a patriarchal system can still profit from the male domination that the system produces in the social, political, and reproductive arenas.

However, despite the male domination that patriarchy supports, not all men can find a comfortable space within patriarchal power structures. Male outsiders abound in patriarchal systems, whether because they are economically unable to found families, or they are incapable of maintaining patriarchal family structures, or because they are excluded from institutions of public authority, or because they are members of a marginalized patriarchy (as, for example, with ethnic minorities or colonized persons), or because they reject the hegemonic masculinity that is supposed to define them. The stakes of exclusion can appear to be very high, since patriarchal systems monopolize institutions of transcendence through their claim on reproductive power. This mono-polized transcendent power is translated into those social and political institutions that are considered to have a transcendent dimension, particularly organized religion and the arts and sciences. Men's dominance in these arenas is legitimized with reference to their vertical connection with one or more gods (or with other transcendent concepts, such as reason). Complementing the transcendent sphere is the horizontal world of "mere" biological reproduction and nurturing, which is performed by women. Since the labor of reproduction, which is done almost entirely by women (in the acts of conceiving, carrying, giving birth to, and raising children), is not in and of itself sufficient to create transcendence, reproduction is understood instead in terms of the wider male-dominated social system. One of the key functions of patriarchy, in fact, is to give men a direct role in the transcendent process of reproduction. It mediates, in other words, what Mary O'Brien has called men's "alienation of the seed."[19] To be a man excluded from the patriarchy is therefore to risk being trapped in a space of alienation, unless one is able to invent new means of establishing transcendence.

One way in which subordinated men cope with the often inflexible verticality of patriarchal power is to create alternative cultures of masculinity. German Social Democrats, for example, who were politically and economically unable to conform to the elite model of masculinity in imperial Germany, instead "situated the representation of their masculinity in the public sphere of political discourse."[20] Men can also mobilize masculinity to effect revolutionary change, as was the case in the American colonies and in France.[21] As Karen Hagemann and Stefan Dudink have pointed out, what all this suggests is that masculinity can be "harnessed to establish, change, and defend relations of power."[22] The case of genocidal masculinity is no different. The men who project genocidal masculinity as a political model seek to replace patriarchal systems of human reproduction with centralized, statist, and militarist variants of male domination that wrest transcendence from the familial realm and place it, instead, squarely within the genocidal project. In this sense they are both revolutionary and anti-patriarchal. Of course, genocidal regimes rely for their meaning systems on pre-existing patriarchal institutions, and especially the hegemonic form of masculinity produced therein, and they often draw liberally from pre-existing patriarchal symbols in crafting their propaganda. But despite their copious references to the past, their commitment to it is superficial. They all seek to make incursions into the semi-autonomous space of families and households in order to claim for the state and the party the transcendent power monopolized within them.

A key feature of genocidal masculinism, then, is a pronounced hostility to the status quo organization of households and the monopoly on transcendent power that these units appear to claim. Because the dominant mode of organizing the reproductive arena in human societies has been patriarchy, genocidal masculinity is an assault on patriarchal social relations, and is understood as such by the true believers. The antagonism for patriarchy that we can identify within genocidal ideologies can be explained by a number of factors. First, the architects of genocide see themselves as revolutionaries and aim to overturn the status quo, which is associated with the old patriarchal order, and especially with those patriarchs who, in the minds of the *génocidaires*, were incapable of protecting the group from the real and imagined threats they identify. Second, patriarchal institutions are conservative in nature, and serve to reproduce the status quo and its cultural values. As much as they often receive tacit support, if not direct empowerment, from old patriarchal systems, *génocidaires* are quite aware of the extent to which their radical policies will require a reworking of basic cultural values in society, which are often based on religious traditions that prohibit murder. The patriarchal family is a prime site for the reproduction of these values. Third, these institutions allow for a degree of autonomy from the kind of state or party interference necessary to the genocidal cause, which requires the reorganization of social relations under the strict control of the *génocidaires*. And finally, patriarchs are seen to be competitors for decision-making power: both secular and religious patriarchal legal regimes generally give fathers wide discretionary powers regarding the women and children under their control, and this can present an obstacle to the reproductive policies pursued by the parties promoting genocide. These four aspects of patriarchy that *génocidaires* seek to undermine point to the extent to which genocidal ideology has as its goal the flattening of the patriarchal distinction between the public (productive) and the domestic (reproductive) spheres, however these realms are culturally defined.

In addition to the overthrow of the old order, genocidal masculinity also informs the image of the new order that is to take its place. In the position of the old patriarchy, which, after all, was responsible for the maintenance of a stable hierarchy and the organization of the "reproductive arena" toward the sustenance of human lives, *génocidaires* seek permanently to organize society around the task of killing, utopian images of a renewed and strengthened people notwithstanding. This creates a very specific culture that is characterized by the valorization of pure martial brutality and cold-heartedness in men, especially toward "outsiders," and the desire, if not always the attempt, to exercise a direct control over the family lives and reproductive choices of "insiders."

The extent to which genocidal leaders can actualize their anti-patriarchal fantasies by forcing themselves into the reproductive arena will depend on several factors, including the degree of control they have over the coercive powers of the state, the proximity of the killing fields to the home front, the length of time they have exercised power, and their level of commitment to ideological transformation. Although in each case, specific historical and cultural factors determine how far civilian life is actually reorganized by *génocidaires*, some reciprocity between the killing fields and the home front will inevitably occur. Perhaps the most extreme example of this reciprocity is the Cambodian genocide, where the home front was collapsed into the killing fields, as the Khmer Rouge abolished the family and forced people into rural collective production sites that were also the space of genocidal atrocity.[23] A similar logic was at work during the civil war in Sierra Leone, in the regions controlled by the Revolutionary United Front (RUF). The typical RUF pattern was to attack villages, commit genocidal atrocities against villagers, and then kidnap boys to be used as child soldiers and girls to be used as sex slaves and domestics.[24] In this case, where, as in Cambodia, much of the violence did not have an ethnic dimension, the civilian world itself was destroyed, appropriated, and converted into the killing field.

In Rwanda, where there was no far-reaching ideological reorganization of political, social, and economic structures in the years preceding the genocide, the proximity of the killing fields to the killers' homes gave *génocidaires* the opportunity to assault old patriarchal hierarchies and institutions on an *ad hoc* basis while simultaneously pursuing mass murder, thereby very quickly creating a new culture – if not a legal regime – of genocidal masculinity. This new culture rested on several things: the complete erasure of the norms of civilian life, the reorientation of group activity around rituals of killing, and the refocusing of public and private values toward murder over the maintenance of life. One witness to the genocide tells us:

Sometimes the men returned from an expedition pushing a fugitive in front of them. They would stop him in the marketplace. They would take off his watch and shoes. Occasionally they would take off his clothes as well – at least at the beginning of the killings, because afterwards the runaways were so tattered, there was nothing left worth taking off.

These doomed victims were usually acquaintances who had tried to cheat – to pass for Hutu, for example. Or people who had been rich and important before. Or acquaintances disliked because of old quarrels.

The killers would call everyone to watch. All the women and children would gather to see the show. There were people still carrying drinks, or nurslings on their backs. The killers would cut off the victims' limbs, they would crush their bones with a club, but without killing them. They wanted them to last. They wanted the audience to learn from these torments. Shouts would rise up from all sides. These were raucous village jamborees, quite rare and quite popular.[25]

A killer from the Rwandan genocide describes the time of genocide as an almost complete inversion of civilian life, along the lines described by Girumuhatse:

During the killing, we had not one wedding, not one baptism, not one soccer match, not one religious service like Easter. We did not find that kind of celebration interesting anymore. We did not care a spit for that Sunday silliness. We were dead tired from work, we were getting greedy, we celebrated whenever we felt like it, we drank as much as we wanted.[26]

GENOCIDAL MASCULINITY AND THE FAMILY

An irony of genocidal masculinism's antagonism to patriarchal institutions and the civilian order they sustain is that some policies of genocidal states appear at face value to be progressive toward women. Such apparent feminism is most striking in the case of the brand of Turkish nationalism furthered by the Committee of Union and Progress (CUP) and the gender-equalizing policies promoted by the Khmer Rouge in Cambodia. In these two very different states, leaders promoted a vision of women's equality, but did so with the goal of eroding the relative autonomy that patriarchal families had from governing institutions. The larger purpose of challenging traditional laws and customs involving women was to exert state control over reproduction in the name of improving the biological power of the nation. The Committee of Union and Progress (CUP) is well known for having relatively republican views about Turkish women. Ziya Gökalp, the best-known intellectual of pan-Turkish nationalism, advocated "democracy in the 'parental' family as opposed to the autocracy of the patriarchal family," as well as women's equality and monogamy, arguing in addition that these were all aspects of an ancient, pure Turkic tribal code.[27] The first secular Family Law, enacted by the CUP in 1917, placed Shari'ah courts under the authority of the Ministry of Justice, giving the state control over family law and personal status for the first time in Ottoman history. It also recognized the right of women to initiate divorce, and both legalized and restricted the practice of polygamy.[28] Nevertheless, these changes were as much part of a self-conscious modernization effort that involved weakening Muslim clerics and creating a uniform national citizenry as a genuine commitment to women's emancipation. "Although Turkism may have provided a new ideological framework to debate these questions [about women's status]," writes Deniz Kandiyoti, "Unionist family policies must ultimately be understood as an attempt to extend state control and intervention into the private realm of the family."[29]

In a much more extreme fashion, the 'gender equity' practiced by the Khmer Rouge regime in Cambodia was also part of an attempt to insert the state into the private realm of the family. Article 13 of the Constitution of Democratic Kampuchea stated that "men and women are fully equal in every respect," which accounts for the high numbers of women in Khmer Rouge militias. This "equality" of course led to a situation of equal terrorization, as distinctions between men and women were officially abolished (along with age distinctions), and all people were subjected to state coercion and violence. The institution of the family itself was abolished, families were torn apart, and members forced to perform collective agricultural labor and practice communal living. Any demonstration of the normal familial sentiments of loyalty and affection were referred to as "family-ism" and considered suspect.[30] In the place of the traditional Khmer family, the Khmer Rouge placed the party, and specifically *Angkar* ("the Organization"), which it considered to be the "dad–mom" of the Khmer people.[31] The Khmer Rouge frequently used forced marriages, which violated the rights of both the women and the men involved.[32] The purpose of these marriages was to increase the population under the total control of *Angkar*. In the process of radically reorganizing society according to a new party-focused familial model, and purifying it of all foreign elements, including the supposedly Western and bourgeois sympathies family members had for one another, the Khmer Rouge created one of the most total and destructive states in human history.

Even in places where political propaganda drew heavily on the imagery of the patriarchal family, such as in Nazi Germany, genocidal states have pursued policies that could appear to liberate women from the restrictions of the patriarchal system. A good example of this is the Third Reich's policies toward single mothers of "Aryan" stock. Nazi laws allowed unwed mothers to use the title *Frau* (Mrs.), and prevented such women from being dismissed from the civil service. Heinrich Himmler established SS "Well of Life" homes that provided help for single women who had given birth to children fathered by soldiers at the front, and he famously advocated polygamy as one way to ensure the perpetuation of his preferred genetic material.[33] Similarly, Nazi divorce laws made it easier for women to obtain divorces, but only in cases where divorce would benefit German racial purity.[34] These policies, of course, must be understood in the context of the dark world of Nazi racial ideology, which aimed to produce "racially valuable" children for the "national community." The same "Well of Life" homes that provided aid to some single mothers also raised those "racially valuable" children who had been kidnapped from their racially unworthy families in Poland and the Soviet Union. In fact, the Nazi Party, while proceeding at a much slower pace than the Khmer Rouge, was on a path to destroying fully the autonomy of families and the institution of marriage, in the name of creating only racially valuable reproductive units overseen by the SS.

Nowhere is this clearer than in the Nazis' abortion, sterilization, and euthanasia policies. Like other genocidal regimes, the Nazis also sought to erode family prerogatives in order to gain access to "valuable" German children while destroying those considered to be "useless eaters."[35] Although initially assuring parents that its youth organizations, the Hitler Youth and the League of German Girls, would not interfere with parental authority, the Third Reich eventually used these organizations precisely to undermine parental rights and claim the nation's youths for party goals.[36] Hitler once announced that:

After these youths have entered our organizations at age ten and there experienced, for the first time, some fresh air . . . we shall under no circumstances return them into the hands of our old champions of class and social standing, but instead place them immediately in the Party or the Labor Front, the SA or the SS . . . And then the Wehrmacht will take them over for further treatment . . . And thus they will never be free again, for the rest of their lives.[37]

Here he was of course talking about boys. Girls were trained to become model mothers, not in the patriarchal sense of the term, but in terms of the radical racism of national socialism, whereby their role was reduced to its mere material element – the production of the genetic material that would further advance the Aryan race, creating stronger soldiers and more fecund and "racially valuable" mothers. Those children who were considered racially inferior were sterilized, sent to concentration camps, or murdered as part of the euthanasia program, with or without the consent of their parents.[38]

Most genocides are not characterized by a *de facto* state penetration into institutions of the family within the preferred group. Often this penetration remains on an ideological level only, and manifests itself in practice only in *ad hoc* ways. In Rwanda, for example, the Hutu Power faction in government shared many of the extremist nationalist preoccupations of the Nazi and Khmer Rouge regimes, but was not in a position, until the genocide was under way, to begin to assault old patriarchal family patterns and values. Ideologically, however, Hutu Power defined the family in clearly genocidally masculinist terms, with its main purpose being defined as the breeding of "pure Hutus." The first three articles of the "Hutu Ten Commandments," published in 1990 in the organ of the radical Hutu Power parties, *Kangura*, mobilized the family as a prime site of the struggle against the Tutsi enemy.[39] Commandment 1 defines as a traitor any Hutu man who marries, befriends, or even employs a Tutsi woman; Commandment 2 reaffirms the value and beauty of Hutu women as daughters and wives; and Commandment 3 encourages Hutu women to "bring your husbands, brothers and sons back to reason" regarding the Tutsi menace. During the genocide, some facets of the killing directly contravened established patriarchal beliefs. For example, it was customary for women to take on the ethnicity of their husbands at marriage, so a Tutsi woman married to a Hutu man would be socially defined as Hutu, as would their children. During the genocide, however, many Tutsi wives of Hutu men were murdered on the basis of the anti-patriarchal racialism of Hutu Power, according to which even ethnically Hutu women could be of Tutsi racial stock.[40] Christopher Taylor has interpreted the genocide as a reassertion of "an imagined past condition of patriarchy as well as the perpetuation of Hutu dominance." This was a revolutionary type of patriarchy, however, a male domination that rested on the unleashing of destructive powers against society in general.[41]

Serbian nationalists imagined breeding utopias similar to those of Heinrich Himmler, but the Yugoslavian/Serbian state under Milošević never tried to implement them. What these schemes nevertheless show is the direct connection between the desire among adherents of genocidal masculinity to reorganize reproduction along materialist lines within their "own" group, on the one hand, and the types of atrocities perpetrators commit against their victims (a subject I will cover in more detail below), on the other. A Serbian academic quoted by Norman Cigar wrote with stunning clarity about the folding of the patriarchal institution of the family into the destructive apparatus of the genocidal state:

In order for the Serbian people to survive, every woman must give birth to at least three children. Let those cliques who take pride in liberty, planned parenthood, and the unquestionable right of women to abortion remember that in a law-abiding state no one is master of his own body, whether male or female. Women must give birth to replacements, while men must go to war when the state calls them.[42]

A Serbian artist went further than this and advocated the creation of a special ministry to increase Serbian births, a "gynecological bus" in every town that would presumably implement the ministry's policies, and the requirement that every woman give birth every nine months, on punishment of being sent to the United Arab Emirates. Regarding the latter, he noted, "Let her have them inseminate her [instead] if she does not want to do so here."[43]

GENOCIDAL MASCULINITY AND LIFE FORCE ATROCITIES

The attempts made by genocidal states to break open the semi-autonomous zone of the patriarchal family demonstrate the tense relationship in which these states find themselves with respect to existing patriarchal institutions. The architects of genocide reject, along with the patriarchal family, the entire peacetime world that patriarchy seeks to organize. Whereas patriarchy creates a dual universe of peace and war that is linked in the figure of the father-warrior, the architects of genocide seek to fold the institutions of peace, including the family, into a new social order that is based entirely on destruction. Their utopian dreams place an eventual time of peace in the transcendent realm, the realm of the goal; the here and now is to be characterized by killing. Genocidal masculinity therefore reflects an effort to shift transcendence from creation to destruction, and indeed, it draws together aspects of men's historical experience to produce a creative destruction. In some cases this transference of transcendence is articulated explicitly. In a famous passage about World War I, the German writer and war veteran Ernst Jünger referred to war as "the male form of procreation."[44] Such a view identifies male creative agency with destruction, and casts killing as an inherently good, generative, and transformative project. In Jünger's work, men live to fight; there is no peacetime masculinity. Although he never joined the Nazi Party, his work on war promoted a kind of cultural masculinism that nurtured "the kinds of fantasies of power and violence from which the Nazis built much of their mass support."[45] Ideological systems like this rest on the denial of the universally accepted transcendent value of bringing children into the world, which the genocidal state or military achieves through the ritual enactment of cruelty against those groups it targets as its victims.

This visceral contempt for family institutions is woven deeply into genocidal ideologies. This has been misunderstood because the pronatalism of many genocidal regimes can serve to mask the hostility that *génocidaires* feel for the reproductive arena. Pronatalism in a genocidal context is nothing more than an effort to empty reproduction of its transcendent power and instead hitch it to the transcendent killing project. Attempts to undermine the independence of family institutions among the preferred group are linked to attempts to destroy the reproductive arena altogether within the targeted victim groups. Leaders who commit genocide often tie the two reproductive realms together by describing the reproductive capacities of the perpetrator and the victim group (or sets of groups) according to a zero-sum logic, which leads them to claim that their people are facing cosmic annihilation. Both Adolf Hitler and Slobodan Milošević felt that their core societies were losing the reproductive battle to their victim groups, whom they endowed with genocidal intentions.[46] Of course we know that the potential for genocide is closely correlated to a perceived threat from the victim group. The Ottoman Empire was losing territory to Europe, Hitler's Germany had lost territory and Great Power status in World War I, Cambodia was facing attack from Vietnam and from the United States, Serbia was losing historically claimed lands as Yugoslavia broke apart, Rwanda was being invaded by refugee Tutsi forces from Uganda. What is important here is that the *génocidaires* interpret these things in cosmic terms, in terms of the potential for their own annihilation. The frequent references one finds among *génocidaires* to this perceived cosmic threat seem to arise directly from their core obsession with being cut off from the life force, something they propose to solve through the "male form of procreation."

The absolute hostility toward the family that is felt by many men engaged in genocide is immediately evident when one examines the methods they use to torture and kill their victims, methods that I have elsewhere called "life force atrocities."[47] What I mean by this is a ritualized pattern of violence that targets the life force of a group by destroying both the physical symbols of the life force as well as the group's most basic institutions of reproduction, especially the family unit. While long considered to be meaningless excesses, these atrocities betray what Alex Hinton has called the "meaning making" potential of genocidal killing.[48] In examining these atrocities, it becomes evident that the final act of murder is merely the end product of genocidal violence. At least as important to the perpetrators – if not more so – are the drawn-out ritual cruelties that occur before the victims are killed. In the genocidal mind, unarmed and harmless civilian populations can pose existential threats precisely because of the strength of their civilian institutions. Their weapons are strong families and communal cohesion, which are interpreted as instruments for the undermining of the *génocidaires'* group. Therefore, *génocidaires* attempt to destroy victim groups in comprehensive ways that target all aspects of the reproductive process – material, symbolic, and metaphysical. As much as *génocidaires* express the wish to erode patriarchal families at home in order to replace them with more efficient reproductive arenas, they still recognize the ultimate power of the patriarchal family as such. This may explain why all genocidal processes are characterized by particularly horrific physical and psychological tortures against people in their family roles.

As I have argued elsewhere, genocidal destruction specifically targets people and institutions in their capacity as actors in the reproductive process.[49] Men are targeted specifically as fathers, husbands, sons, and brothers; women as mothers, wives, daughters, and sisters; children as the group's future; and the elderly as its past. Pregnant women and infants appear to be particularly symbolically loaded victims, since they are the physical evidence of a group's autonomous generative power. Even the destruction of intellectuals and religious figures has a reproductive dimension, as these figures are generally understood to provide both the structure and the content necessary to the coordination of meaningful regeneration. For this reason, genocide really is what Dirk Moses has called a "total social practice." Drawing upon the insights of Raphael Lemkin in his *Axis Rule in Occupied Europe*, the concept of "total social practice" underscores how genocide is a holistic process that targets many different aspects of group life in its destructive efforts.[50]

The "total social practice" of genocide can tell us a great deal about the perpetrators, for it provides evidence of states of mind, motivation, and intent that, combined with other sources, gives us access to a world view that is very hard to reconstruct after the fact, especially for the perpetrators themselves. The "banality of evil" observed by Hannah Arendt at the Adolf Eichmann trial in 1961 is the product in part of the failure of language to be able to capture the emotional state experienced by the architects and the agents of genocide. Our deepest passions are notoriously hard to express; for that, we have our poets, our playwrights, our composers. *Génocidaires* rarely have the insight, the inclination, the honesty, the clarity, the talent, or the freedom to tell us what the crime was for them. But people like Jean Girumuhatse, whose interview with Philip Gourevitch I quoted at the outset, take us a step closer to an unsettling truth – that genocide is, for many people, a creative and dynamic process. It is exciting; it is fulfilling. Evil may be banal from the outside, but for those engaged actively in it, it appears to have a deeply satisfying quality.

The kinds of rituals that make up the total social practice of genocide demonstrate how genocide unfolds within a meaning-system governed by genocidal masculinity. These rituals fall into two categories. The first are inversion rituals that seek to reverse proper hierarchies and relationships within families, and thereby to destroy the sacred bonds that give our lives purpose and meaning. Such acts include forcing family members to watch the rape, torture, and murder of their loved ones, and forcing them to participate in the perpetration of such crimes. Common versions of such atrocities include fathers being forced to rape their children, mothers being forced to kill their children, children being forced to kill their parents, children being pulled screaming from their parents' arms to be killed, and parents being forced to watch as their children are slowly tortured and murdered. The second category of genocidal atrocity is the ritual mutilation and desecration of symbols of group reproduction, including male and female reproductive organs, women's breasts as the sites of lactation, pregnant women as the loci of generative powers, and infants and small children as the sacred symbols of the group's future. The evisceration of pregnant women and the use of infants for target practice are common examples. What ties these two categories of life force atrocity together is that in each, perpetrators betray a pronounced obsession with the destruction of the life force of a group – not just the group's biological ability to bring children into the world, but also the structures of tenderness, love, protectiveness, and loyalty that sustain family, and community, life.

A terrible example of the intentional use of life force atrocities is recounted by Peter Balakian in *Black Dog of Fate* and reprinted in James Waller's *Becoming Evil*. It describes the experiences of a young woman named Dovey, a member of Balakian's extended family. In July 1915, Turkish soldiers first came for Dovey's father, whom they took away, murdered, and then returned to his traumatized family. He had been beheaded and crucified, horseshoes nailed to his feet, his genitals completely mutilated, and his body eviscerated. They left his head propped on the steps where the house met the street. A week later, Dovey witnessed a horrific spectacle at the marketplace. Armenian women had been rounded up by Turkish soldiers and made to dance in the middle of a crowd of Turkish onlookers. The Turkish soldiers beat the women mercilessly with whips. Around the women stood their children, as well as some Armenian children that the soldiers had taken from nearby schools especially to witness this spectacle. The children "were forced into a circle," Dovey tells us:

> and several Turkish soldiers stood behind them with whips and shouted 'Clap, clap.' And the children clapped. And when the soldiers said 'Clap, clap, clap,' the children were supposed to clap faster, and if they didn't, the whip was used on them. Some of the children were two and three years old, barely able to stand up. They were all crying uncontrollably. Crying in a terrible, pitiful, helpless way. I stood next to women in burugs and men in red fezzes and business suits, and they too were clapping like little cockroaches.

The torturers then stepped up their brutality:

> Then two soldiers pushed through the crowd swinging wooden buckets and began to douse the women with the fluid in the buckets, and, in a second, I could smell that it was kerosene. And the women screamed because the kerosene was burning their lacerations and cuts. Another soldier came forward with a torch and lit each woman by the hair. At first all I could see was smoke, and the smell grew sickening, and then I could see the fire growing off the women's bodies, and their screaming became unbearable. The children were being whipped now furiously, as if the sight of the burning mothers had excited the soldiers, and they admonished the children to clap "faster, faster, faster," telling them that if they stopped they too would be lit on fire.[51]

The heavy symbolism of the violence in Dovey's account is clear. The patriarch of the family is killed first, and his position within the family is desecrated through the mutilation of his genitals, through his beheading, and through his crucifixion (a reference not only to Armenians as Christians, but also to men's sacred position in patriarchal families). His head, placed at the boundary between the privacy of the Armenian home and the public world, which was now being claimed only for Turks, is particularly poignant. It represents the end of the Armenian family, the end of Armenian generation, the end of Armenian history. His murder is a symbolic microcosm of the crime of genocide itself. The marketplace massacre of the women and children, which occurred in the light of day amidst gleeful onlookers, rounds out the destruction of the father by destroying the most deeply generative unit – mothers and children. The abjectly cruel ritual played on the love children have for their mothers and mothers' naturally protective response to their children, attempting to destroy one of the deepest bonds within our species.

Examples of life force atrocities abound across genocides and within conflicts that are not generally viewed through the lens of genocide, but which have a genocidal dimension. These include the civil wars in Sierra Leone and the Democratic Republic of Congo, the sex slavery system of the Japanese imperial army in World War II, and the "Rape of Nanking." Many of the pre-genocide massacres that Manus Midlarsky argues provided a necessary continuity to the genocides of the Ottoman Armenians,

European Jews, and Rwandan Tutsis were also rife with life force atrocities.[52] These cases demonstrate that genocidal masculinity can emerge in many different historical contexts, and does not require state-based ideological indoctrination. In other words, genocidal masculinity can predate the emergence of cohesive genocidal ideologies, and its existence does not necessarily result in or require the domination of the state by its adherents. Genocidal thinking may, in fact, be far more common than we would like to believe. While historical prejudices and bigotries determine the groups that will be singled out as victims in cases both of genocidal violence and root-and-branch genocides, one has the feeling that historical prejudices end up focusing rather than creating the rage against families that perpetrators express when they commit life force atrocities.

CONCLUSION

Why would *génocidaires* exhibit such contempt for family institutions? The most obvious answer is that families are the principal reproductive unit for groups. Thus, it is the decision to destroy the group – a category that is at the core of the definition of genocide – that determines the treatment that families receive.[53] But there is reason to believe that the important role played by families in the ideologies and the strategies of *génocidaires* does not merely derive from the hatred that *génocidaires* feel for specific groups. After all, the architects of genocide frequently seek to undermine families within their preferred groups, and genocidal utopias generally promote a wholesale and brutal reorganization of reproduction. It is possible that genocidal masculinity emerges in a deep space of human experience that is rarely brought to words, but frequently evidenced in the kinds of atrocities that take place in processes we call genocidal. It points out the deep extent to which some perpetrators invest themselves in the labor of killing, and helps explain both the process and the symbolic framework that enables them to derive feelings of transcendence and freedom from it.

To return to the example of Jean Girumuhatse, his brief but dense description of killing represents it as a creative act and therefore a route to freedom. It allowed him to become a self-employed and sovereign actor, an agent directly involved in the creation of his own fate. Gourevitch comments that:

> Before [the genocide] he had been a peasant, as he was again now, living in poverty and toil, tending to the fields of slightly less poor peasants for beer money and enough beans and bananas to sustain himself, his wife, and seven children. But for a few months in 1994 Rwanda had become a kingdom of death and he had lived more fully, more like a lord, than he had ever imagined possible. It occurred to me that, just as the genocide had set him free, the *gacaca* process had liberated him to talk about it.[54]

This freedom, as I have argued, was deeply gendered. It was about a man finding for himself a space of transcendence in killing, in organizing his domestic life around this task, in folding the generative power that exists in the reproductive arena – and that was for him an economic burden – into the profitable and independent activity of death. The act of killing demonstrated, again and again and again, his victory over the life force itself. We do not know if Girumuhatse engaged in life force atrocities in the process of killing between eleven and seventy people. Few *génocidaires* will admit to these, but we do know that life force atrocities were quite pronounced in the Rwandan case.

The genocidal investment in the transcendent destruction of families distinguishes genocide from warfare, as well as other forms of massacre that lack this generative dimension. Genocide targets not only civilians, but a specific aspect of civilian life – the institutions of generative power that provide identity, continuity, and cohesion to the group's historical development. So civilians and the civilian world are destroyed in a patterned way that seeks to profane the reproductive arena. While all these processes involve the marshaling of violent masculinity, genocide marshals a specific type, a type that defines male identity and vitality not only in terms of warfare, but also and much more importantly, in terms of a war against the life force itself. Naturally, the same process of desensitization that makes conventional warfare possible, and the coercive institutions that organize war, will lend themselves to the development of genocidal thinking among combatants and the implementation of genocidal policies. But the latter does not derive from the former, and indeed, the type of masculinity that defines genocide pits itself against the patriarchal institutions that pursue conventional warfare.

The insights provided by the framework of genocidal masculinity underscore the "organic" nature of the crime of genocide, to use Scott Straus's useful term. He defines genocide as an "organized attempt to annihilate a group that a perpetrator constitutes as an organic collectivity."[55] As the genocides in Cambodia and Ukraine suggest, groups that objectively may appear to be political, social, or economic in nature may in the mind of the perpetrator take on an essentialist, self-reproducing quality.[56] Life force atrocities are key indicators that violence has taken on this organic, genocidal logic. I would add that focusing on genocidal masculinity gets us closer to understanding what the term "destroy" means in a genocidal context, and how we can identify this type of destruction as it plays out on the ground. *Génocidaires* do not mean simply to destroy the human bodies and other material evidence of a group, but also to get at the very life force responsible for that group's existence. Men's destruction of organic collectivities is truly a crime against humanity. It evidences a contempt for the reproductive process in general, and a desire to annihilate that world in which women and men invest in the painful, back-breaking, joyful, and intimate work that ensures our species continues into the future, meaningfully and with dignity.

NOTES

1 Philip Gourevitch, "The Life After: Fifteen Years after the Genocide in Rwanda, the Reconciliation Defies Expectations," *The New Yorker*, May 4, 2009, pp. 40–41.
2 Dan Stone, *History, Memory, and Mass Atrocity: Essays on the Holocaust and Genocide* (London: Vallentine Mitchell, 2006), pp. 198–199.
3 Ibid., 206.
4 Gourevitch, "The Life After," p. 41.
5 For a succinct discussion of these three approaches to the perpetrator's state of mind during the killing, see Jacques Semelin, *Purify and Destroy: The Political Uses of Massacre and Genocide*, trans. Cynthia Schoch (London: Hurst and Company, 2007), esp. pp. 240–256.
6 Gourevitch, "The Life After," p. 38.
7 Christopher Browning, *Ordinary Men: Reserve Police Battalion 101 and the Final Solution in Poland* (New York: Harper Perennial, 1998); Scott Straus, *The Order of Genocide: Race, Power, and War in Rwanda* (Ithaca, NY: Cornell University Press, 2006).

8   The literature on this is growing rapidly. For the seminal works on the subject, see Adam Jones, "Gender and Genocide in Rwanda," *Journal of Genocide Research*, 4: 1 (2002), pp. 65–94; Alexandra Stiglmayer, ed., *Mass Rape: The War against Women in Bosnia-Herzegovina* (Lincoln, NE: University of Nebraska Press, 1994); Helen Fein, "Genocide and Gender: The Uses of Woman and Group Destiny," *Journal of Genocide Research*, 1: 1 (1999), pp. 43–63.

9   See, for example, James Waller, *Becoming Evil: How Ordinary People Commit Genocide and Mass Killing* (Oxford: Oxford University Press, 2002).

10 Semelin, *Purify and Destroy*.

11 Roger W. Smith, "Women and Genocide: Notes on an Unwritten History," *Holocaust and Genocide Studies*, 8: 3 (Winter 1994), pp. 315–334; Martin Shaw, *War and Genocide* (Cambridge: Polity Press, 2007).

12 Joane Nagel, "Masculinity and Nationalism: Gender and Sexuality in the Making of Nations," *Ethnic and Racial Studies*, 21: 2 (March 1998), p. 243.

13 John Roth, "Equality, Neutrality, Particularity: Perspectives on Women and the Holocaust," in Elizabeth R. Baer and Myrna Goldenberg, eds, *Experience and Expression: Women, the Nazis, and the Holocaust* (Detroit, MI: Wayne State University Press, 2003), pp. 8–9.

14 R. W. Connell, "The Social Organization of Masculinity," in Stephen M. Whitehead and Frank J. Barrett, eds, *The Masculinities Reader* (Cambridge: Polity Press, 2002), p. 34.

15 Michael Kimmel, *The Politics of Manhood* (Philadelphia, PA: Temple University Press, 1996).

16 Michael Kaufman, "The Construction of Masculinity and the Triad of Men's Violence," in Laura L. O'Toole, Jessica R. Schiffman, and Margie L. Kiter Edwards, eds, *Gender Violence: Interdisciplinary Perspectives*, 2nd edn (New York: New York University Press, 2007), p. 42.

17 Judith Halberstam, *Female Masculinity* (Durham, NC: Duke University Press, 1998).

18 R.W. Connell, "The Social Organization of Masculinities," in Connell, *Masculinities*, 2nd edn (Berkeley, CA: University of California Press, 2005), pp. 67–86; Mary O'Brien, *The Politics of Reproduction* (London: Routledge and Kegan Paul, 1981).

19 Ibid., p. 52.

20 Thomas Welskopp, "The Political Man: The Construction of Masculinity in German Social Democracy, 1848–78," in Stefan Dudink, Karen Hagemann, and John Tosh, eds, *Masculinities in Politics and War: Gendering Modern History* (Manchester: Manchester University Press, 2004), p. 258.

21 Joan B. Landes, "Republican Citizenship and Heterosocial Desire: Concepts of Masculinity in Revolutionary France," in Dudink, Hagemann, and Tosh, eds, *Masculinities in Politics and War*, pp. 96–115.

22 Karen Hagemann and Stefan Dudink, "Masculinity in Politics and War in the Age of Democratic Revolutions, 1750–1850," in Dudink, Hagemann, and Tosh, eds, *Masculinities in Politics and War*, p. 6.

23 Ben Kiernan, "External and Indigenous Sources of Khmer Ideology," in Odd Arne Westad and Sophie Quinn-Judge, eds, *The Third Indochina War: Conflict between China, Vietnam and Cambodia* (London: Routledge, 2006), pp. 187–206.

24 Human Rights Watch, *Sowing Terror: Atrocities against Civilians in Sierra Leone*, Vol. 10, No. 3(A) (New York: Human Rights Watch, July 1998).

25 Jean Hatzfeld, *Machete Season: The Killers in Rwanda Speak*, trans. Linda Coverdale (New York: Picador, 2006), pp. 132–133.

26 Ibid., pp. 94–95.

27 Deniz Kandiyoti, *Women, Islam and the State* (Philadelphia, PA: Temple University Press, 1991), pp. 34–35.

28 William L. Cleveland and Martin Bunton, *A History of the Modern Middle East*, 4th edn (Boulder, CO: Westview Press, 2008), p.150.

29 Kandiyoti, *Women, Islam and the State*, p. 36.

30 Kiernan, "External and Indigenous Sources," p. 195.

31 Eric D. Weitz, *A Century of Genocide: Utopias of Race and Nation* (Princeton, NJ: Princeton University Press, 2003), p. 163.

32 Immigration and Refugee Board of Canada, "Cambodia: Forced Marriages; Whether Forced Marriage is Currently Practised; Protection Available from the Government; Consequences for a Woman who Refuses a Forced Marriage," December 9, 2003, UNHCR Refworld. Available at http://www.unhcr.org/refworld/docid/403dd1fd8.html.

33 Michael Burleigh and Wolfgang Wippermann, *The Racial State: Germany 1933–1945* (Cambridge: Cambridge University Press, 1991), p. 252.

34 Ibid., p. 253.

35 Mark P. Mostert, "Useless Eaters: Disability as Genocidal Marker in Nazi Germany," *Journal of Special Education*, 36: 3 (2002), p. 157.

36 Michael H. Kater, *Hitler Youth* (Cambridge, MA: Harvard University Press, 2004), p. 37.

37 Quoted in ibid., p. 37.

38 Michael Burleigh and Wolfgang Wippermann, "The Persecution of the 'Hereditarily Ill', the 'Asocial', and Homosexuals," in *The Racial State*, pp. 136–198.

39 Published in *Kangura*, 6 (December 1990). Available at: http://www.trumanwebdesign.com/~catalina/commandments.htm.

40 Christopher C. Taylor, *Sacrifice as Terror: The Rwandan Genocide of 1994* (Oxford: Berg, 1999), p. 155.

41 Ibid., pp. 176–177.

42 Norman Cigar, *Genocide in Bosnia: The Policy of 'Ethnic Cleansing'* (College Station, TX: Texas A&M University, 1995), p. 79.

43 Ibid., p. 80.

44 Ernst Jünger, *Der Kampf als inneres Erlebnis, Samtliche Werke*, 2 Abt., Essays I, Bd. 7 (Stuttgart: Klett-Cotta, 1980), p. 50.

45 Andreas Huyssen, "Fortifying the Heart – Totally Ernst Jünger's Armored Texts," *New German Critique*, 59 (Spring/Summer 1993), p. 9.

46 Cigar, "Motivating the Perpetrator," in *Genocide in Bosnia*, pp. 62–85; Eberhard Jäckel, *Hitler's World View: A Blueprint for Power* (Cambridge, MA: Harvard University Press, 1981).

47 Elisa von Joeden-Forgey, "The Devil in the Details: 'Life Force Atrocities' and the Assault on Families in Times of Conflict," *Genocide Studies and Prevention*, 5: 1 (2010), pp. 1–19.

48 Alexander Laban Hinton, *Why Did They Kill? Cambodia in the Shadow of Genocide* (Berkeley, CA: University of California Press, 2005), p. 31.

49 von Joeden-Forgey, "Devil in the Details," and Elisa von Joeden-Forgey, "Gender and Genocide," in Donald Bloxham and A. Dirk Moses, eds, *The Oxford Handbook of Genocide Studies* (Oxford: Oxford University Press, 2010), pp. 61–80.

50 A. Dirk Moses, "Empire, Colony, Genocide: Keywords and the Philosophy of History," in A. Dirk Moses, ed., *Empire, Colony, Genocide: Conquest, Occupation, and Subaltern Resistance in World History* (New York: Berghahn Books, 2008), p. 13.

51 Quoted in Waller, *Becoming Evil*, pp. 53–54. Original from Peter Balakian, "Dovey's Story," *Black Dog of Fate: A Memoir* (New York: Basic Books, 2009 [1997]), pp. 217–232.

52 Manus I. Midlarsky, "Continuity and Validation," in *The Killing Trap: Genocide in the Twentieth Century* (Cambridge: Cambridge University Press, 2005), pp. 43–63.

53 Fein, "Genocide and Gender."

54 Gourevitch, "The Life After," p. 41.

55 Scott Straus, "Contested Meanings and Conflicting Imperatives: A Conceptual Analysis of Genocide," *Journal of Genocide Research*, 3: 3 (2001), pp. 349–375.

56 Weitz, "Nation, Race, and State Socialism: The Soviet Union under Lenin and Stalin," in *Century of Genocide*, pp. 53–101; Norman Naimark, *Stalin's Genocides* (Princeton, NJ: Princeton University Press, 2010).

Figure 6.1 Hindiya, a Congolese man wounded in fighting at Mgunga, near Goma, in 2007.

Source: Courtesy Julien Harneis/Flickr.

CHAPTER 6

Invisible Males

A critical assessment of UN gender mainstreaming policies in the Congolese genocide

Paula Drumond

INTRODUCTION

Since 1998, the Democratic Republic of the Congo (DRC) has experienced a succession of foreign invasions, internal conflicts, and mass murders. In approximately 12 years of conflict, it is estimated that more than 4 million people[1] have died, with another 1.5 million displaced. Clashes involving the DRC Armed Forces (FARDC), foreign troops from neighboring countries, and several main militia groups have caused a humanitarian catastrophe on Congolese territory.

After being governed for 30 years by Mobutu Sese Seko's dictatorship (1965–1997), the situation in the DRC was aggravated by the end of the Rwandan genocide, when former *génocidaires* sought refuge in the Congo. There, they formed a Hutu militia, the Democratic Forces for the Liberation of Rwanda (FDLR), increasing ethnic resentments and provoking episodes of violence against the Banyarwanda population (originally Tutsi and Hutus from Rwanda) in North Kivu, and the Banyamulenge (identified as Tutsi) in South Kivu.[2]

The FDLR, like all armed militias involved in the Congolese warfare, has systematically targeted the Congolese civilian population with massacres and sexual violence.[3] Among the most culpable militia actors are the Lord's Resistance Army (LRA), *Le Congrès National pour la Défense du Peuple* (CNDP),[4] and the Mayi Mayi. Apart from the militias, the number of rapes, killings, and other human rights violations perpetrated by the DRC Armed Forces (FARDC) increased during 2009–2010.[5] In addition, the existence of lootable natural resources, such as gold, coltan, and diamonds[6] in the country has contributed to violent disputes involving militias supported by foreign companies and governments that act as spoilers of the peace process.[7]

To deal with this "most deadly conflict since the World War II,"[8] in 1999 the United Nations Security Council approved the deployment of its biggest peacekeeping mission,[9] MONUC (United Nations Organization Mission in the Democratic Republic of the Congo), now renamed MONUSCO (United Nations Organization Stabilization Mission in the Democratic Republic of the Congo).[10] From the start of its operations, MONUC has attempted to deal with patterns of genocidal violence, such as massive killings, the systematic use of sexual violence, and the excess number of civilian deaths by disease and malnutrition, also caused by the prevalent insecurity of the conflict.

The Congolese genocide calls for our attention due not only to the number of civilians affected by violence, but to the systematic use of gender-based violence as a genocidal weapon. The perpetration of sexual violence is so widespread that eastern Congo is now referred to as "the rape capital of the world."[11] This chapter seeks to address how social constructions of gender shape patterns of violence in the genocidal warfare sweeping the Congo, and consider how the United Nations (UN) has addressed patterns of gender-based violence (GBV)[12] in its gender policies.

Without disregarding GBV against women and girls, the chapter will point to a widespread silence on the UN's part with regard to gender-based violence against men and boys. The evidence, derived mostly from analysis of the prevailing UN discourse on gender, shows that although the UN has witnessed patterns of gender-based violence against men and boys in the past, the organization has continued to equate "gender policies" in its peacekeeping operations with the protection of females and their (re)incorporation into post-conflict environments. This is despite the fact that the gender-based violence observable in the DRC suggests that men and boys are also targeted by sexual violence and, especially, by summary executions.

PATTERNS OF GENDER-BASED VIOLENCE DURING GENOCIDE

Though it is not the only significant variable, gender helps to define how men and women are targeted during genocidal violence.[13] Gender-based violence, such as sex-selective massacres and sexual violence, is frequently deployed as a weapon during genocides. In Rwanda, for example, the systematic use of sexual violence targeted approximately 250,000–500,000 Tutsi and moderate Hutu women. According to the International Criminal Tribunal for Rwanda (ICTR):

> Rapes resulted in physical and psychological destruction of Tutsi women, their families and their communities. Sexual violence was an integral part of the process of destruction, specifically targeting Tutsi women and specifically contributing to their destruction and to the destruction of the Tutsi group as a whole.[14]

However, sexual violence is not merely a crime against women. In the former Yugoslavia, for example, there are numerous reports of the use of sexual violence by Serb forces against both sexes.[15] We thus need to attend also to male victims of sexual violence in armed conflict – and to note how sexual violence against females is also directed against community males. Since sexual violence against women and girls violates their socially-constructed image of chastity and purity, it also undermines the masculine identity of male victims. In general, GBV is frequently used to weaken the social fabric of groups considered as enemies. By associating heterosexual masculinity with power, *génocidaires* perpetrate crimes informed by gendered constructions, thereby affirming their group identity as superior in power and masculine prowess (see also Elisa von Joeden-Forgey's Chapter 5 in this volume).

In addition to sexual violence, another pattern of GBV commonly perpetrated during genocide is the sex-selective massacres of civilian males. According to authors such as Adam Jones and R. Charli Carpenter, males are typically the principal victims of such massacres in cases of genocide, due to the imputed masculinization of the enemy, and the resulting identification of all men as combatants or potential combatants. For instance, research carried out for the Gendercide Watch website found that during the genocide in Bosnia, 80 percent of the dead were battle-age males.[16]

In sum, sex-selective massacres and sexual violence are used as weapons to eradicate the masculine underpinning of the victimized group (that is, the source of its supposed strength and bloodline), and to destroy the group's social fabric. These strategies contribute to the main goal of *génocidaires*: the destruction in whole or in part of the targeted collectivity.

GENDER-BASED VIOLENCE IN THE DRC

Rape and sexual violence have also been strategically used in the DRC conflict to attack and to terrorize members of the civilian population suspected of supporting enemy members of a rival ethnic group, or simply identified as political traitors.[17] Since those crimes usually have the effect of making populations flee their territories, this kind of violence is also used to establish control over areas rich in natural resources. As a consequence, rape acts as a demonstration of power in the political and economic spheres. Another motivation for the perpetration of sexual violence in the DRC is impunity, not only because the Congolese criminal justice system has been ineffective in prosecuting perpetrators of sexual violence, but also because the victims are either afraid of denouncing the abuses, fearing reprisals, or are unable to identify the abusers.[18]

The effects of sexual violence in the Congo are physical, psychological, and social. Female rape survivors are frequently rejected by their communities, their families, and their husbands. If they are single, female victims become unmarriageable.[19] In this conflict, sexual violence includes "individual rapes, sexual abuse, gang rapes, mutilation of genitalia, and rape-shooting or rape-stabbing combinations, at times undertaken after family members have been tied up and forced to watch."[20] Sexual violence is so alarmingly systematic and recurring that a new term – "*reviolé*" (or "re-raped") – was created to refer to individuals who were raped more than once.[21] The United States Agency for International Development (USAID) has reported that people aged between 4 months old and 84 years old have been victimized.[22]

Recently, the UN affirmed that after 12 years of conflict, 200,000 women and girls have been victims of sexual violence in the DRC.[23] All international organizations report that figures and statistics are highly unreliable, since victims have difficulty seeking medical and legal assistance, both because of the distance from villages to health centers and numerous other obstacles – including the threat of renewed rape – *en route* to these sources of assistance. They are often also reluctant to file reports, whether from fear of retaliation or because of the stigma that female *and male* rape survivors acquire.

For even though the available figures refer only to the victimization of women and girls, *all extant reports recognize that rape and sexual violence are also systematically perpetrated against males in the DRC*. Amnesty International, for instance, affirms that "a hitherto unreported aspect of sexual violence is the large number of men who are also victims."[24] A 2005 Human Rights Watch report adds that "men and boys in increasing numbers are also reporting having been raped and otherwise sexually assaulted by combatants; however, there are no figures available . . . [and] few [male] victims give detailed statements about attacks they have suffered."[25]

In mid-2009, several international organizations acknowledged that the number of men and boys raped in the DRC was on the increase.[26] According to a report in *The New York Times*, published in June 2009, more than 10 percent of victims reporting sexual violence were men.[27] Researchers agree that such cases are under-reported, since men and boys rarely acknowledge their sexual abuse, due to social constraints regarding constructions of heterosexual masculinity: "real" men do not "let themselves" be raped.[28] In fact, sexual violence against men is under-reported in most societies, especially in settings like the DRC where sexual violence has the effect of excluding the victim from the social life of his or her community.[29] As one male victim told *The New York Times*, "I'm laughed at . . . The people in my village say: 'You're no longer a man. Those men in the bush made you their wife.'"[30] This social construction of masculinity was also evident in a testimony given by a man from Ituri to Human Rights Watch:

> I was arrested on August 31, 2002 in Bunia along with my father. The UPC [militia] arrested us as they thought we were against them because of our ethnicity. I did not understand it as I had done nothing wrong. I spent one month and ten days in prison. When they first arrested us they interrogated us, sometimes every two days. We stood nude in front of UPC officials; one of them was Rafiki Saba [UPC Chief of Security]. I was so shocked. I had never seen my father this way. In our culture, it is not right. First they molested us . . . then they raped us. Even today I cannot really talk about this . . . I am still traumatized by what happened to me.[31]

A 2004 Amnesty International (AI) report also demonstrates how sexual violence against males affects the victim's masculine self-conception. In the words of a fisherman: "I feel that people in the community look down on me. When I talk to other men, they look at me as if I'm worthless now."[32] Another male victim described his attack to AI investigators:

> My wife and I were in bed when the soldiers knocked on the door, saying that the man of the house had to come outside . . . Then they raped me. While they were doing that they kept saying "you're no longer a man, you are going to become one

of our women." My leg and foot still hurt. I'm not able to have sexual relations any more.[33]

Apart from being directly targeted by sexual violence, men and boys are also frequently forced to rape, or to watch the rape of, female family members and, if they refuse, they are executed.[34] However, this psychological violence is not addressed by humanitarian organizations, which focus on the (female) victim directly targeted by rape.[35]

In the Congolese genocide, men and boys are also more frequently victimized by killings and summary executions. This can be inferred from the above-cited reports, which note, for example, that "commonly, groups attack a village, *killing civilian men and boys and raping women and girls*, before making off [with] the community's cattle, tools or clothing . . ."[36]

This pattern can be observed especially in eastern DRC, the most violent and insecure region in the country. The International Rescue Committee (IRC), in its 2001 mortality report on the region, published a mortality graphic that showed that 61 percent of those violently killed were adult males.[37] In another mortality survey conducted in 2004, the IRC indicated another increase in this figure, affirming that in eastern DRC, "adult males aged 15 years and over were at great risk of being killed, constituting 72 percent of all violent deaths, although women and children were not exempt,"[38] constituting respectively 18 percent and 10 percent of violent deaths.[39]

Another survey conducted in 2005 by a group of Médecins Sans Frontières' (MSF) doctors in Ituri illustrated once again the pattern described above. The group investigated living conditions in Internally Displaced Population (IDP) camps in the region by looking at the Tché Camp, in which conditions were considered similar to other two camps (Kakwa and Tchomia) located in the same region. The survey demonstrated that there was a gender asymmetry among the camp population (see the demographic pyramid in Figure 6.2). According to the research, a "*lack of males* was reported for children under 5 years old and for those 15 to 44 years."[40] The researchers could not

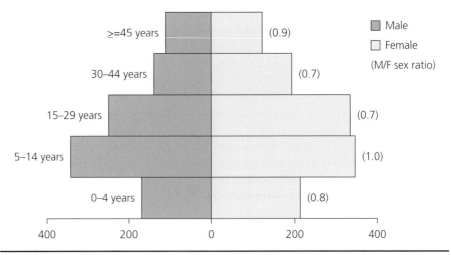

Figure 6.2 The demographic pyramid in the Democratic Republic of the Congo.

Source: *Global Public Health*, 1: 3 (October 2006), p. 199.

point to a reason for this absence of males, but speculated that men were away working or fighting.

However, two years earlier, MONUC's Office of Gender Affairs had affirmed that 80 percent of the IDP from the Ituri Province were *widows and children*.[41] Thus, it is possible to conclude that men are under-represented in the IDP/refugee population *because they are being killed*, while their widows are spared and flee as refugees.

A large number of civilian men and boys are forcibly recruited by Congolese militias. Because of their identification as warriors, males are being captured and forced to fight. If they try to resist the forced enlistment, they are killed. Recently, the *Seattle Times* affirmed the existence of a "new category of displaced people" in eastern Congo: young men trying to escape from forced recruitment by rebel forces.[42] According to a young Congolese, "If they [the rebels] see a young boy, they just give him a weapon and tell him to fight."[43] As Charli Carpenter noted, forced recruitment is a form of gender-based violence, since it is sex-selective, targeting men and boys specifically – and exposing them to death – owing to the militarized masculine identity that they bear.[44]

These patterns of GBV against males are also made visible by the testimony given by a Congolese woman in 2008. When explaining why women still leave IDP camps to collect firewood and search for food despite the risk of being raped, she affirmed: "Our men will be killed or recruited if they leave the camp . . . what choice do we have?"[45] Another research project, conducted by MSF on the security of civilians in Ituri between 2003 and 2007, found an under-representation of certain gender and age groups: that is, children under 5 years old and males, particularly men between the ages of 30 and 44 years. The report affirmed that this situation "illustrates the extent of the cumulative effects of several years of conflict on the populations."[46] But although the research showed the insecurity of civilian males, this is not problematized as an issue *per se*. In this regard, the report stated that "the underrepresentation of men may also contribute to perpetuating the insecurity of families, with single women often heading the household."[47] Thus, the under-representation of men was considered a problem only because of its effects on *women's* lives.

The killing of combat-age males was once again cast into sharp relief with the September 2009 release of a report from the United Nations Joint Human Rights Office in the DRC, addressing human rights violations perpetrated in November 2008 in Kiwanja (North Kivu) by Mayi Mayi and CNDP rebels.[48] During that month, according to the report, CNDP members conducted at least 67 arbitrary executions of Hutu and Nande victims, most of them males.[49] According to the investigations: "CNDP fighters proceeded to systematically *execute mainly adult males, whom they accused of belonging to, or supporting the Mayi Mayi*" (emphasis added).[50] It is important to note that these executions did not take place in a context of fighting. According to the investigations, the executions of men were perpetrated against non-combatants, as retaliation against civilian populations for the alleged support they rendered to the Mayi Mayi fighters.

Another rebel group, the Lord's Resistance Army (LRA), is also involved in these same patterns of GBV. From December 24, 2008 until the beginning of January 2009, the LRA killed more than 860 civilians in a series of coordinated attacks in several villages in the Haut-Uele District, such as Faradje, Batande and Bangadi.[51] The massacres were labeled as the "Christmas massacres" since the worst killings were strategically carried out on December 24 and 25, while civilians were gathered in large groups celebrating

Christmas.[52] Most of the attacks targeted women and girls with sexual violence.[53] Although the killings were mainly indiscriminate – targeting women, men, and children in the villages – in Faradje, for example, the LRA fighters targeted mainly males. According to HRW:

> In the afternoon, as residents gathered for a Christmas concert, a group of about 200 LRA combatants descended on the town and killed at least 143 people, *mostly men*[54] ... The combatants fired shots in the air and began to round up the girls and boys. *They killed the men they managed to capture* with blows to the head.[55]
>
> (emphasis added)

The FARDC also perpetrated sex-selective slaughters of males along with massacres of Rwandan civilians, "either refugees or FDLR dependants," between March and April 2009, in an attempt to eradicate the FDLR presence from the Congolese territory. According to the final report of the UN Group of Experts on the DRC,[56] FARDC Colonel Ngaruye issued the following order: "Any young men found should be killed, while all children, women and elders should be captured and sent back to Rwanda."

In sum, the evidence demonstrates that the social construction of gender influences the way men and women have been targeted during the Congolese conflict. While women and girls are more frequently victimized by rape, and are not exempted from mass killings, civilian men and boys are also vulnerable to these sexual attacks, and tend to be more frequently targeted for summary executions and lethal attack, because as bearers of masculinity they are automatically perceived as a rebel/enemy threat. Despite this, international organizations' reports have failed to problematize this pattern of gendered violence. On the contrary, despite the consistent evidence, the above-mentioned reports continue to affirm that *women and children* are the most vulnerable groups during campaigns of genocidal massacre.[57]

GENDER POLICIES AT THE UN: GENDER MAINSTREAMING?

The United Nations has recognized that gender plays an important role in shaping experiences during conflicts, and in post-conflict peace building, when it adopted as a buttress of its policies the so-called "gender mainstreaming principle." This is:

> the process of assessing the implications for women and men of any planned action, including legislation, policies or programmes, in any area and at all levels. It is a strategy for making the concerns and experiences of women as well as of men an integral part of the design, implementation, monitoring and evaluation of policies and programmes in all political, economic and societal spheres, so that women and men benefit equally, and inequality is not perpetuated. The ultimate goal of main-streaming is to achieve gender equality.[58]

Despite the empirical evidence from numerous wars and genocides that males are also afflicted by specific kinds of gender-based violence, the UN continues to adopt gender mainstreaming policies that, contrary to its own definition, are strongly biased toward violence against women. This bias is evident in UN documents such as *Gender and UN Peacekeeping Operations* (2005), in which the Department of Peacekeeping Operations (DPKO) contextualizes gender's inclusion in peacekeeping missions as follows:

> The priorities of the international community shifted towards assisting women affected by conflict situations and integrating a gender perspective into policies and institutional mechanisms for building peace. These previously neglected issues gained greater urgency following reports of massive crimes against women during conflict in Rwanda and the former Yugoslavia.[59]

Thus, despite the sex-selective massacres against men and boys that the UN witnessed both in Rwanda[60] and in the former Yugoslavia (where "mass graves . . . were filled 'about 90 percent' with 'middle-aged or elderly Muslim men'"),[61] the organization still concentrates its gender policies on the pernicious effects of conflict on women alone. For instance, UN Security Council Resolution 1820 (2008), recognizing rape as a weapon of war, makes no mention of the importance of addressing sexual violence against males, while continuing to stress the presumption that "women and girls are particularly targeted by the use of sexual violence . . ."[62] The reference to "women and girls" is constantly present throughout the document. I will highlight below some of the sections of the resolution which reveal the exclusive focus on females:

> 5. *Affirms its intention* . . . to take into consideration the appropriateness of targeted and graduated measures against parties . . . who commit rape and other forms of sexual violence against women and girls . . .

> 8. . . . and prevent sexual violence against women and girls in conflict and post-conflict situations . . .

> 15. *Also requests* . . . strategies to minimize the susceptibility of women and girls to such violence . . . taking appropriate measures to protect women and girls from all forms of sexual violence.[63]

The document demonstrates not only how the UN marginalizes male victims, but also ends up reifying a dichotomy that opposes the image of the male perpetrator to that of the female victim. This reinforces the perspective of females as vulnerable and always in need of assistance, while fortifying a sense that males are significant only as violent victimizers. This is despite the fact that in August 2009, the UN Secretary-General explicitly recognized that men and boys can also be victims of sexual violence. In the *Report of the Secretary General Pursuant to Security Council Resolution 1820* (2008), Ban Ki-Moon affirmed that:

> while women and girls are particular targets and are the majority of the victims of sexual violence . . . the International Criminal Tribunal for the Former Yugoslavia (ICTY) and the Special Court for Sierra Leone (SCSL) also bears testimony to the use of sexual violence against men."[64]

However, this is the only paragraph in the report to make reference to men and boys. Elsewhere, the focus is exclusively on "proposals for strategies to minimize the susceptibility of women and girls to such violence."[65] In addition, the report does not mention the occurrence of sexual violence against males in current conflicts. It explores only aspects of female victimization, and the causes and consequences of sexual violence in regard to women and girls. In referring to the DRC, for example, the document makes no mention of male victimization, in spite of the wide range of evidence of sexual violence against men and boys in this conflict. In sum, the document suggests that sexual violence is, and should continue to be, regarded as a crime against females. While passing rhetorical reference may be made to males, they do not merit the same kind of specific humanitarian concern.

The silence surrounding male victimization was also acknowledged by a recent documentary called *Gender Against Men*, produced by the Refugee Law Project (RLP) in Kampala, Uganda in 2008. The documentary addresses civilian male vulnerability in the conflicts of the Great Lakes Region, focusing particularly on the cases of the DRC and Uganda. According to RLP staff, humanitarian workers in the area focus on women's victimization and treat gender-based violence as a women's problem, because acknowledging male victimization risks drawing away resources from women. By ignoring male victimization, humanitarian policies are rendered unable to deal with the full panoply of gender and conflict, wherein GBV is embedded in complex ways with masculine constructions.

THE UN'S GENDER POLICIES IN THE DRC

This section analyzes how the UN and its agencies are addressing GBV in the Congolese genocide. To this end, it compares gender policies developed during 2002, the first year of operation for MONUC's Office of Gender Affairs, with more recent work carried out by the organization in the country during 2008–2009. It seeks to assess whether there has been any significant change in MONUC's focus, and any attempt to incorporate a gender-inclusive perspective on GBV.

Gender mainstreaming policies are implemented in the Congo both by MONUC and its Office of Gender Affairs (OGA), and by other UN agencies such as the United Nations Development Fund for Women (UNIFEM), the United Nations Population Fund (UNFPA), the United Nations Children's Fund (UNICEF), and so on. These actors promote meetings, seminars, and workshops for the civilian population and police forces.

During the first year of its activities, MONUC's OGA organized meetings with groups and NGOs that deal with women's issues in the country, such as *Dynamique des Femmes Politiques au Congo Démocratique* (DYNAFEP) and *Résau Action Femmes*, with which the OGA developed a campaign to eliminate violence against women.[66] Joint initiatives were also implemented for radio and television networks (especially Radio OKAPI), with the goal of promoting "discussions on the impact of armed conflict *on women and girls* in the DRC"[67] (emphasis added). The 2002 OGA Activities Report lists several workshops organized by the OGA together with universities and academic institutions. The workshops' topics include: "sexual violence *against women and minors;*

women's political participation; . . . [and] *women* as perpetrators and victims . . ."[68] (emphasis added). These initiatives suggest that the OGA's "gender policies" were constructed to deal almost exclusively with perceived "women's issues."

Research shows that this pattern was unaltered in 2008–2009. MONUC's official website continued to announce workshops[69] and consultations that examined sexual violence as exclusively a women's issue. For example, on June 13, 2008, MONUC published a joint press release regarding a consultation on the eradication of sexual violence in the Great Lakes Region. The consultation sought to encourage an urgent response "to the problem of sexual violence, along with the measures required to ensure the prevention, protection and access to care and justice *for women and children*."[70] One of the aims of the consultation process was to promote "community sensitisation for the reintegration of *women and girl rape victims*, including approaches to change the attitudes and behavior of young people and men"[71] (emphasis added). As usual, the discourse depicted males only as agents of violence, and women and children as the only victimized group.

On October 15, 2008, MONUC issued a press release expressing concern for vulnerable populations in North Kivu where clashes between the FARDC and the CNPD had forced people to seek refuge near MONUC's base. The story highlighted that protecting the vulnerable population was MONUC's main goal. To this end, "MONUC peacekeepers are sharing their food rations with *women and children* from some 400 families"[72] (emphasis added). The news release quoted Alan Doss, the UN Secretary-General's Special Representative for the Congo (SGSR), who stressed the importance of implementing the disengagement plan developed by MONUC. Mr. Doss declared that "only in this way can we hope to put an end to the armed conflict, [and] reduce significantly violence against *women and children* . . ."[73] (emphasis added). Again, both the press release and the SRSG's discourse equated "vulnerable" populations with "women and children," excluding the victimization and vulnerability of civilian males.[74]

The attitude of the United Nations toward male victimization in the DRC was also evident in testimony given by a Congolese man in the documentary *Gender Against Men*. The man denounced the sexual violence that he and his daughter had suffered to UNHCR's office in the country. However, the protection officers, who were females, were only interested in the violence suffered by his daughter, and did not care about him, leaving him with the impression that in their view, men could not be raped. In his words: "They talked a lot more about the rape of my daughter than about my own case. I was tortured, I was raped, but they believe that rape is not done to men. That's what I was able to observe."[75] The UN appears to be disregarding sexual violence against men and boys, and failing to adapt its institutional perspective of rape to the empirical pieces of evidence it confronts in the field.

ACKNOWLEDGING GENDERCIDE

In March 2009, Nicola Dahrendof, the UN Special Advisor on Sexual Violence in the DRC, announced a new policy entitled "The Comprehensive Strategy on Sexual Violence in the DRC" (CSSV), which aimed to create a common platform for action by bringing together and improving the policies on sexual violence implemented by UN agencies in the country.[76] The CSSV apparently adopts a gender-neutral language and, at first glance, does not seem to be a biased document focusing on women alone. However, during an interview for MONUC's website, Ms. Dahrendof demonstrated that the CSSV may still be based on the women-as-victims approach. She mentioned only how women and children were vulnerable to sexual violence, and highlighted, for example, the intention to recruit more female judges and magistrates to deal with the implementation of sexual violence laws in the DRC.

Thus, in practice, the CSSV discourse does not acknowledge GBV against men; nor does it seem to engage with gender constructions and questions of masculinity that influence patterns of sexual violence in the country. More flexible and inclusive gender policies should acknowledge that gender-based violence in conflicts affects both males and females, and deal with the construction of femininity *and* masculinity – since gendered constructions that hierarchize heterosexual masculinities underpin the targeting of both females and enemy males in genocidal warfare.

However, the majority of gender analysis of the Congolese conflict is still carried out with a predominantly feminist perspective, emphasizing violence perpetrated against women and girls. For instance, since 2007,[77] when the UN began the campaign "Stop Raping our Greatest Resource: Power to Women and Girls in the DRC," the occurrence of sexual violence in the country has been constantly referred to as "femicide" by UN news agencies and personnel.[78]

By deploying the concept "femicide," these discourses allow emphasis only on acts directed at the destruction of women and girls in the country. This effectively casts a shroud of silence over gender-based violence against males in the DRC, which is a common characteristic during the occurrence of genocide. Thus, given the widespread occurrence of male victimization, the concept of *gendercide* – coined by Mary Anne Warren in 1985 and revived by Adam Jones in 2000[79] – seems more appropriate for the current situation in the DRC. According to Warren, *gendercide* refers to:

> the deliberate extermination of persons of a particular sex (or gender). Other terms, such as "gynocide" and "femicide," have been used to refer to the wrongful killing of girls and women. But "gendercide" is a sex-neutral term, in that the victims may be either male or female. There is a need for such a sex-neutral term, since sexually discriminatory killing is just as wrong when the victims happen to be male. The term also calls attention to the fact that gender roles have often had lethal consequences, and that these are in important respects analogous to the lethal consequences of racial, religious, and class prejudice.[80]

The concept of gendercide is relevant not only because it addresses how social constructions of gender influence the dynamics of conflict, but also because it offers a neutral term that addresses both male and female victimization.[81] The analysis presented in this chapter has shown how in the Democratic Republic of the Congo, both men and women are suffering the "lethal consequences" of gendered constructions. Men are the most frequent targets of gendercidal killings and forced recruitment because of their perceived gender roles. This does not mean that women and girls are not victims of *gendercide*. In the DRC conflict, rape and other patterns of sexual violence are committed against males and females and, in these cases, gendercide affects especially women and girls when it comes to "combined rape and killing, or raping to death."[82] But "femicide" is inappropriate to define GBV in the DRC, since it renders invisible the violence that is systematically perpetrated against males.

It is important to highlight that the DRC is experiencing patterns of genocidal violence similar to those in Rwanda where men, women, and children were victims of massacres and sexual violence. However, alongside those acts of root-and-branch genocide – which target all members of a group regardless of gender or age[83] – there are also gendercidal slaughters of men and boys, especially during reprisal attacks on villages, seeking enemy combatants and sympathizers.

The international community, and international organizations such as the UN, should thus frame victimization more broadly, addressing atrocities against both sexes. To this end, it is necessary to recognize how men and women alike are vulnerable to different patterns of GBV. It is important to understand gender as a relational identity affecting both men's and women's perception of each other. Gender identities are also infused with power constructions which carry political consequences, especially in conflict settings where gender-based violence is used as a tool for redistributing power among groups. Thus, humanitarian organizations should attend to gender and sexual violence more broadly, by taking into consideration the construction of men's and women's roles in afflicted societies.

CONCLUSION

The analysis of UN activities in the DRC has shown how the organization continues to associate "gender" policies exclusively with the protection of women and girls. This perspective is unwarranted and myopic. It impedes a more critical approach toward the way in which these gendered constructions operate during genocide. In the case of the Congolese conflict, the UN has failed to problematize sex-selective massacres and sexual violence against males. To all intents and purposes, it appears that constructions of masculinity enter the equation only to the extent that they have a negative and destructive impact on women's lives. As a consequence, male vulnerabilities, and the constructions of masculinity that deepen them, are largely absent from the organization's policies.

Although the UN has apparently shown signs of goodwill in its latest documents, adopting more gender-neutral terminology and acknowledging male victims of sexual violence, these treatments remain superficial, rarely amounting to more than a few words in any given source.

It should be stressed that this chapter does not seek to downplay the catastrophic levels of violence suffered by women and girls, in Congo and elsewhere. Rather, the argument offers strong support for the role of international organizations in aiding and empowering female victims of armed conflict and genocide. This is a necessary step to overcome gendered constructions that legitimize representations of women as inherently vulnerable and inferior beings.

However, civilian men and boys are as vulnerable as females, and are also negatively affected by social constructions of gender. If the diverse consequences of gender constructions for both sexes were acknowledged, analysts and policy-makers would have a clearer view of the gender dynamics shaping conflict and genocide in the Democratic Republic of the Congo, and in many other cases of mass violence worldwide.

NOTES

1. Gérard Prunier, *Africa's World War: Congo, the Rwandan Genocide, and the Making of a Continental Catastrophe* (New York: Oxford University Press, 2009), p. xxxvi.
2. Both groups are identified with Rwanda and, as a consequence, they are still considered as foreign invaders, a category of people to whom, histroically, colonizers, and later, the dictatorship of Mobuto Sese Seko granted political and economic privileges, such as land rights. Prunier, *Africa's World War*, pp. 46–58; Lydia Polgreen, "Fighting in Congo Rekindles Ethnic Hatreds," *The New York Times*, January 10, 2008, http://www.nytimes.com/2008/01/10/world/africa/10congo.html.
3. Telephone interview with Ms. Juliane Kippenberg, Human Rights Watch researcher, September 8, 2009.
4. CNDP is a Tutsi militia that claims the right to protect the Congolese-Tutsis in the DRC.
5. It is estimated that 54 percent of rapes reported in the first semester of 2009 were perpetrated by the FARDC. Human Rights Watch, *Soldiers Who Rape, Commanders Who Condone*, July 16, 2009, http://www.hrw.org/en/reports/2009/07/16/soldiers-who-rape-commanders-who-condone.
6. Karen Ballentine and Heiko Nitzschke, *Beyond Greed and Grievance: Policy Lessons from Studies in the Political Economy of Armed Conflict* (New York: International Policy Academy, 2003), p. 1.
7. Dena Montague, "Stolen Goods: Coltan and Conflict in the Democratic Republic of Congo," *SAIS Review*, 32: 1 (2002), pp. 105–107.
8. Polgreen, "Fighting in Congo Rekindles Ethnic Hatreds."
9. See MONUC website, http://www.un.org/Depts/dpko/missions/monuc/index.html.
10. On July 1, 2010, MONUC was renamed MONUSCO. According to the UN, this change reflects "the new phase reached in the country." MONUSCO website states that:

    > The new mission has been authorized to use all necessary means to carry out its mandate relating, among other things, to the protection of civilians, humanitarian personnel and human rights defenders under imminent threat of physical violence and to support the Government of the DRC in its stabilization and peace consolidation efforts.
    > (See: http://www.un.org/en/peacekeeping/missions/monusco/)

    However, constant attacks on civilians still keep being reported by humanitarian agencies and no significant changes seem to be occurring so far in the DRC.
11. Jeffrey Gettleman, "Symbol of Unhealed Congo: Male Rape Victims," *The New York Times*, August 5, 2009, http://www.nytimes.com/2009/08/05/world/africa/05congo.html. In 2008, 4,820 rapes were registered in North Kivu alone according to the latest Human Rights Watch report on the DRC (Human Rights Watch, *Soldiers Who Rape, Commanders Who Condone*).
12. Gender-based violence can be defined as any kind of violence directed to a person because of his/her "sex and/or socially constructed gender role" (Women's Caucus, quoted in R. Charli Carpenter, "Recognizing Gender-Based Violence Against Civilian Men and Boys in Conflict Situations," *Security Dialogue*, 37: 1 (2006), p. 83). Carpenter gives the following examples of patterns of GBV: forced recruitment, sex-selective massacres, and sexual violence (ibid., p. 86).

    Regarding sexual violence more specifically, Sivakumaran provides the following typology: (a) rape; (b) enforced sterilization; (c) other forms of sexual violence including: genital violence, enforced nudity, and enforced masturbation. See Sandesh Sivakumaran, "Sexual Violence Against Men in Armed Conflict," *European Journal of International Law*, 18 (2007), pp. 261–267.

13   Adam Jones, "Problems of Gendercide," in Adam Jones, ed., *Gendercide and Genocide* (Nashville, TN: Vanderbilt University Press, 2004), p. 264.

14   Judgment, *Prosecutor v. Akayesu*, Case No. ICTR-96-4-T, Judgment No. 731 (September 2, 1998), quoted in Rebecca Haffajee, "Prosecuting Crimes of Rape and Sexual Violence at the ICTR: The Application of Joint Criminal Enterprise Theory," *Harvard Journal of Law and Gender*, 29 (2006), p. 207. Available at: http://www.law.harvard.edu/students/orgs/jlg/vol291/haffajee.pdf.

15   Adam Jones, "Gender and Ethnic Conflict in ex-Yugoslavia," *Ethnic and Racial Studies*, 17: 1 (1994), p. 118. See also Carpenter, "Recognizing Gender-Based Violence."

16   See Adam Jones, ed., *Gendercide and Genocide* (Nashville, TN: Vanderbilt University Press, 2004); Adam Jones, "Gender and Genocide in Rwanda," in Jones, ed., *Gendercide and Genocide*, pp. 98–137; Carpenter, "Recognizing Gender-Based Violence"; R. Charli Carpenter, *"Innocent Women and Children": Gender, Norms and the Protection of Civilians* (Aldershot: Ashgate, 2006); http://www.gendercide.org/case_bosnia.html.

17   Amnesty International, *Democratic Republic of Congo: Mass Rape – Time for Remedies* (London: Amnesty International, 2004), http://www.amnesty.org/en/library/asset/AFR 62/018/2004/en/dom-AFR620182004en.html; United Nations Joint Human Rights Office, *Consolidated Report on Investigations Conducted by the United Nations Joint Human Rights Office into Grave Human Rights Abuses Committed in Kiwanja, North Kivu, in November, 2008* (New York: United Nations, 2009), http://www.reliefweb.int/rw/RWFiles 2009.nsf/FilesByRWDocUnidFilename/LSGZ-7VQHJ2-full_report.pdf/$File/full_report.pdf. It should be mentioned that there is a controversy related to the role of ethnic identities within the DRC conflict. While some organizations and news stories highlight how ethnic identity can play a role in the targeting of civilians, some researchers disagree on the importance of ethnic identities in the perpetration of sexual violence and mass killings in the conflict.

18   Human Rights Watch, *Soldiers Who Rape, Commanders Who Condone*, p. 50.

19   Amnesty International, *Democratic Republic of Congo Mass Rape – Time for Remedies.*

20   Marion Pratt and Leah Werchick, *Sexual Terrorism: Rape as a Weapon of War in Eastern Democratic Republic of Congo,* USAID/DCHA Assessment Report, 2004. Available at: http://www.peacewomen.org/resources/DRC/USAIDDCHADRC.pdf.

21   Stephanie Nolen, "Rape Again Rampant in Congo," *The Globe and Mail*, October 17, 2008, http://newsite.vday.org/node/1204.

22   Pratt and Werchick, *Sexual Terrorism.*

23   United Nations News Centre, "Congolese Rape Survivors Break Silence at UN-organized Event," *United Nations News Centre,* September 12, 2008, http://www.un.org/apps/news/story.asp?NewsID=28034&Cr=DRC&Cr1=KIVU.

24   Amnesty International, *Democratic Republic of Congo: Mass Rape – Time for Remedies.*

25   Quoted in Human Rights Watch, *Seeking Justice: The Prosecution of Sexual Violence in the Congo War* (New York: Human Rights Watch, March 7, 2005), http://www.hrw.org/en/reports/2005/03/06/seeking-justice.

26   Gettleman, "Symbol of Unhealed Congo." See also Human Rights Watch, *You Will Be Punished: Attacks on Civilians in Eastern Congo*, December 2009, http://www.hrw.org/sites/default/files/reports/drc1209web_1.pdf, p. 107.

27   Gettleman, "Symbol of Unhealed Congo." This figure ranged between 2 percent and 4 percent in 2007. See Médicins Sans Frontières, *Ituri: Civilians Still the First Victims – Permanence of Sexual Violence and Impact of Military Operations*, October 2007. Available at http://www.doctorswithoutborders-usa.org/publications/reports/2007/Ituri-Civilians-Still-the-First-Victims.pdf.

28   Sandesh Sivakumaran, "Male/Male Rape and the 'Taint' of Homosexuality," *Human Rights Quarterly*, 27: 4 (2005), pp. 1274–1308.

29   Sivakumaran, "Sexual Violence Against Men in Armed Conflict," pp. 253–267.

30   Quoted in Gettleman, "Symbol of Unhealed Congo."

31   Quoted in Human Rights Watch, *Seeking Justice.*

32   Quoted in Amnesty International, *Democratic Republic of Congo Mass Rape – Time for Remedies.*

33 Ibid.

34 See also Human Rights Watch, *You Will Be Punished*, pp. 75–76.

35 This problem was also recognized by the documentary *Gender Against Men*, produced by the Refugee Law Project (2008).

36 Amnesty International, *Democratic Republic of Congo: Mass Rape – Time for Remedies*.

37 International Rescue Committee, *Mortality in Eastern Democratic Republic of Congo: Results from Eleven Mortality Surveys*, 2001, http://www.grandslacs.net/doc/3741.pdf. See also http://www.theirc.org/resource-file/dr-congo-mortality-study-2001-graphs.

38 International Rescue Committee, *Mortality in the Democratic Republic of the Congo: Results from a Nationwide Survey Conducted April–July 2004*, 2004, p. 10, http://www.smallarms survey.org/files/portal/issueareas/victims/Victims_pdf/2004_IRC_DRC.pdf.

39 Benjamin Coghlan, Richard J. Brennan, Pascal Ngoy, David Dotara, Brad Otto, Mark Clements, and Tony Stewart, "Mortality in the Democratic Republic of the Congo: a Nationwide Survey," *The Lancet*, 367 (2006), p. 48.

40 L. Ahoua, A. Tamrat, F. Duroch, R.F. Grais, and V. Brown, "High Mortality in an Internally Displaced Population in Ituri, Democratic Republic of Congo, 2005: Results of a Rapid Assessment under Difficult Conditions," *Global Public Health*, 1: 3 (2006), pp. 198–199.

41 United Nations Organization Mission in the Democratic Republic of the Congo (MONUC), *Activities Report from the Office of Gender Affairs of the United Nations Organization Mission in the Democratic Republic of the Congo*, January 10, 2003, p. 9, http://www.peacewomen.org/resources/Peacekeeping/MONUCOGA2002report.pdf.

42 Stephanie McCrummen, "Congo Rebels Grab Young Men," *The Seattle Times*, November 14, 2009, http://seattletimes.nwsource.com/html/nationworld/2008389457_congo14.html.

43 Ibid.

44 Carpenter, "Recognizing Gender-Based Violence against Civilian Men and Boys in Conflict Situations," p. 92.

45 International Rescue Committee, "Congo Crisis: More Help is Needed for Women and Girls in North Kivu as Sexual Violence Escalates," November 21, 2008, http://www.theirc. org/news/congo-crisis-more-help-needed-women-and-girls-north-kivu-sexual-violence-escalates-4423.

46 Médicins Sans Frontières, *Ituri: Civilians Still the First Victims*, p. 27.

47 Ibid., p. 27

48 Ibid., p. 8.

49 Ibid., p. 12.

50 Ibid., p. 4.

51 Human Rights Watch, *The Christmas Massacres: LRA Attacks on Civilians in Northern Congo*, February 2009, p. 4, http://www.hrw.org/sites/default/files/reports/drc0209web_0. pdf.

52 Ibid., p. 4.

53 Ibid., p. 5.

54 Ibid., p. 34.

55 Ibid., p. 36.

56 The Group of Experts on the DRC is an independent group of external consultants appointed by the Secretary General of the United Nations, in consultations with the Security Council Sanctions Committee on the DRC and mandated to monitor the implementation of the arms embargo imposed on non-governmental armed groups operating in eastern DRC, and, in particular, to investigate the financial and material support given to such armed groups.

    See http://monuc.unmissions.org/Default.aspx?tabid=932&ctl=Details&mid=2070 &Item ID= 6659.

57 Adam Jones, "Gender and Genocide in Rwanda," in Jones, ed., *Gendercide and Genocide*, pp. 98–137; Carpenter, "*Innocent Women and Children*."

58 UN Doc.A/52/Rev.1 (1997) quoted in Dyan Mazurana, Angela Ranven-Roberts, Jane

Parpart, and Sue Lautze, "Introduction: Gender, Conflict and Peacekeeping," in Dyan Mazurana, Angela Ranven-Roberts, and Jane Parpart, eds, *Gender, Conflict and Peacekeeping* (New York: Rowman and Littlefield Publishers, 2005), p. 15.

59 United Nations Department of Peacekeeping Operations, "Women, Peace and Security," in *Gender and UN Peacekeeping Operations*, October 2005, http://www.un.org/Depts/dpko/ gender/.

60 In this regard, see Jones, "Gender and Genocide in Rwanda."

61 Jones, "Gender and Ethnic Conflict in ex-Yugoslavia," p. 125.

62 United Nations Security Council, *UN Security Council Resolution 1820 (2008)*, June 19, 2008. Available at: http://daccessdds.un.org/doc/UNDOC/GEN/N08/391/44/PDF/N08 39144.pdf?OpenElement.

63 United Nations Security Council, *UN Security Council Resolution 1820 (2008)*.

64 United Nations Security Council, *Report of the Secretary General Pursuant to Security Council Resolution 1820 (2008)*, August 20, 2009, pp. 3–4, http://www.reliefweb.int/rw/RWFiles 2009.nsf/FilesByRWDocUnidFilename/MYAI-7UD3DM-full_report.pdf/$File/ full_report.pdf.

65 Ibid., p.1.

66 United Nations, *Activities Report*, pp. 6–8.

67 Ibid., p. 7.

68 Ibid., p. 9.

69 Sy Koumbo, "One Day Workshop Held on the Promotion of New Sexual Violence Law in the DRC," *MONUC report*, April 1, 2008. Available at: http://www.reliefweb.int/rw/RWB. NSF/db900SID/EGUA-7DAS8A?OpenDocument.

70 United Nations Mission in the Democratic Republic of Congo (MONUC), "Great Lakes: Consultation on the Eradication of Sexual Violence and Impunity," June 13, 2008. Available at: http://www.reliefweb.int/rw/RWB.NSF/db900SID/LSGZ-7FNDE5?OpenDocument.

71 Ibid.

72 United Nations Mission in the Democratic Republic of Congo, "The Protection of the Population Remains the Primary Goal for MONUC, Says Alan Doss," *MONUC News*, October 15, 2008. Available at: http://www.congoforum.be/upldocs/MONUC%20News% 2015%20English.pdf.

73 Ibid.

74 For an argument addressing this problem as it was manifested on previous occasions, see Carpenter, *"Innocent Women and Children."*

75 Congolese refugee testimony given to the documentary *Gender Against Men* (2008).

76 Office of the Senior Advisor and Coordinator for Sexual Violence, *Comprehensive Strategy on Combating Sexual Violence in DRC: Executive Summary*, March 18, 2009. Available at: http://www.stoprapenow.org/pdf/SVStratExecSummaryFinal18March09.pdf.

77 See http://www.vday.org/node/999.

78 For example, see Yan Ertürk, quoted in "Silence Surrounding Violence Against Women Has Been Broken – UN Expert," *UN News Centre*, March 5, 2009, http://www.un.org/ apps/news/story.asp?NewsID=30092&Cr=violence+against+women&Cr; Jeffrey Gettleman, "Rape Victims' Words Help Jolt Congo into Change," *The New York Times*, October 17, 2008, http://www.nytimes.com/2008/10/18/world/africa/18congo. html. For more material on the Congolese "femicide," see: http://www.un.org/apps/news/ story.asp?NewsID= 29866&Cr=democratic&Cr1=; http://scotlandonsunday. scotsman.com/ features/Femicide- in-the-Congo-.4980370.jp; http://edition.cnn.com/2008/WORLD/africa/10/15/congo. women/index.html; http://www.vday.org/node/999.

79 Jones, "Gendercide and Genocide."

80 Warren, quoted in Jones, "Gendercide and Genocide," p. 3.

81 Jones, "Gendercide and Genocide."

82 Ibid., p. 11.

83 Ibid., p. 266.

Figure 7.1 At an elevation 705 km (438 miles) above Earth, this September 8, 1999, a Landsat 7 satellite scene captured Dili, capital of East Timor, just days after the pro-independence referendum result was announced. Black smoke produced by fires started by pro-Indonesian militia can be seen streaking southwest across the image.

Source: Originally published by the Genocide Studies Program, Yale University, http://www.yale.edu/gsp.

CHAPTER 7

Tracking Evidence of Genocide through Environmental Change

Applying remote sensing to the study of genocide

Russell F. Schimmer

INTRODUCTION

Can the physical environment reveal evidence of genocide? Can satellite images capturing environmental change corroborate documented eyewitness testimonies, published news reports, and scholarly research describing genocidal events? This chapter presents four case studies suggesting that remote sensing using satellite imagery can be a highly effective tool for studying genocide. Does it have the potential to play a greater role in genocide prevention, intervention, and evidence obtention?

Remote sensing is simply the observation of an object, group of objects, or process from a distance. The sensors used for digitally capturing these images can be generally divided into two categories: airborne and spaceborne. Most airborne sensors are carried on airplanes, whereas spaceborne sensors are fixed to satellites. Data products are categorized by their spatial resolution (pixel size), temporal resolution (the return time to a location on Earth), spectral resolution (the measured portions of the electromagnetic spectrum divided into band groups), and radiometric resolution (the reflective intensity of those spectral band groups).

The technology of remote sensing is not new. But as with many research tools, the development of more efficient computers and advances in sensor technology continue to make remote sensing a robust research tool with a variety of scientific and social applications. A growing number of government and commercial remote sensing platforms offer coherent temporal and spatial collections of data. These images can be used to show large- and small-scale changes to the environment at multiple spatial resolutions in many portions of the light spectrum, as well as by active radar.

All four case studies presented in this chapter – Guatemala, Rwanda, East Timor, and Darfur – revealed substantial corroborating, and sometimes surprising, evidence of systematic genocidal processes. The nature of the violence determined the remote sensing applications, but the availability of suitable satellite imagery sometimes limited the scope of the analysis. At times, the research involved assembling related clues and observations in an attempt to reconstruct each event or course of events. As a result of these findings, a number of questions emerged: How do extreme genocidal events and activities destroy an environment and disrupt the ability of people to extract subsistence materials, as well as sustain vital local and national economies? Can the environment be deliberately and systematically used as a mechanism to commit acts of genocide?

RESEARCH APPROACHES

I identify at least three remote sensing approaches relevant to the study of genocide. First, historical models of past genocides help to illustrate genocidal processes and reveal substantial evidence of the resulting destruction. Proving process is one element in proving intent. Because the images freeze time, remote sensing can examine the historical record. Historical models aid in identifying factors contributing to genocide, and provide corroborating evidence for reconstructing genocidal events. Second, monitoring ongoing genocides provides information not easily obtained by other means because of limited access to locations. This information can be useful for raising public awareness and influencing policy decisions on intervention. The dissemination of revealing images sometimes frustrates perpetrators' attempts to disguise their activities. Third, monitoring environmental change and human activity can help to identify potential genocides by synthesizing a retrospective understanding of process and the multifarious factors often leading to genocide. Fundamental ancillary materials include eyewitness documentation, news reports, academic research papers, court testimonies, and other visual materials.

Temporal land-cover change is a useful method for viewing and assessing the impact of genocide on an environment. The *Normalized Difference Vegetation Index* (NDVI) is a standard remote sensing application for detecting and measuring temporal land-cover changes, especially vegetation.[1] NDVI is related to vegetation because healthy vegetation is absorbed in the 500–700 nm red visible range of the electromagnetic spectrum and reflects very well in the 700–1300 nm near-infrared (NIR) range of the spectrum. NDVI is derived from the ratio (NIR band – Red band)/(NIR band + Red band).

Temporal and spatial continuity, variations in spatial resolution, and overlapping coverage are integral to assembling reliable empirical datasets. Thus, one fundamental limitation of the method is the availability of an adequate number of images that spatially and temporally capture the events. High-spatial resolution commercial satellite images

(~1 m pixel resolution) have become more readily available to the public. Such images have graphically documented the destruction of villages in Darfur since 2003.[2] However, the cost of acquiring the images can be prohibitive for research purposes. Well before these high-resolution technologies became available in the last ten years, a limited number of imagery sources and formats were available. Since the 1970s, one important source has been the National Aeronautics Space Administration (NASA) Landsat program. NASA currently provides Landsat images at no cost to the public. Thus, Landsat remains an important source of temporally and spatially uninterrupted coverage of the globe. For my remote sensing research in Guatemala, Rwanda, and East Timor, I used Landsat imagery exclusively.

Finally, during the process of identifying anthropogenic causal agents of land-cover and vegetation coverage change, I consider other externalities; for example, seasonal and annual climate fluctuations. These were important considerations for my case studies in Guatemala and Rwanda, and were charted annually for Darfur. For Guatemala and Rwanda, no abrupt climate changes were identified that could have affected the findings, whereas in Darfur, climate was a principal component of the research and its results. Furthermore, I made an effort to maintain seasonal continuity among images acquired during different years; this is important regardless of the ecosystem or environment under study.

GUATEMALA

Located in the northern part of El Quiché, the mountainous Ixil and Ixcán regions are the home of Guatemala's Maya, Ixil Indians. Estimated at 80,000 in 1981, the Ixil Indians accounted for nearly 90 percent of the population of El Quiché.[3] During the government-sponsored Guatemalan genocide, *La Violencia*, of the 1980s, these regions experienced some of the highest frequencies and magnitudes of killings – between March 1981 and March 1983, the Guatemalan armed forces carried out 77 massacres, resulting in 3,102 known deaths.[4] The army designated the Ixil area as the "Ixil Triangle" – referring to its three municipal centers, Nebaj, Chajul, and Cotzal, each of which housed a military base.[5]

For the Ixil region, the anthropologist and human rights scholar Victoria Sanford argues that, though the army's scorched-earth campaign is usually dated from 1981 to 1983, the violence continued as the government initiated new genocidal campaigns, which did not end until 1990.[6] The anthropologist and human rights scholar Beatriz Manz states that, even after the 1986 decrease in government-sponsored genocide-type activities, the military remained openly active and present in the area, continuing to implement the relocation of model village policies.[7] Model villages were an integral part of the military's rural development campaign: army-controlled resettlement work camps developed as a means to maintain absolute control over Mayan communities.[8] Sanford identifies three campaigns of genocide: (1) the massacre; (2) the sustained hunt for survivors in flight; and (3) the systematic militarization and deliberate infliction of harm on survivors forcibly relocated into "model villages" (also known as "pole villages").[9]

Guatemalan military violence in the Ixil area began in the late 1970s. One of the more overt examples of this violence occurred on April 21, 1981, in the town of Acul, due west of Nebaj. Typical of the army's system of terror, the violence in the town of Acul began with pre-dawn house-to-house searches and the abduction of young men, who would be interrogated and often murdered.[10] The Acul massacre was one of 79 carried out in the department of El Quiché in 1981.[11] Implementation of President Efrain Ríos Montt's "scorched earth" strategy raised the violence to a peak in 1982–1983. The military systematically destroyed virtually all of the rural subsistence farming settlements among the Ixil Triangle's municipalities. Soldiers massacred unarmed Maya in their villages and pursued survivors into the mountains, where they used fire to force mostly women and children out of hiding.[12]

In late 1983, the army launched a program described as Development Pole Villages. These "model villages" were an important component of the government's *fusiles y frijoles* ("guns and beans") counterinsurgency program. Villagers displaced by the violence and still surviving in the area of their former residences became concentrated in these military-controlled zones.[13] The government offered "amnesty" to survivors in exchange for community acceptance of and participation in army-controlled civil patrols.[14] In towns like Acul, the community remained highly militarized through army-organized civil patrols, which were not disbanded until after the signing of the Peace Accords in December 1996.[15]

My primary research question was whether satellite imagery could reveal evidence of burnings of houses and crops, and the development of model villages in and around the central Ixil municipalities.[16] Using NDVI, temporal-change detection of the study area involved assembling four Landsat MSS and TM satellite scenes acquired during the dry season. The images date from February 6, 1979, March 13, 1986 (two scenes), and January 23, 2000. The findings suggest that the documented temporal changes in vegetation from 1979 to 2000 were the cumulative result of the violence, military activities, and the government-sponsored pole-village campaigns of the 1980s and 1990s. First, most deforestation in the area of interest (AOI) occurred in the Ixil region of El Quiché, at or in close proximity to villages that suffered documented destruction. Second, the findings statistically validated the clearing of forests and other vegetation for the construction of pole villages in the municipal centers of Nebaj, Acul, Chajul, and Cotzal.

By 1986, the findings showed large mountainous areas denuded of forest cover, like scars on the landscape, at or in close proximity to the locations of many villages confirmed to have experienced multiple attacks by government forces. By 2000, these scars were no longer visible and a return of some agricultural vegetation was evident – but not of the dense forests that characterized the area before 1980.

In the area of Nebaj and Acul, as well as other pole settlements (for example Chajul and Cotzal), the findings showed definitive evidence of widespread vegetation clearance by 1986 (Figure 7.2). A reliable remote sensing method used to quantify temporal changes to a landscape requires the user to define land-cover classes based on identified land-cover types appearing on one image, and then to train the computer to identify similar land-cover types based on their spectral characteristics from the same and subsequent images. For the purpose of this research, I designated three supervised classes representing "heavy vegetation" (heavily forested areas), "medium vegetation" (agriculture, mixed vegetation, and dispersed vegetation), and "light-to-no-vegetation" (open ground, exposed soil, urban areas, and roads).

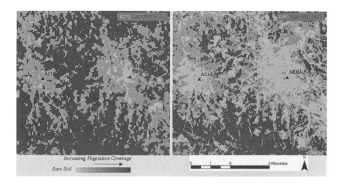

Figure 7.2 Evidence of vegetation clearing in the Ixil townships of Acul and Nebaj caused by the Guatemalan government-sponsored "Pole Village" policies of the early 1980s. Ixil Indians formerly living in rural mountain hamlets were violently concentrated into "development areas" which became work camps controlled by the army.

Source: Originally published by the Yale Genocides Studies Program, www.yale.edu/gsp.

In the Nebaj and Acul municipalities, the statistics showed that in 1979, the land-cover class "heavy vegetation" covered almost 60 percent of the area, whereas "light-to-no vegetation" covered only 4 percent (Table 7.1). However, by 1986, heavy vegetation had declined to 33 percent and light vegetation rose to 29 percent. Moreover, by 2000, the environment had recovered considerably from 1986, but still had not returned to 1979 conditions.[17] I documented similar findings for the entire Ixil region. These findings offer powerful evidence of the genocidal activities conducted by the Guatemalan military in the Department of El Quiché during the period from 1979 through to the mid-1990s.

Table 7.1 Classification results for the Nebaj-Acul municipality for 1979 and 1986

Class/Region	Hectares	Km^2	Acres	$Miles^2$
Area Summary Report for 02/06/1979 MSS NDVI Classified				
Heavy vegetation	3520.1	35.2	8698.4	13.6
Medium vegetation	2223.1	22.2	5493.4	8.6
Light-to-no vegetation	236.7	2.4	585.0	0.9
Total	5981.4	59.8	14780.4	23.1
Area Summary Report for 03/13/1986 MSS NDVI Classified				
Heavy vegetation	1984.0	19.8	4902. 6	7.7
Medium vegetation	2240.2	22.4	5535.6	8.6
Light-to-no vegetation	1742.4	17.4	4305.5	6.7
Total*	5981.4	59.8	14780.4	23.1

*In some categories, the sums reported fall slightly short of the totals. These represent areas of unclassified pixels; i.e. pixels that did not fit into any of the three classes.

RWANDA

The genocide in Rwanda occurred during a twelve-week period in 1994. The most intensive period was from April to May, when hundreds of thousands of Tutsi were murdered. The Bisesero hills, in the Kibuye Prefecture, southwestern Rwanda, became known as the location of some of the most intensive genocidal killing. Thousands of Tutsi from the surrounding communes of Kibuye fled to the Bisesero region, where they staged a staunch resistance. The massacre sites in Bisesero are numerous. The International Criminal Tribunal for Rwanda (ICTR) proceedings dealing with the Bisesero *secteur* mentioned Muyira, Murambi, Ku Cyapa, Kabatwa, and Nyarutovu. Likely no fewer than 14,000 people perished,[18] about 400 corpses per square kilometer of the identified region.

According to one ICTR report,[19] the region was the target of near-daily attacks between April 9 and June 30, 1994. The attackers comprised gendarmes, communal police officers from Gishyita and Gisovu, armed civilians, and Interahamwe (an unofficial paramilitary group made up exclusively of extremist Hutu). They gained daily access to the region using a variety of small and large vehicles. The attackers then used firearms, grenades, machetes, spears, clubs, and other weapons to assault their victims.

As with Guatemala, my research goal was to attempt to identify evidence of fire damage and destruction of vegetation caused by the violence, using NDVI and a temporal assemblage of before-and-after Landsat images.[20] I expected to discover some evidence of changes to the landscape in the Bisesero region that likely resulted from the genocide-resistance event. I used four Landsat scenes to assess land-cover change, dated 1987, 1995, 1999, and 2000. My findings located areas in the Bisesero region which were likely to have been most impacted by the resistance activity. Based on the NDVI analysis, two areas emerged that were characterized by scattered vegetation clearance in 1995 – but not in 1987, 1999, and 2000. The contiguous area containing these two cleared areas was approximately 35 km². The French Ministry of Higher Education and Scientific Research and Culture's map, *Rwanda: Les Grands Sites du Génocide et des Massacres, Avril–Juillet 1994*, corroborated three of these locations as areas of genocide and resistance.[21]

The documented violent activity in this small area would certainly have resulted in discernible evidence on the landscape. In 1995, road- and trail-features appeared to follow the Kirparo River and its tributaries from the local town of Mubuga deep into these cleared landscapes. Like the clearance of vegetation, these road features are most pronounced in 1995 and almost indiscernible in 1987, 1999, or 2000 – thus strongly corresponding to the genocide-resistance event. Eyewitness accounts often speak of their attackers arriving daily *en masse*, in a variety of vehicles including "buses and lorries."[22] In addition, a third feature appeared by 1999: a highly visible bare surface area or "stain" of appendages in close proximity to the hamlet of Rubazo. It is unique within the larger area of undulating, well-vegetated topography. Regardless of the season, the size, shape, and highly reflective qualities of this feature remained unchanged. Eventually, the feature was identified as a monument, although it is uncertain whether any genocide victims are buried at the site.

The genocide had a great impact on the environment, evident in the change in NDVI during and immediately following the 1994 genocide at many confirmed locations of violence in the Kibuye Prefecture. Post-genocide documentation of the region, including reports of the country's agricultural and economic recovery,[23] coincides with my research findings of an abrupt and severe decrease in agricultural activity during the immediate aftermath of the 1994 genocide, evidenced by the overall decrease of vegetation coverage observed in the Kibuye Prefecture in 1995, followed by a full recovery of vegetation by 1999 in those same locations. Thus, the remote sensing findings appear strongly corroborative of genocide and resistance. As in Guatemala, these large-scale violent activities embedded their indelible fingerprint on the landscape, captured and frozen in time.

EAST TIMOR

East Timor lies on the eastern half of the island of Timor, but also includes the Oécussi (Oecusse) Ambeno enclave in the northwest portion of Indonesian West Timor, and the islands of Ataúro north of Dili, and Jaco on the easetern tip of West Timor (Figure 7.3). It is a primarily mountainous terrain. After nearly twenty-four years of Indonesian occupation and despite weeks of being terrorized by the Indonesian military and pro-Indonesian militias, the East Timorese voted overwhelmingly for independence in the UN-supervised referendum held on August 30, 1999. During the ensuing conflicts, roughly 70 percent of the buildings in East Timor were incinerated, leaving thousands homeless. More than 300,000 people fled or were expelled.[24] On September 11, 1999, a United Nations Security Council delegation arrived in Dili, the capital of East Timor, where they reported evidence of mass atrocities, looting, and wanton destruction. Entire neighborhoods had been reduced to ashes.[25] Eyewitness-reports claimed that anti-independence militants had set houses alight with hoses spraying gas.[26]

NASA acquired a single Landsat 7 satellite image on September 8, 1999, during the climax of violence.[27] The scene did not cover the entire island of Timor, but fortunately showed Dili and the center of Timor island, where much of the violence occurred. My goal was to locate areas with the greatest concentration of fires, and to assess these locations' spatial relationships to mapped villages, towns, regions, and the international border with Indonesia. This involved three steps: first, developing a remote sensing method capable of identifying possible fire locations; second, cataloging these locations; and, third, corroborating these findings with eyewitness accounts of locations reported to have experienced destruction when the scene was acquired.

The most intense and easily recognizable fires were those in Dili (Figure 7.3). Using the foci of these Dili fires, I combined the Landsat image's thermal band six and spectral band seven to create an algorithm capable of isolating the specific radiometric intensity of the spectral signature, "fire." I then used this algorithm to identify locations of fire on other parts of the satellite scene. For capturing spectral and thermal information, the spatial resolution of Landsat 7 images is 30 m and 60 m respectively. That is, the specific spectral–thermal signature representing a fire or group of fires would have to dominate at least a 900–3600 m^2 pixel space for it to be positively identified; smaller fires of more scattered grouping would not be detectable using this method. Thus, the results do not give an actual number of fires, but the likely locations of fire. I expected to identify fire signatures unrelated to the genocidal activities, such as brush fires, but posited that a greater concentration of identified fire pixels should be located in areas of reported atrocity as an additional control to test the accuracy of the method.

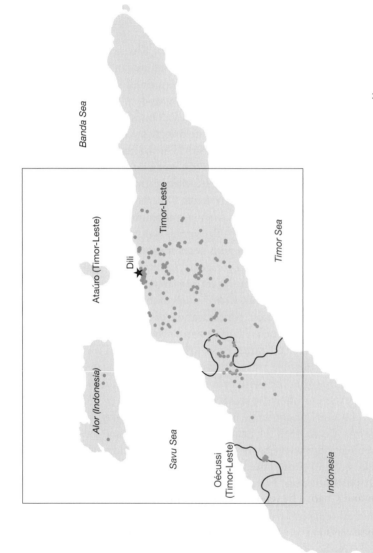

Figure 7.3 On August 30, 1999, Timorese citizens voted overwhelmingly for independence from Indonesia in a UN-sponsored referendum. During the ensuing conflicts, roughly 70 percent of the buildings in East Timor were burned, leaving thousands homeless. The circles represent positively identified locations of fire captured on a September 8, 1999, Landsat 7 satellite image (the rectangle shows the spatial extent of the image). Reports confirm that the Indonesian army and pro-Indonesia militias were responsible for most of the violence.

Source: Originally published by the Yale Genocides Studies Program, www.yale.edu/gsp.

I identified a large number of fires concentrated in an area just west of the East Timor border with Indonesian-controlled central Timor. Further west of the border, the number and concentration of positively identified fires decreased noticeably. The East Timor National Liberation Armed Forces (FALINTIL), a pro-independence insurgent group, said both refugees and the Indonesian military were on the move in the province – many of the refugees fleeing into the mountains. Pro-Indonesian militia leader Herminio da Costa acknowledged the extent of the destruction, telling Portuguese radio he had the right to burn what belonged to him, particularly in light of the sweeping vote for independence.[28]

The Indonesian military forcibly held tens of thousands of refugees in camps just across the border in West Timor. Reports stated that as many as 230,000 refugees had crossed into the western half of the island, some telling aid workers and journalists that retreating Indonesian troops had forced them across the border at gunpoint.[29] The Indonesian government claimed that, by August 30, some 150,000 East Timorese had arrived in West Timor. My application also identified a number of fires on the Oécussi border. An 80 km stretch of road connects this enclave, wholly surrounded by West Timor, to the rest of East Timor. FALINTIL Commander Taur Matan Ruak claimed that Indonesian troops and their militia allies had killed 50 people and raped many women in the enclave.[30]

As expected, my findings did detect a number of fires unrelated to the genocide; for example, on the Indonesian island of Alor. This confirmed my assumption that I would likely find fire locations unrelated to genocide activities, but that the greater number of fires would be concentrated in areas of reported violence. Across East Timor, few buildings had escaped damage, and many had been reduced to smoldering ashes.[31] Because the Landsat scene represents a single moment in time, my findings are evidence of a consistent spatial and temporal symmetry of these fire signatures. As in many other documented cases of genocide, fire offered an inexpensive, readily available, and devastating tool of destruction.

DARFUR

In May 2004, the UN High Commissioner for Human Rights issued the report *Situation of Human Rights in the Darfur Region of the Sudan*.[32] Among its findings, the report described repeated attacks on civilians by the military forces of the government of Sudan and its proxy militia, the *Janjawiid*; the pattern of attacks on civilians included killing, rape, pillage, looting of livestock, and destruction of property. It further reported that much of Darfur's population, especially rural residents, had been forcibly displaced to locations in Darfur and Chad. The report stated three primary factors as precipitating the genocide in Darfur: race and religion, climate change, and competition among ethnic groups for declining available resources, such as water and livestock grazing ranges.[33]

In July 2004, a 7,000-member African Union Mission began to deploy in Darfur. But not until four years of government-sponsored genocidal violence had passed with near impunity did the United Nations Security Council, on July 31, 2007, pass Resolution 1769. It called for the creation of a joint 26,000 UN–African Union (UNAMID) ground force to establish peace in Darfur. The Sudanese government agreed to the deployment and, on December 31, 2007, the first UN forces arrived in Darfur. However, they still faced major obstructions to their operations and remained, three years later, not fully deployed.

Historically, the majority of the Sudanese population has depended on subsistence and commercial agriculture, which, in 2003, employed over 80 percent of the nation's workforce and contributed 35 percent to its GDP.[34] The economy of Darfur is also largely agrarian. Its main subsistence crops are millet and sorghum. Groundnuts, tobacco, vegetables, and watermelons are the main cash crops.[35] An explosive growth in livestock numbers – from 28.6 million in 1961 to 134.6 million in 2004 – resulted in widespread degradation of the rangelands.[36] Sheep- and goat-rearing increased because these herbivores can acclimatize better to dry environments, and have relatively lower water needs than cattle.[37]

The majority of livestock in Sudan are raised in traditional pastoral systems, on community rangelands.[38] Herders raise an estimated 80–90 percent of Sudan's livestock.[39] Almost all Darfurians own some livestock, and almost all of the refugees report the loss of these animals.[40] A typical farmer could own as many as ten goats, five to ten sheep, seven cows, and one camel. A better-off farmer typically owned 200 each of goats, sheep, and cows, as well as horses, donkeys, and camels. Fully-grown camels are worth more than US$1,000, as much as most Sudanese workers earn in a year.[41]

Environmental stress can precipitate and facilitate genocide, as well as attest to its impacts. Remote sensing applications can measure the health and vigor of vegetation and availability of water, as well as the speed of environmental recovery, and judge the stress humans and their activities place on the environment. Agriculture and livestock grazing are historically important economic activities in Darfur. Disruptions to these normal patterns of land use should be evident in changes to land cover. Although fluctuating rainfall can influence long-term changes and adaptations, violence intended to disrupt these systems of land use can have abrupt dramatic impacts. These are observable by aerial and satellite remote sensing.

My primary research goal was to use remote sensing as a tool to detect trends in land-cover change – natural, agricultural, and pastoral – directly related to changes in land use as a result of genocidal activities since 2003 in Darfur.[42] The research integrated ancillary data, using Geographic Information System (GIS) techniques, in order to establish correlations between observed changes to land cover and vegetation coverage in the context of these changes' temporal and spatial relations to documented violence. Based on the climatic, economic, and land use patterns existing in Darfur prior to the 2003 violence, I suggested that the following would take place: (1) the presence of livestock grazing would reduce NDVI vegetation vigor, regardless of water availability; (2) the reduction of livestock grazing would stimulate a rebound in natural vegetation vigor; and (3) the displacement of people would be synonymous with the gradual decline of livestock numbers and activity in a region. The findings show a clear distinction between the effects of rainfall and livestock grazing on environmental stress (Figures 7.4 and 7.5 below). My primary thesis is that this change in vegetation coverage is a result of the displacement of people and the cattle rustling that have substantially reduced livestock numbers, and disrupted semi-nomadic grazing and sedentary horticultural practices.

My research in Darfur required a large volume of satellite data to cover the spatial and temporal requirements of the ongoing violence since 2003. The research area of

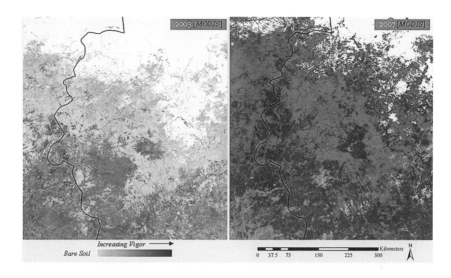

Figure 7.4 In Darfur from 2003 through to 2007, MODIS satellite images showed a steady increase of non-agricultural vegetation coverage and vigor, likely grasses and shrubs, in formerly agrarian and livestock-grazing ranges. The regions experiencing most change have spatial and temporal correlation with systematic local violence during the same period. This trend occurred despite a continuing decrease in annual rainfall, suggesting that a greatly reduced number of livestock is likely the main factor driving the increase in vegetation.

Source: Originally published by the Yale Genocides Studies Program, www.yale.edu/gsp.

approximately 361,000 km² covers those regions of North, West, and South Darfur experiencing the highest impact of reported violence since mid-2003.[43] I began with satellite data collected in 1998 in order to establish a pre-genocide understanding of the observable stresses to the environment as influenced by climatic and anthropogenic factors. I used two satellite imagery products to document change in vegetation coverage: NASA's Moderate Resolution Imaging Spectroradiometer (*MODIS Terra*) and the Centre National d'Études Spatiales's Le Système Pour l'Observation de la Terre (*SPOT Vegetation*); and one to measure annual rainfall: NASA's *Tropical Rainfall Measuring Mission* (TRMM). To measure annual and inter-annual change in vegetation coverage and vigor as detected by the NDVI, I used a *Fourier Classification* method that also distinguishes vegetation phenologies.[44] This method analyzes NDVI based on image stacks (23 for MODIS Terra and 36 for SPOT Vegetation) with temporal coverage of one calendar year each.

From 2004 through to 2007, both MODIS and SPOT images showed a steady increase of non-agricultural vegetation coverage and vigor, likely grasses and shrubs, in formerly agrarian and livestock grazing ranges. The regions experiencing most change correlate spatially and temporally with systematic reported violence. This trend occurred despite a continuing decrease in annual rainfall (Figure 7.5), suggesting that a greatly reduced number of livestock is likely the main factor driving the increase in vegetation.

Traditionally, pastoralists moved north during the rainy season (July to October) and south during the dry season. Since 2003, herds in Darfur have been reported as migrating southwards in search of safety, even during the rainy season.[45] The violence has further

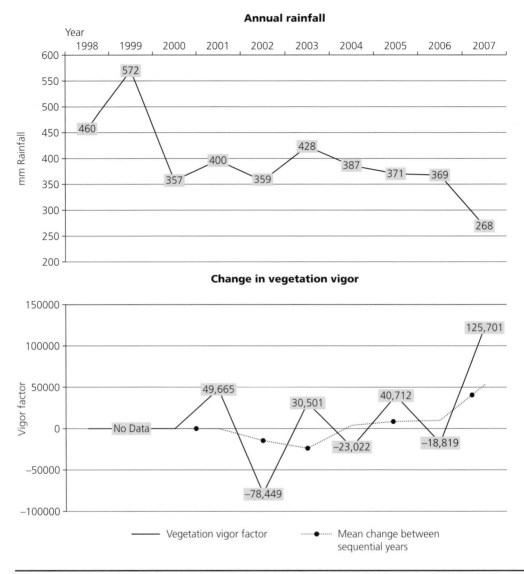

Figure 7.5 Annual rainfall (1998–2007) and vegetation vigor (2000/01–2007) in the study region of Darfur.

Source: Originally published by the Yale Genocides Studies Program, www.yale.edu/gsp.

restricted grazing ranges and, for security reasons, surviving livestock are being contained in concentrated areas, especially in the south, throughout the year.[46] In addition, reported Arab resettlement of traditionally Black African tribes' homelands in western and southern Darfur had been ongoing.[47]

These two factors – the concentration of livestock in the south and the Arab resettlement of some southern and western locations – likely explain the 2008 MODIS findings,[48] which showed a discernible demarcation, running east to west through west-central Darfur, of contrasting vegetation vigor. North of this line, vegetation vigor continued to increase after 2007, but south of this line, it has decreased considerably.

PREVENTION, INTERVENTION, AND EVIDENCE OBTENTION

Remote sensing has played and continues to play an integral role in national security policymaking for many countries. As part of a multidisciplinary approach to monitoring potential or ongoing "hot spots" of violence or the threat of violence, governments have used remote sensing for reconnaissance. Generally, these data have provided the military and policymakers with vital intelligence. One of the first examples of airborne remote sensing was used during the US Civil War, when both the North and South harnessed the technology of gas balloons to observe each other. It was not spying, *per se*, because it was done in full view of the other. It was simply another form of reconnaissance. However, the Cold War generation of U-2 reconnaissance aircraft were obviously designed to be more than conspicuous observers.

Today, the technology of observing earth from a distance has greatly improved. A multitude of nationally, internationally, and commercially owned and operated satellite sensors operate well beyond anyone's view, continuously observing. The space surrounding Earth has become a busy place. It has partly developed into a commercially-driven international marketplace of information exchange and observation, with or without the permission of those being observed.[49] Satellites have become an integral component of global communications and information dissemination, scientific observation, and transportation. We use satellites for global positioning systems (GPS), weather and hurricane monitoring, cell-phone communications, and television broadcasting.

With public accessibility to an increasing amount of satellite data, the public's ability to show and monitor environmental disasters and acts of violence, as well as publish findings, has raised social awareness and aided disaster relief efforts. For example, Google Earth in collaboration with the US Holocaust Memorial Museum and the American Association for the Advancement of Science, and with support from the US State Department, published graphic images of destroyed villages in Darfur,[50] and Crisis Mappers' *Haiti Crisis Map*, published a multimedia GIS disaster response to the 2010 earthquake.[51]

But how much information is enough to prevent genocide? How much proof is required to intervene in ongoing genocide? In his chilling narrative, Canadian General Roméo Dallaire, commander of the United Nations Mission in Rwanda, described how his repeated warnings of possible mass murder went unheeded by UN officials. As he tried to save lives, the UN Security Council withdrew nearly all his troops; his warnings, soon after, became a reality.[52] If there is no political will, what more can remote sensing contribute to preventing genocide? After nearly seven years of violence and genocide in Darfur, none of the publicly available evidence, gathered through remote sensing or by other means, has prevented further atrocities. Thus, rather than for prevention, perhaps remote sensing could be used more effectively for evidence obtention in the investigation and prosecution of genocidal crimes.

A fine line exists between spying and reconnaissance. For national security purposes, governments want or need to protect their technologies and data. But whereas these sources provide useful information for policymaking, this information is often rendered useless as evidence in courts of law, because it lacks full disclosure. An even finer line exists between information published to raise or increase public awareness, and scientific or scholarly research intended to obtain evidence of violence. In the realm of public awareness, conflicts of interest can arise that compromise the use of information in a legal context. This might occur in collaborative efforts in which information is provided by commercial entities or government sources responsible for protecting national interests. Thus, can remote sensing findings, which are scientifically validated, non-political, transparent, and relevant, be admissible evidence in prosecuting crimes against humanity and genocide?

LEGAL APPLICATIONS

Enacted in 1998, the Rome Statute established that the jurisdiction of the International Criminal Court (ICC) would be limited to the most serious crimes of concern to the international community as a whole, including the crime of genocide.[53] In addition, the ICC has jurisdiction over crimes against humanity[54] – a more easily prosecutable crime than genocide, because it lacks the requirement of "acts committed with intent to destroy, in whole or in part, a national, ethnical, racial or religious group."[55] Instead, it requires only that the acts be widespread or systematic, directed against any civilian group, and inflicted with knowledge of a context of a wider assault.[56]

In the legal process of establishing the *actus reus* and *mens rea* of mass atrocity, it is doubtful that a remote sensing finding could be an eyewitness pointing a finger directly at the perpetrator and stating the why, when, where, what, and how. But, as the case studies here demonstrate, remote sensing can corroborate witness testimony or other substantive evidence of criminal activity and intent. With regard to evidence obtention and admissibility, I believe that remote sensing can make significant contributions as a tool for: (1) criminal investigation; (2) witness corroboration; (3) evidence obtainment; and (4) damages assessment.

As an investigatory tool, remote sensing findings can contribute to an investigation of genocide or crimes against humanity by helping to add structure and meaning to other forms of admissible evidence, and revealing information about criminal activities not previously discerned. Because remote sensing data are captured in real time and do not change, even years after an environment has recovered from large-scale destruction, the evidence is not blurred or lost. As a corroborative tool, remote sensing can substantiate other forms of evidence and link events that initially might have appeared random. Thus, it legitimizes testimonies and accounts of the events. As an obtention tool, remote sensing can spatially substantiate the targeting of a group when used in tandem with other types of geographic and demographic data. Finally, as a tool for assessing damages, remote sensing can help to identify the causal agents and quantify the victims' losses.

However, if spaceborne remote sensing is to become a useful tool for evidence obtainment in the pursuit of international justice, it faces two major challenges: (1) it must overcome the historical stigma of image tampering attached to the processes of data acquisition, production, and presentation; and (2) it must overcome questions as to its scientific validity and legal relevance. The historic and ongoing use of spaceborne, remotely-sensed information-gathering for espionage has given rise to suspicions of its legitimate acquisition, distribution, and presentation. In contrast, international space law treaties, such as the UN's Principles Relating to Remote Sensing of the Earth from Space (1986), have striven to assure that remote sensing activities are "carried out for the benefit and in the interests of all countries, irrespective of their degree of economic, social, or scientific and technological development."[57]

Since 1972, through NASA's Landsat program, the USA has worked to maintain the principles of international non-discriminatory access by favoring open-information societies and demonstrating the peaceful uses of space technology.[58] Beginning in the late 1990s, an increasing number of commercial satellite products have become available to the public. However, from a legal perspective, commercially available satellite products can present conflict-of-interest admissibility problems. For example, in September 2008, the American company GeoEye launched GeoEye-1, which has a spatial resolution of 0.41 m or about 16 ins, making it one of the world's highest resolution platforms. The company received $500 million in funding from the US government's National Geospatial-Intelligence Agency (NGA) to help fund completion of GeoEye-1, and the company began delivering images to NGA in early 2009, generating monthly revenues estimated at $12.5 million.[59]

One alternative might be to assemble spatially and temporally overlapping data sets from a variety of sources – commercial and governmental – but processed using similar methods. If the individual findings are consistent, courts might consider a data set admissible as a body of evidence. A second alternative to the stigma problem might be an international framework establishing certification guidelines for satellite products, whether produced by national, international, or commercial entities. It would likely not be in the interest of all satellite producers to pursue certification, but it would offer an incentive for some producers to standardize their products. For example, the US Department of the Interior's Geological Survey at the Earth Resources Observation and Science Data Center (USGS/EROS) archives remote sensing imagery, including Landsat, collected from satellites and other sources. In addition, the Center certifies photographic prints for litigation purposes.[60] A new certification process will provide the same assurances of reliability with digital data.[61]

In addition to the stigma problem, two legal requirements must be met: (1) the validation of remote sensing methodologies as a science; and (2) the establishment of remotely sensed data as relevant evidence. In the US, Federal Rule of Evidence 901(b) (9) allows "evidence describing a process or system used to produce a result and showing that the process or system produces an accurate result."[62] Expert testimony could establish that satellite data were properly collected, transported, handled, and stored. In addition, testimony could validate that the user or technician who processed and interpreted the data applied accepted scientific methods.[63] With respect to "scientific evidence," the trial court judge makes a preliminary assessment of whether it is relevant and material as applied to the facts, and supported by appropriate scientific validation.[64]

The ICC Rules of Procedure and Evidence provide, in part, that "the Prosecutor may seek additional information from . . . other reliable sources that he or she deems appropriate."[65] In addition, they provide that, at any stage of the proceedings, "a Chamber may . . . invite or grant leave to a . . . person to submit in writing or orally, any observation on any issue the Chamber deems appropriate."[66] Thus, the ICC Chamber could determine that remote sensing data are substantive and admissible if they are found to be reliable and relevant to the issues.

In summary, if remote sensing is to have an important role in evidence obtainment for prosecutions of crimes against humanity and genocide, a legal precedent and standard must be established for its use. This standard would likely require that the processes of acquisition, production, and presentation comply with established rules of evidence. If it is shown that remote sensing findings, as evidence of genocide, can be obtained and produced in a way that meets these criteria – using methods that are scientifically validated, non-political, and transparent – remote sensing might have an important future role in the prosecution of these crimes.

CONCLUSION

In a variety of natural and anthropological confluences, environments embody human activities and cultural processes. Humans make choices based on the available resources and environmental behavior – the environment affects humans as much as humans affect the environment. In so many aspects of life, societies are vulnerable to even subtle environmental changes – some induced by nature and others by humans. Sometimes, violence disrupts the environment and the results may supply evidence of a premeditated intent to destroy its inhabitants. Regardless of whether the environment is used as a weapon, however, it always serves as a witness.

Far from being an alternative to the more established approaches to genocide studies, remote sensing is a scientific approach that relies on and must function in synergy with these other approaches. It can show proof of past and present violence, and it has the potential to provide warning signs of violence that may be impending. No amount of technology or proof will ever stop or punish violence in the absence of an international consensus and the necessary political will. But if such a consensus and will exist, remote sensing may aid significantly in future attempts to bring perpetrators of genocide and crimes against humanity to justice.

NOTES

1   P.J. Sellers, "Canopy Reflectance, Photosynthesis, and Transpiration," *International Journal of Remote Sensing*, 6 (1985), pp. 1335–1372; R.B. Myneni, F.G. Hall, P. J. Sellers, and A. L. Marshak, "The Interpretation of Spectral Vegetation Indexes," *IEEE Transactions on Geoscience and Remote Sensing*, 33 (1995), pp. 481–486.
2   See Humanitarian Information Unit (HIU)–US Department of State, *Sudan (Darfur)–Chad Border Region Confirmed Damaged and Destroyed Villages* (August 2004), http://www.usaid.gov/locations/sub-saharan_africa/countries/sudan/images/Darfur_Aug_2_villages.pdf; US Holocaust Memorial Museum, *Museum Mapping Initiative: Crisis in Darfur* (2007), accessed January 2011 at http://www.ushmm.org/maps/projects/darfur.
3   Cultural Survival, "Counterinsurgency and the Development Pole Strategy in Guatemala," *Cultural Survival Quarterly*, 12: 3 (1988), p. 11.
4   Comisión para el Esclarecimiento Histórico, *Memoria*, Vol. 10, cited in Victoria Sanford, *Buried Secrets: Truth and Human Rights in Guatemala* (New York: Palgrave Macmillan, 2003), p. 157.
5   Sanford, *Buried Secrets*, p. 122.
6   Ibid., p. 124.
7   Beatriz Manz, "The Case of the Ixil Triangle Development Pole," Chapter 4 in Beatriz Manz, *Refugees of a Hidden War: The Aftermath of Counterinsurgency in Guatemala* (Albany, NY: State University of New York Press, 1988), pp. 97–125.

8   Sanford, *Buried Secrets*, p. 137.

9   Ibid., p. 78.

10 Ibid., p. 87, 89.

11 Ibid., p. 93.

12 Ibid., pp. 100–101.

13 Beatriz Manz, *Refugees of a Hidden War*, pp. 97–125.

14 Sanford, *Buried Secrets*, p. 106.

15 Ibid., p. 116.

16 See Russell Schimmer, *Environmental Impact of Genocide in Guatemala: The Ixil Triangle and the Mexican Border* (GSP Working Paper No. 31, 2005), http://www.yale.edu/gsp/gis-files/ guatemala/Genocide_in_Guatemala_GSP_WorkingPaperNo.31.pdf.

17 Schimmer, *Environmental Impact of Genocide in Guatemala*.

18 Philip Verwimp, "Death and Survival during the 1994 Genocide in Rwanda," *Population Studies*, 58: 2 (2004), pp. 233–245.

19 Foundation Hirondelle, *Bisesero, The Hills of Death* (ICTR/Bisesero, June 2, 2003).

20 See Russell Schimmer, *Indications of Genocide in the Bisesero Hills, Rwanda, 1994* (GSP Working Paper No. 32, 2006), http://www.yale.edu/gsp/gis-files/rwanda/Indications _of_Genocide_in_the_Bisesero_Hills_Rwanda_1994_GSP_Working_Paper_No.32.pdf.

21 Ministère de L'Enseignement Supérieur, de la Réchèrche Scientifique et de la Culture, *Rwanda: Les Grands Sites du Génocide et des Massacres, Avril–Juillet 1994* (Paris, 1997).

22 International Criminal Tribunal for Rwanda, *Factual Findings: Massacres at Bisesero* (Case No.: ICTR-96-13, January 27, 2000), paragraphs 354–497.

23 Earth Trends Country Profiles, *Agriculture and Food Rwanda* (2003), http://earthtrends. wri.org.

24 James Waller, "The Invasion of Dili," in James Waller, *Becoming Evil: How Ordinary People Commit Genocide and Mass Killing* (New York: Oxford University Press, 2007), p. 133.

25 Matt Frei, "Dili: Back to Year Zero," (BBC World: Asia-Pacific, September 11, 1999).

26 Matt Frei, "Eyewitnesses Speak of Timor Devastation," BBC World, September 10, 1999.

27 See Russell Schimmer, *Violence by Fire in East Timor, September 8, 1999* (GSP Working Paper No. 33, 2006), http://www.yale.edu/gsp/gis-files/east-timor/Genocide_in_East_ Timor_GPS_ Working Paper No.33.pdf.

28 Frei, "Eyewitnesses."

29 Matt Frei, "Timor Refugees Return to Shattered Land," BBC World, September 27, 1999.

30 Matt Frei, "Killings and Rapes in Timor Enclave," BBC World, October 18, 1999.

31 Frei, "Timor Refugees Return."

32 UN High Commissioner for Human Rights, *Situation of Human Rights in the Darfur Region of the Sudan* (May 2004); Treena Hein, *Livestock for Survival in Sudan* (November 2007), http://www.new-ag.info/focus/focusItem.php?a=261.

33 See Julie Flint and Alex de Waal, *Darfur: A Short History of a Long War* (New York: Zed Books, 2005).

34 Hein, *Livestock for Survival in Sudan*.

35 International Committee of the Red Cross, *Food-Needs Assessment DARFUR* (Khartoum: Economic Security Unit, ICRC, October 2004), pp. 5–6.

36 United Nations Environment Programme, *Synthesis Report Sudan Post-Conflict: Environmental Assessment* (June 2007), p. 8, http://postconflict.unep.ch/publications/ UNEP_Sudan_synthesis_E.pdf.

37 Food and Agriculture Organisation of the United Nations in Collaboration with the North Darfur Veterinary Department, *North Darfur Livestock Coordination Workshop: Proceedings and Recommendations* (El Fashir, March, 2005), p. 3.

38 Hein, *Livestock for Survival in Sudan*.

39 Abdel Ghaffar M. Ahmed, Alemayehu Azeze, Mustafa Babiker and Diress Tsegaye, *Post Drought Recovery Strategies Among the Pastoral Households in the Horn of Africa: A Review* (OSSREA: Addis Ababa, 2002), p. 1, cited in Coalition for International Justice, *Soil and Oil: Dirty Business in Sudan* (Washington DC: Coalition for International Justice, February 2006), p. 62.

40 John Hagan and Wenona Rymond-Richmond, *Darfur and the Crime of Genocide* (New York: Cambridge University Press, 2009), p. 25.

41 Ibid., p. 24.

42 See Russell Schimmer, *Tracking the Genocide in Darfur: Population Displacement as Recorded by Remote Sensing* (Genocide Studies Working Paper No. 36, 2008), http://www.yale.edu/gsp/gis-files/darfur/Tracking_the_Genocide_in_Darfur_GSP_Working_Paper_No.36.pdf.

43 See http://siasglobal.com/darfur.html.

44 Roland A. Geerken, "An Algorithm to Classify Vegetation Phenologies and Coverage and Monitor their Inter-annual Change," *Journal of Photogrammetry and Remote Sensing*, 64: 4 (July 2009), pp. 422–431.

45 Food and Agriculture Organisation of the United Nations in Collaboration with the North Darfur Veterinary Department, pp. 3, 4, 6, and 8–9.

46 Southern African Regional Poverty Network (SARPN), "The Livestock Sector in The Darfur Crisis," Chapter 4 in *The Livestock Resource in Sudan* (2005), pp. 20, 34.

47 Hagan and Rymond-Richmond, "The Racial Spark," in *Darfur and the Crime of Genocide*, pp. 161–192; and "Global Shadows," in ibid., pp. 193–218.

48 http://siasglobal.com/darfur.html.

49 See Aylia Lincor, "Satellite Remote Sensing: Commercialization of Remote Sensing. Is the Use of Satellite Derived Information for Military Purposes in Violation of the Peaceful Purposes Provision of the Outer Space Treaty?" *ILSA Journal of International and Comparative Law*, 14 (2007), pp. 222–223.

50 See United States Holocaust Memorial Museum, accessed January 2011 at http://www.ushmm.org/maps/projects/darfur/; American Association for the Advancement of Science, accessed January 2011 at http://shr.aaas.org/geotech/darfur_2/negeha.shtml.

51 See http://hypercube.telascience.org/haiti.

52 See United States Holocaust Memorial Museum, *A Good Man in Hell: General Roméo Dallaire and the Rwanda Genocide*, Videocassette (Committee on Conscience/United States Holocaust Memorial Museum, 2003).

53 Rome Statute of the International Criminal Court, Part 2: Jurisdiction, Admissibility and Applicable Law, Article 5, § 1(a) (1998).

54 Ibid., Article 5, § 1(b).

55 Ibid., Article 6.

56 Ibid., Article 7, § 1.

57 United Nations Treaties and Principles on Outer Space, Principles Relating to Remote Sensing of the Earth from Outer Space, Annex, Principle II, A/RES/41/65, accessed January 2011 at http://www.oosa.unvienna.org/oosa/en/SpaceLaw/gares/html/gares_41_0065.html.

58 Joanne Irene Gabrynowicz, "The Perils of Landsat from Grassroots to Globalization: A Comprehensive Review of US Remote Sensing Law with a Few Thoughts for the Future," *Chicago Journal of International Law*, 45 (Summer 2005), p. 51.

59 Ibid.

60 Ronald J. Rychlak, Joanne Irene Gabrynowicz, and Rick Crowsey, "Legal Certification of Digital Data: The Earth Resources Observation and Science Data Center Project," *Journal of Space Law*, 33: 1 (2007), p. 197.

61 Ibid.

62 Federal Rules of Evidence, Article IX: Authentication and Identification, Rule 901(b)(9), http://www.law.cornell.edu/rules/fre/rules.htm.

63 Rychlak, Gabrynowicz, and Crowsey, "Legal Certification of Digital Data," p .207.

64 Ibid., pp. 200–201.

65 International Criminal Court Rules of Procedure and Evidence, Chapter 5: Investigation and Prosecution, Section I, Rule 104(2) (adopted by the Assembly of States Parties, First session, New York, 3–10 September 2002).

66 Ibid., Chapter 4, Provisions Relating to Various Stages of the Proceedings: Section IV, Rule 103(1).

Figure 8.1 Young boy in poor neighborhood of Coptic Christian quarter, Cairo, Egypt, 1989.

Source: Adam Jones.

CHAPTER 8

Genocide and Structural Violence

Charting the terrain

Adam Jones

INTRODUCTION

Jean Ziegler, the UN Special Rapporteur on the Right to Food, has a distinctive perspective on mass murder.

By Ziegler's estimate, one hundred thousand people die worldwide *daily* from starvation – more than thirty times as many people as died in Al-Qaeda's attacks on US cities on September 11, 2001. Ziegler describes this as a "massacre of human beings through malnutrition," and has stated: "Every child who dies of hunger in today's world is the victim of assassination."[1] Nor does he balk at identifying the actual or potential "assassins." He has denounced the initiative by the World Trade Organization (WTO) to render "food aid, especially that distributed by the United Nations . . . subject to certain rules in order to avoid any distortion of commercial markets."

Ziegler's comments, like the millions of victims of starvation every year, have passed almost unnoticed. His claims that the victims of such processes do not passively "die" but are actively murdered, and that victims of WTO trade policy are "wittingly condemned to starve to death," sit poorly with most commentary on human rights and mass crimes. Do they, in fact, have substance? Is human agency central to such large-scale mortality? Can such cases of structural suffering and mortality qualify as mass atrocities? If so, to what extent, and under what circumstances, might they be considered genocidal? And which strategies of intervention and prevention may be available?

STRUCTURAL VIOLENCE AND THE GENOCIDAL CONTINUUM

In the 1970s, Norwegian peace researcher Johan Galtung initiated the study of structural violence. He defined violence in general

> as the *avoidable impairment of fundamental human needs* or, to put it in more general terms, the impairment of human *life*, which lowers the actual degree to which someone is able to meet their needs below that which would otherwise be *possible*.[2]

Galtung described structural violence as indirect, distinct from "*personal* or *direct*" violence "at the hands of an *actor* who *intends* this to be the consequence." "Can we talk about violence," he asked, "when nobody is committing direct violence, is acting?"[3] His answer was yes: certain *inherently violent* structures had become so reified that "no personal violence or threat of personal violence is needed." Galtung cited, for example, "the typical feudal structure," which "is clearly structurally violent regardless of who staffs it and regardless of the level of awareness of the participants." But he also acknowledged that structures influenced individuals to commit direct, personal violence:

> These important perspectives are regained if a person is seen as making his decision to act violently not only on the basis of individual deliberations but (also) on the basis of expectations impinging on him as norms contained in roles contained in statuses through which he enacts his social self; *and*, if one sees a violent structure as something that is a mere abstraction unless upheld by the actions, expected from the social environment or not, of individuals. . . . The distinction that nevertheless remains is between violence that hits human beings as a *direct* result of . . . actions of others, and violence that hits them *indirectly* because repressive structures . . . are upheld by the summated and concerted action of human beings . . . The question is . . . whether violence is structured in such a way that it constitutes a direct, personal link between a subject and an object, or an indirect structural one, not how this link is perceived by the persons at either end of the violence channel.[4]

In accordance with the broad thrust of Galtung's argument, I contend that:

(a) structures and institutions, by definition, are created and perpetuated by the collective actions and agency of human beings;[5]

(b) as "background" features of social relations, structures and institutions influence individual actions, whether conscious or unconscious;

(c) *all* violence is the product of human agency; and

(d) such agency therefore underpins "structural violence," by maintaining the structures and institutions that channel and facilitate violence.

These formulations are consistent with other scholars' explorations of structural and institutional violence; for instance, Steven Lee's exploration of the question, "Is Poverty Violence?" Lee writes:

Poverty results in a whole range of serious physical and psychological harms: higher risks of disease, shortened life spans, stunted mental and emotional development, and inadequate opportunity to lead a meaningful life. These are primarily institutionally imposed harms, because they are the result of the enforcement of systems of social, political, legal, and economical [*sic*] rules. But, though the harms are institutional, they are caused by individuals, in the sense that the acts of other individuals could avoid them. It is individuals who enforce the unjust legal norms of the social order and refrain from seeking to change these norms to achieve a fairer redistribution of wealth and power.[6]

An important feature of the violence that human agency produces when supported by ideological structures and institutions is that violent outcomes arrive by a more indirect route than the direct, highly personal actions we standardly label as "violent." This is true in both a temporal and an empirical sense. Structural and institutional forms of violence tend to be inflicted more slowly, often through gradual impoverishment and debilitation. They also tend to result from human actions and decisions, *the proximate purpose of which is other than to cause death or debilitation*; these consequences may be incidental or even accidental, rather than integral to the purposive project. To cite an example, industrial pollution may be seen as a form of structural and institutional violence, in that it is: (1) an outgrowth of a human institution (industrialism), embedded in pervasive, enduring economic and social structures; and (2) objectively harmful to human life and health. However, pollution is not released in order to damage human beings and the ecosystem that sustains them. It is released as part of the pursuit of profit, or of personal utility, or even accidentally (as with a toxic chemical spill). Likewise, the looting of state assets and resources through corruption does not have the purpose of creating social conditions that result in mass immiseration and rising mortality: its perpetrators simply aim at self-enrichment. None of this, however, means that the death and debility linked to institutionalized corruption are unintentional – motive and intent are conceptually distinct, as I explore next.

STRUCTURAL VIOLENCE AND GENOCIDAL INTENT

With Nancy Scheper-Hughes, we can point to a *continuum* of structural and institutional violence:[7] from less to more destructive; from less to more empirically manifest; from less to more traceable to the actions of individual human agents. To the extent that structural and institutional violence is more amorphous and diffuse, it is less amenable to a genocide framing, in which intentional human agency is central. To the extent that it is more manifest and direct, it may be more amenable to such a framing – and to interventions and attempts at amelioration based upon that framing.

The language of "intent to destroy" in Articles 2(b), (d), and (e) of the UN Genocide Convention suggests that group destruction can be accomplished by means other than physical killing. For the purposes of this chapter, I limit the application of 2(b) to serious physical debility (i.e. setting aside the question of "mental harm"), and exclude 2(d) and (e) entirely. This is not because these strategies are necessarily less central to the Convention definition – although genocide in the absence of killing has failed to arouse much in the way of outrage and intervention – but because it is harder to tie structural and institutional violence to outright "killing," "physical destruction," and "serious bodily" harm. If such a link can be made credibly, then most would probably accept that it can also be made with regard to "mental harm," or "imposing measures intended to prevent births within the group." (I am not sure about 2(e), "forcibly transferring children.")

Summarizing the recent finding of the Akayesu trial chamber of the International Criminal Tribunal for Rwanda (ICTR) in his study *The Genocide Convention: An International Law Analysis*, John Quigley wrote: "If an actor does violence to immediate victims, understanding that thereby harm is brought to the group, or even having reason to know that harm is thereby brought to the group, the elements of genocide would seem to be satisfied."[8] *Even "wilful blindness"* may suffice to demonstrate genocidal intent, referring to "a situation in which an actor lacks actual knowledge but is aware of a high probability of the existence of a fact and fails to inquire into circumstances that would have made him aware of the existence of the fact." The tribunals find it a fair reading of Article 2 to include persons who do not have actual knowledge of the consequences, but who should, on the basis of facts they knew, have understood the consequences.[9]

Quigley even touches upon the theme of structural and institutional violence in the context of massive mortality inflicted by environmental degradation:

> One can imagine situations of potential environmental harm that could constitute genocide if the culpability standard requires less than a purpose to bring about a result. Allowing a nuclear generator to operate in the face of knowledge that it is emitting radioactive material to the surrounding area might be taken as evidence of an intent to destroy a group.[10]

What seems important in determining the degree of genocidal intent is whether a reasonably short causal chain exists; the destruction wreaked is readily apparent; and the evidence shows that actors were aware of the impact of their policies and decisions, or should have been. I return to these elements in the closing section of the chapter.

CASES (1): A BRIEF SUMMARY

What unites the exceedingly diverse phenomena examined in this section? First, all have resulted, or (in the case of global warming) may well result, in large-scale human suffering and mortality. Second, all have been denounced, often repeatedly, by public commentators employing the language and framework of genocide and/or mass human-rights atrocity. Third, all have been linked to underlying social, political, and economic *structures*, and to *institutions* in both the broader (ideological) and narrower (formal/ bureaucratic) sense. Fourth, none constitutes a discrete "event" of the kind normally examined in genocide studies; they are instead *processes*, *aspects*, *features* – that is, phenomena both more amorphous and usually more enduring than "events."

Global poverty and inequality

Despite considerable advances on a number of fronts, the death toll inflicted by the core structural inequalities in the international system continues to be incomprehensibly large – and almost invisible. In his article "Structural Violence as a Form of Genocide," Nafeez Mosaddeq Ahmed writes that "the international economic order's systematic generation of human insecurity . . . has led to the deaths of countless hundreds of millions of people, and the deprivation of thousands of millions of others."[11] The UN's Food and Agriculture Organization (FAO) contends that "nearly six million children die each year as a result of hunger or malnutrition."[12] A global economic crisis, such as the one that descended worldwide in 2008, "will condemn 53 million more people to extreme poverty and contribute to 1.2 million child deaths" in the half-decade that follows, according to the World Bank and the International Monetary Fund (IMF). The same authorities estimate that "more than a billion people, or one in six people on the planet, are still struggling to meet basic food needs, leading to increased instances of disease – and ultimately death – in young children and pregnant women," with "1.2 million children . . . likely to die between 2009 and 2015 as a result . . ."[13]

S.P. Udayakumar's 1995 essay for *Futures*, "The Futures of the Poor," coined the terms "structural genocide" and "poorcide" to describe a global assault by the privileged upon the poor. His essay included a section, "Poverty is Genocide," that merits extended quotation:

> Although race, ethnicity, gender, generation and political powerlessness all contribute considerably to poverty, the "economic worth" factor forms the basis in "poorcide," the genocide of the poor. It is an economic group (or class) who [is] discriminated against in poorcide. A particular group of people is massacred in genocide, but poverty kills indiscriminately, irrespective of the group identity.
>
> Genocide just kills you, but poverty tortures you and condemns you to a slow and painful death. . . . Genocide prompts physical elimination, but poverty causes physical pain, mental agony, moral degradation and spiritual dissipation. Extending the analysis of physical violence and structural violence to genocide, we can distinguish between direct and indirect, or physical and structural, genocide. Genocide means not just massive killing (which we can call direct or physical genocide) but also includes calculated attacks on and constant efforts at undermining the basic human dignity and life-support systems of a particular group of people (which may be described as the indirect or structural genocide). Poorcide may not be actual physical elimination of the poor [on] a massive scale, but it is a slow-pace[d] silent holocaust.[14]

Udayakumar's focus on Article 2(c) of the Genocide Convention, i.e., "calculated attacks on and constant efforts at undermining the basic human dignity and life-support systems of a particular group of people," seems especially relevant to our analysis of structural and institutional genocide. Article 2(c) focuses on the kind of indirect, but intentional and "calculated," infliction of debility and death which scholars of structural violence from Johan Galtung to Udayakumar and Paul Farmer have emphasized.[15]

Debt crisis in the South

In *The Collapse of Globalism*, John Ralston Saul describes "the Third World debt crisis [now] stretching on toward the end of its third decade" as an example of "crucifixion economics" inflicted on poor countries. "The debt is unpayable, unserviceable, of no use to a stable free market or to the debtors." Respect for it, Saul writes, "must unfortunately trump disease, suffering and social order."[16]

According to some observers, the surplus mortality that can be linked to ruinous debt payments, often exceeding 20 percent of a country's gross domestic product, is of holocaust proportions.[17] Jeffrey D. Sachs, an economist who previously urged "stabilization" programs on economically vulnerable governments, more recently has emphasized the destructive impact of prioritizing macroeconomic stability over subsistence needs. Writing in August 2005, he argued that "these policies have left [made?] hundreds of millions of people even more desperately poor and hungry. Millions die each year, either of outright starvation or from infectious diseases that their weakened bodies cannot withstand . . ."[18]

"Austerity programs" and privatization measures

"Just as war can be a form of politics carried on by other means, so can genocide represent economic policy carried out by means of mass murder."[19] So writes Hannibal Travis, one of the brightest of the new generation of genocide scholars.

The requirement that poor countries service their debt is an essential element of the austerity programs and "structural adjustment" policies imposed upon Southern economies, especially in the 1980s and 1990s, as a condition for loans and other aid. Such programs, also referred to as "shock therapy," "call for nations to deregulate their economies, by opening up to international investment, privatize services, lowering labor and environmental standards, and use a significant portion of government funds to service their debt."[20] Such "sado-monetarism"[21] (in Gerard Baker's memorable phrase) likely reached its zenith – or, rather, its nadir – in post-communist Russia under the government of Boris Yeltsin. Nothing less than "the wholesale, complete replacement" of Soviet institutions by "an alternative, market-based system," would suffice.[22] By 2006, *The Los Angeles Times* was reporting that "the end of the Soviet healthcare system and the debut of free-market medicine have added to the slide":

> In the new Russia, millions are born sick. Many succumb to poisons in the air and water around them, or are slowly killed by alcohol, cigarettes or stress. Most are too poor to buy back their health. The overwhelmed healthcare system can't help much. Although medical care still is nominally free, in practice all but the most basic services are available only to those able to pay hefty fees . . . The Scientific Center of Children's Health, a branch of the Russian Academy of Medical Sciences, estimates that 45% of Russian children are born with "health deviations," including problems of the central nervous system, faulty hearts, malformed urinary tracts and low birth weight.[23]

A *Lancet* study published in 2009 found that "rapid mass privatization as an economic transition strategy was a crucial determinant of differences in adult mortality trends in post-Communist societies," with its effects "reduced if social capital was high" (and sharpened where it was low). According to the report, "only a little over half of the ex-Communist countries have regained their pretransition life-expectancy levels."[24] Russia specialist Stephen F. Cohen of Princeton, one of the leading critics of the "structural adjustment" measures inflicted on post-Soviet Russia, has estimated the death toll exacted by the "nihilistic zealotry" of proponents of "savage capitalism" as in the *tens of millions* ("the lost lives of perhaps 100 million Russians seem not to matter . . .").[25] "I don't think . . . it is unfair," stated Russian commentator Aleksander Prokhanov, "to call it genocide."[26]

Maternal mortality

The global plague of maternal mortality inflicts approximately half a million deaths a year, frequently in agony paralleling that of the worst tortures. The non-governmental organization that I co-founded, Gendercide Watch, declares itself "skeptical of including individual-level killings, let alone 'agentless' ones, under the rubric of 'gendercide,'" and hence of genocide. Nonetheless, the broader framing of genocidal intention that has come to predominate in international case-law, in which "reckless disregard" and "wilful blindness" can qualify as genocidal, can be "'gendered' to encompass the institutional discrimination, leading to physical victimization, that occurs on a massive scale with maternal mortality in the underdeveloped world." I alleged that "those primarily responsible" for the mass mortality

> are the governments and ruling elites who can always find money for weapons, but only rarely for hospitals and clinics and midwives; who systematically deny other resources (educational, legal, contraceptive) to women; and who thereby deny them rights that every human being should have to control their bodies and their destinies. The failure of the developed world to contribute meaningfully to the development of the poorer countries is [also] obviously an important factor.[27]

AIDS in the Global South

"By some estimates," according to Edward O'Neil Jr., "AIDS will claim more lives by the year 2025 than the total of lives lost in all of humanity's wars since the first century."[28] Both state and nonstate actors have been accused of complicity in the massive excess mortality afflicting the African continent, and elsewhere, in the age of HIV/AIDS. The accusation that this is tantamount to genocide and/or crimes against humanity has regularly featured. Especially outspoken on this count has been Stephen Lewis, the UN Special Envoy for HIV/AIDS in Africa, who denounced "those who watch [the epidemic] unfold with a kind of pathological equanimity," and demanded they be held to account: "There may yet come a day when we have peacetime tribunals to deal with this particular version of crimes against humanity."[29]

While the world's wealthiest countries, and particularly pharmaceutical companies,[30] have come in for their share of condemnation, the most vitriolic denunciations have been reserved for a government in the developing world: the South African regime under President Thabo Mbeki. The Mbeki government's "disastrous and pseudo-scientific" health policy had resulted in "many people . . . dying unnecessarily," according to an open letter issued by sixty experts in September 2006.[31] Richard Branson, the British mogul, went a step further in ceremonies commemorating the opening of a health center he had funded in a South African township. He declared (in a media outlet's paraphrase) that government inaction "is killing thousands of its own people"; "this government is not doing enough . . . [and] the little that they are doing could be seen as genocide."[32]

Climate change and global warming

A strong scientific consensus now exists that human activity – notably the burning of fossil fuels – is decisively altering the global climate, resulting in average temperature increases not seen for thousands of years. The implications are profound for animal species,[33] including human beings. As early as 2001, the Canadian Broadcasting Corporation cited estimates that "global warming may have killed between 50,000 and 100,000 people in the past three years and made up to 300 million people homeless."[34] In 2006, the non-governmental organization Christian Aid concluded that:

> climate change will devastate poor countries. [The group] estimates that up to 182 million people in sub-Saharan Africa could die of diseases directly attributable to climate change by the end of the century. Many millions more people throughout the world face death, disease and penury if nothing is done . . .[35]

According to Andrew Pendleton of Christian Aid, "Knowing what we know, if we don't respond, we're committing a very serious crime . . . It would be the climate change version of Rwanda,"[36] "a death sentence for many millions of people."[37] The renowned genocide scholar Mark Levene in the UK supplied his endorsement, and that of the Crisis Forum he co-founded, for a conference in which a looming "environmental genocide" was denounced.[38]

Corruption and stripping of state resources

What is one to make of countries where a regime, or a series of regimes, have effectively stripped the country of resources that could have brought enormous benefits to a society, leaving the population in penury and facing malnutrition and early death? On its face, this would seem to meet the UN Convention definition of genocide as including the infliction of conditions "calculated" to destroy a national group. Nuhu Ribadu, a Nigerian anti-corruption activist, estimates that successive Nigerian kleptocracies have stolen or squandered in excess of US$380 billion since the country achieved independence in 1960.[39] A more severe, or at least more intensive, example of out-of-control looting and stripping of state assets is Zimbabwe under the regime of President Robert Mugabe. In a critique published in *The Sunday Times* in January 2007, R.W. Johnson described a system not only of pervasive political persecution, but of "general economic meltdown"; a "health system [that] has collapsed"; and "a populace now weakened by five consecutive years of near-starvation." "A vast human cull is under way in Zimbabwe," Johnson alleged:

> it is a genocide perhaps 10 times greater than Darfur's and more than twice as large as Rwanda's . . . Genocide is not a word one should use hastily, but the situation is exactly as described in the UN Convention on Genocide, which defines it as "deliberately inflicting on the group conditions of life calculated to bring about its physical destruction in whole or in part" . . . Mugabe . . . [has] already been responsible for far more deaths than Rwanda suffered and the number is fast heading into realms previously explored only by Stalin, Mao and Adolf Eichmann.[40]

David Coltart, a member of Zimbabwe's opposition Movement for Democratic Change, claimed that "Zimbabwe has the lowest life expectancy in the world: 34 for women and 37 for men," and that Mugabe's tyranny had rendered him culpable for the country's structural collapse. "To use a legal term, I would say this amounts to genocide with constructive intent. In terms of a complete disregard for the plight of people, not caring whether there is wholesale loss of life, it amounts to genocide."[41]

Economic sanctions and embargo

The structural dislocation associated with punitive economic actions, and the mass mortality allegedly caused by them, have hovered at the margins of comparative genocide studies since the beginning of the 1990s. It was at that point that the United Nations Security Council, led by the United States and Great Britain, imposed sanctions on Iraq as punishment for its May 1990 invasion of neighboring Kuwait. The destruction of civilian infrastructure caused by the ensuing Gulf War "wrought near apocalyptic results on the economic infrastructure" of Iraq, in the estimation of a March 1991 UN report. The mixture of sanctions and war had returned Iraq to a "pre-industrial age but with all the disabilities of post-industrial dependency on an intensive use of energy and technology."[42] The 1996 International Court on Crimes Against Humanity Committed by the UN Security Council on [*sic*] Iraq, headed by former US Attorney General Ramsey Clark, charged and found that:

> The United States, its President Bill Clinton and other officials, the United Kingdom and its Prime Minister John Major and other officials have committed genocide as defined in the Convention against Genocide against the population of Iraq including genocide by starvation and sickness through use of sanctions as a weapon of mass destruction . . .[43]

In December 1996, after more than five years of unparalleled privation, the "Oil for Food" program was established, ostensibly to alleviate the worst of the damage caused by sanctions, to allow the Iraqi regime to purchase essentials for the population through carefully-managed oil sales and disbursements of revenue. However, two successive overseers of the program resigned, and *both* subsequently adopted the framing and vocabulary of genocide to denounce what was occurring under the sanctions regime.[44] In her 2010 treatment, *Invisible War: The United States and the Iraq Sanctions*, Joy Gordon stated her belief "that the sanctions on Iraq [do not] constitute genocide or crimes against humanity, as these are defined in international law"; but contended that if understandings of genocidal intent could be expanded to place greater emphasis on *general* rather than *specific* intent, the term would be apt:

> Under this standard, it is clear that dozens of U.S. officials had the necessary intent and knowledge to be found criminally responsible under the Rome Statute, were there a prosecution . . . There is a terrible and obvious cost to using the higher level of [specific] intent that the Genocide Convention and the Rome Statute require for genocide and crimes against humanity, rather than the general intent standard . . . It may be that the specific intent requirement does not provide the means to punish genocidal murderers in general, but only tactically inept ones.[45]

Dumping of hazardous waste

When toxic wastes and poisonous products or by-products are dumped into an ecosystem, in the knowledge that they will cause widespread death and debilitation – or when such consequences are likely and should be seen to be likely – can a genocide framework be useful? Among the high-profile cases in recent decades are:

- The death and deformity caused by "a historically unprecedented level of chemical warfare," namely "the indiscriminate spraying of nearly 20 million gallons [of herbicides] on one-seventh the area of South Vietnam" during the Vietnam War. The devastating human impact of the chemical "Agent Orange," produced by Dow Chemical and other US-based corporations, was the subject of a legal claim for genocide filed in US courts. In the words of the judgment:

  > It is contended that the acts against plaintiffs constitute genocide, in violation of customary international law which prohibits the following acts committed with intent to destroy, in whole or in part, a national, ethnic, racial or religious group, as such: killing members of the group; causing serious bodily or mental harm to members of the group; deliberately inflicting on the group conditions of life calculated to bring about its physical destruction in whole or in part; or imposing measures intended to prevent births within the group.[46]

- The explosive growth of cancer rates in China in recent years – the disease is now the leading cause of death – has been persuasively tied to the country's extraordinary economic transformations and pell-mell industrialization over the past two decades. According to a detailed 2010 report by Lee Liu, published in *Environment*, "China appears to have produced more cancer clusters in a few decades than the rest of the world ever has," the result of the country's "'grow first and clean up later'" approach to development, which led to an acceleration of environmental pollution and serious environmental health problems. The result is the so-called "cancer-village phenomenon," which is likely to worsen in the future, partly because the health impact of environmental pollution tends to be long-lasting . . . The poor, such as the cancer villagers, will remain poor or may get even poorer . . . What does development mean to these villages? . . . Pollution causes diseases that lead to absolute poverty and death.[47]

CASES (2): PARAMETERS OF EVALUATION

What are the conditions under which it is reasonable to contend that a structural and institutional form of violence is genocidal? I point to three main factors:

- *Convincing evidence of severe, large-scale debility and/or premature death.* In the absence of serious harm of the type mentioned in Article 2(b) of the Genocide Convention – especially physical harm, and especially life-threatening physical harm – an allegation of genocide is less likely to prompt recognition and intervention.
- *A reasonably short and direct causal chain, traceable to identifiable actors.* In order for a genocide framework to be preferred in instances of structural violence, it is important to establish a reasonably clear connection between human agency/actions and possibly genocidal outcomes. Although diffuse/collective agency does not rule out an allegation of genocide, it is certainly the case – given the Genocide Convention's emphasis on individual responsibility – that allegations made against more easily identifiable agents, acting in a more direct and calculated fashion, are more likely to persuade a tribunal of their soundness.
- Related to both of the above factors is *actors' evidence of awareness of the impact of policies and decisions*; or a failure to seek or acknowledge such an awareness that is so egregious as to amount to negligence. Where strong evidence exists and the causal chain is reasonably direct, a perpetrator's responsibility and liability are more firmly established. Consider a standard aspect of structural-adjustment measures: so-called "shock therapy." This euphemism, *employed by those imposing it* as well as by critics, recognizes that at least in the short-to-medium term, the socioeconomic impact will inflict a shock, defined by the *Concise Oxford Dictionary* as a "violent collision, concussion, or impact" and a "great disturbance of organization or system"; it adapts a psychological treatment strategy based on "inducing coma or convulsions." It is not merely the case that the policies are imposed in the reasonable expectation that they will inflict a severe shock, which is all that would be required to demonstrate *mens rea* and, thus, intent; in fact, they are explicitly *designed* to inflict a "great disturbance of organization or system" (thus motive and purpose). Where actors are aware or should have been, but fail to heed or respond adequately to available evidence, they may also be genocidally culpable. "If you have evidence your inaction is responsible for millions of deaths, you promise to correct that situation, then you fail to deliver, what do you call that?" asked Julio Montaner in the context of the AIDS crisis. "It's not ignorance. It's not mere negligence. It's more than a crime against humanity. It can only be characterized as genocide."[48]

Beyond these empirical issues, we need to distinguish between forms of structural violence in which *a greater or lesser degree of voluntary agency* is evident among those apparently victimized by the phenomenon in question. For example – to cite a case that I have not explored in this chapter – how are we to evaluate the role of tobacco companies? On one hand, the product they sell kills tens of millions of people every year – possibly more than any of the phenomena considered in this chapter, with the exception of global poverty. Extensive evidence also suggests that the companies are fully aware of the dangers of the product they sell, and have often employed deception to downplay those dangers. Nonetheless, the destruction wreaked by tobacco-related illness is also closely tied to the independent agency of the consumers, and, since tobacco dependence and addiction can be voluntarily broken (I personally did so on January 1, 2010), to their voluntary decisions to keep purchasing and consuming the product.[49]

On the basis of these criteria, which of the cases examined here appear to be more amenable to a comparative-genocide framing, and intervention strategies derived from it? Which are less amenable? See Table 8.1.

The "ideal case" of a clear responsibility for genocide in cases of structural/institutional violence would thus be found where the evidence in Table 8.1 in column (1) is high, the causal chain and agency in column (2) are short, direct, and centralized/individualized, the actors' awareness (*mens rea*, column (3)) is high, and victims' agency in column (4) is low. Only one case on our list is "ideal" in this respect: that of the Iraq sanctions and economic embargo. There would appear to be very strong support for a charge of genocide in this instance.

Table 8.1 Evaluation of cases of structural/institutional violence

Event/Process	(1) Evidence of debility and death as result of event/phenomenon (high, moderate, low)	(2) Causal chain (direct/indirect); agency (centralized–individualized/decentralized–diffuse)	(3) Actors' awareness (high, moderate, low) of policies' destructive impact	(4) Degree of agency/voluntarism among victims
Global poverty and inequality	High	Indirect/decentralized–diffuse	Moderate	Low
Global debt crisis	Moderate	Direct/centralized–individualized	High	Low
Austerity programs and privatization measures	Moderate	Direct/centralized–individualized	High	Low
Maternal mortality	High	Indirect/decentralized–diffuse	Low	Low
AIDS in the developing world	High	Direct/centralized–individualized	Moderate	Through transfusion: low Through sexual transmission: moderate
Corruption and stripping of state resources	Moderate	Indirect/centralized–individualized	Low–moderate	Low–moderate
Iraq sanctions and embargo	High	Direct/centralized–individualized	High	Low
Dumping of hazardous waste	Moderate	Direct/centralized–individualized	High	Low

In other cases, where requisites (2), (3), and (4) are satisfied, there would appear to be a strong case for a charge of genocide. Thus, with regard to the global debt crisis, transmission of AIDS by blood transfusion, austerity programs and privatization measures, and dumping of hazardous waste, support for an allegation of genocide appears moderate to strong. At least, this would be true *at times*; all of these phenomena are of an "umbrella" character, and responsibility for genocide could be more readily demonstrated in some instances than in others.

In several cases (global poverty and inequality, maternal mortality, corruption, AIDS through sexual transmission), powerful obstacles appear to impede a persuasive charge of genocide – at least to the extent that such a charge is to be directed against a limited set of identifiable actors. Evidence may be lacking of debility and death *resulting reasonably directly* from the event or phenomenon at hand. Responsibility and agency may be highly decentralized or diffuse. Evidence of actors' awareness of the damage their policies are apparently causing may be lacking. Some victim agency may be present, even decisive in the equation. However, in my view, this does not entirely rule out a deployment of a genocide framework. For example, it may be quite legitimate to refer to the huge mortality inflicted by global poverty and inequality as "genocidal," even though, in a real sense, most of us in the Global North – and a good number of those in the Global South – share responsibility for perpetuating unequal and poverty-producing structures and institutions.

STRATEGIES OF INTERVENTION AND PREVENTION

In 2001, the International Commission on Intervention and State Sovereignty (ICISS) released its report, *The Responsibility to Protect*, which immediately became a *cause célèbre* among proponents of a more vigorous interventionist stance in the face of mass atrocity. The commission's members declared that, in their view,

> military intervention for human protection purposes is justified in two broad sets of circumstances, namely in order to halt or avert:
>
> - *large scale loss of life, actual or apprehended, with genocidal intent or not, which is the product either of deliberate state action, or state neglect or inability to act, or a failed state situation; or*
> - *large scale "ethnic cleansing," actual or apprehended, whether carried out by killing, forced expulsion, acts of terror or rape.*[50]

Upon reading the statement of the first "broad set of circumstances," my mind leapt in a perhaps unexpected direction: to the phenomenon of *maternal mortality*. Here we clearly have a case of "large scale loss of life," "actual" in the sense that it produces hundreds of thousands of female deaths annually, and enormous attendant suffering. Maternal death on this scale is at the very least a product of "state neglect or inability to act." The majority of such deaths occur in the poorer states of the "Third World." Most of these states could readily devote resources that they currently squander, for example, on high-tech weaponry, to establishing the institutions and mechanisms that would reduce maternal mortality to First World levels or below. Cuba, for example, has done so.[51] For those unable to generate the necessary resources and expertise, transfers of resources from the First World could readily fill the gap.

As the ICISS emphasized, "genocidal intent" need not be present in order to trigger military intervention. But as it happens, a case for such intent could easily be made. Drawing upon the arguments advanced in John Quigley's reading of the case-law spawned by the UN Genocide Convention, the "reckless disregard" and "wilful blind-ness" that underpin maternal mortality worldwide could qualify as genocidal.

My purpose in making this argument is not to call for military intervention and the trampling of state sovereignty in order to address the crisis of maternal mortality. Rather, I question the readiness with which we, like the ICISS commissioners, leap to a defini-tion of "broad . . . circumstances" that centers on the notion of *event-based* humanitarian emergencies, rather than *process-based* or *institutional* ones. The commission was driven by the discrete and time-bound developments in Bosnia, Kosovo, East Timor, and elsewhere during the 1990s. There is no mention anywhere in its text of structural emergencies.

The ICISS constructs "intervention" broadly. It includes not only (or principally) military intervention, but emphasizes as well "political, economic and judicial measures." One can imagine a range of such measures being instituted to address maternal mortality and other forms of structural violence. On the judicial front, for example, a simple assertion and activation of the basic subsistence rights guaranteed under the Universal Declaration of Human Rights could radically transform the prevailing language of human rights. This has concentrated, for most practical purposes, on direct violence by state agents and others. What other "political" and "economic" measures might be required to intervene effectively in structural violence? These are very much open to discussion and debate; but the debate cannot occur unless the question is first raised, and a persuasive case made that it should be taken seriously.

With regard to *intervention through legal mechanisms and systems*, one should first ask what is the likelihood and viability of bringing charges against the alleged perpetrators. As the case-law of genocide has evolved, the formidable challenges to making a charge of genocide stick in the courts have become more evident. Even in more clear-cut cases of individual responsibility for mass murder of members of a sharply-defined group, the difficulty of securing a verdict of genocide has resulted in other prosecutorial strategies being preferred – such as bringing charges of *complicity* in genocide and, most commonly, of war crimes and/or crimes against humanity. The difficulty of widening the legal framing of genocide to address adequately, for example, malfeasance by multi-national corporations or international organizations does not seem insurmountable. But it is unlikely to generate positive outcomes proportionate to the enormous investment of energy required.

It is likely, in my view, that the best use of a genocide framework is as a political and rhetorical instrument, to *denounce and shame alleged perpetrators*. It could, in fact, be a powerful tool in *mobilizing popular movements* to confront structural and institutional atrocities. Where interventions through publicity campaigns and demonstrations fail to generate results, direct action, notably peaceful civil disobedience, can be tried.

What of *strategies of violent resistance*? In extreme cases, these may be justified. Consider the case of Freeport's Grasberg gold mine in Papua New Guinea, which has apparently bought the complicity of Indonesian government officials in order to undertake operations that are projected to result in the dumping of "*six billion tons of waste*," much of it "into what was once a pristine river system."[52] Do downstream populations have the right not only to protest, petition, and launch legal proceedings, but if this fails, to conduct acts of sabotage against mining operations – destroying material plant, say, or seizing and sequestering mine officials and administrators? Such tactics have been adopted by rebel groups among the Ogoni people of Nigeria, to confront Shell Oil's rampant destruction of their Niger Delta territories.[53] Since both the state and the oil company have refused to stage an effective intervention in the pattern of ecocidal – and arguably genocidal – destruction, it seems hard to gainsay such measures. However, it seems reasonable to argue that a strategy of violent resistance should only be adopted in the most extreme cases: where definable actors are demonstrably responsible for the structural and institutional violence in question; and where permanent injury to human beings can be avoided.

A substantial redistribution of wealth, both within and between societies, seems central to interventions in structural violence. In addition to "internal redistributions," writes Henry Shue:

> The only feasible source of the amounts now needed . . . are transfers from the countries that are now wealthy . . . One can responsibly acknowledge subsistence rights, including duties to aid, only if one is willing to support, where necessary, substantial transfers of wealth or resources to those who cannot provide for their own subsistence and willing to support any structural changes necessary nationally and internationally to make those transfers possible.[54]

At the very least, the prevailing pattern, *under which transfers of wealth are massively greater from poor countries to rich ones than vice versa*, must be abandoned. According to Linda McQuaig, from 1982 to 1999, "a net transfer of $1.5 *trillion* from South to North" occurred.[55] Forgiveness of the debts of highly-indebted countries, tied perhaps to increases in the provision of services and development of social-oriented infrastructure, is indispensable.

Attention to structural and institutional forms of violence also encourages a shift away from the state-centric orientation that has long reigned in comparative genocide studies. States do, probably, remain the primary actors, given the power they exert not only directly vis-à-vis their domestic populations, but collectively through the international (inter-state) organizations they comprise. But other institutional actors – notably international organizations as distinct bureaucratic bodies; corporate entities, both national and multinational; and "third-party states" indirectly complicit in atrocities – also figure prominently in the equation.

Another important aspect of a focus on structural and institutional violence is that it forces us to confront the *collective agency* often required to inflict it. Each of us is duty-bound to examine the institutions and structural arrangements in which we participate, many of which we are born into; to determine the extent to which they are violent, even genocidal; to understand how we act, in concert with others, to buttress and perpetuate them; and to consider *how we can and should act*, again alongside others, to impede and erode them. This is particularly relevant to those of us in western countries, who both dominate the world and its resources and enjoy democratic freedoms that enable us to influence socio-political outcomes.

We might also heed Nancy Scheper-Hughes's advice, cited earlier, to focus on daily practices and discourses of exclusion, anathematization, and marginalization:

> It is essential that we recognize in our species (and in ourselves) *a genocidal capacity* and that we exercise a defensive hypervigilance, a hypersensitivity to the less dramatic, *permitted*, everyday acts of violence that make participation (under other conditions) in genocidal acts possible, perhaps more easy than we would like to know.[56]

And we should not overlook the role that victims may play in intensifying and perpetuating their own victimization. In cases where the destruction would be on a lesser scale without the voluntary or semi-voluntary contribution of a victim class – the cigarette smoker, the irresponsible sexual partner – a corresponding responsibility may exist to monitor one's own complicity with an oppressive social formation, and to transcend it.

CONCLUSION

This chapter has argued that patterns and processes of structural and institutional violence have tended to be downplayed in the genocide studies literature. In part, this reflects the state-centric orientation of the field, which grew out of the ultimate state-planned and -administered genocide, the Nazi Holocaust. However, a consistent thread runs through discourse on mass atrocity, broadly defined – one in which "holocaust," and other genocide-inflected terminology, is used to convey the massive mortality of structural and institutional forms of violence, and the human agency underpinning it.

I have argued that this marginal discourse deserves to be taken seriously, and moved closer to the mainstream of genocide studies. There is nothing in the UN Genocide Convention that rules out such forms of violence as genocidal mechanisms. A standard sticking point has usually been the issue of agency and intent. But there is much in the evolving case-law to suggest that the understanding of intent can legitimately be extended to cases where motives are quite different from the destruction of a population for destruction's sake – for example, personal or corporate profit. The evolving interpretation also acknowledges "wilful blindness" and "reckless disregard" as falling under the rubric of genocidal intent.

Genocide studies, and international case-law, are presently at the stage of an extended "plausibility probe," pushing the boundaries of the destructive actions, targeting of definable groups, and degrees of *mens rea* that can legitimately be termed genocidal. It is far from clear that questions of structural and institutional violence will be readily incorporated into the emerging legal framing. It is probable, in fact, that the genocide framework will be more effective at the level of political mobilization and popular discourse than in a more formal courtroom setting. Where a short causal chain, direct responsibility, and individual perpetrators are present, legal remedies may be viable. However, they are unlikely to prove a decisive strategy of genocide prevention and intervention, even in the context of the political–military events usually prosecuted as "genocide." Not until a transformation in public opinion and popular mobilization is brought about, on an international and indeed global scale, is genocide likely to be effectively confronted. In this broader transformation and mobilization, framings of genocide and structural/institutional violence may play a notable part.

NOTES

1 Jean Ziegler quoted in "UN Expert Decries 'Assassination' by Hunger of Millions of Children," UN News Center dispatch, October 28, 2005. This article began life many years ago as a conference presentation to the International Association of Genocide Scholars (biennial meeting in Boca Raton, FL, 2005). It has undergone extensive revisions and new permutations since. I am grateful to Edwin Hodge for capable and proactive research assistance, and to Jo and David Jones for proofreading and editorial suggestions.

2 Johan Galtung cited in "D@dalos – Peace Education: Basic Course 2 – Violence Typology," http://www.dadalos.org/frieden_int/grundkurs_2/typologie.htm.

3 Johan Galtung, "Violence, Peace, and Peace Research," in Galtung, *Peace: Research – Education – Action* (Copenhagen: Christian Ejlers, 1975), p. 111.

4 Ibid., p. 123.

5 This is close to Peter Prontzos's definition of structural violence as "deleterious conditions that derive from economic and political structures of power, created and maintained by human actions and institutions." Prontzos, "Collateral Damage: The Human Cost of Structural Violence," in Adam Jones, ed., *Genocide, War Crimes and the West: History and Complicity* (London: Zed Books, 2004), p. 299.

6 Steven Lee, "Is Poverty Violence?," in Deane Curtin and Robert Litke, eds, *Institutional Violence* (Amsterdam: Rodopi, 1999), p. 9.

7 Nancy Scheper-Hughes, "The Genocidal Continuum: Peace-time Crimes," in Jeannette Marie Mageo, ed., *Power and the Self* (Cambridge: Cambridge University Press, 2002), pp. 29–47. See also my application of Scheper-Hughes's continuum to cases of subaltern genocide in Adam Jones, "'When the Rabbit's Got the Gun: Subaltern Genocide and the Genocidal Continuum," in Nicholas A. Robins and Adam Jones, eds, *Genocides by the Oppressed: Subaltern Genocide in Theory and Practice* (Bloomington, IN: Indiana University Press, 2009), pp. 185–207.

8 John Quigley, *The Genocide Convention: An International Law Analysis* (London: Ashgate, 2006), p. 119.

9 Ibid., p. 119.

10 Ibid., pp. 111–112.

11 Nafeez Mosaddeq Ahmed, "Structural Violence as a Form of Genocide: The Impact of the International Economic Order," *Entelequia: Revista Interdisciplinar*, 5 (2007), p. 4.

12 "Hunger Kills '6m Children a Year,'" *BBC Online*, November 22, 2005.

13 Ed Cropley, "Economic Crisis Adds Millions to Ranks of Poorest," Reuters dispatch, April 23, 2010.

14 S.P. Udayakumar, "The Futures of the Poor," *Futures*, 27: 3 (1995), p. 342.

15 Johan Galtung, "Violence, Peace, and Peace Research," in Galtung, *Peace: Research – Education – Action*; Paul Farmer, *Pathologies of Power: Health, Human Rights, and the New War on the Poor* (Berkeley, CA: University of California Press, 2005). See also Thomas Pogge, *World Poverty and Human Rights* (Cambridge: Polity Press, 2002).

16 John Ralston Saul, *The Collapse of Globalism and the Reinvention of the World* (Toronto: Viking Canada, 2005), pp. 12, 103–104, and 107.

17 Ross P. Buckley, "The Rich Borrow and the Poor Repay: The Fatal Flaw in International Finance," *World Policy Journal*, 19: 4 (Winter 2002/03), http://www.worldpolicy.org/journal/articles/wpj02-4/buckley.html. Buckley states:

> According to UNICEF, over 500,000 children under the age of five died each year in Africa and Latin America in the late 1980s as a direct result of the debt crisis and its

management under the International Monetary Fund's structural adjustment programs. These programs required the abolition of price supports on essential food-stuffs, steep reductions in spending on health, education, and other social services, and increases in taxes. The debt crisis has never been resolved for much of sub-Saharan Africa. Extrapolating from the UNICEF data, as many as 5,000,000 children and vulnerable adults may have lost their lives in this blighted continent as a result of the debt crunch.

18 Jeffrey D. Sachs, "Alive Today, Desperate Tomorrow," *Tompaine.com*, August 19, 2005, http://www.truthout.org/docs_2005/081905G.shtml.

19 Hannibal Travis, *Genocide in the Middle East: The Ottoman Empire, Iraq, and Sudan* (Durham, NC: Carolina University Press, 2010), p. 4.

20 Robin Fenske, John G. Bell, and Erich Albrecht, "Affinity Group: 'International Relations and Systems Thinking,'" http://www.arlecchino.org/ildottore/palod/paper_-_international_relations.html.

21 Quoted in William Keegan, "This is No Time to Flirt with Fiscal S&M," *The Observer*, April 4, 2004, http://politics.guardian.co.uk/economics/comment/0,11268,1185543,00.html.

22 Richard E. Ericson, "The Classical Soviet-Type Economy: Nature of the System and Implications for Reform," *The Journal of Economic Perspectives*, 5: 4 (Autumn 1991), pp. 25–26.

23 Kim Murphy, "For the Sick, No Place to Turn," *The Los Angeles Times*, October 9, 2006.

24 Cited in Judy Dempsey, "Study Looks at Mortality in Post-Soviet Era," *The New York Times*, January 16, 2009; see David Stuckler, Lawrence King, and Martin McKee, "Mass Privatisation and the Post-Communist Mortality Crisis: A Cross-National Analysis," *The Lancet*, 373: 9661 (January 31, 2009), pp. 399–407.

25 Stephen F. Cohen, *Failed Crusade: America and the Tragedy of Post-Communist Russia* (New York: W.W. Norton & Company, 2000), pp. 38, 50. The collapse of health care in post-Soviet Russia has been especially catastrophic. See Murphy, "For the Sick, No Place to Turn."

26 Prokhanov, quoted in Mark G. Field, "The Health and Demographic Crisis in Post-Soviet Russia: A Two-Phase Development," in Mark G. Field and Judyth L. Twigg, eds, *Russia's Torn Safety Nets: Health and Social Welfare during the Transition* (New York: St. Martin's Press, 2000), p. 17.

27 Gendercide Watch, "Case Study: Maternal Mortality," http://www.gendercide.org/case_maternal.html.

28 Edward O'Neil Jr., "Poverty, Structural Violence, and Racism in a World Out of Balance," *Race/Ethnicity: Multidisciplinary Global Perspectives*, 3: 1 (Autumn 2009), pp. 115–138.

29 Stephen Lewis, quoted in Michael Mann, *Incoherent Empire* (London: Verso, 2005), p. 61.

30 Criticizing "superpatents" which prolong US pharmaceutical companies' patents on drugs for AIDS and other conditions, Pedro Chequer, chief of Brazil's national AIDS program, stated: "If you prevent countries from using generic drugs, you are creating a concrete obstacle to providing access to drugs. You are promoting genocide, because you're killing people." Quoted in Dr. Peter Rost, "The Genocide Election," *Counterpunch.org*, November 6, 2006, http://www.counterpunch.org/rost11062006.html.

31 Open letter quoted in "Aids Experts Condemn SA Minister," *BBC Online*, September 6, 2006.

32 Zinkie Sithole, "Govt's HIV Policy 'Is Genocide,'" *News24.com*, October 30, 2006.

33 See Alister Doyle, "Humans Spur Worst Extinctions Since Dinosaurs," Reuters dispatch in *The Scotsman*, March 20, 2006.

34 Cited in Peter Prontzos, "Collateral Damage: The Human Cost of Structural Violence," in Adam Jones, ed., *Genocide, War Crimes and the West: History and Complicity* (London: Zed Books, 2004), p. 303.

35 John Vidal, "Africa Climate Change 'Could Kill Millions,'" *The Guardian*, May 15, 2006.

36 Andrew Pendleton, quoted in Gerry Smith, "Climate Change 'Genocide' Threatens Kenyan Herders: Aid Groups," Agence France-Presse dispatch, November 12, 2006.

37 Andrew Pendleton, quoted in Michael McCarthy, "The Century of Drought," *The Independent*, October 4, 2006. Emphasis added.

38 I am thinking, for instance, of an event held in the mid-2000s, "How Can Jews Help Prevent Environmental Genocide and Save the Planet?," with Levene as panelist.

39 "Nigerian Leaders 'Stole' $380bn," *BBC Online*, October 20, 2006, http://news.bbc.co.uk/2/hi/africa/6069230.htm.

40 R.W. Johnson, "Zimbabwe, the Land of Dying Children," *The Sunday Times*, January 7, 2007.

41 Sebastien Berger, "Starving in Zimbabwe 'Amounts to Genocide,'" *The Daily Telegraph*, August 21, 2007, http://www.telegraph.co.uk/news/worldnews/1560933/Starving-in-Zimbabwe-amounts-to-genocide.html.

42 Quoted in *BBC Online*, "A Country Suffering under Sanctions," February 3, 1998, http://news.bbc.co.uk/2/hi/events/crisis_in_the_gulf/road_to_the_brink/53003.stm.

43 Ramsey Clark, "Criminal Complaint against the United States and Others for Crimes against the People of Iraq," in Jones, ed., *Genocide, War Crimes and the West*, p. 271.

44 The first, Denis J. Halliday, stated in a speech in Spain in 1999 that was based on a careful reading of the UN Genocide Convention:

> Some including myself consider that by the deliberate continuation of the UN sanctions regime on Iraq, in full knowledge of their deadly impact as frequently reported by the Secretary-General and others, the member states of the Security Council are indeed guilty of intentionally sustaining a regime of genocide.

He added sardonically: ". . . I have observed that the term 'genocide' offends many in our Western media and establishment circles when it is used to describe the killing of others for which we are responsible, such as in Iraq." Denis J. Halliday, "US Policy and Iraq: A Case of Genocide?," in Jones, ed., *Genocide, War Crimes and the West*, pp. 264, 265–266. Halliday's successor, Hans-Christian von Sponeck, likewise resigned, writing subsequently in *A Different Kind of War: The UN Sanctions Regime in Iraq* (Oxford: Berghahn Books, 1996), p. 171:

> The conclusion that . . . the Genocide Convention . . . was violated by the UN Security Council from the beginning of the Oil-for-Food Programme in 1996 by, for example, severe limitations of rights of children to health, development of their personalities and education is therefore sound.

See also the statement of genocide scholar Alan Kuperman on the H-Genocide academic list, March 5, 2003.

> I realize it is hard for Americans, some of whom are Holocaust survivors, to accept that their own government would knowingly pursue a policy that killed hundreds of thousands of innocent civilians, mainly children. But it happened. Admittedly, killing the civilians was not the U.S. government's ultimate goal, but merely a means to an end and a type of "collateral damage" deemed acceptable. But it is important to understand that this is the case in *most* genocides. The Holocaust, while not unique, is an exceptional case of genocide, where killing the population was the ultimate end. In most cases of genocide, it is a means to an end or a type of "collateral damage" deemed acceptable, such as when putting down an armed rebellion by clearing rebel-infested areas (draining the sea), or punishing a fifth column that has sided with an external aggressor, etc. To term it "scandalous" when someone raises the undeniable facts of the U.S. genocide in Iraq is, ironically, itself a type of genocidal denial.

45 Joy Gordon, *Invisible War: The United States and the Iraq Sanctions* (Cambridge, MA: Harvard University Press, 2010), p. 227. See also Thomas Nagy, "A Reluctant Genocide Activist," describing aerial bombing of Iraq as *prima facie* prohibited by Article 2(c) of the Genocide Convention and by "extermination" provisions of crimes against humanity legislation; in

Adam Jones, ed., *Evoking Genocide: Scholars and Activists Describe the Works that Shaped Their Lives* (Toronto, ON: The Key Publishing House Inc., 2009), pp. 215–218.

46 United States District Court, Eastern District of New York, Memorandum in re: Order and Judgment "Agent Orange," MDL No. 381, p. 51, http://www.nyed.uscourts.gov/pub/rulings/cv/2005/moj-04-cv-400-mdl381.pdf. The decision of the court, however (p. 181), was that "The use of herbicides in Vietnam did not constitute genocide as defined by either the Genocide Convention Implementation Act or the Genocide Convention . . ."

47 Lee Liu, "Made in China: Cancer Villages," *Environment*, (March/April 2010), http://www.environmentmagazine.org/Archives/Back%20Issues/March-April%202010/made-inchina-full.html. The institutional analysis in this report makes plain how much human agency and carefully structured injustice shape these outcomes:

> Due to economic, social, and political disparities, the poor rural people . . . have no healthcare and rarely do physical exams, so cancer is usually found at a late stage, and they are too poor to pay for treatments, leading to the high death rate. Compared to their urban counterparts, the villagers are more likely to be excluded in the decision-making process when a potentially polluting factory is put in their areas; they are powerless against the alliance of corporation and government. As a result, polluters get rich quickly and are not concerned with destroying the local environment . . . Since governmental officials are not democratically elected, they do not work for the villagers, who in turn have little influence on government policies . . . China has established many environmental laws, but they are seldom enforced . . . Cancer victims have filed many lawsuits against the polluters, but few have been successful. There are no government reports that establish a direct link between a factory's pollution and villagers' cancers. As a result, it is impossible for the victims to obtain compensation.

See also Jonathan Watts, "China's 'Cancer Villages' Reveal Dark Side of Economic Boom," *The Guardian*, June 7, 2010, http://www.guardian.co.uk/environment/2010/jun/07/china-cancer-villages-industrial-pollution.

48 André Picard, "Political Leaders Accused of AIDS Genocide," *The Globe and Mail*, August 18, 2006.

49 As my father David pointed out (written comments, March 2011), the question of death and debility inflicted through second-hand smoke would be a separate question. It might best be classed together with other instances of pollution and contamination; but unlike most such cases, the principal perpetrators would be individuals at the grassroots (i.e. smokers), rather than corporate actors.

50 The International Commission on Intervention and State Sovereignty, *The Responsibility to Protect* (Ottawa, ON: International Development Research Centre, 2001), p. 32. Emphasis in original.

51 See Gendercide Watch, "Case Study: Maternal Mortality," http://www.gendercide.org/case_maternal.html.

52 See Jane Perlez and Raymond Bonner, "Below a Mountain of Wealth, a River of Waste," *The New York Times*, December 27, 2005, http://www.nytimes.com/2005/12/27/international/asia/27gold.html.

53 On the ecocidal dimension of the assault on the Niger Delta, see Daniel Howden, "Visible from Space, Deadly on Earth: The Gas Flares of Nigeria," *The Independent*, April 27, 2010, http://www.independent.co.uk/news/world/africa/visible-from-space-deadly-on-earth-the-gas-flares-of-nigeria-1955108.html.

54 Henry Shue, *Basic Rights: Subsistence, Affluence and U.S. Foreign Policy*, 2nd edn (Princeton, NJ: Princeton University Press, 1996), pp. 103–104.

55 McQuaig, cited in Prontzos, "Collateral Damage," p. 307.

56 It may also be fairly contended that individual responsibility is greatest where individual capacity is greatest; and so the recent resurgence of mega-philanthropy in the developing world, by billionaires like Microsoft chairman Bill Gates and investor Warren Buffett, is to be welcomed.

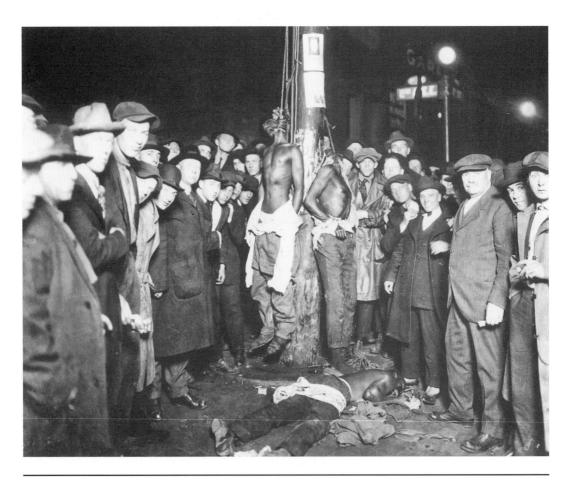

Figure 9.1 "[Lynching of] Isaac McGhie, Elmer Jackson, and Elias Clayton . . . on June 15, 1920, when three black circus workers were attacked and lynched by a mob in Duluth, Minnesota. Rumors had circulated among the mob that six African Americans had raped a teenage girl. A physician's examination subsequently found no evidence of rape or assault." Contemporary postcard.

Source: Courtesy Brown University.

CHAPTER 9

Moral Bystanders and Mass Violence

Ernesto Verdeja

> The fact that man is capable of action means that the unexpected can be expected from him, that he is able to perform what is infinitely improbable.
>
> (Hannah Arendt)

The modern study of political violence has largely focused on the roles of perpetrators and victims, and for understandable reasons.[1] In the aftermath of the Holocaust, historians, psychologists, and others sought to explain how a nation could systematically exterminate an entire people, and whether there were particular historical, dispositional, or situational factors that could lead to such an enormous crime.[2] The publication of survivor testimonies in the decades following World War II, as well the Eichmann and Auschwitz trials, generated renewed interest in the experiences of victims and the nature of the Nazi cataclysm. Following the genocides in Rwanda, Bosnia-Herzegovina, and now Sudan, further attention has been paid to analyzing the role of human rights violators and the plight of victims. Significantly less attention, however, has been given to understanding the role of bystanders, those ostensibly "passive" agents who remain unwilling to intercede in situations of mass violence.[3]

This chapter examines the normative status of moral bystanders in cases of extreme political violence. By re-inscribing the moral domain to exclude outgroups from moral consideration, bystanders carry a special, though rarely a legal, responsibility for violations. My goal here is to sketch the basic elements of a normative theory of bystanders that differs from some prevailing understandings, and to provide a partial phenomenology that traces the complexity of bystander behavior and motivation. As a phenomenology, it focuses on concrete instances of bystander behavior, rather than theorizing from abstract principles. As will become evident, the character, roles, and motivations of moral bystanders are complex, and thus in practice it can be difficult to define precisely the contours of "bystanding." Indeed, the boundaries between bystanders and perpetrators, or bystanders and victims, are often unclear, and can change over time and across space.

As difficult as it may appear, theorizing about this question has political and moral consequences, for without a satisfactory understanding of bystanding, responsibility remains either woefully under-theorized – essentially focusing blame for mass crimes on a relatively small number of perpetrators while the rest of society escapes moral scrutiny – or crudely overdetermined, placing everyone who is not a direct victim into the category of perpetrator, and thus falling into unhelpful and dangerous conceptions of collective guilt that have little historical nuance.

This chapter begins with a definition of the bystander, and then proceeds to examine two of its constituent components: individual knowledge and acknowledgment of crimes, and agency to intervene proactively. I then problematize the bystander category by exploring variations in bystander behavior that are missed in many contemporary accounts, and finally turn to some difficult questions surrounding the relationship between action and motive in assessing moral behavior.

THE BYSTANDER

We often think of a bystander as someone who is uninvolved in a particular event, and thus largely free of responsibility for its consequences. A bystander is not the object or target of an action, nor is she its author. Rather, she merely observes events passively, having no tangible effect on them. In American law a bystander is normally excused from criminal liability, since she is not directly involved in a crime. And yet this passivity requires further scrutiny. Edmund Burke allegedly said, "the one condition for the triumph of evil is that good men do nothing,"[4] capturing the fact that inaction carries consequences, and can be understood as itself a form of action. Indeed, observing an event, particularly some moral transgression, implicates the bystander, if only because her unwillingness to intercede can facilitate the commission of a wrong. Ervin Staub defines bystanders as "those members of society who are neither perpetrators nor victims, or outside individuals, organizations, and nations," noting that "the support, opposition or indifference of these people largely shapes the course of events."[5]

My focus is more circumscribed, and concentrates on members of the society that is experiencing violence. I define bystanders as those individuals in a given territory, such as a country, who do not actively participate in violence, but who share the same politically salient identity as direct perpetrators (ethnicity, "race," class, etc.), or whom the perpetrators consider political allies. Bystanders are neither members of the victim group, nor associated with victims, though I will argue that these boundaries can be rather ill-defined in practice. (In this discussion, I do not explicitly discuss institutional and international actors, though many of the points raised here would also apply to them.)

Moral bystanders are those who bear some responsibility by virtue of being in a position to intercede and consequently alter the direction of events, and yet fail to act. Those who were *unable* to intervene because of given circumstances cannot be considered "moral" in quite the same sense, as they cannot exercise morally meaningful agency. Thus, in the remainder of this chapter, I use the term "bystander" to refer to moral bystanders in the sense given here. Admittedly, this distinction between the ability and inability to intervene is theoretically rather neat. There can be many constraints to action, some legitimate and others not, and we may prefer to see ourselves as incapable of intervening for a variety of reasons. But the distinction does allow us to separate, if only for a brief theoretical moment, passive moral agents from mere observers.

This idea of bystander responsibility is not without its detractors. Certain strands of political thought do not see bystanding as a moral problem because of the way they understand what it means to be a person, morally speaking. Rather, they conceive of subjects in radically individualistic terms: that is, a sense of self arises not from inter-subjective relations of being or responsibility, but from the exclusion of others.[6] Early modern thought, particularly that of John Locke and Thomas Hobbes, understands personhood not in intersubjective terms, but as monadic and self-contained. For these thinkers, freedom means the lack of dependence on others, and can be limited only through those contractual relations that are entered into rationally and voluntarily (those necessary, for example, for establishing society and the state).[7] Similarly, H.D. Lewis believes that holding someone blameworthy for the actions of another with whom he is associated is barbaric, and inappropriate for an enlightened society.[8] A tacit conception of tolerance functions here as the primary form of social interaction. There are relatively few ethical claims placed on citizens, who pursue their own interests and life plans as they see fit.

But tolerance itself includes a number of ambiguities,[9] and in certain contexts it can collapse into moral indifference. One can tolerate the suffering of others without any sense of remorse, precisely because one remains a monadic ego, devoid of socially or emotionally meaningful relations with fellow humans. This conception of tolerance offers little insight into a sense of communal obligations toward others, collective respon-sibility for the actions of the state or fellow members of the community, or indifference that facilitates state-authored crimes. Tolerance can quickly become a form of passivity and indifference toward the plight of the vulnerable.

In a similar way, bystanders rarely accept that they are implicated in the events around them, preferring to see themselves as occupying a "neutral territory, suspended above the agonistic world of non-innocence."[10] This is misleading, for they are in fact part of a larger moral domain that includes perpetrators and victims. Indeed, they are "often *both* [perpetrators and victims] at the same time, and project their own struggles, interests and expectations onto the conflicts they either observe or try to resolve."[11] I begin, then, from a different premise: namely, that we are *social* beings, defined at least partly, and in important ways, by our relations with others and the psychological and emotional security and benefits we gain from these relations. We gain a sense of value and self-respect from the moral *recognition* of others, and derive meaning in our lives from the communities in which we live and the groups to which we belong. Recognition is a reciprocal relation through which subjects see each other as equals entitled to moral respect. Formally put, recognition is a primary – though not exclusive – aspect of healthy moral subject formation, and thus our relations with others are, in an important sense, moral.[12] To be a social creature also means that we are embedded in relations with others, and thus it is impossible to separate ourselves from the events around us or the behavior of other people.

But the nature of shared identity is more specific than this. As citizens of a nation, for example, we identify with fellow citizens in complex ways. It is not that we identify with their every concrete act; rather, our bonds are based on certain emotional connections we have with the nation. Speaking of "national pride," Farid Abdel-Nour argues that it "is a sign of a very specific way in which participants in national belonging connect themselves to select actions performed by others. These are actions of which they imaginatively identify themselves as agents."[13] The extreme individualism of Locke, Hobbes, and Lewis, with its emphasis on a tolerance that hews distressingly close to moral indifference, misses this fundamental point about identity.

This idea that we are socially embedded creatures with identities shaped through group membership, and thus are responsible for what happens around us, is powerfully articulated by Karl Jaspers. Jaspers examines various forms of moral responsibility, or "guilt" as he terms it, which arise from this embedded conception of being. Criminal guilt arises from the commission of acts that are prosecutable under recognized laws, while political guilt connotes the extent of political acquiescence among the population to a despotic or authoritarian regime. Moral guilt concerns the individual's awareness of serious wrongs, or her participation in unethical decisions that led to specific wrongs. Finally, and perhaps most contentiously, there is metaphysical guilt:

> There exists a solidarity among men as human beings that makes each co-responsible for every wrong and every injustice in the world, especially for crimes committed in his presence or with his knowledge. If I fail to do whatever I can to prevent them, then I too am guilty.[14]

There is an "inevitable guilt of human existence," rooted in the fact that "every human being is fated to be enmeshed in the power relations he lives by."[15] Jaspers correctly notes that we live in complex relationships with others. But metaphysical guilt risks draining responsibility of any normative content, for it treats everyone as guilty by virtue of their membership in the human race, regardless of their specific actions. Considering the scope of metaphysical guilt – all humanity – it is difficult to draw distinctions between perpetrators, victims, and bystanders, for all are implicated equally. The guilt that comes with being a person overshadows actual instances of wrongs or righteous behavior. When all bear guilt merely by existing, the concept is empty, for no one is responsible in any morally significant way.

Larry May provides a more compelling conception of responsibility. He correctly notes that our identities are partly formed through the communities to which we belong, as is evident in the fact that we are proud of the accomplishments of the groups with which we identify, and dismayed by their failings. For May, we carry a vicarious moral liability rooted in our membership in these groups. Thus, while we may not be directly guilty for specific transgressions committed by particular members of our society, the fact that we share an identity – that we recognize bonds of solidarity among us – means we are implicated, in some ways, in the failings of our groups. The "collective inaction of a group of persons may make members of that group at least partially responsible for harms that the group could have prevented."[16] We are morally *tainted*, in other words, by the wrongs of our fellow members. Thus, vicarious moral liability is based on group solidarity. What is important is not the fact of membership in itself – a point where

May diverges from Jaspers – but rather how we *react* to what members of our group do: "what is under one's control, and hence the subject of appropriate feelings of responsibility, is how one positions oneself in terms of that group."[17] Responsibility is rooted in our membership in particular communities, but ultimately what matters morally are the actions we take to distance ourselves from other members. May's thesis is more convincing than Jaspers's, for it explicitly specifies the importance of behavior, something that in Jaspers's metaphysical guilt risks being eclipsed.

The main difficulty here, however, is that many of these philosophical accounts of responsibility are largely static. They outline the parameters of responsibility through group membership, but say little about how particular actors may change their behavior over time, for a variety of reasons and in response to changing circumstances. Thus, in Jaspers, we are provided with overarching categories of guilt that encompass increasingly larger populations, yet there is little insight into the ways in which bystanders reposition themselves in relation to one another, and to perpetrators and victims. But bystanders continuously react to their environments, and their behavior evolves over time. A bystander may be faced with numerous ways to respond to a situation. She may, for example, remain unmoved by the events around her, yet later intervene. She may be emotionally conflicted, feeling she can do little to change the course of events, but nevertheless recognizing that she should do "something"; she may side with victims while fearing what might happen to her, or harbor feelings of mistrust and even outright scorn for those victims. Moreover, all these emotions may (and probably will) change along with transformed circumstances. Jaspers and May do not address these shifting relations and behaviors, instead opting to sketch general categories of responsibility in rather fixed and abstract terms.

Zygmunt Bauman's important book, *Modernity and the Holocaust*, goes some way toward addressing these issues, and attempts to ground discussions about bystanders by tracing the specific nature of responsibility for the Holocaust. Bauman proposes that "moral behavior is conceivable only in the context of coexistence, of 'being with others,' that is, a social context."[18] He argues that the Nazis' sophisticated bureaucratization of death created a form of moral compartmentalization, so that extermination was institutionalized and routinized, while the possibility of moral empathy was subverted. The Nazis' putatively scientific, systematic categorization of the population into desirable and undesirable elements, combined with the division of exterminationist labor into minute and technical tasks, meant that individual perpetrators carried out highly rationalized and specific functions in killing Jews and others, but remained psychologically protected from exposure to the overall effects of the Holocaust, for very few of them were confronted with the end result of their actions. This bureaucratic rationalization effectively ensured that the boundary between perpetrator and bystander would be blurred, providing each perpetrator with a rationalization to show that he or she was not a murderer. Given a highly anomic social environment in which Jews and others were already dehumanized, the authorization and routinization of violence, as well as insulation from a direct confrontation with the consequences of one's actions, effectively undermined moral resistance.

Bauman's theory of moral distancing through bureaucratized murder has strongly influenced contemporary theorizings of bystander and perpetrator responsibility. It is debatable, however, whether the Holocaust is best described as "bureaucratic," given that a sizeable number of Jews – perhaps one million – were slaughtered by German mobile killing units (*Einsatzgruppen*) in wild massacres, rather than in the extermination and concentration camps. In any case, this technological–bureaucratic understanding does not translate well to other cases of contemporary mass atrocity. Most contemporary genocides are not highly institutionalized, as the Holocaust was. Rather, the killing process is less rationalized, and is rarely separated into formally discrete tasks. The genocides in Cambodia, Rwanda, Bosnia, Darfur, and elsewhere were not the result of a careful division of labor that shielded individuals from the process of murder, but instead were carried out through the coordinated efforts of the armed forces, para-militaries, and party cadres who directly exterminated their targets "in the field" and looted their property. In any event, the "modernity" thesis of mass murder provides little insight into the dynamics of modern violence or bystanding beyond the Holocaust.

In the following sections, I sketch an alternative model of bystanding. It is a dynamic model that places bystanders on a spectrum ranging from near-perpetrator to near-victim. I will focus on two elements of moral bystanding: the epistemological component of the knowledge of wrongs, and the practical component of agency and the ability to intervene. Unlike Jaspers and May, I emphasize how bystanders may shift along the spectrum, depending on changing conditions.

ELEMENTS OF MORAL BYSTANDING

I noted earlier that a bystander's moral responsibility is partly rooted in membership in a group with a distinct identity and solidaristic bonds. But shared identity at best presents us with the broad parameters of potential responsibility. Here, I would like to investigate individual knowledge and behavior: that is, whether one knows crimes are being committed, and what one does about this.

First, consider the question of *knowledge*. Bystanders may be unaware of events or their importance, or remain unclear about the consequences of their own actions. Unsurprisingly, ignorance is a common bystander response to subsequent revelations of crimes. Although these claims are frequently self-serving, ascertaining whether someone knew of the crimes at the time of their commission is often difficult. Only in retrospect can one judge whether an individual was sufficiently informed, and thus whether he bears any responsibility. But even basic information about atrocities can prove to be a somewhat inaccurate measure of knowledge. It is not uncommon for individuals to receive information about massacres or atrocities and remain incredulous, considering them simply too outlandish to be true. Much more morally problematic, these individuals may work to place themselves in positions where they knowingly remain ignorant. This, of course, is different from simply being unaware of events, for it betrays an *effort* – conscious or not – to avoid taking on a moral obligation to respond to events.

We should distinguish, then, between knowledge and acknowledgment. The former refers to a set of facts about a crime, and the latter to the process of understanding a crime *as such* – whether it was interpreted correctly, internalized, and finally believed. Petar L., a Bosnian Croat whom I met in Sarajevo, stated that it took some time to realize that the violence that tore his country apart from 1992 to 1995 was not merely a civil war between identifiable armed groups, but also included widespread attacks against civilians:

I lived near Mostar at the time, and the tensions between Croats and Muslims were high. While I certainly did not participate in attacking Muslims, we did not know the extent of the violence that was happening. We heard about shootings and killings, but I never saw anything. Mostly, we just tried to keep to ourselves. Only later, in the summer of 1993, did we realize what was happening and tried to do something to help our Muslim neighbors.[19]

Petar's reflections on the war are telling, and not uncommon. He knew of violence against civilians, but claimed he was unaware of its extent until much later. It is impossible to verify these claims, but Petar's comments show how acknowledgment of the killings may come in stages: the information first had to be interpreted accurately, then internalized, and finally believed. Only after it had been accepted, could there be a possibility of changing one's behavior. Acknowledgment, then, is based on a fundamental transformation in one's perception of events. This shift from knowledge to acknowledgment, from exposure to events to understanding, also traces a shift in responsibility. We do not normally consider someone morally responsible for failing to act when he clearly lacks information about what is happening around him. It is only when a particular threshold of knowledge is met that we can begin to speak of a moral component; for it is at this point that a subject can no longer deny the evidence before him. And as this knowledge is properly grasped in its totality and its consequences – as the enormity of events are acknowledged – the bystander's inaction becomes a moral issue. This first point, then, concerns knowledge and its transformation into acknowledgment as a fundamental aspect of moral bystanding.

Second is the question of *agency*. We often think of action in a binary way, as including only the interested parties – in this case, the perpetrator and victim. Certainly it is true, at least to an extent, that the act of killing occurs between perpetrator and victim. This is chillingly captured in the words of a Rwandan Hutu *génocidaire*:

At the marketplace I saw a man running toward me. He was coming down from Kayumba, all breathless and scared, looking only for escape, and he didn't see me. I was heading up, and in passing, I gave him a machete blow at the neck level, on the vulnerable vein . . . I kept chasing after runaways all day long.[20]

Léopord's confession evokes the frightening immediacy of death, the awful manner in which the fate of two people is determined through the swing of a machete. But this binary way of framing mass murder is also misleading, for while certainly Léopord bears direct responsibility for the killing, the murder occurred in the context of mass, genocidal violence, planned and executed through the concerted effort of an organized group targeting another well-defined group, with the acquiescence of a significant portion of the population. Although we can certainly identify a specific killing (or killings) in time and location, its consequences reverberate well after the event. This binary formulation of killer and killed underpins the broader context – political, social, moral – in which political violence occurs, and the ways in which a third party may facilitate violence.

A more complete understanding of perpetrator–victim interaction needs to take into account bystander action. Moral bystanding implies the ability to act, to intervene meaningfully. It assumes a range of possible actions that could have altered events, but which were not taken. It is precisely this lack of action that lends moral resonance to bystanding, for inaction is still an act. Of course, bystanders frequently emphasize that coercive conditions – and thus a lack of agency – excuse their behavior, or claim that their non-participation had no bearing on events. Even if they knew what was happening, they deny any ability to have influenced the course of events. And indeed, they may be so constrained that they lack the possibility of action in any important sense. Often, however, the sense of inaction may also be a rationalization for an unwillingness to intervene, to place oneself in a position of vulnerability between perpetrators and victims.

Given that the moral component of bystanding hinges on the assumption that one could and should have acted, it is important to define agency. By agency, I mean the ability of an individual to act or refrain from acting intentionally in a particular context. It is a volitional concept, for it assumes that individuals can make decisions on how to behave and interact with one another and with their surroundings. Paul Ricoeur notes that: "on the level of interaction, just as on that of subjective understanding, not acting is still acting: neglecting, forgetting to do something, is also letting things be done by someone else, sometimes to the point of criminality."[21]

Speech is itself a form of action, as Hannah Arendt rightly noted, and speaking against violence can constitute a particularly powerful form of intervention, forcing fellow citizens to confront what they may well wish to ignore.[22] None of this means that bystanders have an unlimited set of choices, for there is no such thing as "pure" agency. The actions of bystanders, as socially embedded actors, are both constituted and constrained by their particular contexts, or the "structural" conditions in which they find themselves.[23] "Bystander" is thus a relational concept: it implies that there is a particular set of actors with particular relations between them – perpetrator and victim, for example. A bystander intervenes in the context of existing relations and behavior, and this context affects the options available to her. The interplay between agency and structure, however, is a dialectical one: social structure and volitional action continuously shape one another, for just as particular contexts may influence the choices available to individuals, when individuals act, they fundamentally alter those contexts.

More specifically, in adapting themselves to particular situations, actors adopt specific roles. They internalize assumptions and expectations about proper behavior, assumptions that are later externalized through their interactions – including inaction – with others. The relationship between structure and agency, therefore, is likewise dialectical, for while agents internalize social norms and expectations, through their behavior, they shape and reshape those social dynamics.

Structure and agency are thus inextricably connected. While structural conditions constrain potential actions, they also make action possible. Indeed, action is inconceivable without a context which lends meaning to an act. Intervening to stop a Nazi Brownshirt from beating a Jewish man, for example, should be interpreted in the context of prevailing anti-Semitism and Jewish persecution. Nevertheless, it would be wrong to assume that structure overdetermines actions, for the structure only makes it *possible* for agents to act. Social actions are tied to highly generalized motivations and beliefs (such as anti-Semitism, Hutu Power, and so on), but how these are interpreted in particular situations can rarely be known in advance, and the interpretations may be enacted in diverse ways.

Bystanders, then, not only react to the situation in which they find themselves, but through their behavior help to constitute that situation. Inaction allows wrongs to occur, for it signals to perpetrators that their actions will provoke no serious sanctions. "Once one is aware of the things that one could do, and one does not do them, then lack of action is something one has chosen."[24] Indeed, bystander inaction can sometimes be taken as an endorsement of perpetrator behavior.

And yet, bystanders do differ from one another. Although knowledge and inaction form the basis of complicity, there are important distinctions between the relative responsibility of different bystanders. They are implicated in various ways, with some closer to violence than others, and thus possessing a potentially greater influence on events. Testimony from Rwanda shows that in at least some Hutu roadblocks where Tutsis were detained, remarkably few *génocidaires* carried out the massacres, while many others simply watched the carnage, sometimes encouraging the killers and at other times observing passively.[25] In other cases, "local businessmen or other well-to-do people sponsored barriers, which meant supplying the guards with food, drink and sometimes marijuana as well."[26] These examples, and many others, seem to buttress Bauman's argument that "responsibility arises out of proximity to the other. Proximity means responsibility, and responsibility is proximity."[27]

Nevertheless, proximity need not only be spatial; new technologies and media have rendered physical conceptions of space virtually meaningless for assessing responsibility, as people have new ways of staying informed and intervening. Political leaders, clergy, intellectuals, and others, who by virtue of their status may be informed and command some authority, may potentially exert greater influence on events than those who directly witness specific atrocities, but are otherwise incapable of intervening. Thus, given that leaders tend to be informed and influential – that is, they are knowledgeable and possess agency – they are also complicit if they fail to denounce brutality and violence. In fact, their responsibility may be greater than that of low-level perpetrators, given the broad influence they could exert. All of this is to say that *moral* proximity – the degree to which someone can affect circumstances, regardless of her physical location – is a particularly important consideration in assessing bystander agency and responsibility.

Although knowledge and ability to act certainly characterize the bystander category, this category is by no means uniform. This point is often under-appreciated in philosophical treatments that focus more on shared identity as the wellspring of moral responsibility than on the complex ways in which bystanders may situate themselves in relation to other actors.[28] In the following section, I want to examine this complexity, looking first at behavior and then at motivation.

COMPLEXITY IN BYSTANDER BEHAVIOR

Within the bystander domain, there are differing degrees of action and moral responsibility, depending on how particular bystanders position themselves with respect to perpetrators and victims. Here, I sketch some of these varying positions along a continuum of bystanding. One end of the continuum stops short of direct participation in violence, while the other is characterized by resistance, rescue, and possible victimhood. These extremes blend into the categories of perpetrator and victim, respectively.

Furthermore, the distinctions *within* the bystander continuum are fluid and dynamic. An individual may shift position depending on particular circumstances or choices. Nevertheless, we can draw some distinctions that may help to highlight the broad range of bystander behavior.

At one end is *near-direct complicity*, where someone actively supports the elimination of victims without directly participating in the violence. This lies just short of direct participation, and entails active support for the extermination process and the policies of the perpetrator force or regime. One may be a radical supporter of the perpetrators without a prior history of direct participation in violence; but over time, through a steady acculturation to violent behavior and a deepening of ideological commitment, one may come to endorse the systematic exclusion of the targeted group from social, political, and economic life and legal protection, and eventually support its destruction. These bystanders are normally ardent supporters of the genocidal forces, and are frequently motivated by a deep fear or hatred of the victims (or, as is often the case, both). They may or may not be members of the genocidal forces themselves, but they identify strongly with them – indeed, they may feel that their destinies are shared – and also share in the blame commonly ascribed to the victim for her status. In Rwanda, for example, the Hutu government enlisted the support of university professors in developing policies for winning the civil war against the Tutsi insurgents, creating civilian "self-defense" groups, and producing reports about Tutsi treachery for public dissemination. One professor, Eugène Rwamucyo, urged increasingly violent tactics against Tutsi. He and other intellectuals reportedly received "complete support" from their students, some of whom "condemned vigorously the diabolical intentions of the inyenzi inkotanyi [a disparaging term for Tutsi meaning 'cockroaches'] to eliminate the popular democratic mass."[29] Here, there is no clear boundary between perpetrator and bystander. Apportioning responsibility is difficult, because often those who wholly support genocidal policies seem to us as guilty, or nearly as guilty, as those who actually order and carry out mass murder. Indeed, these bystanders directly facilitate mass violence through their support of the regime's most radical policies, making their status as "mere" bystanders contestable.

Alternately, some bystanders are distinguished by the *qualified support* they may provide to a genocidal regime. One may support some of a regime's positions – such as economic or foreign policies – or its nationalist and symbolic rhetoric, which may speak directly to a shared sense of wounded pride or victimization. One need not support the persecution of targeted groups *per se*, but only privilege other issues above the fate of victims. When qualified support is combined with the moral exclusion of the victim, the effect is to sanction the conduct of the regime.[30]

Other bystanders may be significant *beneficiaries* of regime policies, and thus receive certain privileges or patronage from the government, but maintain some distance from the active process of destruction. Beneficiaries are perhaps best viewed as a subset of qualified supporters, but unlike those who endorse the regime for ideological reasons, beneficiaries' support is largely instrumental. They are often tied to the government in some substantial way, and are unlikely to oppose a regime that is a source of political, economic, or other benefits, even if these are clearly at the expense of victims. This does not necessarily require endorsement of the state's more violent policies toward victims, for unlike radical supporters, beneficiaries' focus is on cultivating and maintaining particularly useful relations with the state; they show little concern for the plight of victims. What is important for them is whether lucrative relations with the state can be nurtured and sustained, regardless of broader moral and social consequences.

The theoretical center of the bystander continuum is characterized by *indifference and inaction*. These individuals attempt to remain separated from unfolding events, neither providing support for the regime nor extending aid to victims. When we speak of bystanders, it is normally this idea that we have in mind: a kind of balanced indifference, both in act and perhaps in thought, toward both victims and perpetrators. Nevertheless, this idea of suspending oneself above a conflict, of maintaining a rarefied indifference, is misleading. As I have argued, bystanders are socially embedded, and their inaction shapes events around them. They cannot remain neutral to surrounding developments, particularly in situations of significant flux and instability like genocide and war.

The reasons for indifference are often hard to discern. A bystander may remain externally indifferent to the suffering around him because he supports the targeting of victims, and yet finds other aspects of the regime objectionable, tempering his support for the government. Or indifference may reflect a deep fear of both the state and the out-group, a profound sense of self-preservation combined with an unwillingness to become enmeshed in unpredictable cycles of violence. Acquiescence in practice, then, does not necessarily tell us much about motive.

What all of these positions on the bystander continuum have in common, however, is the general moral abandonment of victims. Regardless of the motives or specific behavior of bystanders, they have all redrawn the constellation of moral obligation to exclude victims. One can hate victims, fear them, find them distasteful, or be largely indifferent toward them, but in all cases bystanders reject their moral status.

As we move away from overt complicity and beyond "neutrality," we find a wide array of *oppositional behavior*, often covert but occasionally explicit. In some instances, bystanders may extend limited support to victims, such as refusing to divulge to authorities the victims' whereabouts, or passing along information about impending persecutions. This type of behavior is particularly difficult to track, since it is often clouded in secrecy and episodic, leaving little historical trace. Nevertheless, sporadic and piecemeal opposition is likely the most common form of resistance, pursued under conditions that do not require continued or sustained exposure to repression by the authorities.

Oppositional behavior is transformed when resistance becomes sustained. Bystanders who are actively engaged in protecting victims position themselves in radical opposition to the regime, shedding much of the protection from condemnation and persecution that anonymity can afford. Some bystanders may be in solidarity with victims, and work actively to protect them, distancing themselves from the inaction of their fellow citizens to take an explicitly oppositional stance toward the regime. This may be covert, as in the case of a Hutu policeman who hid eleven people in various locations, including in ceilings and pits. When asked why he thought others in the surrounding area had not rescued Tutsi, he simply said: "People don't have the same mind."[31] The justly famous case of the Hotel Mille Collines in Rwanda vividly illustrates this transformation from acquiescence to resistance. As the genocide rapidly engulfed the country in the early weeks of April, 1994, over a thousand threatened Tutsi and Hutu sought sanctuary at the luxury hotel in downtown Kigali. Paul Rusesabagina, a Hutu who was temporary manager of the hotel, repeatedly spoke to international news sources to secure protection for the terrified residents of the hotel.[32] Under siege, with no guards or arms to protect them, and with threat of massacre at the hands of Hutu militia, Rusesabagina deceived, flattered, and cajoled the killers into restraining their attack, while begging his international contacts to pressure the Hutu government to spare the residents. No attack occurred, and no one who took refuge at the hotel died during the genocide.

Rusesabagina's story is notable not only for his impressive heroism and courage, but also for illustrating how a bystander may resituate himself along the continuum and adopt an oppositional stance toward the regime.[33] The shift toward active resistance transforms bystanders into potential targets of state repression, placing them outside of the domain of protection afforded to those who are assumed to be supporters. As we move further along the bystander continuum into active opposition, it becomes clear that the traditional perpetrator–victim dyad is unsatisfactory for understanding political violence.

Of course, active resistance need not be motivated by a concern for victims. Bystanders may engage in increasingly confrontational practices for reasons that have little to do with victims. Against the backdrop of the Rwandan genocide, Hutu support for the regime – which was never total – began to show significant strains about four weeks into the slaughter, and in the southern region around Butare intra-Hutu conflict broke out. In at least some instances, both Hutu loyal to the regime and those who came to oppose its increasingly chaotic violence (as it often targeted Hutu as well) employed a genocidal discourse against one another. Regime supporters and their opponents accused each other of being "*ibyitso*," or accomplices of the invading Tutsi insurgents. The distinction between perpetrator and bystander broke down as violence among Hutu became anarchic, and paramilitaries and soldiers encountered greater resistance from the Hutu population.

There were already profound cleavages among the Hutu in Butare, partly political, but also geographic, class-based, and occasionally even personal, which further complicated the perpetrators' efforts to exterminate local Tutsi.[34] Some of this Hutu-on-Hutu violence followed its own logic, motivated by attempts to seize power over local institutions or wage personal vendettas. In any case, while there are certainly documented cases of Hutu protecting Tutsi,[35] some of the Hutu opposition in Butare was born not of solidarity with the Tutsi, but of a sense that the victims were simply not part of their concern. They fought the regime for other reasons.

MOTIVE AND ACTION

This last point on motive requires further attention. Scholars and survivors often assume that bystander motivation tracks relatively unproblematically with behavior. Those bystanders who seem more complicit with the process of destruction are assumed to support the regime, while those who are "passive" in practice are neutral in attitude, and those who resist the regime do so out of solidarity with victims.[36] Indeed, it would appear, intuitively, that one who resists the regime for honorable reasons, like solidarity with victims, is more praiseworthy than one who does so for purely self-interested reasons, such as to preserve personal wealth or business opportunities. Presumably, the worse the behavior, the more morally suspect the motives, and vice versa.

The assumption that motive can be deduced from behavior, and that one can evaluate moral responsibility from this deduction, raises a host of questions. What do we make of those Hutu who resisted the regime for reasons other than a concern for Tutsi? Should we judge these resisters as morally praiseworthy for fighting a genocidal regime, even if their motives were not victim-centered? Even if the protection of the Tutsi was not a prime concern for them, should we consider feelings toward victims at all in our assessment? The question ultimately revolves around the relationship between action and motivation, and whether moral evaluation should take into account resisters' motives. In a certain sense, the answer is "no." Resisting a genocidal regime is morally admirable, for it represents opposition to an incontrovertible evil, the very essence of which is the systematic destruction of human beings. Certainly, many resisters have morally defensible reasons for fighting that have little do to with protecting the primary targets of genocide.[37]

Framing it in this way, however, focuses only on the relationship between resister and perpetrator, and fails to locate the resister in the broader context of violence. We must still inquire into the resister's behavior toward victims: whether she also targets them or not, or acts in ways that further endanger them. That is to say, an exploration of resistance should not be confined merely to the dynamics of conflict between perpetrators and resisters (who obviously become potential victims when resisting), but must also include the primary victims as well. The failed German coup attempt of July 1944 carried out by conservative military officers was motivated by a concern that Hitler was leading Germany to catastrophe. Most of the officers were not particularly moved by the extermination of the Jews and Roma, or by the use of slave labor to fight the war. (Indeed, the mastermind of slave labor, Albert Speer, was seen as a potential ally.) And yet, these officers are today celebrated as heroes, and rightly so, for sacrificing their lives to end Hitler's rule. But should their attitudes toward Jews and other victims play a role in how we appraise their actions? Does the fact that some of them largely ignored persecutions and massacres of marginalized groups for years, and only became opponents of the Nazis when Germany began losing the war, affect our understanding of their heroism? It seems that any adequate account of responsibility ought to take motive seriously, and expand our understanding of resistance to include behavior toward victims.

This discussion shows that individuals can occupy a range of positions on the bystander spectrum, and do so for a variety of reasons. Indeed, one of the points that emerges is that we *cannot deduce motive from action*; one may support the regime, or at least not resist it, for a variety of reasons, including fear, indifference, hatred, personal gain, or other reasons. Given the environment of terror and insecurity typical of war and genocide, it is frequently difficult and on occasion impossible to discern the real reasons why individuals behave as they do.[38]

The upshot is that bystander behavior and motivation do not fit neatly with one another. In moral evaluations of bystanders, then, we may feel that the focus should remain on their (in)actions and practical constraints, as May argues, rather than on motives.[39] While motives may provide some insights into behavior, retrospective justifications frequently present past choices in the most positive – or least culpable – light, and require rendering a judgment on the inner life of individuals, which is practically impossible to divine.

Admittedly, this does not satisfactorily address the concern that eliminating motives from the process of moral assessment equalizes the moral status of actors who behave rather similarly, yet do so for radically different reasons – some praiseworthy and others not. If we dismiss the importance of reasons, we risk establishing an equivalence between those who worked unselfishly to protect victims and undermine the regime, and those who resisted for personal reasons unrelated to the needs of the most vulnerable. Conversely, this approach makes it difficult to draw distinctions between those who support the regime for strongly ideological reasons, and those who are largely apolitical, yet in their acquiescence encourage increasingly more radical policies. Of course it may be the case, as Saul Friedländer argues, that there is really no morally meaningful difference between them.[40]

CONCLUSION

This chapter has explored a number of issues around the bystander phenomenon, and sought to demonstrate its complexity. I have argued that any discussion of moral bystanding must take into account knowledge and agency, and furthermore that the bystander category is highly dynamic. Behavior does not necessarily tell us much about justifications, raising difficult questions about the proper role of motive in examining moral responsibility. Many of these issues underscore the difficulty in assessing responsibility when acquiescence can mean so many things, but they do establish the basic parameters in which any discussion about responsibility should take place. With this in mind, we can join with Camus, who pleaded: "All I ask is that, in the midst of a murderous world, we agree to reflect on murder and to make a choice."[41]

NOTES

1 Hannah Arendt, *The Human Condition* (Chicago: Chicago University Press, 1958), p. 178. Special thanks to Matthew Goldfeder, Eileen Botting, Gene Halton, Fred Rush, and the Social and Political Theory Faculty Workshop at the University of Notre Dame, IN.

2 Raul Hilberg, *The Destruction of the European Jews* (New York: Holmes & Meier, 1985); Theodor Adorno, Else Frenkel-Brunswick, Daniel Levinson, and Nevitt Sanford, *The Authoritarian Personality* (New York: Harper & Brothers, 1950); Victor Frankl, *Man's Search for Meaning* (Boston: Beacon Press, 1992); Stanley Milgram, *Obedience to Authority: An Experimental View* (New York: Harper & Row, 1974).

3 Victoria Barnett, *Bystanders: Conscience and Complicity during the Holocaust* (Westport, CT: Greenwood Press, 1999); Robert Ehrenreich and Tim Cole, "The Perpetrator-Bystander-Victim Constellation: Rethinking Genocidal Relationships," *Human Organization*, 64: 3 (2005), pp. 213–224; Arne Vetlsen, "Genocide: A Case for the Responsibility of the Bystander," *Journal of Peace Research*, 37: 4 (2000), pp. 519–532.

4 Ronnie Landau, *The Nazi Holocaust* (London: Ivan R. Dee, 1992), p. 222.

5 Ervin Staub, *The Roots of Evil* (Cambridge: Cambridge University Press, 1989), p. 20.

6 Norman Geras, *The Contract of Mutual Indifference: Political Philosophy after the Holocaust* (London: Verso, 1999).

7 Thomas Hobbes, *Leviathan* (New York: Penguin Books, 1985); John Locke, "The Second Treatise of Government," in John Locke, *Two Treatises of Government* (Cambridge: Cambridge University Press, 1988).

8 H.D. Lewis, "Collective Responsibility," in Larry May and Stacey Hoffman, eds, *Collective Responsibility* (Savage, MD: Rowman & Littlefield, 1991).

9   Michael Walzer, *Toleration* (New Haven, CT: Yale University Press, 1999).

10   Miroslav Volf, *Exclusion and Embrace* (Nashville, TN: Abingdon Press, 1996), p. 83.

11   Ibid., p. 83.

12   Axel Honneth, "Integrity and Disrespect: Principles of a Conception of Morality Based on a Theory of Recognition," in Axel Honneth, *The Fragmented World of the Social* (Albany, NY: SUNY Press, 1995); Ernesto Verdeja, *Unchopping a Tree: Reconciliation in the Aftermath of Political Violence* (Philadelphia, PA: Temple University Press, 2009), Chapter 2.

13   Farid Abdel-Nour, "National Responsibility," *Political Theory*, 31: 5 (2003), p. 702. But see George Kateb, "Notes on Pluralism," *Social Research*, 61: 3 (1994), p. 527.

14   Karl Jaspers, *The Question of German Guilt* (Westport, CT: Greenwood Press, 1947), p. 32.

15   Ibid., p. 34.

16   Larry May, *Sharing Responsibility* (Chicago, IL: University of Chicago Press, 1992), p. 105.

17   Larry May, "Metaphysical Guilt and Moral Taint," in Larry May, ed., *Collective Responsibility* (Lanham, MD: Rowman and Littlefield, 1992), p. 245.

18   Zygmunt Bauman, *Modernity and the Holocaust* (Ithaca, NY: Cornell University Press, 1989), p. 179.

19   Petar L., interview with the author, Sarajevo, Bosnia-Herzegovina, July 2006.

20   Jean Hatzfeld, *Machete Season: The Killers in Rwanda Speak* (New York: Picador, 2005), p. 26.

21   Paul Ricoeur, *Oneself as Another* (Chicago, IL: University of Chicago Press, 1992), p. 157.

22   Hannah Arendt, *The Human Condition* (Chicago, IL: University of Chicago Press, 1989), p. 178.

23   Pierre Bourdieu, *The Logic of Practice* (Stanford, CA: Stanford University Press, 1992).

24   May, *Sharing Responsibility*, p. 105.

25   Jean Hatzfeld and Linda Coverdale, *Life Laid Bare: The Survivors in Rwanda Speak* (New York: Other Press, 2007). Though see Scott Straus, *The Order of Genocide: Race, Power and War in Rwanda* (Ithaca, NY: Cornell University Press, 2006), pp. 145–148.

26   Alison Des Forges, *Leave None to Tell the Story: Genocide in Rwanda* (New York: Human Rights Watch, 1999), pp. 213–214.

27   Bauman, *Modernity*, p. 194.

28   Cassie Striblen, "Guilt, Shame and Shared Responsibility," *Journal of Social Philosophy*, 38: 3 (Fall 2007), pp. 469–485.

29   Des Forges, *Leave None to Tell the Story*, p. 544.

30   Michelle D. Wagner, "All the Bourgemestre's Men: Making Sense of Genocide in Rwanda," *Africa Today*, 45: 1 (January–March 1998), pp. 25–36.

31   Mahmood Mamdani, *When Victims Become Killers: Colonialism, Nativism and the Genocide in Rwanda* (Princeton, NJ: Princeton University Press, 2001), p. 220.

32   Paul Rusesabagina, *An Ordinary Man: An Autobiography* (New York: Viking Books, 2006).

33   Also see Philip Hallie, *Lest Innocent Blood Be Shed: The Story of Le Chambon and How Goodness Happened There* (New York: Harper Colophon Books, 1979).

34   Des Forges, *Leave None to Tell the Story*, pp. 554–561.

35   Ibid., p. 565.

36   See Frances Henry, *Victims and Neighbors: A Small Town in Nazi Germany Remembered* (South Hadley, MA: Bergin and Garvey Publishers, 1984); and victim testimonies in Donald Miller and Lorna Touryan Miller, *Survivors: An Oral History of the Armenian Genocide* (Berkeley, CA: University of California Press, 1999); Gideon Hausner, *Justice in Jerusalem* (New York: Schocken Books, 1968).

37   Consider the Polish nationalist (largely Catholic) underground Home Army fighting the Nazis, whose main concern was not the plight of Polish Jews. The partisans were, of course, victims themselves, but nevertheless they often had strained relations with Jews. See Norman Davies, *Rising '44: The Battle for Warsaw* (New York: Viking, 2004).

38   Berel Lang, "The Decision Not to Decide," in Berel Lang, *Act and Idea in the Nazi Genocide* (Chicago: Chicago University Press, 1990).

39 May, "Metaphysical Guilt."
40 Saul Friedländer, *The Years of Extermination: Nazi Germany and the Jews 1939–1945* (New York: HarperCollins, 2007).
41 Albert Camus, *Neither Victims Nor Executioners* (New York: World Without War, 1968), p. 34.

PART 3 CASES

TOLOWA TATTOOING

From Copyright Photograph 1923 by E.S.Curtis

Figure 10.1 Edward Curtis, "Tolowa Tattooing" (Tolowa woman), photograph, 1923. In Edward Curtis and Frederick Hodge, eds, *The North American Indian, XIII* (Norwood, MA: Plimpton Press, 1924), plate opposite p. 100.

Source: Courtesy the Beinecke Library, Yale University.

CHAPTER 10

When "The World Was Turned Upside Down"

California and Oregon's Tolowa Indian genocide, 1851–1856

Benjamin Madley

Del Norte County – in California's northwest corner – is a quiet region of towering redwoods, rugged coastline, and clear, free-flowing rivers. Known for weathered barns, fishing boats, and pristine forests, the region draws visitors seeking calm in a world of change. The shadows beneath its redwoods are particularly evocative of tranquil constancy. Some of these titans have stood for a thousand years or more; they were seedlings when Rome fell. Dwarfed by them, it is easy to imagine that history might involve little change over time. Yet to those who know the region's nineteenth-century past, the crack of a single falling branch can recall cataclysmic upheaval.

Like many California Indian peoples, the Tolowa of northwestern California and southwestern Oregon were nearly obliterated following the arrival of Anglo-Americans. From as many as 5,000 people in 1851, their population fell to perhaps 900 by 1856, a decline of as much as 82 percent or more in just five years.[1] European diseases probably played some part in this catastrophe, but genocide also played a role that, until now, has remained largely unexamined.[2]

Scholars have studied the Tolowa for over 130 years, generally emphasizing Tolowa culture, resistance, and survival.[3] Yet, while four scholars have briefly suggested that the Tolowa suffered genocide, no one has yet written a detailed history of the Tolowa demographic decline, or carefully evaluated whether or not this decline was the result of genocide.[4] While researching the broader question of genocide in California, for

"American Genocide: The California Indian Catastrophe, 1846–1873," it became clear that the Tolowa genocide question merited further detailed study.[5]

Using written and oral history sources – many new to Tolowa studies – this chapter will first describe the pre-1851 Tolowa world before narrating the three phases of the Tolowa genocide, which lasted from 1851 to 1856. The chapter will then explore the potentially genocidal conditions imposed upon the Tolowa in federal reservations from 1856 on. Finally, the chapter will explain how the Tolowa catastrophe constituted genocide according to the 1948 United Nations Genocide Convention and what this means for the Tolowa, genocide scholars, and our understanding of both Native American and United States history.

TAA-LAA-WAA-DVN BEFORE 1851

For perhaps eighty centuries or more, the Tolowa inhabited a place they call "Taa-laa-waa-dvn," meaning "Tolowa place/homeland."[6] According to Tolowa theology, the Tolowa originally emerged from a specific place on this land after genesis.[7] Many Tolowa today claim pre-contact borders extending from Oregon's Sixes River to California's Wilson Creek and "east to [Oregon's] Applegate watershed," while defining themselves as part of a larger Dee-ni' community, Athabascans who spoke mutually intelligible languages and shared a culture and religion before contact.[8] Most scholars, however, have described the Tolowa as a distinct tribe, probably due to the mid-nineteenth-century deportation of all Oregon Dee-ni' to reservations. Thus, most scholars generally agree that pre-contact Taa-laa-waa-dvn extended from Oregon's Winchuck River to near California's Wilson Creek, while interior boundaries were less clearly defined. According to these borders, Taa-laa-waa-dvn was roughly contiguous with modern-day Del Norte County and covered between 640 and 955 square miles, a region somewhat smaller than Rhode Island (Figure 10.2).[9] This chapter will address the Tolowa of this area.

Before whites arrived, the Tolowa employed a complex legal system, used sea-shell currency, and constructed permanent rectangular redwood houses in politically autonomous villages bound together by a shared language.[10] From the Pacific, Tolowa harvested crustaceans, seals, sea lions, and stranded whales. From rivers and streams they collected salmon, smelt, and trout. From the land they took elk, deer, and other game while harvesting berries, seeds, tubers, and that California Indian staple, the acorn.[11] In combination, these varied and abundant food sources supported 2,400 to 5,000 Tolowa in some 23 settlements.[12]

The discovery of gold all around Taa-laa-waa-dvn prefigured the near-obliteration of this world. In 1850, prospectors found gold 30 miles south, on Trinity Bay, and 60 miles east, on the Shasta River. The next year they struck gold 40 miles to the northeast, in southern Oregon. Surrounded by these strikes to the north, east, and south, Taa-laa-waa-dvn became a destination for gold-seekers. Their arrival proved particularly devastating to the Tolowa, in large part because California legislators had imposed anti-Indian measures just prior to prospectors' arrival.

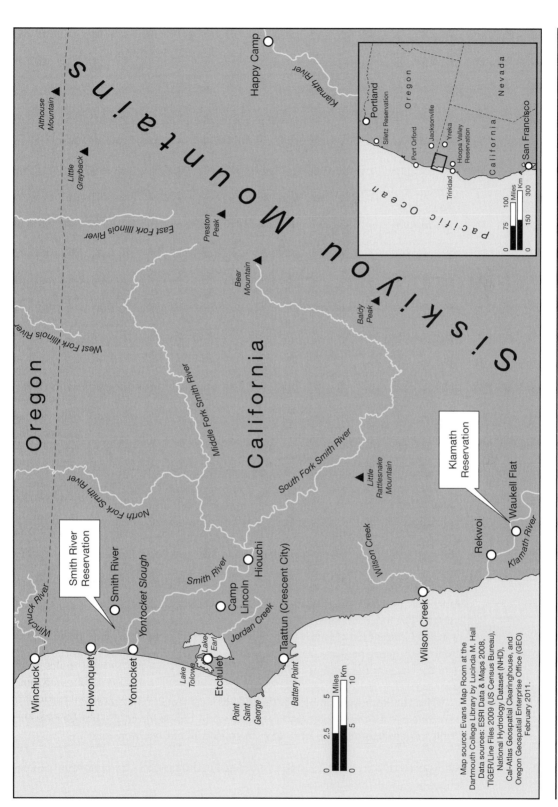

Figure 10.2 Map of Tolowa territory, 1850s.

PHASE I: THE KILLINGS BEGIN, 1851–1853

In a January 1851 speech, California's first civilian United States governor, Peter Burnett, helped set the course of the new state's American Indian policies when he declared "that a war of extermination will continue to be waged . . . until the Indian race becomes extinct," and warned that what he called "the inevitable destiny of the race is beyond the power or wisdom of man to avert."[13] California state legislators then put the power of the purse behind Governor Burnett's declaration. In February of 1851 they appropriated $500,000 to pay for past and future Indian-hunting campaigns by volunteer California state militia units.[14] Three months later, whites began killing Tolowa.

In May 1851, some prospectors entered Taa-laa-waa-dvn's Smith River Valley and encountered "about fifty Indians." The prospectors then met "Captain J.B. Long, Commandant and three privates of the Shasta Volunteers," heading north "to chastise the Rogue River Indians" of southern Oregon. After failed negotiations, during which Long demanded that the Tolowa surrender a gun he believed stolen, Tolowa men trained their weapons on the whites. Although the Tolowa were probably only covering their retreat, "The [ten] whites then commenced firing" and pursued the retreating Tolowa. Ultimately, "They found four dead Indians . . . and it is supposed several were wounded but . . . None of the whites were hurt." The prospector's narration ended with a postscript: "We have discovered good diggings on a creek emptying into this river, which yields on an average about fifty cents per pan."[15] Whites, guns, and gold would prove an explosive mixture.

In the spring of 1852, whites pitched tents on the beach near Ta-at-tun (Taa-'at-dvn), the village where Jedediah Smith's exploring party had made the first known white visit to Taa-laa-waa-dvn 23 years earlier.[16] The newcomers displaced the Tolowa community – perhaps violently – and, on its remains, built Crescent City, which quickly became the distributing seaport for booming gold-mining towns like Jacksonville, Oregon, and Happy Camp, California. Many of these newcomers had little use for Native Americans.

In about 1852 or 1853, the Tolowa apparently suffered their first major massacre at white hands. In 1880, former United States Indian Affairs Commissioner, George Manypenny, who had served from March 1853 to March 1857, wrote that "[a]t an early day . . . a gold hunting expedition" landed "near the southern boundary of Oregon," i.e. presumably in Taa-laa-vaa-dvn. "About thirty" Indians then "at the request of the 'Americans' proceeded to help unload the vessel." Unaware of some whites' annihilationist enmity, "The Indians labored faithfully." Meanwhile, as unloading continued in what was probably Crescent City Harbor – the only good harbor in the immediate vicinity of the California/Oregon border – the prospectors placed two cannons on "a large rock" located "[i]n the bay near the landing and close to the vessel." Then,

> When the work was completed, the Indians were requested to come on the rock to receive pay for their labor. As they passed up in Indian file, at the proper moment, the guns were brought to bear upon them, and all but two were killed.

Manypenny thus reported 28 Indians murdered in this massacre, heretofore unacknowledged as part of Tolowa history.[17]

By 1853, "people were constantly arriving at Crescent City, and the place was rapidly growing from a small collection of tents to a good-sized town."[18] One of these new arrivals was 44-year-old Ward Bradford, an important yet all-but-forgotten observer of the Tolowa ordeal. He arrived at Smith River, 13 miles north of Crescent City, in March 1853, and described the region as "thickly inhabited by Indians, who lived chiefly in villages along the coast, subsisting mainly on fish. They were shy at first, but soon became acquainted with us, and were quite trustworthy."[19] As it turned out, the Tolowa were wise to be wary.

PHASE II: ORGANIZED MASSACRES, 1853

White attacks on the Tolowa multiplied in 1853, continuing a period that modern Tolowa recall as "the time the world was turned upside down."[20] The year brought the birth of the "first white child ever" in what would become Del Norte County, the establishment of Crescent City's first two churches, and frequent organized massacres.[21]

According to J.M. Peters' recollections – which do not appear in academic literature on the Tolowa – "about the 1st of May, 1853 California Jack and two other men started from Crescent City for the purpose of prospecting on Smith River"; "after a week or two it was reported that an Indian had been seen in town carrying a revolver, and several men started for the Indian ranch at Battery Point," near Crescent City. When they arrived, a Tolowa showed Peters and the others a pistol engraved: "California Jack." Assuming that the Tolowa had acquired the revolver by nefarious means, "the party at once made a charge upon the camp, killing the one who had the pistol and eight others" before burning the hamlet.[22] This massacre of nine Tolowa, a death toll scholars have never before quantified, initiated a series of similar organized killings, more of which would be precipitated by events in Oregon three months later.

In August 1853, the on-again-off-again Rogue River War – between southwestern Oregon Indians and whites – began north of Taa-laa-waa-dvn. Crescent City whites, who traded extensively with southwestern Oregon immigrants and miners, soon marched north to join the conflict. In 1877, Benjamin Dowell of Jacksonville, Oregon – another source new to Tolowa studies – recalled that, in August or early September of 1853, "a company . . . marched from Crescent City through Jacksonville and Rogue River valley to the council ground on Rogue River near Table Rock waving a flag on which was inscribed in flaming colors Extermination." According to Dowell, these men "threatened to Carry out their favorite idea of Extermination after they joined the Oregon volunteers." Fortunately, Rogue River Indian leaders and General Joseph Lane signed a peace treaty soon thereafter, thwarting the plan.[23] Returning south, however, these Crescent City men unleashed their "favorite idea" – extermination – on the Tolowa.

Why did Oregon's Rogue River War trigger a campaign against uninvolved Tolowa who lived mainly in California? Because the war involved Dee-ni' tribes that were ethnically, culturally, and linguistically linked to the Tolowa, some whites apparently feared the Tolowa might join the war and attack whites. Thus, they launched preemptive search-and-destroy sorties in northern Taa-laa-waa-dvn.

Just north of the California border, where the Winchuck River flows into the sea, whites attacked the northernmost Tolowa village of Winchuck (Duu-srxuu-shi'). "[A]n

Indian of the Chetco River" later wrote that while most of its inhabitants were upriver, hunting and gathering, the attackers "burned about forty houses and the old people in them."[24] That same year, Howonquet (Xaa-wan'-k'wvt) "was burned and about seventy people were killed" at the Smith River's mouth.[25] Army regulars also stuck to the east. In late October a correspondent reported that soldiers had attacked an Indian camp in the Siskiyou Mountains, near "Illinois creek," killing "from 8 to 15" Tolowa fleeing coastal violence.[26] Five weeks later, San Francisco's *Daily Alta California* reported: "The Indians of Illinois Valley (the extreme south) have been troublesome, but were quieted by a brush with some US troops, in which 8 Indians were killed."[27] A lethal pattern was emerging.

That November, Austrian travel writer Ida Pfeiffer arrived in Taa-laa-waa-dvn to "visit the Indians." Her four-day-long "excursion" from Crescent City to the Smith River region and back provided a vivid picture of the autumn anti-Tolowa campaign. Pfeiffer initially described a people in retreat: "they are retiring further and further into the interior since the settlement of the whites, and to see a large village you have to go at least twelve miles." She soon discovered why: "These Indians are represented as treacherous, cowardly, and revengeful, and only attacking the whites when they find one alone." Pfeiffer then reported that Tolowa resistance had left at least three and perhaps five white men dead.

Traveling north, Pfeiffer's portrait of devastation sharpened.

In the [Smith River region] I saw several burnt and devastated wigwams, whence the people had been driven out by force because they would not willingly give up their native soil to the stranger; and besides taking their land, the whites seduce their wives and daughters, and, when they can not succeed in this, sometimes seize them by open violence.

For example:

Three miles from [Crescent City] Americans had settled as farmers; and one day, when a native was passing by their door with his wife, on his way to the town, these ruffians sprang out of their dwelling, snatched the woman from the side of her husband, dragged her into the house, and locked the door. The poor Indian screamed, and yelled, and struck the door, demanding his wife; but, instead of giving up their prey, these civilized men rushed out again, beat the Indian furiously, and drove him away.

Such abductions were apparently common. At one ranch, Pfeiffer noted: "These farmers, it seems, lived in a state of constant strife with the Indians, on account of their [abductions of Tolowa] women."[28] In fact, abductions seem to have been an important contributing factor in the Tolowa cataclysm.

In 1850, a California state law – which legalized white custody of Indian minors while barring Indian testimony against whites in California courts – had opened the door to abductions. The abductions, in turn, tended to separate Tolowa males and females, thus exacerbating Tolowa population decline.[29] Then, in 1852, California legislators passed an "Act to Prevent the Sale of Fire-arms and Ammunition to Indians," thus limiting Tolowa ability to protect themselves and their families from raiders.[30] The result seems to have been the abduction of both Tolowa women and children. According to the 1983

Tolowa Federal Acknowledgment Petition, "youngsters stolen from their parents under California law became indentured servants [and were taken to] San Francisco, Los Angeles and Portland."[31]

Meanwhile, burned villages, suggesting possible massacres, were a common sight as Pfeiffer continued her journey. On November 9, she visited a "settlement of about a dozen whites" and noted,

> Here also the first thing I saw was the remains of a wigwam that had been burned to ashes [and Tolowa] naturally revenged themselves when they could, and had at last killed one of the white men, whereupon the rest set fire to the village and drove away its inhabitants.

Pfeiffer concluded: "The great fault of the government is over-indulgence toward the white settlers . . . who shamefully abuse the indulgence." To her, the solution lay in a more robust and equitable legal system:

> As long as there are so few courts of justice in the country that it is very difficult for a native to find his way to one, and until these courts show some more just severity to the misconduct of the settlers, the poor Indian will remain the sport of the insolent white.[32]

Pfeiffer's words proved prescient.

In the late autumn of 1853, large numbers of Tolowa pilgrims proceeded to Yontoket (Yan'-daa-k'wvt), the largest Tolowa town and "the spiritual center of the Tolowa world."[33] Located on the west end of Yontocket Slough, south of Smith River, Yontocket lay some 13 miles north of Crescent City. There, Tolowa pilgrims rendezvoused with Yuroks, from the south, and other Dee-ni' from the north.[34] The pilgrims came to pray and celebrate the World Renewal Dance, the *Nee-dash*, or "Feather Dance."[35] The Tolowa were not at war with whites that autumn. Nevertheless, while the celebrants slept, whites led by veteran Tolowa-killer J.M Peters stealthily encircled them.

According to Peters – whose recollections shed fresh light on these events – when it became known that survivors of his Battery Point massacre were at Yontocket, he formed a 33-man company, "well armed and resolved upon the extermination of all the Indians concerned in the killing of" California Jack and his companions. Peters's men then surrounded Yontocket and opened fire as "the first rays of morning began to streak the Eastern horizon."

> Immediately the Indians came creeping out of their huts, armed with bows and arrows. But these primitive weapons were no match to the improved arms of the whites . . . On all sides as the savages attempted to escape they were shot down and the crack of rifles and Indian yells, intermingled with the screams of the women and children, made the scene one of wild confusion.

Peters's men burned the village to the ground and "Scarcely an Indian was left alive." Attempting to dignify this atrocity, Peters reported no women or children intentionally killed. Still, he called the attack – in which he lost no men – "a saturnalia of blood."[36]

In 1923, the 34-year-old Tolowa Sam Lopez, his wife, and father-in-law briefly summarized that nightmare dawn: "a large number of Indians were caught during a ceremonial dance and ruthlessly slaughtered."[37] In 1963, 87-year-old Eddie Richards related another Tolowa perspective based on "stories told to him by" relatives and an eyewitness:

> The white people got all around them, around that farm, along that big slough. Most of them got on the other side, and when the Indians come across they get him. The others started in around that house. Every time someone go out, never come back in . . . They set fire to the house, the Indians' house. You could see them just cutting heads off. They stick them things into them; pretty soon they pick them up and throw them right into the fire. Some of 'em tried to get away, run down the slough. Soon as they get down there, if they don't get 'em right away, they get 'em from the other side when they come up.

Richards quoted a survivor reporting "hundreds and hundreds" of Indians at Yontocket, and explaining that after the massacre, "the water was just red with blood, with people floating around all over." Also in 1963, 93-year-old Amelia Brown related another Tolowa view based upon what she had been told: "The white people were all around, they just watched. Then they set fire to the place. Women try to get away, they grab 'em, throw 'em in fire. Take pot shots at 'em when they try to run. Just two men got away."[38] In 1966, Sam Lopez added that attackers "killed so many Indians they could not bury them all, so they took the bodies and tied rocks around their necks and took them in the slough . . . and buried them that way."[39] In 1979, Loren Bommelyn related another harrowing Tolowa view of the massacre's conclusion: "Over 450 of our people were murdered or lay dying on the ground. Then the whitemen built a huge fire and threw in our sacred ceremonial dresses, and regalia, and our feathers, and the flames grew higher." Then, "they threw in the babies. Many of them were still alive."[40]

Because so many victims were incinerated, submerged, or floated away, the attackers probably could not obtain an accurate body count. In Ernie Coan's unpublished 1933 manuscript, Peters recollected "a score or more" killed, but an unsigned 1880 *Del Norte Record* article – almost certainly an earlier recollection by Peters, given nearly identical wording – stated that, "an eye witness says that he stood in one place and counted seventy bodies," presumably after the killing had concluded, and thus after many victims had already been immolated or thrown into Yontocket Slough. These conditions help explain why this 1880 estimate concluded that "[p]erhaps the souls of as many more were sent to . . . the Great Spirit" – for a total of as many as 140 killed – and why Bledsoe later estimated "a large number" killed.[41] These circumstances also help to clarify why Smith River resident Asa Crook reported, in a forgotten 1916 essay, that: "The number killed, including men, women and children is estimated at one hundred fifty."[42]

Still, this may have been an underestimate (Table 10.1). Tolowa sources insist that whites murdered between "several hundred" and 600 people at Yontocket.[43] Even if we halve the latter estimate, the attack killed a substantial portion of the Tolowa, and may rank among the most lethal massacres in United States history, rivaling the approximately 270–300 Miniconjou Sioux killed at Wounded Knee, South Dakota, in 1890.[44] Yet, the Yontocket massacre remains unknown except to a few scholars, locals, and, of course, Tolowa.

Table 10.1 1853 Yontocket massacre death toll estimates, 1880–1999

Source and date	Estimated Native American death toll
Peters(?) in *Del Norte Record*, 1880	70–140
Bledsoe, 1881	"a large number"
Crook in Baldwin, 1916	~150
Lopez (Tolowa), his wife, and her father, 1923	"a large number"
Peters in Coan, 1933	"a score or more"
Lopez (Tolowa), 1966	"several hundred"
Bommelyn (Tolowa), 1979	450
Tolowa Sources summarized by Thornton, 1984*	450–600
Reed (Tolowa), 1999*	~500

*For sources, see note 43.

Despite its magnitude, Yontocket was only part of the wider 1853 anti-Tolowa campaign. The local historian John Childs later explained that in "1853, the Indians at Burnt Ranch (Yontocket) and the ranches at the mouth of the Smith river were nearly annihilated and their houses burned by the determined whites."[45]

The "determined whites" continued their operations the following year. On January 18, 1854, the purser of the steamer *Crescent City* arrived in San Francisco and described how, just before sailing from Crescent City, "seven Indians were killed . . . about ten miles up the" Smith River. A Mr. McCombe arrived in San Francisco on the same day as the purser, having sailed on a different ship from Humboldt. McCombe reported eight Indians killed in the "vicinity" of "the mouth of Smith's River."[46] Whites may also have slain other Tolowa along Jordan Creek.[47] Finally, "In 1854 some Indians from Crescent City, accompanying as guides a party of three miners, capsized the canoe in crossing Smith river and killed the miners." In retaliation, whites "attacked the Tátatténi [Tolowa] at Crescent City, burned their houses, and killed many of them."[48]

PHASE III: STATE-SUPPORTED KILLING

Until 1854, California state officials were only indirectly involved in killing Tolowa. Governor Burnett had set the tone by proclaiming "a war of extermination . . . inevitable," and legislators created the legal frameworks that denied California Indians full protection under state law, barred them from owning firearms, encouraged Indian killing, and thus facilitated violence against the Tolowa. Still, while state officials had armed and paid for militia campaigns against other California Indians, they had not yet directly supported Tolowa-killing. That changed during the third phase of the time when "the world was turned upside down." State decision-makers now officially recognized local volunteer state militia units, armed and supplied them, and, after one search-and-destroy campaign, paid them.

On April 27, 1854, Crescent City men organized the Klamath Mounted Rangers as a California state militia cavalry unit.[49] By May 2, 66 men had joined up.[50] Eleven days later, rival Crescent City men formed the Coast Rangers and elected D.W. Thorpe their captain. Thorpe soon told Governor John Bigler that he planned to quell "the Indians between [Crescent City] and Wyreka [Yreka] threatening the peace." Thorpe then requested rifles, formal recognition, and commissions for his officers. By July 11, 49 men had joined up. The next day Thorpe requested of Bigler "thirty five U.S. Rifles + all other accoutrements belonging to a Rifle company."[51]

The state of California armed these two Crescent City volunteer militia units and their community to an extent scholars have never before documented. In an undated petition, Klamath County men asked Governor Bigler for ten rifles, 20 muskets, and 1,000 cartridges for use against "hostile Indians."[52] Bigler approved this request while also granting – and adding to – Thorpe's request.[53] On January 31, the state militia Quartermaster General, William Kibbe, sent the Klamath County judge "20 Muskets, 10 Rifles and 1000 Rifle Cartridges."[54] By November 14, Kibbe had sent the Coast Rangers 35 each of "Percussion Rifles and Appendages [,] Cartridge Boxes[,] Cartridge Boxes Plates[,] Cartridge Boxes Belts[,] Cartridge Boxes Belts Plates[,] Gun Slings[,] Cones" as well as "3,000 Percussion Caps[,] 2,000 Rifle Ball Cartridges [and] 4 Non-commissioned Officers' Swords and Belts."[55] Meanwhile, Kibbe sent the Klamath Rangers "50 Percussion Rifles; 50 Cartridge Boxes; 50 do. Belts and Plates; 50 Cap Pouches; 50 Gun Slings."[56]

This stockpiling of over a hundred rifles and muskets, as well as swords, accoutrements, and thousands of rounds of ammunition, complemented local whites' existing arsenal and suggested the presence of a clear danger or at least a credible threat. Yet a June 10 letter in the first *Crescent City Herald* insisted: "our country [has] neither wild beast nor Indian formidable as an enemy." Unfortunately, militiamen and their advocates soon overwhelmed such voices of reason.

On November 1, 1854, the 36-year-old Klamath Mounted Rangers' Second Lieutenant, Alfred French, joined a hunting trip on the Smith River's south fork.[57] During the trip, he disappeared. On November 8, *The Crescent City Herald* reported: "It is supposed by some that he has been killed by the Indians on the South Fork, as several months ago Mr. French had occasion to punish one of them for some misdemeanor."[58] Soon thereafter, French's corpse was found near an Indian camp and three Indians, "Black Mow, his son Jim . . . and a Chetcoe [*sic*] Indian named Narpa" were accused of murdering him.[59]

Some locals now began clamoring for the obliteration of the Tolowa. On November 15, *The Crescent City Herald* reported that "a feeling of resentment against the Indians began to rise in the community, and an indiscriminate punishment of the whole of them was advocated by many."[60] Exterminationists now became increasingly vocal. The possibility that Tolowa might have killed a Klamath Mounted Ranger who was also a recent county sheriff candidate provoked public meetings in Crescent City.[61] Some whites called for "an indiscriminate slaughter of the Indians:"

> To precipitate matters and prevent any peaceful solution to the case, some white men of the baser sort, went among the Indians who had been gathered at [Battery Point] and caused them to fly by telling them that the Whites were going to kill them all, thus to give color to the assertion that all were guilty and should be exterminated.[62]

As the debate divided whites, Klamath Mounted Rangers captured Black Mow, Jim, and Narpa and brought them to Crescent City on November 17. The following day, "the citizens of Crescent City assembled *en masse* at the El Dorado saloon," selected 12 jurors and watched while the vigilante jury sentenced the three men "to be hung." On

November 20, Black Mow, Jim, and Narpa were hanged near Battery Point, as 24 Klamath Mounted Rangers stood by.[63]

Ironically, the hangings – meant to punish, deter, and thus minimize a perceived Tolowa threat – only intensified white anxieties. On December 20, *The Herald* described white fears and the desire to assuage those fears with either federal management or mass murder. The article first suggested that failing federal intervention, annihilation was the only possible course of action: "We . . . would regret our being driven to the necessity of waging a war of extermination against the red men in this quarter, before even an attempt could have been made by the Government to provide for them." The piece then sought to explain this bizarre equation:

> From appearances it would seem that the Klamath and Chetcoe [*sic*] Indians seek revenge for the three Indians lately hung here . . . They steal more frequently, appear in squads as if on the war-path, assume a bold impudence and not seldom use threats . . . A committee is even now investigating these matters and if it should appear that the Indians really concert new mischief nothing can save them from destruction . . . if [whites] make a clean sweep of the Indians, who can blame them?

Following this endorsement of extermination, the journalist claimed that salving anxieties justified annihilation:

> It cannot be expected that the community will suffer continual threats from the Indians and keep itself on the *qui vive* against them all the time. We have done our best to live in peace with them, and if now we should be forced to harsher measures, the fault will not be ours.[64]

Of course, it was just not true that local whites had done their "best" to achieve peaceful cohabitation. This threat of preemptive strike was, in effect, a veiled declaration of extermination.

On December 27, *The Herald* published the report of the four-man committee sent to investigate the possibility of an Indian attack emanating from the Smith River region. The committee found no evidence of planned Tolowa hostility, but fearful and murderous whites required scant evidence to launch another preemptive massacre.[65]

In late December, the Tolowa and their Indian neighbors gathered on the shores of Lake Earl to again celebrate their annual World Renewal ceremonies, in keeping with tradition.[66] Not wanting to revisit the Yontocket killing fields, celebrants relocated the sacred gathering to the "large" town of Etchulet ('Ee-chuu-le'), about four miles north of Crescent City.[67] As James Collins has theorized, "whites feared Indian retaliation for the . . . hangings, and they were alarmed that Chetco, Rogue River, and Yurok Indians had joined Tolowa" at Etchulet.[68] Militia leaders thus targeted Etchulet for a surprise attack on all-but-unarmed civilians.

In the early morning of December 31, 1854, as many as 50 Coast Rangers and 66 Klamath Mounted Rangers, units armed with state-supplied weapons and ammunition, and accompanied by an unknown number of Smith River Valley whites, surrounded Etchulet.[69] According to oral histories gathered in the 1960s, these men "went out . . . and hid in the brush surrounding the village, agreeing that nobody would shoot until the Indians came out of their houses in the morning." The rangers waited in position.

Finally at day break a single shot was fired by a nervous white man and the whole Indian village was awakened. As the Indians, men, women and children, came from their homes they were shot down as fast as the whites could reload their guns. The Indians were unable to defend themselves as the attackers were hidden in the brush.[70]

The Crescent City Herald reported that the Indians had only three guns, that they were offered no quarter, and that they "swam to the other side of the lake, only to encounter the fire of another party who lay in wait."[71] Oral histories report: "The angered whites followed, shooting at every head that appeared above water," and after the attackers had killed large numbers on land, "they had to take many bodies and bury them in the lake."[72]

Just how many people died at Etchulet remains, as at Yontocket, difficult to estimate, since many victims were killed in the water or thrown into it after being killed. Thus, attackers again probably had difficulty obtaining a complete body count. In January the *Herald* reported that whites had engaged "some thirty-five Indians" and killed "some thirty."[73] That same month, San Francisco's *Daily Alta California* reported that, "the Indians were nearly all killed."[74] Then, on March 10, the Coast Rangers' First Lieutenant, Anderson Myers, reported that between "about" December 27, 1854 and January 25, 1855: "Coast + Klamath Rangers Volunteer Citizens +c under my Command" killed "about thirty" Indians "In the different skirmishes with them [with] but one of our men wounded.[75] Bledsoe echoed this estimate.[76] However, other whites claimed more than "sixty-five Indian deaths" at Etchulet, not including "those who were shot in the water and sank."[77]

Tolowa, probably more familiar with Etchulet's victims, produced much higher estimates. According to Russell Thornton, twentieth-century Tolowa "assert that some 150 Tolowa were killed."[78] Other "Indian accounts" claimed that, "only one or two escaped alive from the hundreds gathered."[79] Like Yontocket, Etchulet may rank among the larger massacres in US history (Table 10.2). Yet it too has been all but ignored.

Whatever the death toll, Etchulet was a carefully planned operation aimed at placing the Tolowa and their Indian neighbors in the cross-hairs of maximum firepower. Planners had to coordinate two competing militia units as well as Smith River auxiliaries. All three forces then had to meet under cover of darkness and surround Etchulet without alerting their intended victims. This required significant planning, communication, and secrecy. The fact that not a single white person seems to have warned the Tolowa, despite the operation's scale and complexity, suggests permissiveness, if not complicity, toward massacring Indians on the part of the many local whites involved.

Table 10.2 1854 Etchulet massacre death toll estimates, 1855–1998

Source and date	*Estimated Native American death toll*
Crescent City Herald (1855)	~30
Bledsoe (1881)	~30
Warburton and Endert (1966)	65+
Tolowa in Thornton (1984)	~150 Tolowa
"Indian accounts" summarized in Collins (1998)	"hundreds"

Two days after the slaughter, a *Crescent City Herald* article on Etchulet opened with a frank and chilling leader: "The die is cast and a war of extermination commenced against the Indians." Still, some whites opposed it. That same day, the *Herald* observed: "As to the expediency or necessity of an attempt to exterminate the Indians, various views are held by our citizens, and some deprecate very much the course taken." Others opposed only what they saw as excesses. The following week, an editorial censured killing Indians within city limits and the rumored public display of "an Indian scalp."[80]

Still, many locals defended Etchulet's perpetrators and the extermination war. On January 3, 1855, Smith River Valley whites "*[r]esolved*, That the citizens of Smith river valley concur in the proceedings of the volunteers and Coast Rangers against the Lagoon Indians, so far as they understand the proceedings." Three weeks later, the *Herald* attempted to justify the massacre as a meritorious act:

> the descent upon the Lagoon Ranch [Etchulet] happened to prove fatal to the very worst class of Indians. It would be unjust to blame the companies for acts of cruelty, reported to have been perpetrated by individuals, without giving them credit for their readiness in lending assistance to the settlers when the safety of the latter was considered to be in imminent danger.[81]

In other words, a potential but unspecified and unsubstantiated threat supposedly justified the preemptive mass-murder of Tolowa and other Indian civilians.

In 1894, John Childs continued with this line of reasoning in attempting to rationalize the massacres of late 1854 and early 1855: "To these prompt measures taken by the early settlers of Del Norte county is due their immunity from the terrors and privations of Indian wars. Eastern sentimentalists perhaps condemn such actions and style them massacres, but they insured safety."[82] As Childs suggested, this was no war. The "prompt measures" were serial preemptive massacres. They constituted, in sum, methodical annihilation.

Days after Etchulet, Tolowa headmen "CHY-LUS, COSE-TOOTTI, [and] YUT-SAY" signed a local treaty with white Smith River leaders, agreeing to surrender "all their fire-arms." Still, white violence continued. On January 17, the *Herald* reported that another white committee seeking to make "the Lagoon Indians" sign a treaty had killed "three of them."[83] Two days later, the *Sacramento Daily Union* reported that Klamath Mounted Rangers had killed "several" more Indians on the Smith River.[84] Three days after that, a correspondent reported that, between Trinidad and "Crescent City . . . whites are shooting them whenever an opportunity offers."[85] The Coast and Klamath Mounted Rangers took the field – officially – for only four weeks, until January 25, 1855, but they killed dozens, and perhaps hundreds, of Tolowa at Etchulet and beyond. According to the *Yreka Herald*, it was a "war of extermination" while the *Sacramento Union* warned: "The Indians must and will inevitably be annihilated by force, unless the United States Government adopts a different policy towards them."[86] Unfortunately, federal decision-makers took no action, and the killings continued.

Some whites seem to have employed trickery in their quest to annihilate the Tolowa. According to local historian Doris Chase:

> In January, 1855, some of the whites told some of the Indians they would furnish them with meat for a feast if they would invite Indians from another village. The

Indians invited their neighbors and had a big feast. Then, in the very early morning, the whites came and killed all the Indians they could find.[87]

Chase's statement suggests another well-orchestrated massacre. Other killers were less creative. On February 4, 1855, a correspondent reported: "Yesterday the ranches at the Lagoon, nine miles from here, north, were set on fire and consumed by a private war party."[88]

Responding to the example of this violence and to the possibility of the Rogue River War spilling south, on February 9, 1855, whites formed yet another volunteer militia unit: the "Crescent Guards." By February 21, it had 31 members.[89] Eight months later, an October issue of the *Herald* reported "the opening of an[other] Indian war in Rogue River Valley" and local whites again began discussing preemptive extermination.[90] On November 14, the *Herald* ran an editorial ominously entitled, "A War of Extermination," which reported: "we hear it is often said that nothing short of exterminating the Indians will give us peace and security."[91] Such sentiments were apparently well disseminated. On January 19, 1856, Pacific Department Commander Major General, John Wool – the highest ranking army officer in California – warned United States Army Headquarters that, "In Oregon, as well as in the northern part of California, many whites are for exterminating the Indians."[92]

Meanwhile, whites marshaled forces for action. In late November 1855, 90 men formed yet another Crescent City militia unit.[93] On January 9, 1856, "fifty [United States] soldiers" landed at Crescent City, presumably to protect local whites.[94] Nevertheless, six days later, some of the town's men began petitioning the California Governor, J. Neely Johnson, to officially enroll a volunteer militia company.[95] Then, after three petitions, on March 12, state legislators passed "An Act to Call out a Company of Volunteers for the Suppression of Indian Hostilities in Klamath County," appropriating $15,000 for the campaign.[96]

Recognizing another potentially murderous state-supported militia campaign in the making, other whites now stepped in. They relocated hundreds of Tolowa to an island in Crescent City Harbor, probably Taa-'at-nin'-le'.[97] According to the *Herald*, "These, partly of their own accord, partly on the representations of the Whites, came to the city for protection, and for their own safety were transferred to the little Island in our bay." J.B. Rosborough reported that, based upon the rations issued on March 2, 1856, their numbers included Indians from: Smith River, 179; Lagoon, 58; Ottegon, Chacha, Kohpay, and Neckel, 79; Total, 316. Rosborough also reported, "A few from each rancheria absent, more than a rateable [*sic*] portion of whom are squaws and old men unable to travel, and some sick."[98]

Still, many whites remained deeply frightened, perhaps fearing that un-incarcerated Tolowa might avenge past atrocities. Thus, Daniel White reached Crescent City on March 7 and pronounced it "a d—d hard place nothing done or to be done. Excitement still raging about the Indians."[99] Tolowa not "removed to the island" clearly remained in peril.[100]

On April 7, 1856, Governor Johnson finally called out a volunteer state militia company. Three days later, he countermanded the order, probably upon receiving news that General Wool had ordered "50 [soldiers] to the forks of Smith River."[101] Nevertheless, Rosborough used the April 28 burning of two houses near the Smith's mouth to rally 50 volunteers. The governor's local representative then enrolled 30 of them, on May 3, for

30 days.[102] Most surviving, un-incarcerated Tolowa eluded them, but state militia documents recorded five Indians killed between May 5 and May 31.[103] This "Klamath Expedition" disbanded on June 3. California legislators eventually spent $6,190.07 on related salaries and supplies, not counting armaments, thus endorsing the "Klamath Expedition" after the event. Congress did likewise, in 1861, voting to reimburse California for expenses related to the campaign, and ultimately paying California $2,953.77.[104]

Killings continued in June and July of 1856. Smith River Valley farmer Ward Bradford later recalled that: "Just before the close of the [Rogue River] war, in July, 1856, five or six roughs engaged in killing all the bucks they could find. They had already surrounded two small villages and killed twenty or thirty of the inhabitants." Bradford explained that, "One town of this character was located on my land near the beach, and was very ancient. This village contained about one hundred persons. The roughs threatened this town also." Bradford then reportedly armed himself and escorted these Tolowa to "the light-house island in front of the city," on whose "fifteen acres" he thought they could find "shelter" (Figure 10.3). According to Bradford, "If I had been caught in the act by the roughs, it would have cost me my life, as they still threatened me until peace was proclaimed . . . which was about six weeks after the Indians moved to the island."[105]

A new chapter of the Tolowa ordeal was beginning. On June 6, 1856, the *Herald* reported "about 1500 Indians" being held at the Klamath Reservation, near the mouth of the Klamath River, by "[s]ome thirty soldiers."[106] Then, in July, the reservation agent reported, "500 recently removed on to the reserve . . . from the country adjacent to the Oregon line," and his intention to "remove to the reservation . . . about forty Indians from Smith's river – the remnant of the Talawa [*sic*] tribe."[107] Eventually, some 600 Tolowa were taken to the Klamath Reservation.[108] Perhaps several hundred others remained unaccounted for. Thus, by mid-1856, the Tolowa had been reduced from perhaps 5,000 to probably not more than 900 people.

MAOR BRADFORD CONDUCTING INDIANS TO A PLACE OF SAFETY.

Figure 10.3 Unknown artist, drawing of "Major Bradford Conducting Indians to a Place of Safety," in Ward Bradford, *Biographical Sketches of the Life of Major Ward Bradford, Old Pioneer, As Related by the Author Who is Eighty-three Years of Age and Nearly Blind* (NP: Self-published, 1892?), p. 50.

Source: Courtesy the Beinecke Library, Yale University.

AFTERMATH: RESERVATIONS

Federal authorities' removal of most surviving Tolowa initiated a destructive new cycle of incarceration, escape, recapture, and re-incarceration – punctuated by deportations to other reservations – that would last until 1871.[109]

Tolowa today recall Klamath Reservation as the "Klamath Concentration Camp."[110] A June 1856 army report explained:

> The Indians . . . say that lies have been told them; that they have been told . . . that if they came here they would be protected from the whites [and] given fisheries[,] helped to build new houses, and that they would be fed . . . but that no such thing had been done, that no preparations have been made, and that they . . . will not . . . come down here to freeze and starve; that they own no land on this portion of the river, and that if they fish at the fisheries of other Indians they would be killed.

Moreover, "All 'cultivation' that has been done on the 'reservation,' that I am aware of, is a small piece of land at Wak-ell, near the mouth of the river, and the produce of which might support about twenty persons." Finally, reservation Indians, "are continually exposed to the brutal assault of drunken and lawless white men; their squaws are forced, and, if resented, the Indians are beaten and shot."[111]

In response to these conditions, many Tolowa fled. Reservation personnel shot some escapees, but by July 1857, the reservation agent reported "[i]n the vicinity of Crescent City and Smith's River some six hundred Indians."[112] Many were then re-deported to Klamath Reservation that summer.[113]

Desperate Tolowa now organized an uprising. On November 17, "an old squaw came to the station and told the Agent that the *Yon-tak-et Mow-e-ma* was very sick and wanted to see him." The agent and a Mr. Goodspeed then walked into a trap. Scarcely had they "entered the house of the supposed sick man" when "*Requa Mike* . . . presented a yager [gun] to the breast of the Agent and fired," just missing him. "The Tolowas [now] rushed upon them" and "a fight ensued." Fifteen minutes later, soldiers "arrived from the station and the Indians were completely routed, with the loss of ten of their number killed."[114] Lieutenant George Crook specified that his troops killed "ten, besides a number wounded," but three others – who met with reservation Agent H.P. Heintzleman the day after the uprising – reported that regulars "killed fifteen [while] others are supposed to have died of their wounds."[115] Thus, Bledsoe's claim of "fifteen or twenty" killed may well be accurate.[116] Whatever the death toll, most Tolowa eventually escaped. By Christmas, 1857, Crook reported 600–700 "on Smith River" and in March 1858, Crescent City was reportedly "full of" Indians.[117]

For the 80 Tolowa still at Klamath Reservation in 1858, the situation remained perilous.[118] In July, the *Humboldt Times* warned: "Government must take some steps to provide for these [reservation] Indians or they will be exterminated", and in October, insisted: "no attempt has ever been made by the officers in charge . . . to look after, or care for any" of the Indians relocated to Klamath Reservation.[119]

In 1860, federal forces again removed the Tolowa. Perhaps 600 were marched up the coast and incarcerated near Port Orford, Oregon. Most escaped to Taa-laa-waa-dvn, but some were later taken to northwestern Oregon's Siletz Reservation, with its reported diseases and poor conditions.[120]

Determined to hold the Tolowa on a reserve by force, but stymied by Tolowa resolve to live on ancestral lands, on May 3, 1862, federal decision-makers created the Smith River Reservation in Taa-laa-waa-dvn and established Fort Lincoln to "supervise" it. During its first year, the reservation contained some 2,000 Indians, including "about 300 . . . Tolowas."[121] Conditions were often lethal. In July 1863, California's Indian Affairs Superintendent lamented: "The unsettled condition of three-fourths or more of the Indians, who have been compelled to lie on the cold, damp ground . . . has [in combination with venereal pathogens transmitted by soldiers] caused disease, and death in many instances." Neglect compounded these conditions. Inmates received "no hoes or other farming tools" while "only an occasional Indian wear[s] a whole garment, and not a whole blanket could be found among 100 Indians." Thus, "their constant inquiry was: 'When *Captain* Lincoln, *big chief*, send Indian plenty blankets?'"[122] Unsurprisingly, the population declined. That October, the Commissioner explained: "the number of Indians at Smith river has decreased, not only by escapes but by severe sickness among them; measles, diarrhœa, and other epidemics."[123]

In a July 1868 cost-cutting move, Congress authorized the abandonment of the Smith River Reservation. That winter, the Indian Office moved its 320 inmates 134 miles southeast through the mountains to the Hoopa Valley Reservation on the Trinity River.[124] Still, "by 1871 not one Tolowa remained at Hoopa, for they had all . . . returned to Smith River."[125]

The cycle of repeated removals – in combination with reservation conditions – seems to have created a demographic disaster. Forced marches likely caused considerable mortality, and while many escaped, not everyone returned home, thus severing relationships and retarding demographic recovery. As Russell Thornton explained, Tolowa "population losses from the relocations are unknown. However, relocations have typically been quite severe for Indian peoples, for example, the Cherokee suffered huge population losses during the 'Trail of Tears.'"[126] Reservation conditions, meanwhile, seem to have caused many deaths. Writing in 1881, Bledsoe estimated 270 remaining Indians in Del Norte County "besides 82 on . . . Klamath Reservation."[127]

From 1851 to 1856, murders, abductions, and massacres had already reduced the Tolowa from as many as 5,000 people to perhaps 900 (Table 10.3). In those five years, individuals, groups, state militiamen, and United States soldiers nearly exterminated an entire people. Willful federal neglect, continuing violence and repeated forced removals then probably led to further demographic decline in succeeding decades.

The Tolowa were pushed to the edge of oblivion but held their ground. They survived by escaping, hiding, intermarrying, and tenaciously holding onto their culture and traditions against tremendous odds. Today, 1,526 Tolowa live in Del Norte County and beyond. They have won federal recognition, and 1,444 are enrolled members of the

Table 10.3 Tolowa population decline, 1851–1881

Year	Estimated total Tolowa population
1851	2,400–5,000+
1856	900(?)
1881	352 + some at Siletz = 400(?)

ON THE SHORES OF THE PACIFIC — TOLOWA

Figure 10.4 Edward Curtis, "On the Shores of the Pacific – Tolowa," photograph, 1923. In Edward Curtis and Frederick Hodge, eds, *The North American Indian, XIII* (Norwood, MA: Plimpton Press, 1924), opposite p. 98, plate. The woman in this photograph is Dorothy Lopez Williams, according to Loren Bommelyn, personal communication.

Source: Courtesy the Beinecke Library, Yale University.

Smith River Rancheria near Howonquet while 82 are members of the Elk Valley Rancheria near Crescent City.[128] Contemporary Tolowa are the descendants of people who survived "the time the world was turned upside down." Are they also the descendants of genocide survivors?

Figure 10.5 Edward Curtis, "Tolowa Dancing Head-dress," photograph, 1923. In Edward Curtis and Frederick Hodge, eds, *The North American Indian, XIII* (Norwood, MA: Plimpton Press, 1924), plate 455. The man in this photograph is Sam Lopez.

Source: Courtesy the Beinecke Library, Yale University.

GENOCIDE

To evaluate whether or not the Tolowa suffered genocide, it is crucial to understand the legal definition of this highly charged word. In 1943, the Polish Jew and legal scholar Raphael Lemkin minted a new word for an ancient crime. Defining the concept in 1944, he combined "the Greek word *genos* (tribe, race) and the Latin *cide*," or killing, to describe as genocide any attempt to annihilate an ethnic, national, religious, or political group either physically or culturally.[129] Four years later, the United Nations Convention on the Prevention and Punishment of the Crime of Genocide, defined genocide as: "Acts committed with intent to destroy, in whole or in part, a national, ethnical, racial or religious group, as such," including:

(a) killing members of the group;
(b) causing serious bodily or mental harm to members of the group;

(c) deliberately inflicting on the group conditions of life calculated to bring about its physical destruction in whole or in part;

(d) imposing measures intended to prevent births within the group; and

(e) forcibly transferring children of the group to another group.[130]

The Genocide Convention thus provides a clear, internationally recognized rubric for evaluating possible instances of genocide, including historical cases not subject to legal jurisdiction. First, perpetrators must evince "intent to destroy." Second, perpetrators must commit at least one of the five genocidal acts against one of the four protected groups.

The Tolowa catastrophe fits the two-part legal definition set forth in the 1948 UN Genocide Convention. First, various perpetrators articulated, in word and deed, their "intent to destroy, in whole or in part, a national, ethnical, racial [and] religious group as such." High-ranking California state officials, meanwhile, were also culpable because, despite repeated warnings, they failed to intervene, and because they supplied state militia death-squads with arms, ammunition, and accoutrements. Finally, state and federal legislators approved the 1856 Klamath Expedition, after the fact, by helping to pay for it. Such culpability, at the local, state, and federal levels, was typical of the genocide campaigns waged against California Indians in the 1850s and 1860s.[131]

Second, at various times, perpetrators committed acts of genocide. "Killing" included executions, homicides, and massacres committed by civilian groups, volunteer California militia units, and professional United States soldiers. In total, extant primary and secondary sources provide evidence suggesting that perhaps as many as 1,065 Tolowa people – and possibly many more – were burned alive, beheaded, hanged, killed by artillery fire, impaled, or shot dead by whites (Table 10.4). By way of contrast, Tolowa seem to have killed fewer than 20 whites.

In addition, rapes and beatings amounted to "causing serious bodily harm" on the basis of group identity. These two crimes of "killing" and "causing serious bodily harm," perpetrated against many California Indian tribes under mid-nineteenth-century United States rule, are irrefutable.[132]

However, more work needs to be done to determine whether or not the Tolowa suffered other genocidal crimes. Was malnutrition institutionalized on some or all of the reservations where the Tolowa were interned and, if so, did substantial numbers of Tolowa starve to death in federal custody? Was malnutrition inflicted with the requisite "intent to destroy" them? How much violence did the Tolowa suffer on the reservations? If reservation employees and Washington officials had ample evidence of either Tolowa malnutrition or sustained white violence on the reservations, but took no corrective action, then some of these officials were "deliberately inflicting on the group conditions of life calculated to bring about its physical destruction in whole or in part." This point requires further exploration. Additionally, because malnutrition and overwork predictably lower fertility, while increasing miscarriages and stillbirths, federal decision-makers may have been guilty of "imposing measures intended to prevent births within the group." This too needs further research. Finally, significant numbers of Tolowa children seem to have been abducted. Kidnapping California Indian children was common during this period, so this would not be surprising and would constitute "forcibly transferring children of the group to another group."

Table 10.4 Reported Tolowa killings, 1851–1857

Year	Location	Reported number of Tolowa killed	Reported number of whites killed in same incident
1851	Smith River Valley	4+	0
1852 or 1853?	Crescent City Harbor?	28	0
1853	Battery Point, near Crescent City	9	0
1853?	Winchuk	"burned about forty houses and the old people in them" (40+)	0
1853	Howonquet	70	0
1853	Near Illinois Creek in the Siskiyou Mountains	8 to 15	0
1853	"Illinois Valley (the extreme south)"	8	0
1853	Yontocket	"a score or more" to 600	0
1854	About "ten miles up the" Smith River	7	0
1854	Near "the mouth of Smith's River"	8	0
1854	Jordan Creek	?	0
1854	Crescent City	"killed many of them" (10+)	0
1854	Near Battery Point	2	0
1854	Etchulet	~30 to "hundreds" (200+)	0
1855	Unknown location	3	0
1855	Smith River	"several" (3+)	0
1855	Unknown location	"killed all the Indians they could find" (3+)	0
1856	Three different locations	5	0
1856	Coast near Smith River	20 to 30	0
1857	Klamath Reservation	10 to 20	0
Totals		288 to 1,065	0

In light of the United Nations definition, there is at least sufficient evidence of "intent to destroy," of "killing," and of "causing serious bodily harm" to designate the Tolowa case genocide.

Understanding the Tolowa catastrophe as genocide has important ramifications for the Tolowa, for genocide scholars, and for all Americans. For Tolowa community members, many of whom helped to make this chapter possible, documenting their ancestors' ordeal and labeling it genocide helps corroborate and complement existing Tolowa oral histories.[133] This information, in turn, can be used in education, commemoration, memorials, and in addressing the connection between "intergenerational/historical trauma" and related contemporary life-and-death tribal health issues.[134] For scholars, this study of Tolowa history suggests a new direction in genocide research: the need to undertake similarly detailed case studies exploring the possibility of genocide in other times and places in United States history. Such case studies may have a powerful cumulative impact on how all Americans – both Native American and non-Indian – understand US history. Careful examinations of possible genocides in United States history have the potential to help us re-evaluate the accepted emphasis on disease and warfare in Native American population decline and, ultimately, to create a more detailed, varied, and nuanced understanding of both Native American and United States history.

ACKNOWLEDGMENTS

The author thanks Joan Berman, Lena and Loren Bommelyn, John Faragher, Theresa Ferrer, Joseph Giovanetti, Lucinda Hall, Adam Jones, Ben Kiernan, Timothy Macholz, Dale Miller, George Miles, LaWanda Quinnell, Laura Roe, Jerry Rohde, Susan Snyder, Russell Thornton, Shannon Tushingham, Devon White, and the members of the Elk Valley and Smith River Rancherias for their help and guidance.

NOTES

1   Late twentieth-century pre-contact Tolowa population estimates range from 2,400 to 5,000+. Sherburne Cook, "The Aboriginal Population of the North Coast of California," *University of California Anthropological Records*, 13: 3 (1956), p. 101; Martin Baumhoff, "Ecological Determinants of Aboriginal California Populations," *University of California Publications in American Archaeology and Ethnology*, 49: 2 (1963), p. 231 [hereafter, "Ecological Determinants"]; Russell Thornton, *American Indian Holocaust and Survival: A Population History since 1492* (Norman, OK: University of Oklahoma Press, 1987), p. 207; Loren Bommelyn, *Now You're Speaking Tolowa* (Arcata: Humboldt State University, 1995), p. x; Annette Reed, http://www.csus.edu/pubaf/journal/spring2005/12research.htm.

2   Richard Gould, "Tolowa," in Robert Heizer, ed., *Handbook of North American Indians, Vol. VIII* (Washington, DC: Smithsonian, 1978), pp. 130, 135.

3   The first study appeared in Stephen Powers, *Tribes of California* (Washington, DC: GPO, 1877), pp. 65–71.

4   Jack Norton, *Genocide in Northwestern California: When Our Worlds Cried* (San Francisco: Indian Historian Press, 1979), pp. xviii, 54–57 [hereafter, *Genocide*]; Thornton, *American Indian Holocaust and Survival*, p. 206; David Stannard, *American Holocaust: The Conquest of the New World* (New York: Oxford University Press, 1992), p. 128; Bommelyn, *Now You're Speaking Tolowa*, p. x.

5   Benjamin Madley, "American Genocide: The California Indian Catastrophe, 1846–1873" (Ph.D. dissertation, Yale University, 2009).

6   Shannon Tushingham, "The Development of Intensive Foraging Systems in Northern California" (Ph.D. dissertation, University of California at Davis, 2009), p. ii, Table 21, p. 234. Gould reported 22 centuries of habitation in Gould, "Tolowa," p. 135. Translation provided by Loren Bommelyn.

7   Conversation with Loren Bommelyn; James Collins, *Understanding Tolowa Histories: Western Hegemonies and Native American Responses* (New York: Routledge, 1998), p. 10.

8   *Constitution of the Howonquet Indian Council of the Smith River Rancheria* (June 10, 2008), p. 1 [hereafter, *Constitution . . . of the Smith River Rancheria*]; Russell Thornton, "Social Organization and the Demographic Survival of the Tolowa," *Ethnohistory*, 31: 3 (Summer 1984), p. 188 [hereafter, "Social Organization"].

9   Gould, "Tolowa," p. 128; Thornton, "Social Organization," p. 188; Sharon Malinowski, Anna Sheets, Jeffrey Lehman, and Melissa Walsh Doig, eds, *The Gale Encyclopedia of Native American Tribes* (4 vols., Detroit: Gale, 1998), Vol. 4, p. 181; Richard Gould, "Ecology and Adaptive Response Among the Tolowa Indians of Northwestern California," *The Journal of California Anthropology*, 2: 2 (Winter 1975), p. 153; Baumhoff, "Ecological Determinants," p. 231.

10 Philip Drucker, "The Tolowa and their Southwest Oregon Kin," *University of California Publications in American Archaeology and Ethnology*, 36: 4 (1937), pp. 241–244 [hereafter, "Tolowa"]; Doris Chase, *They Pushed Back the Forest* (Sacramento: Self-published, 1959), pp. 11–12; Annette Reed, *"Neeyu Nn'ee min' Nngheeyilh Naach'aaghitlhni: Lha't'i Deeni Tr'vmdan' Natlhsri* – Rooted in the Land of our Ancestors, We Are Strong: A Tolowa History" (Ph.D. dissertation, University of California at Berkeley, 1999), p. xiii [hereafter, *Neeyu*].

11 Drucker, "Tolowa," pp. 231–235; Richard Gould, *Archaeology of the Point St. George Site, and Tolowa Prehistory* (Berkeley, CA: University of California Press, 1966), pp. 80–85.

12 Drucker, "Tolowa," pp. 226–227. According to Gould, "in 1828 the Tolowa resided for most of the year in eight villages." Gould, "Tolowa," p. 128.

13 California, *Journals of the Legislature of the State of California; at its Second Session* (NP: Eugene Casserly, 1851), p. 15.

14 California, *The Statutes of California* (Sacramento: Eugene Casserly, 1851), pp. 520–521.

15 *Daily Alta California*, July 2, 1851, p. 2 [hereafter, *DAC*].

16 A.J. Bledsoe, *History of Del Norte County, California with a Business Directory and Traveler's Guide* (Eureka, CA: Wyman & Co., 1881), p. 13 [hereafter, *History*]; Chase, *They Pushed Back the Forest*, p. 24.

17 George Manypenny, *Our Indian Wards* (Cincinnati: R. Clarke & Co., 1880), pp. 154–155.

18 Bledsoe, *History*, p. 12.

19 Ward Bradford, *Biographical Sketches of the Life of Major Ward Bradford, Old Pioneer, As Related by the Author, Who is Eighty-three Years of Age and Nearly Blind* (NP: Self-published, 1892?), p. 46 [hereafter, *Biographical Sketches*].

20 Reed, *Neeyu*, p. 46.

21 Bledsoe, *History*, p. 19; Esther Smith, *The History of Del Norte County, California* (Oakland: The Holmes Book Company, 1953), p. 12.

22 Peters(?) in *Del Norte Record*, June 26, 1880, p. 2. Peters was quoted using nearly identical language in Ernie Coan, "The Del Norte Indian" (manuscript, Humboldt State University Library, 1933), p. 20. Jerry Rohde provided this source. See also Collins, *Understanding Tolowa Histories*, 35.

23 B.F. Dowell, "Benjamin Franklin Dowell Papers, 1855–1886," Bancroft Library, pp. 5–6. Emphasis original.

24 Sam Van Pelt in *The Oregonian*, Sunday Magazine, February 5, 1939, p. 8. E.A. Schwartz identified these victims as "Chetcoes." Schwartz, *The Rogue River War and Its Aftermath, 1850–1980* (Norman, OK: University of Oklahoma Press, 1997), pp. 18–19.

25 Edward Curtis and Frederick Hodge, eds, *The North American Indian, XIII* (Cambridge: Cambridge University Press, 1924), p. 91.

26 *The Oregon Statesman*, November 22, 1853, p. 4.

27 *DAC*, December 1, 1853, p. 1.

28 Ida Pfeiffer, *Lady's Second Journey Round the World: From London to the Cape of Good Hope, Borneo, Java, Sumatra, Celebes, Ceram, the Moluccas, etc., California, Panama, Peru, Ecuador, and the United States* (New York: Harper & Brothers, 1856), pp. 312–320 [hereafter, *Lady's Second Journey*].

29 California, *The Statutes of California, Passed at the First Session of the Legislature* (San José: J. Winchester, 1850), pp. 408–410. For more on this act, see: Michael Magliari, "Free Soil, Unfree Labor: Cave Johnson Couts and the Binding of Indian Workers in California, 1850–1867," *Pacific Historical Review*, 73: 3 (August 2004), pp. 349–389.

30 Theodore Hittell, *The General Laws of the State of California, from 1850–1861* (San Francisco: H.H. Bancroft and Company, 1865), p. 532.

31 *Tolowa Federal Acknowledgment Petition* (Draft Version, 1983), p. 52. A final draft of this petition, which documents written and oral Tolowa history, was never submitted.

32 Pfeiffer, *Lady's Second Journey*, pp. 321–322.

33 Drucker, "Tolowa," p. 226; *Constitution . . . of the Smith River Rancheria*, p. 1.

34 Bommelyn, *Now You're Speaking Tolowa*, p. x.

35 Reed, *Neeyu*, p. xiii.

36 Peters(?), in *Del Norte Record*, June 26, 1880, p. 2; Peters in Coan, "Del Norte Indian," pp. 20–22.

37 C. Hart Merriam, notes in Martin Baumhoff, "California Athabascan Groups," *University of California Anthropological Records*, 16: 5 (1958), p. 226.

38 Richards and Brown in Richard Gould, "Indian and White Versions of 'The Burnt Ranch Massacre': A Study of Comparative Ethnohistory," *Journal of the Folklore Institute*, 3: 1 (June 1966), pp. 32–36.

39 Sam Lopez in Barbara Clausen and Beverly Spitzner, *Del Norte Bites: History and Recipes* (NP: Babe Publications, 1996), p. 11 [hereafter, Clausen and Spitzner, *Del Norte Bites*]. Jerry Rohde provided this source.

40 Bommelyn, in Norton, *Genocide*, pp. 54–56.

41 Peters, in Coan, "Del Norte Indian," p. 21; Peters(?) in *Del Norte Record*, June 26, 1880, p. 2; Bledsoe, *History*, p. 20.

42 Asa Crook in Marian Baldwin, "History of Smith River, California" (unpublished essay, Humboldt State University, 1916). Jerry Rohde introduced the author to this source.

43 Lopez in Clausen and Spitzner, *Del Norte Bites*, p. 11; Bommelyn in Norton, *Genocide*, p. 54; Thornton, "Social Organization," p. 192; Reed, *Neeyu*, p. 61.

44 Jeffrey Ostler, *The Plains Sioux and U.S. Colonialism from Lewis and Clark to Wounded Knee* (Cambridge: Cambridge University Press, 2004), p. 345.

45 John Childs, *Del Norte County as it is; Giving its History, Growth, Wealth and Attractions, Embracing a Political, Physical, Social and Financial History, from its Settlement to the Present Year, 1894* (Crescent City: *Crescent City News* Job Office, 1894), pp. 109–110.

46 *DAC*, January 19, 1854, p. 2.

47 *Tolowa Federal Acknowledgment Petition*, p. 16.

48 Curtis, *North American Indian, XIII*, pp. 91–92.

49 See http://www.militarymuseum.org/KlamathMounted%20Rangers.html.

50 *Sacramento Daily Union*, October 30, 1855, p. 2 [hereafter, *SDU*].

51 D.W. Thorpe, W.W. Armstrong, and A. Myers, May 13, 1854; D.W. Thorpe to John Bigler, ND; Muster Roll of the Coast Rangers of Klamath County, California, USA; Requisition, Coast Rangers; and D.W. Thorpe to John Bigler, July 12, 1854, all in Militia Companies Records, California State Archives, B3409-3 [hereafter, MCRB3409-3].

52 S.G. Whipple, W.D. Aylett, and A.J. Butler to John Bigler in California Adjutant General's Office, Military Department, Adjutant General, Indian War Papers, California State Archives [hereafter, IWP], F3753: 228. Del Norte County was then part of Klamath County.

53 John Bigler, September 11, 1854, MCRB3409-3.

54 Wm. Kibbe to Judge of Klamath Co., January 31, 1854, IWP, F3753: 229. Kibbe's 1854 Annual Reports list only "20 Percussion Muskets" sent to the judge.

55 Invoice of Ordnance + Armament . . . for use of the Coast Rangers, MCRB3409-3.

56 "Annual Report of Quarter-Master & Adjutant-General," 1854, p. 7, in California, *Journals of the Legislature of the State of California; at its Sixth Session* (NP: R.R. Redding, 1855).

57 *Crescent City Herald*, November 15, 1854, p. 2 [hereafter, *CCH*]; Klamath Mounted Rangers Muster Roll, June 5, 1854, in Militia Companies Records, California State Archives, B3415-1.

58 *CCH*, November 6 and 8, 1854, p. 2.

59 Bledsoe, *History*, p. 30.

60 *CCH*, November 15, 1854, p. 2.

61 *CCH*, June 24, 1854, p. 3.

62 *CCH*, November 29, 1854, p. 2.

63 *CCH*, November 22 and 29, 1854, p. 2. Emphasis original.

64 *CCH*, December 20, 1854, p. 2. Emphasis original.

65 *CCH*, December 27, 1854, pp. 1–2.

66 Reed, *Neeyu*, p. 66.

67 Drucker, "Tolowa," p. 227.

68 Collins, *Understanding Tolowa Histories*, p. 36.

69 *CCH*, January 3 and 10, 1855, p. 2.

70 Austin Warburton and Joseph Endert, *Indian Lore of the North California Coast* (Santa Clara: Pacific Pueblo Press, 1966), pp. 167–168 [hereafter, *Indian Lore*].

71 *CCH*, January 3, 1855, p. 2.

72 Warburton and Endert, *Indian Lore*, pp. 167–168; Lopez in Clausen and Spitzner, *Del Norte Bites*, p. 11.

73 *CCH*, January 3, 1855, p. 2.

74 *DAC*, January 18, 1855, p. 2.

75 *DAC*, March 18, 1855, p. 2; Anderson Myers to Adjutant General, March 10, 1855, MCRB3409-3.

76 Bledsoe, *History*, p. 32.

77 Warburton and Endert, *Indian Lore*, p. 168.

78 Thornton, "Social Organization," p. 192.

79 Collins, *Understanding Tolowa Histories*, p. 36.

80 *CCH*, January 3 and 10, 1855, p. 2.

81 *CCH*, January 17 and 24, 1855, p. 2.

82 Childs, *Del Norte County*, p. 110.

83 *CCH*, January 17, 1855, p. 2.

84 *SDU*, January 19, 1855, p. 2.

85 January 22, 1855 letter in *SDU*, February 3, 1855, p. 2.

86 *Yreka Herald* and editorial in *SDU*, January 19, 1855, p. 2.

87 Chase, *They Pushed Back the Forest*, p. 44.

88 *CCH*, February 14, 1855, p. 2.

89 *CCH*, February 21, 1855, p. 2.

90 *CCH*, October 17, 1855, p. 2.

91 *CCH*, November 14, 1855, p. 2.

92 John Wool to L. Thomas, January 19, 1856, in S. Ex. Doc. 26, 34 Cong., 1 Sess., 1856, p. 50.

93 *CCH*, November 21, 1855, p. 2.

94 *CCH*, January 16, 1856, p. 2.

95 J.D. Cosby, S.G. Whipple, C.A. Hillman, L.D. Watkins to J. Neeley Johnson, January 10, 1856 in California, *Journal of the Seventh Session of the Senate of the State of California* (Sacramento: James Allen, 1856), p. 132.

96 California, *Statutes of California: Passed at the Seventh Session of the Legislature* (Sacramento: James Allen, 1856), pp. 42–43.

97 For possible locations, see map in *CCH*, January 16, 1856, p. 1. Loren Bommelyn believes that the island was Taa-'at-nin'-le' (personal conversation).

98 *CCH*, March 5, 1856, p. 2.

99 Daniel White, March 7, 1856 entry in "Diary . . . and Life in the Northern Mines," Huntington Library.

100 Bledsoe, *History*, p. 44.

101 Order Calling out a Company . . . April 7, 1856; Order Countermanded, April 10, 1856; Order Countermanding Order, ND; and David Gilman to J. Johnson, April 9, 1856, IWP, F3753: 281–283.

102 J.B. Rosborough to J. Johnson, May 16, 1856; Gilmore to Johnson, May 5, 1856, IWP, F3753: 286, 284.

103 May 6, 1856 postscript in Gilmore to Johnson, May 5, 1856, IWP, F3753: 284; E.Y. Naylor to Wm. Kibbe, August 26, 1856, in California, Quarter-Master General's Office, *Report* (Sacramento: James Allen, 1856), pp. 10–11.

104 Klamath County Expedition, 1856, in Comptroller of California, "Expenditures for Military Expeditions against Indians during 1851–1859," California State Archives.

105 Bradford, *Biographical Sketches*, pp. 48–51.

106 *CCH*, June 6, 1855, p. 2. Northern California's Klamath Reservation should not be confused with the Klamath Reservation later established in southern Oregon.

107 Jas. Patterson to T.J. Henley, July 15, 1856, in US Office of Indian Affairs, *Report of the Commissioner of Indian Affairs, Accompanying the Annual Report of the Secretary of the Interior, for the Year 1856* (Washington, DC: A.O.P. Nicholson, 1857), pp. 249–250.

108 Report in William Strobridge, *Regulars in the Redwoods: The U.S. Army in Northern California, 1852–1856* (Spokane: Arthur Clark Company, 1994), p. 155.

109 According to Reed, "The first . . . removal took place from 1852 to 1856 when the federal government . . . removed some Tolowa to Wilson Creek." Reed, *Neeyu*, p. 80.

110 Ibid., p. 81.

111 C.H. Rundell to F.H. Bates, June [ND], 1856, in H. Ex. Doc.1, No.4, 34 Cong., 3 Sess., 1856, p. 151.

112 Jasper Janes in *Northern Californian*, reprinted in *Humboldt Times*, June 23, 1860, p. 2; H.P. Heintzelman to T.J. Henley, July 13, 1857, in US Office of Indian Affairs, *Report of the Commissioner of Indian Affairs, Accompanying the Annual Report of the Secretary of the Interior, for the Year 1857* (Washington, DC: William A. Harris, 1858), pp. 391–392.

113 *CCH*, August 5 and 12, 1857, p. 2.

114 Reservation Clerk in *CCH*, December 2, 1857, p. 2. Emphasis original.

115 George Crook and Martin Schmitt, eds, *General George Crook: His Autobiography* (Norman, OK: University of Oklahoma Press, 1946), p. 57; Mathews, Parris, and Stephens in *Humboldt Times*, November 28, 1857, p. 2.

116 A.J. Bledsoe, *Indian Wars of the Northwest* (San Francisco: Bacon & Company, 1885), p. 225.

117 George Crook to W.W. Mackall, December 25, 1857, in Robert Heizer, *The Destruction of California Indians: A Collection of Documents from the Period 1847–1965 in which are Described Some of the Things that Happened to Some of the Indians of California* (Lincoln, NE: University of Nebraska Press, 1974), p. 110; *CCH*, March 10, 1858, p. 2.

118 H.P. Heintzelman to Thomas Henley, July 1, 1858, in US Office of Indian Affairs, *Report of the Commissioner of Indian Affairs, Accompanying the Annual Report of the Secretary of the Interior, for the year 1858* (Washington, DC: William. A. Harris, 1858), p. 287.

119 *Humboldt Times*, July 17, 1858, p. 2 and October 2, 1858, p. 2.

120 Reed, *Neeyu*, p. 87; B.R. Biddle to H. Rector, August 13, 1862, in US Office of Indian Affairs, *Report of the Commissioner of Indian Affairs for the year 1862* (Washington, DC: GPO, 1863), pp. 272–278.

121 Reed, *Neeyu*, p. 91; Frances McBeth, *Pioneers of Elk Valley, Del Norte County, California* (Angwin: Pacific Union College Press, 1960), p. 11.

122 George Hanson to William Dole, July 18, 1863, in US Office of Indian Affairs, *Report of the Commissioner of Indian Affairs, for the Year 1863* (Washington, DC: GPO, 1864), p. 94. Emphasis original.

123 B.C. Whiting to N.G. Taylor, October 10, 1868, in US Office of Indian Affairs, *Annual Report of the Commissioner of Indian Affairs, for the Year 1868* (Washington, DC: GPO, 1868), p. 127.

124 B.C. Whiting to E.S. Parker, August 1, 1869, in US Office of Indian Affairs, *Report of the Commissioner of Indian Affairs, Made to the Secretary of the Interior, for the Year 1869* (Washington, DC: GPO, 1870), pp. 195–198.

125 Reed, *Neeyu*, p. 96.

126 Thornton, "Social Organization," p. 192.

127 Bledsoe, *History*, p. 108.

128 "Query Results Summary – Tribal Membership," in "Age Range Newsletter," provided by Theresa Ferrer in January 2011; LaWanda Quinnell provided Elk Valley Rancheria enrollment data in January 2011.

129 Raphael Lemkin, *Axis Rule in Occupied Europe: Laws of Occupation, Analysis of Government, Proposals for Redress* (Washington, DC: Carnegie Endowment for International Peace, 1944), Chapter IX, pp. xi–xii.

130 The United Nations, *Convention on the Prevention and Punishment of the Crime of Genocide. Adopted by the General Assembly of the United Nations on 9 December 1948, Treaty Series, Vol. 78: No. 1021*, p. 280.

131 Madley, "American Genocide."

132 See ibid.

133 The author made presentations on the Tolowa genocide to the Smith River Rancheria community in 2006 and 2007, and to the Elk Valley Rancheria community, in 2011.

134 Eduardo Duran, Judith Firehammer, and John Gonzalez, "Liberation Psychology as the Path toward Healing Cultural Soul Wounds," *Journal of Counseling & Development*, 86: 3 (Summer 2000), p. 292. In 2007, several hundred Tolowa, non-Tolowa Indian and non-Indian participants at the 37th Annual United Indian Health Services Annual Board and Staff Meeting for northwestern California discussed this issue following the author's Tolowa genocide presentation.

Figure 11.1 Pirinççizade Aziz Feyzi (1878–1933) was a regional politician and genocide perpetrator in the Ottoman province of Diyarbekir. He was an ardent Young Turk nationalist and Armenophobe who organized large-scale massacres in Diyarbekir city and the wider region.

Source: Courtesy Cahit Sıtkı Tarancı Museum, Diyarbakır.

CHAPTER 11

Fresh Understandings of the Armenian Genocide

Mapping new terrain with old questions

Uğur Ümit Üngör

INTRODUCTION

This chapter has two main aims. First, for analytical purposes, it divides the Armenian genocide into three levels (macro, meso, and micro) that are fleshed out and discussed, applying theoretical insights on comparative genocide. This overview incorporates recently published and forthcoming studies on the destruction of the Ottoman Armenians. Second, the chapter suggests new research directions, with a particular focus on existing problems in comparative genocide research. This part consists of two thematic sections, on regional differentiation and low-ranking perpetrators. This outline attempts to survey what is known, what remains unknown, and what is desirable in these areas of research.

In the past decade, studies of the Armenian genocide have proliferated in a way that has significantly expanded our knowledge. Although it may be premature to compare this development to the post-Soviet "archival revolution," which cleared several important bottlenecks in the scholarship on Stalinism, the gains are not to be underestimated. They have rendered the Armenian genocide less "controversial," depoliticized its study, and established a rough consensus among scholars.[1] An implicit division of labor among students of comparative genocide has been that whereas German scholars (for example) have mostly studied the perpetrators, Israeli scholars have tended to focus on the victims. A series of conferences by Müge Göçek and Ronald Suny bridged this gap by bringing together scholars of different backgrounds and producing an edited volume.[2] Wolfgang Gust's massive efforts continue to document the genocide in German sources, and make those sources available on an important website, http://www.armenocide.de, and in a seminal source book.[3] In Armenia, the director of the Armenian Genocide Museum Institute in Yerevan, Hayk Demoyan, has deepened the sophistication of the debate and unearthed new Russian and Armenian materials.[4] All in all, on the eve of the centenary of the event, the field of Armenian genocide studies is thriving as never before.

THE STRUCTURE OF THE GENOCIDAL PROCESS

Much like other modern genocides, the Armenian genocide can be examined as a complex process of sequential and overlapping developments. At the outbreak of World War I, persecution of Armenians, stigmatization, expropriation of their property and goods, and emigration ushered in the first phase of the process. It continued with an economic and social boycott, and exclusion from the civil service, in the early winter of 1914. Harassment and sporadic violence became commonplace as the Young Turk regime launched its policy of cultural and economic "nationalization." The Young Turk military failures in the Caucasus and Persia sparked a severe radicalization of anti-Armenian policy at the political center. The second phase was prompted by the threat of defeat in the face of invasions by the British in the west and the Russians in the east. It is no exaggeration to state that the effect of these threats on the Ottoman political elite was apocalyptic. It fueled a fear of collapse, and spurred persecutions in the winter of 1914–1915 when, for example, all Armenian civil servants were fired from their positions and Armenian soldiers were disarmed and consigned to labor battalions.[5]

The third phase developed out of the delusional fear of an organized Armenian insurrection, which reached boiling point when Allied forces launched the Gallipoli campaign on the night of April 24, 1915. That same night, Interior Minister Mehmed Talaat Pasha (1874–1921) ordered the arrest of Armenian elites across the entire Ottoman Empire. In Istanbul, between 235 and 270 Armenian clergymen, physicians, editors, journalists, lawyers, teachers, and politicians were rounded up and deported to the interior, where most were murdered.[6] Other provinces followed suit. This effectively decapitated the Armenian community of its political, intellectual, cultural, and religious leadership. Armenian men in the labor battalions were subsequently disarmed and massacred. By that time, sporadic deportations had already been launched. The fourth phase began on May 23, 1915, when the regime, seeking a territorial solution to the "Armenian question," officially authorized the general deportation of all Ottoman Armenians.[7] From spring 1915 onward, the Ministry of the Interior began deporting Armenians, first to Central Anatolia, then to the Syrian desert. These mass deportations developed into veritable death marches. There were no proper provisions for those *en route* to the scorching desert and those who reached it; exposure and starvation were the norm. This final phase of the process consisted of two pillars: first, an escalation into outright mass murder, as special units began murdering Armenian soldiers, elites, and convoys of deportees; and second, the extension of the massacres to full-scale genocide, targeting the group as a whole: *all* Armenians, loyal or disloyal, were deported and massacred. By the end of the war, approximately 2,900 Anatolian Armenian settlements (villages, towns, and neighborhoods) were depopulated, and about a million Armenians were dead.[8]

The structure of this genocidal process can metaphorically be imagined as a three-tiered Matryoshka doll, with the tiers consisting of macro, meso, and micro levels, bearing in mind the significant connections between them. The macro level comprises the international context and structure of geopolitical power relations that led to war. It is usually binary international conflicts that escalate into war and potentially genocidal situations: Serbia–Croatia, Rwanda–Burundi, Germany–USSR, and for our purposes: the Ottoman Empire versus the Russian Empire. When war becomes a fact, the main condition for genocide is often met. Violence is already extensive, but at first tends to be confined to armies engaged in "legitimate" military operations.

At this point, the second tier of the Matryoshka doll is revealed. Within the structure of war are nestled state developments such as the ideological self-hypnosis of political elites, complex decision-making processes, the necessity and logic of a division of labor, the emergence of paramilitary formations, and mass mobilizations for the segregation and destruction of victim groups. At the heart of the Matryoshka is the smallest but most malevolent doll: the large-scale killings of defenseless victims by genocidal perpetrators. This is the point at which ordinary people become involved in mass killing. Horizontal pressure (group conformism), vertical pressure (coercion in a military command structure), and routinization are major mechanisms propelling massacre.

Viewed as a whole, the image of a Matryoshka doll (as opposed, say, to that of a pyramid) allows us to perceive certain larger contextual layers as conditions for smaller ones. Without the war, there would have been no radicalization of the Ottoman political elite. Without that radicalization, the violent measures against Armenians would not have been amplified and expanded to distant provinces, where tens of thousands of individual perpetrators murdered hundreds of thousands of individual victims in micro-situations of killing. If we take this structure as our starting point, a great deal is already revealed about the Armenian genocide. In what follows, I discuss these three contexts in greater detail, basing the analysis on recent and forthcoming studies of the genocide.

THE MACRO (INTER-STATE) CONTEXT

The largest of our Matryoshka dolls consists of the overarching relations between states. The inter-state pressures on the Ottoman Empire were manifold: economic, military, and cultural. From 1912 to 1923, the empire was waging war almost continuously in an existential struggle for survival. In such a constellation of wars in different locations, polarization and extremism easily took hold. But the debate over the international context has been as politicized as that surrounding the mass murder of Ottoman Armenians. Turkish-nationalist authors have pointed their fingers at western diplomacy as an alleged source of ethnic polarization.[9] Armenian-nationalist historians have accused Germany of outright complicity in the genocide.[10] Neither of these positions, however, captures the ambivalence of internal state disagreements over foreign policy, the complexity of power fluctuations, and the unpredictability of the international state system in which the Armenian genocide was carried out. Most importantly, such preoccupations with the non-analytical (indeed, un-analyzable) categories of guilt and blame have failed to advance the debate significantly.

Donald Bloxham's sophisticated study of imperial pressures on the Ottoman Empire highlighted this hitherto insufficiently problematized issue. From the perspective of genocide studies, his comparative analysis of British, American, and German responses to the Armenian genocide addresses two central questions: What is the influence of inter-state relations on intra-state ethnic polarization? Moreover, once a genocidal process is initiated, which states are able to put a halt to it? Bloxham argues that whereas the Ottoman Empire's military allies wavered between condemning the genocide and turning a blind eye to it, the imperial ambitions of the Ottomans' wartime enemies indirectly escalated the genocide by aggravating Young Turk fears, and providing them with a pretext for maltreating the Armenians even more.[11] What on the surface, from the Allies' perspective, appeared as noble motives of "humanitarian intervention" produced counterproductive, if unintended and probably unforeseen, consequences. This prompts a further conclusion: once the Young Turks launched the genocide under extreme wartime conditions, no state, whether ally or enemy, was in a position to prevent it or intervene in it. The genocide was thus a relatively autonomous process.

Studies on the conduct of the Ottoman Empire's allies, Germany and Austria-Hungary, paint a complex and nuanced picture. Whereas German involvement in the planning and execution of Ottoman war maneuvers has been studied in depth, German responses to the genocide are still a topic of a lively debate. Recent studies on the German role include detailed examinations of the German state, military, and business spheres. The annotated (re-)publication of relevant source materials has helped greatly to clarify the topic.[12] The picture that emerges from this research is compelling and complex: German responses to the Armenian genocide oscillated between resistance and complicity. The locus of resistance was mostly at the lower level: diplomats, military officers, and private individuals. These were people who witnessed the persecution of Armenians at first hand, and who had interacted personally with individual victims. For them, Armenians were real people who suffered, rather than anonymous pawns in a game of global strategy. At the very top levels of the German political elite, however, the conditions and conduct of war militated against concern for a powerless minority. All that mattered to the German ambassador, the German chief-of-staff, and ultimately the Kaiser was keeping the Ottoman Empire in the war.[13] This is a compelling argument that invites comparative reflections on how allies of genocidal regimes comport themselves, and why they do what they do.

The United States of America also figured prominently in the unfolding genocidal scenario. As the USA was neutral until 1917, American diplomatic personnel enjoyed unfettered access to cities and towns in the Anatolian hinterland. Ambassador Morgenthau and his team of diplomats produced hundreds of reports detailing the daily conduct of the genocide from the provinces, in particular Harput, Aleppo, Izmir, Beirut, Damascus, Urfa, Edirne, Samsun, Trabzon, and Adana.[14] Whereas American diplomatic responses are relatively well documented, an edited volume has shed light on the multifaceted nature of American responses to the Armenian genocide. These include American missionary relief efforts, discussions in Congress, postwar commissions, Wilsonian diplomacy, US business interests, and the American media.[15] All in all, the American position has been fairly thoroughly researched. During the genocide and in its immediate aftermath, America's position was consistent in denouncing the "race extermination," and condemning the Young Turk regime. But in the face of business and geopolitical interests, this policy was quickly abandoned in favor of *Realpolitik*, as the Young Turks recovered and consolidated their power base in a strong Anatolian nation-state.

Conversely, we are less fully informed about the Russian position on the genocide. But thanks to recent efforts, this is changing. Russia's southward imperial ambitions were aimed primarily at securing a warm-water harbor and gaining control of the Dardanelles Straits. Imperial policy toward Russian and Ottoman Armenians shifted from tacit support to open repression in the nineteenth century.[16] In 1914, Russia played a leading role in drafting the reform plan by which the six eastern provinces of the Ottoman Empire would be grouped into two provinces with European or Ottoman Christian inspectors-general. What seemed like a benign humanitarian plan was in fact a thinly-veiled attempt to justify the annexation of the eastern provinces.[17] A recent study by Michael Reynolds has examined how the Ottoman–Russian competition over Eastern Anatolia and the Caucasus severely politicized the demographic composition of this large swathe of territory.[18] Deportation and genocide were not only a product of Young Turk humiliation and fear of destruction in a losing war. They were also an attempt to create new demographic realities on the ground at a future peace treaty, and to gain the upper hand over these regions. Peter Holquist's recent work on the Russian occupation of the eastern provinces between 1915 and 1917 supplements this approach. It demonstrates how Russia's impact on the region was "both direct, through its own conduct on the ground, as well as indirect, through its sanction of various irregular formations and its (ambivalent and tactical) endorsement of ethnic politics in this region."[19] These studies demonstrate that the dynamic of inter-state polarization was so powerful as to carry over to intra-societal relations as well. As the competition and animosity between the Russian and Ottoman empires grew, so too did the polarization between Turks and Armenians within the Ottoman Empire itself.

Before, during, and after the Armenian genocide, several non-governmental organizations (NGOs) played notable roles. The conduct and impact of these organizations and individuals have left an indelible imprint on our understanding of the genocide. Matthias Bjørnlund has studied the genocide through Danish sources, including diplomats, but especially missionaries and humanitarian aid workers. The latter two groups' relief efforts were a drop in the ocean, and they could not significantly oppose the Young Turks' policy of destruction.[20] This scenario clearly underlines the powerlessness of non-governmental organizations in conditions of international crisis and war.[21] Similar conclusions can be drawn for those transnational organizations with professional or financial ties to genocide victims. A recent study of western insurance companies adds to our knowledge of how these companies conducted, and conduct, themselves during genocide. From 1915 on, western insurance companies and banks, driven by corporate competition and clinical cost-benefit considerations, cared little for the murder of their Armenian clients. They merely sought compensation for the financial losses they incurred as a result of the Young Turk government's criminal policies.[22]

All in all, we have a relatively clear picture of the largest Matryoshka doll – international relations and transnational contacts. Yet we are still missing a properly researched account of responses to the genocide by certain states. Persia had consulates in critical locations such as the city of Van, but so far we lack an empirically-grounded account of Persian responses to, and accounts of, the genocide. Our understanding of the Vatican's perspective could be expanded as well, since many Catholic missionaries lived through the genocide, and the Armenian Catholic community was attacked and destroyed as well. Finally, Bulgaria presents an interesting case. During the Balkan wars,

Bulgaria fought a bitter war against the Ottoman state and committed violence against Ottoman Muslim civilians, deeply alienating the Ottoman political elite. Only two years later, this constellation changed, when in October 1915 Bulgaria found itself allied with the Central Powers, including the Ottoman Empire. There is some evidence that Bulgaria denied entry and asylum to Armenian refugees from Thrace, and delivered them back to the Young Turk authorities.[23] Did the wartime Bulgarian government do so to keep Istanbul content? Further research could usefully address this question.

THE MESO (INTRA-SOCIETAL) CONTEXT

The second tier of our Matryoshka doll concerns the intra-societal context of changing power relations and structures, extremist ideologies, decision-making processes, and the actual organization of persecution and mass murder. These processes are of course decisive for the deadly outcome. Accordingly, not only does this level link the macro with the micro, but it is also here that the inter-state polarization is reproduced within a society by various political actors and groups. It signifies a recognizable relationship: a similar process, albeit on a smaller scale.

For the Armenian genocide, this is an important level to investigate, because whereas parts of the landscape are relatively well-lit, other regions – including this one – are still shrouded in darkness. For example, Jacques Sémelin has underlined the importance in genocidal processes of the construction of an imagined "internal enemy."[24] How was this figure constructed in the Ottoman case? One line of thought has placed it in the context of the Turkish nation-formation process of the long nineteenth century. The definition and demarcation of the nation occurred under severe inter-state and intra-state pressures, frequently causing crises of identity. During such crises, external enemies like the Russian Empire were equated with upstart internal groups accused of disloyalty by virtue of their supposed religious or political proximity, or upward social mobility. The Armenian upper and middle classes in the Ottoman cities thus bore the brunt of Ottoman state decline.[25] This collective-identity-based model accounts for the vital process of constructing the internal enemy group.

A second theme at this middle level could be Turkish–Armenian polarization, beginning with the polarization of political elites. Dikran Kaligian's study of the Armenian Revolutionary Federation (*Dashnaktsutiun*) on the eve of the war has examined how the international crisis of the Ottoman Empire sparked the deterioration of relations between the ARF and the Committee of Union and Progress (CUP).[26] Young Turk radicals such as Mehmed Talaat en Bahaeddin Shakir perceived Armenian political leaders as a security liability for the state. When war broke out, the Young Turks limited themselves to threats against the Dashnaks. But as the war grew radicalized, at some point in the winter of 1914, they decided to murder the entire membership of the ARF, from top to bottom.[27] Another form of Turkish–Armenian polarization could be ethnic and social, between groups within the empire, as well as in different provinces and cities. As a result of national political polarization, Armenians and Turks locally came to imagine themselves as part and parcel of an overarching conflict. Bedross der Matossian's study of the Adana region takes on the challenging task of describing this inter-ethnic polarization in one of the most important regions of the Ottoman Empire.[28]

Although the scholarship on the Young Turk dictatorship is developing rapidly, we know relatively little about it compared to other genocidal regimes. So far, the Young Turks have been studied in a fragmentary way, with a focus on specific aspects rather than as a coherent whole, and with their violence peripheralized. A series of studies by Şükrü Hanioğlu has sketched a compelling portrait of a ruthless, clandestine revolutionary cabal. On the threshold of state power, the CUP was an uncompromising party that visualized politics mostly as a dichotomy of friends versus enemies, applying terror, threats, and assassination to the latter.[29] But we still await a thorough analysis of the period from 1913 to 1918, and a more contextualized one, embracing the first half of the twentieth century in general. We need to understand better how the regime gained, held, and lost power during this period, including a systematic exploration of important themes such as leadership, governance, ideology, violence, and socialization.[30] A recent analysis by Ayhan Aktar focused on the enormous concentration of executive power in the hands of the party in 1914. Aktar argues that: "The administrative elite of the empire had been transformed into a young, energetic group of officials who had adopted the Turkish nationalist ideology." This development made the exercise of violence on a mass scale possible, and greatly facilitated the genocide.[31] These studies go a long way toward analyzing the regime, but we still require greater depth (a comprehensive empirical recreation) and breadth (an implicit and explicit comparison with other genocidal regimes).

We also still lack explanations founded on collective emotions. Studies of ethnic violence through a prism of affective disposition have identified three major emotional responses triggering ethnic violence in the twentieth century: fear, hatred, and resentment. At the meso level of analyses of genocide, this is a very useful point of departure. According to emotion-based theories, political elites construct identity narratives based on group experiences of structural changes. Shifting socio-economic conditions and patterns of social mobility alter power and status relations among groups, as they overturn time-honored hierarchies in ranked ethnic systems. These changes can precipitate collective emotions such as hatred, fear, and resentment.[32] This is a recognizable scenario in late Ottoman history. Given how Ottoman Christians benefited from modern developments in education, trade, and technology, how did ordinary Turks perceive their ascendance? The young Turkish journalist Ahmed Şerif toured the Anatolian provinces in 1909, and noticed the striking jealousy among Turks toward Armenians and Greeks. He compared the tidy organization of the Armenian schools with the deplorable state of Turkish schools, and admitted that the relative advancement of Armenians saddened him. He warned that "if this continues, we have no future," and urged Turks: "Attempt to imitate your Christian neighbors! They are more advanced than you are in every way, they live more prosperous lives."[33] In such conditions, it is not unthinkable that the genocide emerged as a golden opportunity to make a "great leap forward" by manipulating Turkish collective emotions and absorbing Armenian wealth, property, and infrastructure. This aspect of the genocide certainly warrants greater attention from researchers as well.

It is also important to consider another issue relevant to the meso level as well: regional variations in the genocide. Regionalism, and the transcendence of regionalism, are important themes in recent genocide research. Genocide scholars have examined the relationship between central decision-making processes and the implementation of mass murder at the local level. In-depth research on how genocidal processes evolve at the provincial, district, city, or even village level has proven most fruitful. It can teach us a great deal about how local power shifts influence the course and intensity of genocidal processes, since we know that some genocides are more regionally varied than others. Local political or social elites can anticipate, expedite, intensify, or delay and resist processes of genocidal destruction directed from above. A micro focus can also follow the deterioration and ultimate disintegration of inter-communal relations in the face of external pressures, amidst drastically worsening security and life conditions for the victims.[34]

The broad regionalization of the Armenian genocide can be studied at two levels: regional and provincial. The regional approach examines rough territorial divisions beyond the provincial level, but still within state borders. Here, the genocide presents us with three differing scenarios: the eastern provinces, the Arab south, and Anatolia. First, there is the geopolitical aspect in which the eastern provinces are seen as a classically contested "shatterzone," or imperial borderland. This territory had no natural borders with the surrounding states, as well as lower levels of state formation; during the genocide it witnessed higher levels of violence.[35] Second, Syria under Cemal Pasha can be examined as another region, in which the course of the genocide depended on friction within the regime, in particular diverging agendas and ambitions. Owing to his competition with fellow Young Turk Enver Pasha, Cemal Pasha more and more became a near-independent ruler of his portion of the empire. Under his jurisdiction, many Armenians survived in Damascus, Beirut, and Jordanian towns like Jeresh.[36] We could certainly benefit from a properly-researched account of how and why this happened. Lastly, the CUP's plans for the future of Anatolia were vital for the direction of its anti-Armenian policy. To the Young Turks, Anatolia was the last bastion of "Turkishness", which should never be "Balkanized," that is, dismembered by subaltern groups like Armenians or occupied by the western powers. Recent studies have illustrated how, to that end, the CUP instituted so-called "Turkification zones" where ethnic homogenization was carried out to the fullest extent, according to an ideological vision of ethnic hierarchy.[37] Rough as they are, these territorial delineations deserve greater attention, and seem to offer fertile ground for analysis.

A second form of regionalization lies below the regional level, but above the urban level. In a provincial context, the Armenian genocide demonstrates isomorphism but also disparities in initiation, execution, and development of the persecutions.[38] The source of these differences and changes is the official Ottoman administrative unit of the province. Possible explanations include the personal whims of the governors; the conduct of local elites; and structural factors such as proximity to the front, social stratification, settlement patterns, and opportunity structures. In this sub-field of genocide studies, the Armenian genocide lags behind; the few notable case studies have used different approaches, developed different interpretations, and drawn different conclusions.[39] We need more detailed studies on specific areas – provinces, cities, and if possible villages – employing the full range of source materials.[40] An interesting comparative study could be conducted of provincial governors. Whereas some moderate governors, such as Celal Bey in Konya, Hasan Mazhar Bey in Ankara, and Rahmi Bey in Izmir/Smyrna, delayed and obstructed the destruction, others – including Mustafa Abdülhalik Renda in Bitlis, Cemal Azmi Bey in Trabzon, and Dr. Mehmed Reshid in Diyarbekir

– accelerated and intensified it. In the former provinces, Armenians were treated less violently, and found more possibilities for escape. In the latter ones, comprehensive *in situ* mass murder was the rule. In the spirit of setting an example, I hope to contribute to this burgeoning and promising field of provincial studies with a monograph on Diyarbekir under four decades of Young Turk rule.[41]

Regionalization is not simply a matter of territorial differentiation. It is closely related to the morphology of the organization, coordination, and implementation of the crime. Recent studies have challenged the convention that the genocide had a unipolar pyramidal structure. On the contrary, the genocide was a multipolar process: radicalization came from within and without, and emanated from different perpetrating *clusters*, such as civil and military organizations, the ruling triumvirate itself, and local elites.[42] Competition and conflict among these sectors shaped the genocide. For example, the confiscation of Armenian property and its allocation to Turks became a bone of contention between the Ottoman army and the Interior Ministry. The army attempted to acquire movable and immovable Armenian property for its military ends, but the ministry followed its ideological prescription of forging a "national economy," adamantly assigning confiscated property to the upstart Turkish middle class.[43] Another example is those local elites who shaped the Armenian genocide at the provincial level as a reflection of competition among Turkish families. The competition between urban elites for political and economic power was a structural factor easily manipulated by the CUP dictatorship for its own ends. Local Turkish notables emerged victorious in this competition by volunteering for the death squads and actively collaborating in the campaign that the CUP regime deemed most salient: the murder of their Armenian neighbors.[44] These insights at the meso level of analysis illustrate how dynamics within the perpetrator group can account for variations during the genocide. They also remind us that even if the Armenian genocide unfolded on a twisted course, the result was nevertheless generalized destruction. Future research ought to penetrate deeper into these complexities.

THE MICRO LEVEL: ORDINARY PEOPLE

Let us now turn to the smallest Matryoshka doll, which concerns the extraordinary things that occurred with ordinary people on the ground. Compared to other genocides, it is at this level that the field of Armenian genocide studies suffers most from significant lacunae, beginning with the perpetrators. In studies of the Armenian genocide and accounts of the killings, the perpetrators, including the organizing elites but especially the rank-and-file executioners, have too often figured as faceless killers, undifferentiated and unexplained. The guerrillas, tribesmen, and villagers appear in the Anatolian killing fields *ex nihilo*, and murder people for no apparent reason other than innate (Turkish, Kurdish, or Muslim) cruelty and malignance. This essentialist convention needs to be challenged by problematizing the experience of Ottoman Muslims and Young Turk elites through biographical investigation and sociological contextualization. Following Alexander Hinton, we have to ask: Why did they kill? More research on rank-and-file perpetrators may facilitate further integration of the Armenian genocide into comparative genocide studies.

Comparative research on perpetrators of genocide is gradually reflecting common ground and increasing sophistication.[45] One of the cornerstones in the field was undoubtedly Christopher Browning's bestseller, *Ordinary Men*. This powerful study is famous for adopting a social-psychological model of obedience to authority to explain the behavior of German perpetrators. For our purposes, it might be relevant to highlight another aspect of the book. Browning's research was based on a substantial primary source base – records from the Central Office for State Justice Administrations (*Zentrale Stelle der Landesjustizverwaltungen*) in Ludwigsburg near Stuttgart. He benefited from an extensive collection of records that included later interrogations of the perpetrators who carried out the massacres. Browning writes:

> Never before had I encountered the issue of choice so dramatically framed by the course of events and so openly discussed by at least some of the perpetrators. Never before had I seen the monstrous deeds of the Holocaust so starkly juxtaposed with the human faces of the killers.[46]

Another example of exemplary perpetrator research can be drawn from the Yugoslav wars. In a chapter of her book, *They Would Never Hurt a Fly*, the Croatian author Slavenka Drakulić uses court transcriptions from the International Criminal Tribunal for the former Yugoslavia (ICTY) to paint a moving picture of Dražen Erdemović – a Bosnian Serb who passed through various trials and tribulations, and ended up shooting Bosniak men in the Srebrenica massacre of 13–22 July, 1995.[47] What emerges from Browning's and Drakulić's treatment of perpetrators is a nuanced and complex discussion of dispositional and situational factors. Understanding and explaining the process of perpetration require a source base that is nearly lacking in the Armenian case.

In 2003, Norman Naimark wrote: "As far as I know, we have learned next to nothing about the 'ordinary' Turk or Kurd who engages in this murderousness and why."[48] Eight years later, we are still in the dark as to the actual perpetration of the genocide. What do we even know about ordinary gendarmes, militiamen, and soldiers charged with deportation and massacre? In comparison with other cases, we notice a dire lack of rank-and-file sources on the Armenian genocide perpetrators. If we assume that, in general, the perpetrators were around 20 to 25 years old during the deportations, they could have lived well into the 1960s or 1970s. However, I am not aware of any useful material that can shed light on the grassroots of the genocide. Despite the rising literacy levels, it would be naïve to expect diverse manuscripts to have surfaced, especially because we know that perpetrators tend to keep their silence about their violent pasts. With four decades of subsequent Young Turk censorship, the memory of the genocide was erased and silenced. Armenian and Syriac survivor materials might be much more useful in shedding light on the perpetration aspect of the genocide. Research into oral history materials and memoirs might also be able to move the debate further on.

There are a few exceptions. Having studied the political elites of Diyarbekir, I was able to trace their political maneuvers from the 1890s to the 1940s. Deeply embedded within Diyarbekir's social structure were overlapping and competing networks of influential families of Muslim notables who had historically played the role of local power brokers. These were, for example, the very powerful Cizrelizâde, Pirinççizâde, and Müftüzâde, as well as the Ocak, Ekinci, Zazazâde, Yasinzâde, Ensarizâde, and Cemilpaazâde. The rivalry between these families generated fierce competition over local government. This often resulted in severe forms of corruption and nepotism in the local political culture.[49] Of these extended families, the Pirinççizâde merit particular attention for their role in the genocide. MP Aziz Feyzi (1878–1933) was a Young Turk hardliner known for his anti-Armenian sentiments. He had often verbally assaulted prominent Armenian MP Vartkes Serengulian (1871–1915) in parliament, and reportedly had Ohannes Kazazian, a Catholic Armenian from Mardin and his political rival in the elections, assassinated in 1913. During the genocide, Aziz Feyzi played a crucial role in the organization of the destruction process in Diyarbekir, along with his cousin, Pirinççizâde Bekir Sıdkı (1888–1973) (Figure 11.2). In May and June 1915, the cousins recruited the Kurdish tribesmen who murdered the Armenian elite of the city; expanded the genocide into the vast countryside; and amassed a fortune by plundering the Diyarbekir Armenians. Following the 1918 Ottoman surrender, the Pirinççizâde maintained their support for the Young Turk Party. Aziz Feyzi was promoted to minister, and was assigned a spacious house in Istanbul's upscale Kadıköy neighborhood.[50] During the 1925 Kurdish conflict and ensuing massacres and deportations of Kurdish civilians, he provided logistical support and manpower to the government. In May 1927, Aziz Feyzi was decorated with the Red Independence Medal by the chairman of the Turkish Grand National Assembly, Mustafa Abdulhalik Renda (1881–1957), for his "devoted service to the National Struggle."[51]

His cousin, Pirinççizâde Bekir Sıdkı, enriched himself from Armenian property to the extent that he could afford to send his son to Paris for higher education, amidst the economic crisis of the 1930s. (The young man grew up to become Cahit Sıtkı Tarancı [1910–1956], one of the most celebrated poets of modern Turkey.) According to friends of the family, in the 1930s and 1940s, Sıdkı owned apartments and shops in Istanbul's Eminönü and Beyoğlu districts, where all accoutrements reflected "the fashion of the day: seats, comfortable and high-backed chairs; from the fork in your hand to the tablecloth; from the chandelier that catches the eye to the crystal vase, everything displayed indulgence and money." The family was living in "glaring wealth" (*göze batan zenginlik*).[52] They went on to play a vital role in Diyarbekir's political life and open a lucrative travel agency in Istanbul. The lives of low-level genocide perpetrators like Aziz Feyzi and Bekir Sıdkı are relatively well documented. But accounts of their acts of killing are very rare.

Therefore, for lack of sources, we might have to resort to perpetrator accounts of other episodes of Young Turk mass violence, of which I will provide one example. In the late 1980s, the Kurdish journalist Ahmet Kahraman traveled through Anatolia in search of Turkish soldiers who had served during the interwar anti-Kurdish campaigns. In Trabzon, he found one of his respondents, Dursun Çakıroğlu, a retired sergeant living in Ankara. After initial reservations, Çakıroğlu began to trust Kahraman, and spoke of an operation in a valley in which he participated in 1925:

We besieged the valley in the middle of the night. Movements were detected early in the morning in the valley. One way or the other they found out about us. They started to flee with cries of "The soldiers are coming!" Our commander Deli Kemal Pasha ordered breakfast to be served. We had breakfast. Then we thoroughly surrounded the valley and advanced slowly. It was evident that there were very few

Figure 11.2 Pirinççizade Bekir Sıdkı (1888–1973), shown here with his family, was a regional politician and genocide perpetrator in the Ottoman province of Diyarbekir. He was the cousin of Aziz Feyzi (see Figure 11.1) and his right-hand man in the implementation of mass killings, personally committing torture and massacres.

Source: Courtesy Cahit Sıtkı Tarancı Museum, Diyarbakır.

men among them. They had probably fled. There were women, children, and elderly around. Some young men among them . . . When they finally saw us in front of them, a sudden outcry broke out. Women and children were running around, crying, groaning. Deli Kemal Pasha ordered the soldiers: "Take position!" We took position. Then he yelled: "Fire at will!" We let loose at random. The valley turned into doomsday. Screams, moans, cries, fleeing, flights, yelling . . . It was very bloody. Many died. Afterwards they said 600 casualties. I think there were more. There were tiny children among them . . . For four hours we combed the place with rifles and machine guns. Except for the 20 to 30 people we captured, nobody got out alive. In the volley fire even dogs and horses were shot. I don't know what those valley people had done wrong. They said they were Kurds. They rebelled against the government. When the sounds and twitches died down we entered the tents. Corpses everywhere . . . Children, women and elderly had clung on to each other, dropped everywhere and died. Some friends searched the clothes of the dead and took their gold and money . . . We set fire to the tents and left.[53]

Çakıroğlu also noted that prisoners were taken away and executed at a nearby ravine. According to the interviewer, the old man's body language and facial expression – not captured in the text – revealed feelings of guilt and shame. This example suggests top-down coercion, an argument that points to the obedience-to-authority model. The mass killing was not gender-differentiated, but categorical, including children. We know little about the chain of command: was it the commander who gave the order on his own behalf, or did he act upon central orders? Further research on Turkish perpetrators needs to address such questions.

CONCLUSION

The Armenian genocide is rooted in the wider political and social crisis in the modern history of the Near East. In the process of Habsburg, Ottoman, and Russian imperial collapse, roughly in the period 1912–1923, millions of soldiers were killed in war. But hundreds of thousands of unarmed civilians were also victimized as a result of expulsions, pogroms, and other forms of persecution and mass violence. The Balkan wars of 1912–1913 erased the Ottoman presence in the Balkans, and marked a devastating blow to Ottoman political culture. The years 1915–1916 witnessed the destruction of the Anatolian Armenians, and the period from 1917 to 1923 is of great significance for the history of the Caucasus, both north and south, encompassing wars of annihilation and massacres of civilians. All three processes occurred amidst a critical depacification of inter-state relations and societal conditions, as well as a profound crisis of inter-ethnic relationships between and within states.[54] The Matryoshka model presented here, with its three levels of analysis, can be viewed as a complex whole: a process that triggered the initiation and execution of violence in this period. The Armenian genocide can best be seen as a major link in this transnational chain of violence.

The research desiderata identified in this chapter could expand both our knowledge and enhance our understanding of the Armenian genocide. They by no means constitute an exhaustive evaluation or comprehensive program, but are merely suggestions for relevant new directions in genocide research.

NOTES

1 For an overview of the scholarship, see Donald Bloxham and Fatma Müge Göçek, "The Armenian Genocide," in Dan Stone, ed., *The Historiography of Genocide* (London: Palgrave Macmillan, 2008), pp. 344–372.

2 Fatma Müge Göçek, Norman Naimark, and Ronald Grigor Suny, eds, *A Question of Genocide: Armenians and Turks at the End of the Ottoman Empire* (New York: Oxford University Press, 2011).

3 Wolfgang Gust, ed., *Der Völkermord an den Armeniern 1915/16: Dokumente aus dem Politischen Archiv des deutschen Auswärtigen Amts* (Hamburg: Zu Klampen, 2005).

4 See: http://www.genocide-museum.am/.

5 Uğur Ümit Üngör, "When Persecution Bleeds into Mass Murder: The Processive Nature of Genocide," *Genocide Studies and Prevention*, 1: 2 (2006), pp. 173–196.

6 Mikayel Shamtanchian, *The Fatal Night: An Eyewitness Account of the Extermination of Armenian Intellectuals in 1915* (Studio City, CA: H. and K. Majikian Publications, 2007).

7 Donald Bloxham, "The Beginning of the Armenian Catastrophe: Comparative and Contextual Consideration," in Hans-Lukas Kieser and Dominik J. Schaller, eds, *Der Völkermord an den Armeniern und die Shoah* (Zürich: Chronos, 2001), pp. 101–128.

8 For an early bibliography of the Armenian genocide, see Hamo B. Vassilian, *The Armenian

Genocide: A Comprehensive Bibliography and Library Resource Guide (Glendale, CA: Armenian Reference Books Co., 1992).

9 Salahi R. Sonyel, *The Ottoman Armenians: Victims of Great Power Diplomacy* (London: K. Rustem and Brother, 1987).

10 Vahakn N. Dadrian, *German Responsibility in the Armenian Genocide: A Review of the Historical Evidence of German Complicity* (Watertown, MA: Blue Crane Books, 1996).

11 Donald Bloxham, *The Great Game of Genocide: Imperialism, Nationalism, and the Destruction of the Ottoman Armenians* (Oxford: Oxford University Press, 2005).

12 The following publications were all usefully annotated by Hilmar Kaiser: Eberhard Wolffskeel von Reichenberg, *Zeitoun, Mousa Dagh, Ourfa: Letters on the Armenian Genocide* (London: Gomidas Institute, 2004); Harry Stürmer, *Two War Years in Constantinople: Sketches of German and Young Turkish Ethics and Politics* (London: Sterndale Classics, 2004); Paul Leverkuehn, *A German Officer during the Armenian Genocide: A Biography of Max von Scheubner-Richter* (London: Gomidas Institute, 2008).

13 For a critical overview, see: Hilmar Kaiser, "Germany and the Armenian Genocide: A Review Essay," *Journal of the Society for Armenian Studies*, 8 (1995 [1997]), pp. 127–142.

14 Ara Sarafian, ed., *United States Official Records on the Armenian Genocide, 1915–1917* (London: Gomidas Institute, 2004); Ara Sarafian, *United States Diplomacy on the Bosphorus: The Diaries of Ambassador Morgenthau, 1913–1916* (London: Gomidas Institute, 2004).

15 Jay Winter, *America and the Armenian Genocide of 1915* (Cambridge: Cambridge University Press, 2003).

16 Ronald G. Suny, *Looking toward Ararat: Armenia in Modern History* (Bloomington, IN: Indiana University Press, 1993), pp. 31–51.

17 Manoug Joseph Somakian, *Empires in Conflict: Armenia and the Great Powers, 1895–1920* (New York: I.B. Tauris, 1995), p. 46 ff.

18 Michael Reynolds, "The Ottoman-Russian Struggle for Eastern Anatolia and the Caucasus, 1908–1918: Identity, Ideology and the Geopolitics of World Order" (unpublished Ph.D. thesis, Princeton University, 2003), pp. 83–181.

19 Peter Holquist, "Forms of Violence during the Russian Occupation of Ottoman Territory and in Northern Persia (Urmia and Astrabad), October 1914–December 1917," in Eric Weitz and Omer Bartov, eds, *Borderlands: Peoples, Nations, and Cultures in the Shatterzone of Empires since 1848* (Bloomington, IN: Indiana University Press, 2010).

20 Matthias Bjørnlund, *Scandinavia and the Armenian Question, 1890–1940* (forthcoming).

21 The conclusion can be extended to British and international humanitarian NGO responses as well: see Jo Laycock, *Imagining Armenia: Orientalism, Ambiguity and Intervention* (Manchester: Manchester University Press, 2009); Keith David Watenpaugh, "The League of Nations' Rescue of Armenian Genocide Survivors and the Making of Modern Humanitarianism, 1920–1927," *American Historical Review*, 115: 5 (2010), pp. 1315–1339.

22 Hrayr S. Karagueuzian and Yair Auron, *A Perfect Injustice: Genocide and Theft of Armenian Wealth* (New Brunswick, NJ: Transaction Publishers, 2009).

23 Lewis Einstein, *A Diplomat Looks Back* (New Haven, CT: Yale University Press, 1968), p. 146.

24 Jacques Sémelin, *Purify and Destroy: The Political Uses of Massacre and Genocide* (London: Hurst, 2007), pp. 22–33.

25 Taner Akçam, *Türk Ulusal Kimliği ve Ermeni Sorunu* (Turkish National Identity and the Armenian Genocide) (Istanbul: Su, 2001); Taner Akçam, *Armenien und der Völkermord: die Istanbuler Prozesse und die türkische Nationalbewegung* (Hamburg: Hamburger Edition, 1996), translated into Turkish (1999), English (2006), and Dutch (2007).

26 Dikran M. Kaligian, *Armenian Organization and Ideology under Ottoman Rule: 1908–1914* (New Brunswick, NJ: Transaction Publishers, 2009), Chapter 3.

27 Hratch Dasnabedian, *History of the Armenian Revolutionary Federation, Dashnaktsutiun, 1890–1924* (Milan: Oemme Edizioni, 1990), pp. 109–116.

28 Bedross der Matossian, "Ethnic Politics in Post-Revolutionary Ottoman Empire: Armenians, Arabs, and Jews in the Second Constitutional Period (1908–1909)," unpublished Ph.D. dissertation, Columbia University, 2008.

29 M. Şükrü Hanioğlu, *The Young Turks in Opposition* (Oxford: Oxford University Press, 1995); M. Şükrü Hanioğlu, *Preparation for a Revolution: The Young Turks, 1902–1908* (Oxford: Oxford University Press, 2001).

30 See my book, *The Young Turk Dictatorship, 1913–1950: Problems and Perspectives* (London: Palgrave, forthcoming 2012).

31 Ayhan Aktar, "On Ottoman Public Bureaucracy and the CUP: 1915–1918," paper presented at the conference on "The State of the Art of Armenian Genocide Research: Historiography, Sources, and Future Directions," Center for Holocaust and Genocide Studies, Clark University, 8–10 April 2010.

32 Roger D. Petersen, *Understanding Ethnic Violence: Fear, Hatred, and Resentment in Twentieth-Century Europe* (Cambridge: Cambridge University Press, 2002).

33 Ahmed Şerif, *Anadolu'da Tanin: Birinci Gezi* (Tanin in Anatolia: The First Journey) (Istanbul: Kavram, 1977), p. 123.

34 Recent examples of innovative local studies of genocide include: Tomislav Dulić, *Utopias of Nation: Local Mass Killing in Bosnia and Hercegovina, 1941–42* (Uppsala: Uppsala University Press, 2005); Wendy Lower, *Nazi Empire-Building and the Holocaust in Ukraine* (Chapel Hill, NC: University of North Carolina Press, 2005); Lee Ann Fujii, *Killing Neighbors: Webs of Violence in Rwanda* (Ithaca, NY: Cornell University Press, 2009); François-Xavier Nérard, "The Levashovo Cemetery and the Great Terror in the Leningrad Region," in *Online Encyclopedia of Mass Violence* (February 27, 2009), http://www.mass violence.org/The-Levashovo-cemetery-and-the-Great-Terror-in-the-Leningrad-region.pdf.

35 Mark Levene, "Creating a Modern 'Zone of Genocide': The Impact of Nation- and State-Formation on Eastern Anatolia, 1878–1923," *Holocaust and Genocide Studies*, 12: 3 (1998), pp. 393–433.

36 Hilmar Kaiser, "Regional Resistance to Central Government Policies: Ahmed Djemal Pasha, the Governors of Aleppo, and Armenian Deportees in the Spring and Summer of 1915," *Journal of Genocide Research*, 12: 3–4 (2010), pp. 173–218.

37 Fikret Adanır and Hilmar Kaiser, "Migration, Deportation, and Nation-Building: The Case of the Ottoman Empire," in René Leboutte, ed., *Migrations et migrants dans une perspective historique: permanences et innovations* (Florence: European University Institute, 2000), pp. 273–292; Hilmar Kaiser, "The Ottoman Government and the End of the Ottoman Social Formation, 1915–1917," paper presented at the conference on "*Der Völkermord an den Armeniern und die Shoah*", University of Zürich, November 7, 2001, available at: http://www.hist.net/kieser/aghet/Essays/EssayKaiser.html; Fuat Dündar, *Modern Türkiye'nin Şifresi: İttihat ve Terakki'nin Etnisite Mühendisliği (1913–1918)* (The Cipher of Turkey: The Ethnic Engineering of İttihad ve Terakki [1913–1918] (Istanbul: İletişim, 2008).

38 For an excellent narrative study with a provincial approach, see Raymond H. Kevorkian, *Le genocide des Armeniens* (Paris: Odile Jacob, 2006), translated as *The Armenian Genocide: A Complete History* (London: I.B. Tauris, 2010). See also the chapters in Richard Hovannisian's series on historic Armenian communities in Ottoman cities and provinces.

39 On Erzurum: Hilmar Kaiser, "'A Scene from the Inferno': The Armenians of Erzerum and the Genocide, 1915–1916," in Kieser and Schaller, eds, *Der Völkermord an den Armeniern und die Shoah*, pp. 129–186; on Aleppo: Hilmar Kaiser, *At the Crossroads of Der Zor: Death, Survival, and Humanitarian Resistance in Aleppo, 1915–1917* (London: Gomidas, 2002); on Urfa: Kerem Öktem, "Incorporating the Time and Space of the Ethnic 'Other': Nationalism and Space in Southeast Turkey in the Nineteenth and Twentieth Centuries," *Nations and Nationalism*, 10: 4 (2004), pp. 559–578; on Trabzon: Kevork Yeghia Suakjian, *Genocide in Trebizond: A Case Study of Armeno-Turkish Relations during the First World War* (Lincoln, NE: University of Nebraska Press, 1981); on Cilicia: Raymond H. Kévorkian, *La Cilicie (1909–1921): Des massacres d'Adana au mandat français* (Paris: RHAC III, 1999); on the South Marmara region: Ryan Gingeras, *Sorrowful Shores: Violence, Ethnicity, and the End of the Ottoman Empire, 1912–1923* (Oxford: Oxford University Press, 2009); on Izmir: Hervé Georgelin, *La fin de Smyrne: du cosmopolitisme aux nationalismes* (Paris: CNRS, 2005).

40 The lack of provincial studies is closely tied to sources: major Ottoman provincial capitals

such as Sivas, Diyarbekir, Erzurum, Van, Konya, Bitlis, and Trabzon hold no provincial archives on the war. This seriously cripples regional studies as scholars become dependent on the central Ottoman archives in Istanbul.

41 Uğur Ümit Üngör, *The Making of Modern Turkey: Nation and State in Eastern Anatolia, 1913–1950* (Oxford: Oxford University Press, 2011).

42 Hilmar Kaiser, "Genocide at the Twilight of the Ottoman Empire," in Donald Bloxham and A. Dirk Moses, eds, *The Oxford Handbook of Genocide Studies* (Oxford: Oxford University Press, 2010), pp. 365–385.

43 For an introduction to the plunder of Armenian property, see Uğur Ümit Üngör and Mehmet Polatel, *Confiscation and Destruction: The Young Turk Seizure of Armenian Property* (London: Continuum, 2011).

44 Uğur Ümit Üngör, "Family Matters: Local Elites and the Structures of Genocide," *The Armenian Weekly*, April 25, 2009, pp. 32–35.

45 Alexander Laban Hinton, *Why Did They Kill? Cambodia in the Shadow of Genocide* (Berkeley, CA: University of California Press, 2005); Olaf Jensen and Claus-Christian W. Szejnmann, eds, *Ordinary People as Mass Murderers: Perpetrators in Comparative Perspectives* (London: Palgrave Macmillan, 2008).

46 Christopher R. Browning, *Ordinary Men: Reserve Police Battalion 101 and the Final Solution in Poland* (New York: HarperCollins, 1992), p. xvi.

47 Slavenka Drakulić, *They Would Never Hurt a Fly: War Criminals on Trial in The Hague* (New York: Viking, 2004), p. 106 ff.

48 Norman Naimark, "The Implications of the Study of Mass Killing in the 20th Century for Analyzing the Armenian Genocide," paper presented at the conference *Vectors of Violence: War, Revolution, and Genocide: Turkish-Armenian Workshop*, University of Minnesota, 27–30 March 2003.

49 Uğur Ümit Üngör, "Genocide en lokale elites: over massaal geweld in Turkije, 1913–1918," in Ward Berenschot, ed., *Etnisch Geweld: Groepsconflict in de Schaduw van de Staat* (Amsterdam: Amsterdam University Press, 2009), pp. 27–52.

50 For details on Pirinççizade family life in the 1930s, see the correspondence between Tarancı and a close friend: Ziya Osman Saba, "Cahit'le Günlerimiz," ("Our Days with Cahit") in Cahit Sıtkı Tarancı, *Ziya'ya Mektuplar 1930–1946* (Letters to Ziya, 1930–1946) (Istanbul: Varlık, 1957), pp. 5–6.

51 *Başbakanlık Cumhuriyet Arişivi* (Turkish Republican Archives, Ankara), 030.10/196. 342.11, decree dated May 26, 1927.

52 Saba, "Cahit'le Günlerimiz," p. 27.

53 Interview conducted with Dursun Çakıroğlu by Ahmet Kahraman in Ankara in 1990, transcribed in Ahmet Kahraman, *Kürt İsyanları* (The Kurdish Uprisings) (Istanbul: Evrensel, 2003), pp. 215–216.

54 Benjamin Lieberman, *Terrible Fate: Ethnic Cleansing in the Making of Modern Europe* (Chicago, IL: Ivan R. Dee, 2006), Chapters 2, 3 and 4; Donald Bloxham, *Genocide, the World Wars and the Unweaving of Europe* (Edgware: Vallentine Mitchell, 2008); Donald Bloxham, *The Final Solution: A Genocide* (Oxford: Oxford University Press, 2009); Cathie Carmichael, *Genocide Before the Holocaust* (New Haven, CT: Yale University Press, 2009).

Figure 12.1 Displaced persons in the Vanni region in January 2009, shortly before the end of the Sri Lankan civil war.

Source: Courtesy trokilinochchi/Flickr.

CHAPTER 12

Sri Lanka and Genocidal Violence

From retrospective to prospective research

Benita Sumita

Genocide, as a "grave crime" threatening the peace and security of a country or region, and a "serious concern to the international community as a whole,"[1] is not often used to describe the conflict-ridden history of Sri Lanka – or so many commentators would argue. And indeed, this chapter is not concerned with labeling the many forms of collective and armed violence in this island nation. The benefits of such labeling extend only so far, and genocide scholars continue to deliberate *ad infinitum* the definitional dilemmas and dangers of the concept of genocide. Luke Glanville even wonders: "Is 'genocide' still a powerful word?"[2] Helen Fein's characterization of a "fuzzy concept," with unclear borders and overlapping phenomena, best encapsulates the problem.[3] The aim of this chapter is not to assess the usefulness and limitations of a conceptually debatable phenomenon, but to understand better the link(s) between research and praxis, and to explore the possibilities of making the "genocide" concept *actively useful* through research.

For a concept to be "actively useful," it cannot remain retrospective. It cannot remain merely a means of labeling outcomes, notably outcomes that result in the physical destruction of groups, communities, or societies. The question to be raised, then, is: What is the need to evaluate or investigate post-mortem the violence or conflicts in a region or country? What purpose does it serve?

The purpose, I contend, is twofold. First, academically, it is an effort to instigate new directions into genocide research. Second, it is an attempt to answer Martin Shaw's crucial questions – "How important is the changed context of political violence in the twenty-first century? Is the problem of genocide posed differently today compared with the period when the concept was developed?"[4] To answer Shaw in a few words: yes, the context has changed in the twenty-first century, and genocide is indeed difficult to recognize today. Instances of genocidal violence are not labeled in an academically rigorous way, but are filtered through a legal and pragmatic framework: one that I will argue is inapplicable in South Asia because of its limited and outcome-based conceptualization.

At the heart of the problem of the prevailing genocide framework and its aim both to prevent genocide and punish perpetrators, is the question of proving genocidal intent. Scholars[5] have criticized the rigidity of the traditional genocide framework, but to little avail. The legal and academic spheres remain divided and function independently of each other. Most of the innovative contributions in the field of genocide studies – the academic sphere – have thus failed to influence how the genocide framework is applied in practice – that is, in the legal sphere. While the 1948 Genocide Convention has in certain cases proved a successful instrument in punishing *génocidaires*, the two spheres, academic and legal, need to work much more closely in tandem to render the genocide concept "actively useful."

For its part, academic research must both seek a greater impact on practice, and move to explore the emancipatory potential of the genocide framing. This involves not only understanding genocidal "intent," but identifying the "means" of violence along a continuum – to borrow from Scheper-Hughes[6] and Bourgois[7] – and recognizing violence as a *process* (see also Jones's Chapter 8 in this volume). The main contribution of this chapter is to demonstrate how a historical, sociological, and politico-economic study of protracted social conflicts in countries like Sri Lanka can enhance the conceptual framework of genocide studies and the application of research to praxis.

Why protracted social conflicts, and why Sri Lanka? Incorporating Edward E. Azar's protracted social conflict framework[8] into genocide research can underpin a social-scientific theory of a genocidal continuum, without limiting itself to a single-track focus on outcomes. "Protracted conflicts are not specific events or even clusters of events at a point in time; they are processes."[9] The nearly 30-year armed conflict in Sri Lanka came to a bloody end in May 2009, under the gaze of the media and other national and international actors such as the United Nations, human rights advocates, and national governments. President Mahinda Rajapakse reaped the fruits of the military victory with an electoral triumph in January 2010. However, observers and commentators on Sri Lanka stress that while the war may have been won, the peace has not been. The conflict in Sri Lanka consisted of more than the exchange of fire and bloodshed between the Sri Lankan Army (SLA) and the Liberation Tigers of Tamil Eelam (LTTE). It also consisted of the years of social, political, and economic policies and strategies of Tamil marginalization that paved the way for decades of bloodshed, and destroyed a community "in whole or in part."[10]

After a brief discussion of the conceptual limitations of prevailing genocide frameworks, this chapter uses the Sri Lankan case to demonstrate the importance of investigating the means of violence as a way, in turn, of enhancing the genocide framework and promoting useful research in the field. The case-study shows, I believe, that the strategies used by successive Sri Lankan governments and the LTTE were akin to acts of genocide – except that from a legal point of view, the element of physical destruction is exceedingly difficult to prove and quantify.

CONCEPTUAL LIMITATIONS

It took the international community over a decade to realize that Raphael Lemkin was right in proposing in 1933 to criminalize "the destruction of racial, religious and social collectivities under the law of nations."[11] But their delayed recognition – in the form of the 1948 Genocide Convention – was only a compromise,[12] one that arguably has been ineffectual in its practical implementation and has impeded academic progress. As Huttenbach[13] stated, "this admittedly pragmatic definition of genocide is more in the order of a *descriptive* formula rather than a *conceptual* definition."[14] In Article II of the Genocide Convention, the crime is defined "as five specific acts[15] committed with the intent to destroy a national, ethnical, racial, or religious group as such."[16] First, the focus of the legal framework on the outcome of mass atrocity impedes a holistic approach toward investigating genocides, understanding their intent and motives, and, most of all, preventing such atrocities from recurring. Second, the focus of the framework on the state alone as perpetrator is too limiting. In the case of Sri Lanka, genocide would be legally and practically difficult to prove within the framework of "intent to destroy", based on outcomes. Therefore, the legal framework will not take precedence in this chapter.

Instead, this chapter analyzes the case of Sri Lanka by applying a combination of three theoretical frameworks. First, Robins and Jones's theory of genocides by the oppressed, is used to frame the case of Sri Lanka to look beyond violence and oppressive measures by the state. Robins and Jones's theory highlights cases where "subaltern actors – those objectively oppressed and disempowered – adopt genocidal strategies to vanquish their oppressors."[17] Second, I use Shaw's theoretical framework, defining genocide as "a form of violent social conflict, or war, between armed power organisations that aim to destroy civilian social groups and those groups and other actors who resist this destruction."[18] Third, I combine Scheper-Hughes's genocide continuum and Azar's protracted social conflict concepts. Robins and Jones's and Shaw's frameworks are innovative and unique, but they can be enhanced when used complementarily in understanding the historical and socio-economic aspects of conflict and violence in Sri Lanka. In turn, the case of Sri Lanka can enhance the conceptual analysis presented in these frameworks. In Robins and Jones's theory, Sri Lanka can serve as a case of genocide by the oppressed, because of the violence inflicted by the now-defeated rebel group – the Liberation Tigers of Tamil Eelam (LTTE). The armed and violent LTTE, originating in the late 1970s, promoted the demand for a separate homeland for the minority Tamils who had been oppressed since independence in 1948. However, the limitation of the subaltern-genocide theory is that it emphasizes the infliction of genocidal strategies on the oppressor, and this is not entirely true in the case of the LTTE. They were quite unbiased in inflicting harm. Tamil civilians faced spiralling violence for close to 30 years, even at the hands of the LTTE.

This limitation is addressed by Shaw's framework, which recognizes "*multiple* perpetrators and/or targets."[19] There is also some merit to Shaw's claim that his framework "restores Lemkin's original aim . . . to restore the concept of genocide as a general category, capable of serving as a framework for understanding violent action against civilian populations."[20] Additionally, Shaw's conceptualization does not reduce destroying social groups to killing their individual members, but understands genocide "as destroying groups' *social power* in economic, political and cultural senses."[21] However, the limitation of both frameworks is the lack of attention, or in Robins and Jones's case adequately nuanced attention, to Scheper-Hughes's (2002) genocidal continuum.

To actualize the true potential of an alternative conceptualization of genocide, such as that of Robins and Jones, and Shaw, the basic tenet of genocide as acts or actions and outcomes must shift to means and processes. The 'politics of oppression' is the identifying factor here. However, unlike Scheper-Hughes's anthropological quest to identify sites of oppression such as nursing homes and mental institutions, this chapter locates the genocidal continuum in historical and socio-economic processes and policies that have fertilized the ground, in Shaw's words, for social conflicts "that aim to destroy civilian social groups and those groups and other actors who resist this destruction."[22] This means that the 'politics of oppression' is not limited to "permitted everyday acts and atrocities" or "acts of everyday resistance,"[23] but expands the scope of the genocide continuums – beyond Jones's pre-genocidal and proto-genocidal points of reference and Scheper-Hughes's attempt to localize genocidal practices – to macro-level politics and policies. To actualize such an expansion one would have to employ the genesis and dynamics components of the protracted social conflict framework that Azar developed in the late 1970s. The genesis component identifies the conditions that transform a non-conflictual situation into a conflictual one. This includes the emergence of an ethnically-divided society, the emergence of economic or developmental grievances, and the role of the state in enabling the emergence of divided societies and their grievances through the enactment of political, social, economic, and cultural policies. The dynamics component is constituted by the strategies that sustain – in peaceful and violent times – the genesis of the conflict.[24] Identifying the dynamics of such conflicts is a crucial component that needs to be absorbed into genocide studies. In the case of Sri Lanka, as will be explored in the rest of this chapter, the dynamics of the politics of oppression are clear in the macro-policies successive governments enacted aiming to marginalize and dehumanize the minority Tamil community. This included the Sinhala Only Act 1956, the quota system in higher education, differential allocation of irrigation and development projects, and so on.

Furthermore, and rather unfortunately, the case of Sri Lanka provides evidence of a twin politics of oppression; or twin genocides confronted by the Tamil people of the country. One was physical and psychological at the hands of the LTTE, while the other was direct – as well as structural – at the hands of successive governments. An investigation into the case of Sri Lanka will provide further evidence of these phenomena.

SRI LANKA: A HISTORICAL AND SOCIO-ECONOMIC INVESTIGATION

With the killing of Vellupillai Prabhakaran, leader of the Tamil Tigers, in May 2009, the war in Sri Lanka may have come to an end. However, the conflict continues. It consists of more than an exchange of fire between the LTTE and the Sri Lankan Army (SLA). It consists also of decades of structural and systematic oppression by both sides, directed mostly against Tamil civilians in Sri Lanka. Writing in the *Tamil Guardian* in February 2009, Bruce Fein, former Associate Deputy Attorney General in the Reagan administration and counsel for Tamils against Genocide, stated that in reporting on the conflict, national and international media had "overlooked the grisly Sinhalese Buddhist genocide of innocent Hindu or Christian Tamil civilians . . ."[25] Several international advocacy groups, such as the International Crisis Group and Human Rights Watch, as well as national organizations within Sri Lanka, have urged the government to "cooperate fully with international efforts to investigate alleged war crimes, including a UN-mandated international inquiry."[26] These organizations claim that in the late stages of the war, government forces subjected civilians to "repeated and increasingly intense artillery and mortar barrages and other fire,"[27] after confining them to "smaller government-declared no-fire zones."[28] The claims were rejected by Sri Lankan Defense Secretary Gothabaya Rajapakse in his testimony before the government-commissioned war panel.[29] But Rajapakse did admit that close to 6,000 members of the LTTE may have been killed in the war's climactic stage.[30] The United Nations has also accused the SLA of executing members of the LTTE in 2009,[31] a violation of international humanitarian law.

Fein is not entirely wrong, but he is not wholly right, either, when he characterizes the conflict in Sri Lanka as genocide. The mass atrocities and inhuman conditions that the Tamil civilians of Sri Lanka have suffered are on a genocidal scale and of a genocidal character. However, they do not fit well with traditional conceptual frameworks of genocide. A Sri Lankan academic, Muttukrishna Sarvananthan,[32] has observed that it is difficult to consider any anti-Tamil riot as genocidal: in the first place, because of the relatively small number of casualties that generally result; and in the second place, because the non-state party in the Sri Lankan conflict, the rebel LTTE, itself inter-mittently murdered Sinhalese and Tamil people in border villages in the north and east of the island nation throughout the conflict. The reciprocal violence of the LTTE means that the Sri Lankan case is less likely to attract international legal attention, since perpetrators and victims have not always been clear-cut. Viewed from the perspective of subaltern genocide and social conflict theory, however, there is a case to be probed. Such a probe is only possible by examining the continuum of violence in Sri Lanka since independence, to determine the processes and politics of oppression that led to the infliction of a genocidal social conflict on the Sri Lankan population.

Ironically, in retrospect, unlike the rest of South Asia which erupted in violent nationalist outbursts, Sri Lanka in the late colonial period was an island of peace and stability.[33] The Tamil issue had been a concern for centuries, but violent clashes during the colonial era were of a different nature, and cannot be considered as forerunners of the ethnic and communal violence between Sinhalese and Tamils that began in 1956.[34] At the time of independence in 1948, Tamil concerns seemed to have been ironed out when the British transferred power to the Sri Lankan people and its dominant Sinhala majority.[35] The transfer of power went smoothly, perhaps reflecting the sense of unity that the Sinhala and Tamil bourgeoisie had established against the common enemy, the British.[36]

This sense of an amicable political settlement was bolstered when G.G. Ponnambalam, who had led the Tamils in their political campaigns, became a member of the Senanayake-led United National Party (UNP) Cabinet in 1948. However, as K.M. de Silva points out,[37] the political compromise was far less stable than it appeared. The illusion of a secular–nationalist Sri Lanka, tolerant of the island's many ethnic and religious groups and with an overall sense of equality, was confined to the political establishment. It was in these echelons of political power, too, that the breakdown of secularism and equality later began, reflecting popular pressures and ethnic tensions which had been brewing in the nascent independence years. Sinhalese believed they had not received their fair share of economic opportunities, while Tamils feared for their political, social, and economic rights as a constitutionally-defined "minority" population. Historical analyses of Sri Lanka noted claims "by the Sinhalese that Tamils have been over-represented in the universities and civil service due to preferential treatment by the British,"[38] though assertions that the Tamils held as much as 60 percent of all government posts, and many similar allegations of Tamil advantage, were baseless.[39]

Ethnic tensions and economic inequality were two sides of the same coin in the Sri Lankan case. The reality of economic inequality came to the fore after S.W.R.D. Bandaranaike departed the Sinhala-dominated UNP in mid-1951. In this way, a seemingly secular nationalism gave way to Sinhalese nationalism with the formation of the Sri Lanka Freedom Party (SLFP). This split demarcated class distinctions in Sri Lanka, especially in the Sinhalese community. The majority Sinhalese now had a political choice, and Sinhala political parties and their leaders marched to the tune of their supporters – the electorate. The majority of the voting base was the rural Sinhalese-educated non-westernized class[40] who lent their support to the SLFP, while the English-educated urban and plantation bourgeoisie among the Sinhalese aligned mostly with the UNP. The former group believed that the most rewarding careers were closed off to them, as English was the language of administration, something that was also true within the Tamil community.

Unemployment was an especially worrying issue for Sri Lankans. It stood at just 0.8 percent of the total work force in 1953, but approached 12 percent by 1959–1960.[41] The finger of blame was pointed at the Tamils, with their historical educational advantage. The ethno-economic cleavage deepened when the then-government enforced the use of the mother tongues – Sinhala and Tamil – as the medium of instruction in schools in 1953 following the nationalization of educational institutions, to the disappointment of the Hindu and Christian establishments. They saw the tactic as a political move by the Sinhala-dominant government to drive the ethnic wedge even deeper. And indeed the divide was sharpened by the enactment of the Sinhala Only Act of 1956. The move to make Sinhala the only official language of Sri Lanka was driven by "religious revival among the Buddhists", and was "in part a reaction against Christian missionary teaching. It was also a revolt by people literate in Sinhala, but not in English, against the privileges of the English-speaking elite."[42] The movement for *swabhasha* (own language) began during Britain's colonial rule. However, the driving force behind the *swabhasha* movement was the politics of the Buddhist nationalists. Therefore, in the post-independence period, "the official language controversy shifted from an attack on the privileged position of the English-educated multi-communal elite to a clash between ethnic communities."[43] Potent twin nationalisms – Sinhala and Tamil – materialized around the political establishment's linguistic and religious fervor. As Sidney Tarrow[44] and other social scientists have noted, the right "political opportunity structures" can trigger a movement. In the case of Sri Lanka, the structures were those of the Sinhala and Tamil nationalist movements triggered, in their turn, by the opportunity structures of language and religion.

The foundations of the appropriate "political opportunity structure" were laid with the ascent to power of the SLFP-led coalition, and Prime Minister S.W.R.D. Bandaranaike's prompt declaration that Sinhala would become the sole official language in July 1956. Meanwhile, Prime Minister Bandaranaike also tried to appease the Tamils by entering into a pact with the leader of the Tamil-dominant Federal Party (FP) – S.J.V. Chelvanayakam – a year later. The uproar led by Buddhist nationalists and the UNP, then in opposition, finally ended in the demise of the Bandaranaike–Chelvanayakam pact in April 1958. The same year witnessed a bloody riot that was instigated by demands from Buddhist nationalists for the consolidation of the Sinhala-only language policy.

Over the years, the Sinhala Only Act has been watered down, and constitutional provisions have been made to accommodate Tamil. But even recent media reports have quoted the Chairman of the Official Language Commission as saying "there is an enormous gap between the constitutional provisions and their application."[45] A district quota system was adopted for university admissions, under which Tamils dropped to 19 percent of students in universities in 1975, from the 40–45 percent rate which had prevailed until roughly 1970. Tamils employed in the public sector also fell to 12 percent by 1980.[46] Tamils who already feared the rising tempo of Sinhala nationalism came to believe that they were relegated to second-class citizenship through the systematic denial of seats in educational institutions by language barriers and quotas. These restrictions meant, in turn, that Tamils would have fewer job opportunities.[47] Tamils already in government service felt especially threatened by the need to sit for mandatory Sinhala language exams that would then determine their future in the job as well as their continued salary.[48]

These socially marginalizing and economically oppressive policies of successive Sri Lankan governments were akin to "deliberately inflicting on the group conditions of life calculated to bring about its physical destruction in whole or in part."[49] Although the strategies are *akin* to the acts in the Genocide Convention, it would be difficult to prove or quantify *physical* destruction. The strategies fit neatly, however, within the concept of genocide as a protracted social conflict.

The development project in contemporary Sri Lanka has further exacerbated ethnic and economic cleavages. Development in contemporary Sri Lanka is much more than the introduction of new technologies and financial supplements to the agrarian and domestic economies, as Woost points out.[50] It is a complex array of scarce and unequally distributed material resources, and social and cultural practices, which provide fertile soil for the dissemination of nationalist ideologies.[51] The history of Sri Lanka's economic development is a story of contradictions. The welfare state that the island inherited from the British boosted social development – adult life expectancy (72 years), literacy rates (90 percent) – to a level on a par with industrialized countries. But this has not translated into economic well-being,[52] though the country's GDP growth in the period of active conflict between 1983 and 2000 was a seemingly impressive 4–5 percent per annum.[53] The growth rate was maintained by tea and garment exports and worker remittances. However, it has to be taken with a grain of salt, because calculations left out the provinces of the north and east of the country since the 1990s, where the conflict raged. This is just one of several reasons why a high growth rate in a war-torn country may not translate or trickle down into effective development and well-being for its people. Scholars like Kelegama,[54] and Grobar and Gnanaselvam[55] pay special attention to the toll of the civil conflict. Heavy military spending was the cost the government, its people and the LTTE had to bear. The defense budget continued to eat into the GDP every year since 1983, rising from 1.4 percent of GDP to 6 percent in 1996.[56] A look at the average GDP before the conflict also shows a dismal picture. Sarvananthan[57] calculated that annual average real GDP growth remained stuck in the neighborhood of 4.4 percent from 1961 to 1982. Both the pre-conflict and conflict-period economic situations were fodder for deepening ethnic discriminations.

In the pre-conflict phase, successive governments were unable to generate enough employment to absorb the burgeoning educated masses. Apart from an economically irrational welfare economy, the state's expenditure was also oriented toward the plantation sector that fed the economy with its export income.[58] The high investment into this sector, however, did not generate proportionate employment.[59] A state-led welfare-centric development agenda in the first decades of independence, with increasing concentration of productive resources in the state sector and political clientelism and patronage toward Sinhalese capitalists, shifted slowly toward an open economy policy in the 1970s. Sweeping reforms aimed at liberalizing the economy were instituted in 1977.

Opening the economy only widened the class disparities. These material inequalities should have strengthened class identities, or perhaps regional ones. Instead, ethnicized politics took precedence.[60] Social engineering, for example, was woven into many of the irrigation-related development plans in Sri Lanka. In an attempt to solve the increasing basic needs of a growing population, irrigation development and land settlement schemes were implemented from the 1970s.[61] These state-sponsored resettlement schemes, transplanting Sinhalese to Tamil-dominant regions (north and east), raised Tamil fears of further marginalization.[62] In the contemporary period, the Accelerated Mahaweli Development and Irrigation Programme (MDIP) was especially infamous. Initiated in the late 1960s, this grand plan aimed to settle and resettle 700,000 people in six years – about 5 percent of the country's population at the time.[63] These large-scale settlement-resettlement programs drastically altered the ethnic demography of regions that were mostly Tamil-dominated. For instance, in Trincomalee, the ethnic distribution of Tamil, Sinhalese, and Muslims in 1911 was 65:4:26 respectively. Following the implementation of the Accelerated MDIP, the ratio shifted to 33:33:29 in 1981.[64] Muggah considers this fundamentally a project of ethnic hegemony, with the hydropower development merely a diversion.[65]

It was also in this period that Sri Lanka witnessed the rise of Tamil nationalism. The Tamil political umbrella outfit the Tamil United Liberation Front (TULF) won 48 percent of the seats in the north and east on a platform of separation and the establishment of an independent Tamil Eelam (homeland). Educated but unemployed Tamil youth formed an important wing of the TULF. They would go on to constitute an important sector of the LTTE. The Sinhala government's gradual marginalization of Tamil students pushed disgruntled young men to violent forms of political expression. "Out of the 20,000 who had passed the A levels, only 50 Tamils got into university. It was thus seen as more profitable to turn into a militant," observed the LTTE leader Kittu, interviewed by Rajanayagam in 1994.[66] So the politically, economically, and socially aggrieved Tamil youth, primarily in the north, became the resource-base of the LTTE. This helped the group grow in strength and numbers through the 1970s.

Simultaneously, the 1970s witnessed the emergence of a radical Sinhalese youth movement – the Janatha Vimukthi Peramuna (JVP). These disillusioned youths emerged in the background of a stagnating economy that failed to absorb them into the mainstream development process.[67] On both sides, the members were educated, unemployed youth disgruntled at the state. Animosity between the youth groups flared into violent outbursts on several occasions. Although Jayawardene, Prime Minister in 1977 and the country's first Executive President in 1978, made changes and amendments to the constitution to appease Tamils, violence flared further. The violent right-wing Sinhala groups, such as the JVP, were easier to appease, and soon gravitated toward the political mainstream. The LTTE, however, was further marginalized, leading to 30 years of violence against civilians, who were physically, structurally, psychologically, and systematically targeted and oppressed by both the LTTE and the government.

It is clear in the case of Sri Lanka, that the political, social, and economic politics and policies of successive governments deepened the divide between the Sinhala and Tamil communities that led to years and generations of violence and bloodshed in the country. The consequences of this violence fell especially on the minority Tamils and Muslims – not only at the hands of the LTTE rebels, but also at the hands of their governments.

There have been several instances of violence and impromptu outbursts of rioting in the fraught history of the island nation. But nationalist aggression turned armed and protractedly violent from the early 1980s. The anti-Tamil riots of July 1983, which later came to be known as Black July, marked the beginning of the deadly spiral of armed conflict in Sri Lanka. Some sources claim that Black July witnessed the deaths of 3,000 Tamil civilians, leaving 160,000 Tamil refugees and 300,000 internally displaced.[68] After the first attempts at peace talks failed between the Government of Sri Lanka (GOSL) and the LTTE, the Sri Lankan army took on the rebel group in a fierce battle in 1987. This was followed by an agreement to allow India to send troops to monitor a ceasefire. The dispatching of the Indian Peacekeeping Force (IPKF) turned out to be India's worst foreign-policy decision in years, if not decades. It led, among other things, to the assassination of the then Indian prime Minister, Rajiv Gandhi, in 1991 by an LTTE suicide bomber.

The IPKF had to withdraw from the island in 1990 as violence escalated. This early phase of the 1990s also witnessed the forced displacement of over 60,000 Tamil Muslims from the north by the LTTE; they remain internally displaced to this day. The violence of the 1990s left Tamils, especially in the north and east, deprived of developmental, economic, and other social opportunities. The decade also saw the growing strength of the LTTE, which "brought extensive areas under its control and created a certain military parity of status with the Government of Sri Lanka."[69] The rebel authority took on the functions of security, welfare, and representation, functions that the government had failed to fulfill. State-building by the LTTE therefore had a two-fold agenda.

> On the one hand, it is contingent on the discursive framing of LTTE as the sole representative and guardian of Tamil nationalism. On the other hand, LTTE's hegemony in Tamil politics is closely related to their military capacity to confront the GOSL and thereby provide a degree of external security, but also [to] their repressive capacity in regard to internal anti-LTTE political and militant forces.[70]

While the LTTE seemed to put on a façade of the benevolent state, they were also squeezing dry an already impoverished population through their taxation policies. Collected as direct or indirect taxes – a percentage of government servants' incomes, a percentage of businessmen's income, a percentage of farmers' and fisherfolk's output, a vehicle registration tax, a tax on any goods entering LTTE territory, and more – the forced tributes sizably swelled rebel coffers.[71] According to Sarvananthan's estimate of the LTTE economy, taxes alone added up to about 10 million Sri Lankan rupees daily in 2003.[72] This was not only seen as stifling the economy in the north and east, but also frightening away entrepreneurs, investment, and much-needed development in the region.

The rebel group delivered its most severe blow – militarily, politically, and economically – in 2001, when it attacked the international airport in Colombo, destroying half the fleet of the national flagship carrier, Sri Lankan Airlines. This represented "a body blow to the political establishment, the security forces, to the economy, and to the prospects for peace."[73] According to the Asian Development Bank (ADB), the outlook for the following year was bleak. The ADB not only drew a dismal picture for the tourism sector, but warned of a hefty rise in war-risk insurance that severely hit the shipping industry as well. Unemployment in the early 2000s increased, especially in the manufacturing and tourism sectors. The dissolution of parliament in July 2001 also impacted on new investments and savings. Consequently, as a proportion of GDP, fixed capital investment fell from 28 percent in 2000 to 25.1 percent in 2001, while the savings rate remained at 17.3 percent.[74] After several failed attempts to draw the parties into peace negotiations, the latter half of the decade grew bloody, especially after the Mahinda Rajapakse government reimposed in 2006 the tough Prevention of Terrorism Act (PTA), which had been revoked in 2002 when Ranil Wickremasinghe's government signed a ceasefire agreement with the LTTE. The revived PTA gave the Sri Lankan armed forces unrestricted power to detain, arrest, and interrogate terrorist suspects. The net of terrorist suspicion fell ever more widely.

The Minority Rights Group (MRG) supplies one of the best overviews of the years of violence that followed the resumption of the war in 2006.[75] Beginning with a military offensive in the east using multi-barrelled rocket launchers, the army took over large areas of land, leaving at least 3,500 civilians dead and 290,000 more displaced.[76] The internally displaced were then forcibly returned in contravention of international humanitarian and human rights laws. Human rights violations continued even after the displaced returned to homes they could no longer recognize. In the name of fighting terrorism, "returnees are put through intense security measures and face routine checks by the Sri Lankan military," the MRG reported.[77] Accounts by the Jaffna University Teachers for Human Rights (UTHR(J)) provide further details of the atrocities of both government and rebel forces.[78] As reported by a person who escaped an LTTE prison in Batticaloa, 46 out of 74 prisoners were executed between February and April 2007.[79] Meanwhile, the Sri Lankan Army was grabbing land from the civilians in the east to set up high-security zones as part of the war on terror. Displacing another 15,000 people, mostly Tamil civilians, the army took over 35 square miles of land – covering 15 villages – in Sampur, a town close to the port city of Trincomalee.[80] The MRG noted that this drastically impeded the livelihoods of the local residents, mostly Tamils and Muslims, as access to their means of livelihood – fishing or agriculture – was limited as a security measure, or completely restricted. To add insult to injury, Human Rights Watch noted that "since March 2008 the government . . . confined virtually all civilians displaced by the war in military-controlled detention camps, euphemistically called welfare centers."[81]

In the final stages of the armed conflict in the first half of 2009, civilians faced increased atrocities. A Human Rights Watch (HRW) report alleged that "the Sri Lankan armed forces and the LTTE appear to be engaged in a perverse competition to demonstrate the greatest disregard for the civilian population."[82] During these final stages, the Rajapakse government ordered humanitarian and media organizations to leave the war zone, which not only made information difficult to obtain, but left civilians caught in the war zone stranded without any means of meeting their basic needs. The 2009 HRW report counts over 5,000 civilian casualties, of which over 1,000 were killed and over 4,000 were injured between 20 January and 13 February alone. Conditions grew still grimmer because of a lack of basic necessities – food, medical supplies, and so on – from the government, the LTTE, or the humanitarian organizations which were barred from gaining access to civilians. Even six months after the end of the armed conflict, more than 129,000 civilians, including 80,000 children, were still held in camps, allegedly for their own "welfare."[83]

The military victory of the Sri Lankan Army was echoed in the political victory won by incumbent Mahinda Rajapakse in the 2010 presidential elections. Peace, though, remains to be won. The military and political victory of the Sinhala-majority government has only papered over the deeper conflict based on the marginalization and oppression of the minority peoples – Tamil and Muslim – that continue to chafe under Sinhala domination and discrimination.

CONCLUSION: RESEARCH IMPLICATIONS

Tracing oppression in Sri Lanka historically and socio-economically makes it clear that genocide and genocidal violence must be understood as a continuum. The field of genocide studies should incorporate diverse "means of violence" in its analytical framework. Enhancing the framework in this way could increase the effectiveness of preventive measures devised by scholars of genocide studies. These means of violence are of two kinds: structural and direct. But these are not mutually exclusive layers of oppression. Nor are they limited to acts of physical violence and destruction, though these are usually prominent, as the preceding analysis suggests.

Direct means of genocidal violence include bombing areas known to be inhabited by civilians, the use of civilians as human shields, forced displacement, abduction, killing, disappearances, and limited or lack of access to basic necessities in times of war and peace. These means have been adopted against civilians, mostly minority Tamils and Muslims, at one time or another by both the Sri Lankan Army and the LTTE. Measures taken by the government administration and Sri Lankan armed forces to isolate civilians in war zones, denying them access to humanitarian assistance and resources, are also a violation of the basic right to life, and of the 1948 Geneva Conventions and the 1977 Additional Protocol II. Forcibly detaining those internally displaced in camps, thereby restricting their freedom of movement, is also a violation of basic rights.

Direct violence can generally be defined by its momentary impact and short-term effects. However, direct means also have a bearing over the long term. The creation of large-scale militarized high-security zones in civilian agricultural or residential zones, for example, not only infringes on people's right to own property in the short term, but causes enduring damage to the social and economic structures of local communities and societies.

Structural means of genocidal violence are characterized by oppressive political and socio-economic strategies. In Sri Lanka, such strategies have subjugated and marginalized at least two generations of Tamils. Social and economic policies – such as the Sinhala Only Act of 1956 and the Accelerated MDIP of the 1960s – have created and sustained ethnic rifts that fuel social violence and armed conflict. The LTTE's forced recruitment tactics, meanwhile – especially of children – have destroyed Tamil families and local communities, who lived in constant fear of their lives. The rebel group's state-building measures of taxation threatened entrepreneurship and weakened economic livelihoods and social structures in ways that will also be felt for another generation at least. Now that the armed conflict has ended, Tamil communities must struggle to survive and eke out an existence in a state in which they are still second-class citizens.

In an armed conflict that lasted close to three decades, nearly 70,000 people have been killed in Sri Lanka. In terms of sheer numbers, this would not constitute genocide by many scholars' preferred (Holocaust-centric) definitions. Within a legal framework, it would be difficult to demonstrate genocidal intent, as the strategies of oppression and destruction were inflicted over several decades. Moreover, they were inflicted not only by successive Sri Lankan governments, but by the non-state party in the conflict – the LTTE – as well. While each party fought to destroy the other, those who suffered – not collaterally, but directly and structurally – were the people of Sri Lanka, especially the marginalized Tamil minority.

Two notable research implications arise from the Sri Lankan case. First, the legal and practical genocide framework should be distinguished from academic frameworks. The two approaches aim at two different ends. The legal and practical framework seeks to punish, and perhaps also to prevent, though its efficacy in this respect is debatable. The academic approach, meanwhile, seeks to understand, explain, and explore violence on a genocidal scale, while also working to prevent the recurrence of such atrocities.

Second, existing methods of conflict analysis and genocide studies can be greatly enhanced by investigating the history of a conflict and the continuum of violent strategies that underpins it. A more nuanced identification of the dynamics and means of violence will allow more early warning signs to be identified, which might otherwise pass undetected. It is these early and symptomatic points on the continuum of violence and oppression that can generate protracted social conflict and lead, eventually, to full-scale genocidal violence.

NOTES

1   The phrases "grave crime" and "serious concern to the international community as a whole" are found in the preamble of the Rome Statute of the International Criminal Court.
2   Luke Glanville, "Is 'Genocide' Still a Powerful Word?," *Journal of Genocide Research*, 11: 4 (2009), pp. 467–486.
3   Cited by Alex Alvarez, *Governments, Citizens, and Genocide: A Comparative and Interdisciplinary Approach* (Bloomington, IN: Indiana University Press, 2001), pp. 34–35.
4   Martin Shaw, *What Is Genocide?* (Cambridge: Polity Press, 2007).
5   Shaw, *What Is Genocide?*; Nancy Scheper-Hughes, "The Genocidal Continuum: Peace-time Crimes," in Jeanette Maric Mageo, ed., *Power and the Self* (Cambridge: Cambridge

University Press, 2002), pp. 29–47; Nicholas A. Robins and Adam Jones, eds, *Genocides by the Oppressed: Subaltern Genocide in Theory and Practice* (Bloomington, IN: Indiana University Press, 2009); Frank Chalk and Kurt Jonassohn, *The History and Sociology of Genocide: Analyses and Case Studies* (New Haven, CT: Yale University Press, 1990); and many others.

6 Scheper-Hughes, "The Genocidal Continuum," pp. 29–47.

7 Philippe Bourgois, "The Continuum of Violence in War and Peace: Post-Cold War Lessons from El Salvador," in Nancy Scheper-Hughes and Philippe Bourgois, eds, *Violence in War and Peace: An Anthology* (Oxford: Blackwell, 2004).

8 Edward E. Azar, *The Management of Protracted Social Conflict: Theory and Cases* (Aldershot: Dartmouth, 1990).

9 Edward E. Azar, Paul Jureidini, and Ronald McLaurin, "Protracted Social Conflict: Theory and Practice in the Middle East," *Journal of Palestine Studies*, 8: 1 (1978), pp. 41–60.

10 United Nations Convention on the Prevention and Punishment of the Crime of Genocide (1948), Article II.

11 Raphael Lemkin, "Genocide as a Crime Under International Law," *The American Journal of International Law*, 41: 1 (1947), pp. 145–151.

12 Chalk and Jonassohn, *The History and Sociology of Genocide*, p. 11.

13 Henry R. Huttenbach, "From the Editor: Towards a Conceptual Definition of Genocide," *Journal of Genocide Research*, 4: 2 (2002), pp. 167–175.

14 Emphasis in original.

15 The five specific acts are: killing members of the group, causing serious bodily or mental harm to members of the group, deliberately inflicting on the group conditions of life calculated to bring about its physical destruction in whole or in part, preventing births within the group, and forcibly transferring children from the group to another group.

16 William Schabas, *An Introduction to the International Criminal Court*, 2nd edn (Cambridge: Cambridge University Press, 2004).

17 Nicholas A. Robins and Adam Jones, *Genocides by the Oppressed*, p. 3.

18 Shaw, *What Is Genocide?*, p. 154.

19 Ibid., emphasis in original.

20 Ibid.

21 Ibid., emphasis in original.

22 Shaw, *What Is Genocide?*, p. 154.

23 Robins and Jones, *Genocides by the Oppressed*, pp. 185–186.

24 Azar, *The Management of Protracted Social Conflict*, p. 7.

25 Bruce Fein, "Genocide in Sri Lanka," *Tamil Guardian*, February 18, 2009.

26 International Crisis Group, *War Crimes in Sri Lanka: Executive Summary and Recommendations*, May 17, 2010, http://www.crisisgroup.org/en/regions/asia/south-asia/sri-lanka/191-war-crimes-in-sri-lanka.aspx.

27 Ibid.

28 Ibid.

29 "Sri Lanka Leader's Brother Testifies Before War Panel," BBC, August 17, 2010, http://www.bbc.co.uk/news/world-south-asia-11003815.

30 Ibid.

31 "S Lanka Execution Video 'Authentic'," Al-Jazeera.net, January 8, 2010, http://english.aljazeera.net/news/asia/2010/01/20101718331516260.html.

32 Muttukrishna Sarvananthan, Principal Researcher, Point Pedro Institute of Development, Colombo, Sri Lanka. Mr. Sarvananthan's views were expressed in e-mail correspondence with the writer.

33 Kingsley M. de Silva, *A History of Sri Lanka* (Colombo: Vijitha Yapa Publications, 1981).

34 Elizabeth Nissan and R.L. Stirrat, "The Generation of Communal Identities," in Jonathan Spencer, ed., *Sri Lanka: History and the Roots of the Conflict* (London: Routledge, 1990), pp. 19–44.

35 de Silva, *A History of Sri Lanka*, p. 490.

36   Sunil Bastian, "University Admission and the National Question," in *Ethnicity and Social Change in Sri Lanka* (Colombo: Social Scientists' Association of Sri Lanka, 1985), p. 168.

37   de Silva, *A History of Sri Lanka*, pp. 489–509.

38   Azar, *The Management of Protracted Social Conflict*, p. 68.

39   Dhananjayan Srikandarajah, "Socio-economic Inequality and Ethno-political Conflict: Some Observations from Sri Lanka," *Contemporary South Asia*, 14: 3 (2005), pp. 341–356.

40   Nissan and Stirrat, "The Generation of Communal Identities," p. 35.

41   Pradeep Bhargava, *Political Economy of Sri Lanka* (New Delhi: Navrang, 1987).

42   Walter Schwarz, "The Tamils of Sri Lanka", *The Minority Rights Group Report No. 25*, 1983, p. 6.

43   Robert Kearney, "Language and the Rise of Tamil Separatism in Sri Lanka," *Asian Survey*, 18: 5 (1978), p. 527.

44   Sidney Tarrow, *Power in Movement: Social Movements, Collective Action and Politics* (Cambridge: Cambridge University Press, 1994).

45   V.S. Sambandan, "Language Barrier," *Frontline*, 23: 4 (2006), available at: http://www.hinduonnet.com/fline/fl2304/stories/20060310001305500.htm.

46   Jehan Perera, "Political Development and Ethnic Conflict in Sri Lanka," *Journal of Refugee Studies*, 5: 2 (1992), pp. 136–148.

47   Azar, *The Management of Protracted Social Conflict*, p. 68.

48   Schwarz, "The Tamils of Sri Lanka," p. 8. An executive clerk in the government, one Mr. Kodiswaran, refused to take the Sinhala exam. In 1962, his increment was stayed. He sued the government for discrimination and violation of the protection of minorities provided by Section 29 of the Constitution. This section was dropped when the Constitution was redrafted in 1972.

49   Article III of the Convention on the Prevention and Punishment of the Crime of Genocide (1948).

50   Michael D. Woost, "Rural Awakenings: Grassroots Development and the Cultivation of a National Past in Rural Sri Lanka," in Spencer, ed., *Sri Lanka*, pp. 164–185.

51   Ibid.

52   See United Nations Development Programme, *National Human Development Report 1998: Regional Dimensions of Human Development* (Colombo: UNDP, 1998).

53   Saman Kelegama, "Transforming Conflict with an Economic Dividend: The Sri Lankan Experience," *The Round Table*, 94: 381 (2005), pp. 229–242.

54   Ibid.

55   Lisa Morris Grobar and Shiranthi Gnanaselvam, "The Economic Effects of the Sri Lankan Civil War," *Economic Development and Cultural Change*, 41: 2 (1993), pp. 395–405.

56   Nisha Arunatilake, Sisira Jayasurya and Saman Kelegama, "The Economic Cost of the War in Sri Lanka," *World Development*, 29: 9 (2001), pp. 1483–1500.

57   Muttukrishna Sarvananthan, "Economic Imperative for Peace in Sri Lanka," Working Paper No. 3 (Point Pedro: Point Pedro Institute of Development, 2003).

58   See Donald Snodgrass, "The Economic Development of Sri Lanka: A Tale of Missed Opportunities," HIID Development Discussion Paper No. 637 (Cambridge, MA: Harvard Institute of International Development, 1998).

59   Bhargava, *Political Economy of Sri Lanka*.

60   See Mick Moore, *The State and Peasant Politics in Sri Lanka* (Cambridge: Cambridge University Press, 1985).

61   Jehan Perera, "Political Development and Ethnic Conflict in Sri Lanka," *Journal of Refugee Studies*, 5: 2 (1992), pp. 136–148.

62   Benedikt Korf, "Functions of Violence Revisited: Greed, Pride and Grievance in Sri Lanka's Civil War," *Progress in Development Studies*, 6: 2 (2006), pp. 109–122.

63   See Robert Muggah, *Relocation Failures in Sri Lanka: A Short History of Internal Displacement and Resettlement* (London: Zed Books, 2008).

64   Ibid.

65   Ibid.

66 Dagmar Hellmann-Rajanayagam, *The Tamil Tigers: Armed Struggle for Identity* (Stuttgart: Franz Steiner Verlag, 1994), p. 36.

67 Sirimal Abeyratne, "Economic Roots of Political Conflict: The Case of Sri Lanka," *The World Economy*, 27: 8 (2004), pp. 1295–1314.

68 Schwarz, "The Tamils of Sri Lanka", p. 12.

69 Kristian Stokke, "Building the Tamil Eelam State: Emerging State Institutions and Forms of Governance in LTTE-Controlled Areas in Sri Lanka," *Third World Quarterly*, 27: 6 (2006), pp. 1021–1040.

70 Ibid.

71 Ibid.

72 Muttukrishna Sarvananthan, "What Impedes Economic Revival in the North & East Province of Sri Lanka," PPID Working Paper Series, No. 2 (Point Pedro, Sri Lanka: Point Pedro Institute of Development, 2003).

73 Nirupama Subramaniam, "Terror at Katunayake," *Frontline*, 18: 6 (2001). Available at: http://www.hinduonnet.com/fline/fl1816/18160510.htm.

74 Asian Development Bank, *Asian Development Outlook 2002: Economic Trends and Prospects in Developing Asia: South Asia*, http://www.adb.org/documents/books/ado/2002/sri.asp.

75 Minority Rights Group, "One Year On: Counter-terrorism Sparks Human Rights Crisis for Sri Lanka's Minorities," Briefing Paper, 2007, http://www.minorityrights.org/?lid= 4585.

76 Ibid.

77 Ibid.

78 University Teachers for Human Rights (Jaffna), "Can the East Be Won through Human Culling? Special Economic Zones – An Ideological Journey Back to 1983," Special Report, 2007, http://www.uthr.org/SpecialReports/spreport26.htm#_Toc173926096.

79 Ibid.

80 Ibid.

81 Human Rights Watch, *World Report 2010* (New York: Human Rights Watch, 2010), p. 348.

82 Human Rights Watch, *War on the Displaced: Sri Lankan Army and LTTE Abuses against Civilians in the Vanni* (New York: Human Rights Watch, 2009), p. 1.

83 Human Rights Watch, *World Report 2010*, p. 350.

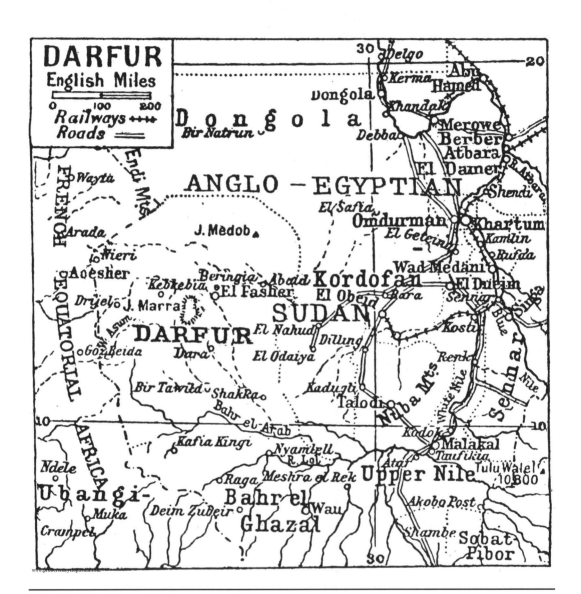

Figure 13.1 Colonial map of Darfur.

Source: Wikimedia Commons.

CHAPTER 13

Researching Genocide in Africa

Establishing ethnological and historical context

Carol Jean Gallo

INTRODUCTION

In my experience as a student of Africa, there appear to be two disparate and sometimes competing approaches to the study of conflict and human rights on the continent, which derive from broader debates over cultural relativity and "modernity." While a Western political-science-based approach tends to be framed in terms of universality, particularly with regard to human rights, a contemporary anthropological approach emphasizes diversity and cultural equality.[1] Yet both areas have evolved, in a general sense, toward a more relativist perspective that recognizes nuance and the importance of questioning assumptions. This transformation is relatively nascent with regard to the human rights movement in comparison to anthropology.

Critical insights can be gained from considering alternative understandings of, for example, economic systems and social structures as manifested in the West. These mechanisms, as they exist in Africa, differ tremendously from the environments in which international policies and scholarship on Africa are formulated. Understanding ethnological context requires incorporating findings from the field of history, and can only benefit the international community's attempts to manage genocide prevention, cessation, and recovery. Historical context will be key in understanding the conflict in Darfur, examined below.[2] One of the major challenges lies in simply understanding what kinds of questions to ask in the first place.

In this chapter, I first review the scant literature available on anthropological approaches to genocide,[3] including a brief history of the field and some of the problems with its initial focus on a universal concept of modernization. I link this to the human rights movement's traditional emphasis on universality. I then provide a case study of Darfur, beginning with an overview of the conflict as it is generally understood in the West by scholars and popular media. An ethnological perspective on racial constructions in Darfur is then presented, examining social patterns as they existed in more stable political and ecological environments, and how these structures crumbled with the onset of war. Finally, I draw some conclusions with regard to new ethnological approaches to genocide research.

THE ANTHROPOLOGY OF GENOCIDE

Historically, anthropology as a discipline grew out of Enlightenment ideas about modernity and progress.[4] While "modernization" was first used to frame the changes that took place in Europe during the Enlightenment (1660–1770), it was soon seen by European intellectuals as a universal phenomenon rather than a contextual one. Non-industrialized, non-Western civilizations were implicitly equated with Europe as it was in the Dark Ages and placed on a lower rung of the modernization/developmental ladder.[5] (This conveniently overlooked the contributions of the medieval Middle Eastern Muslim scholars to the Enlightenment itself.[6]) Modernization theory asserts that the process is an inevitable and evolutionary one that will eventually, everywhere, lead to modern industrialized societies, such as those found in Europe and North America.[7] These industrialized societies are considered the apex of "development" within this framework. In the Western collective imagination, this creates a set of dichotomies centered on notions of traditional versus modern, advanced versus backward, and civilization versus barbarity, *inter alia*.[8] This has historically enabled and justified all manner of colonial projects, the subjugation of indigenous cultures, slavery, and – not infrequently – genocide.[9]

Yet quite early on, anthropology also produced scholars who questioned this received wisdom, and reworked the discipline to challenge racist assumptions and defend the rights of indigenous peoples. These pioneers "demonstrate[d] that categories like race are social constructs situated in particular historical and social contexts."[10] Today, the cornerstone of this approach is the recognition that culturally specific ethics and morals are products of history, and as such, one cannot assume that the cultural values of one group of people are universal or more legitimate than others.[11]

In one of the first volumes specifically to address the anthropology of genocide, Alexander Laban Hinton confronts the problematic nature of "modernization" when he notes that "traditional" peoples are not simple recipients of a foreign, exogenous modernism and its attendant technologies. Instead, they actively adapt these influences to their own social structures and cultural meanings consciously, as they see fit, and through more organic processes of synthesis and syncretism.[12]

Until recently, the field of human rights has also taken, quite literally, a universalist approach. This is rooted in the idea that, as human beings, we are all entitled to certain fundamental rights.[13] This is in contrast to the essentialized humanity that is supposed to be the product of modernization in early anthropological frameworks; rather, it posits a universal humanity that all are born with. Yet what those universal rights should be, and who should decide, remain contentious. The Universal Declaration of Human Rights was passed by the United Nations General Assembly at a time when its membership consisted of just 57 countries, to the exclusion of non-members, colonies, and other territories.[14] After the Declaration was passed, the American Anthropological Association criticized it as a "statement of rights conceived only in terms of the values prevalent in the countries of Western Europe and America."[15]

As the field has grown since its current incarnation was formed after World War II, human rights research has increasingly come to resemble the work of anthropologists and ethnographers.[16] Human rights reports have become more comprehensive, examining not only political and historical dynamics but also ethnic and social ones.[17] In the Foreword to *Annihilating Difference,* Kenneth Roth, the Executive Director of Human Rights Watch, highlights two major potential relationships between anthropology and human rights. The first is the explanatory use of anthropology to illuminate the local meanings of human rights abuses. The second is that understanding social structures and local knowledge within an anthropological framework can help to provide a "blueprint for change."[18]

Hinton's *Anthropological Reader* and many of the cases in *Annihilating Difference* focus primarily on the first human rights–anthropology relationship alluded to by Roth, using anthropological research to explain genocidal violence itself. Many scholars – and Hinton counts himself among them – "believe that genocide remains a human behavior, albeit an extreme one, that can and must be explained to whatever extent is possible."[19] There are few cases, however, of scholarship that explores the second relationship that Roth suggests can lead to a blueprint for change. In this chapter, I will attempt to contribute one such case, examining pre-conflict social structures and conflict resolution mechanisms in Darfur, and the factors that contributed to their collapse. The local knowledge I have chosen to guide the story centers on the concept of race.

The main limitation of this endeavor is my inability to draw on personal fieldwork, in the face of a dismally small selection of historical and anthropological literature on this particular region. Of the scholarly works on western Sudan that I was able to find, most analyze the history of Darfur and the conflict through political science methodologies that fail to take into account the deeper meanings of grievances, or explain the local knowledge surrounding cultural practices and social structures. Most were published only after Darfur became a trendy cause in the West, coloring its content despite the supposed obligation of political scientists to maintain objectivity. Adding to this challenge is the highly diverse and complex nature of society in Darfur and the ways in which various groups have interacted over time, making it difficult to synthesize varying and sometimes contradicting accounts of the history and ethnology of the region. There are, however, a number of valuable resources from which core themes can be extrapolated.

ARAB VERSUS AFRICAN: THE WESTERN POP NARRATIVE OF DARFUR

The conflict in Darfur should first be understood within the context of Sudanese conflicts in general. Briefly, there are two other major conflicts that, in addition to Darfur (see map, Figure 13.2), are sometimes confused with one another. The least reported conflict is that between the multi-ethnic Nuba of Kordofan and the government, which began in 1987.[20] The government scapegoated the Nuba as supporters of the insurgency in the south; in the mid-1990s, Sullaiman Rahhal of Nuba Mountains Solidarity Abroad described the government's attacks on Nuba communities as genocide.[21]

The other conflict is the civil war between the north and south. Civil war began almost immediately after independence in 1956, when a contingent of southerners sent north to become part of the national army mutinied. The forces of nationalism – northern Arab nationalism in particular, which drove the independence movement – essentially became, for the south, a replacement for British colonialism.[22] In 1969, Colonel Jaafar Nimeiry came to power in a military coup.[23] The first phase of civil war with the south came to an end in 1972 when Nimeiry negotiated the signing of the Addis Ababa peace agreement, which granted Southern Sudan a measure of autonomy.[24] But by 1982, the government was reneging on the terms of the agreement with a view to enlisting the support of the growing Islamist movement and its political parties. The growth of these parties was largely the result of Western pressure on Sudan to democratize, allowing the political space for these parties to emerge.[25]

The National Islamic Front (NIF) was one of the parties opposed to the peace agreement, feeling that it was an unacceptable ideological compromise. In the 1970s, the NIF and the Muslim Brotherhood rallied substantial electoral support and began to gain influence in the government. This movement culminated in the imposition of Islamic law on the whole of Sudan in 1983, including the south, effectively revoking its autonomy.[26] John Garang, a southerner and Lieutenant Colonel in the national army, was sent south to quell a mutiny, but instead encouraged it, spurring the establishment of the Sudan People's Liberation Army (SPLA).[27] The NIF, led by General Omar Al Bashir,[28] took power in a coup in 1989 and escalated the agendas of "Arabization" and Islamicization of the country.[29] For the northern elite, Arab and Muslim together constituted the essence of what it meant to be "Sudanese."[30] This phase of the war was effectively brought to an end with the signing of the Comprehensive Peace Agreement in 2005.[31]

The onset of the recent war with Darfur is usually recognized as occurring in the Spring of 2003, when the two main rebel movements – the Sudan Liberation Army (SLA) and the Justice and Equality Movement (JEM) – attacked government military bases.[32] In order to stem the tide of rebellion, hardliners in the government chose to repeat the strategy used in Kordofan and Southern Sudan – in which pastoral Arab groups were mobilized into proxy militias to fight the rebels.[33] As in Kordofan and the south, civilians belonging to the same ethnic groups as the rebels were seen as conspirators, and were also attacked in order to weaken what the government saw as the rebels' bases of support. The following is a relatively typical representation of the conflict and its origins in terms of Arab versus African, as portrayed by Western scholars:

Roughly the size of Texas, Darfur . . . is split between two main groups: those who claim black "African" descent and primarily practice sedentary agriculture, and those who claim "Arab" descent and are mostly semi-nomadic livestock herders. As in many ethnic conflicts, the divisions between these two groups are not always neat;

Figure 13.2 Sudan, showing Darfur, and surrounding countries.

Source: Modified from United Nations, *Sudan* [2004], Map No. 3707 Rev. 7/Wikimedia Commons.

many farmers also raise animals, and the African-Arab divide is far from clear. All Sudanese are technically African, Darfurians are uniformly Muslim, and years of intermarriage have narrowed obvious physical differences between "Arabs" and black "Africans." Nonetheless, the cleavage is real, and recent conflicts over resources have only exacerbated it. In dry seasons, land disputes in Darfur between farmers and herders have historically been resolved peacefully. But an extended drought and the encroachment of the desert in the last two decades have made water and arable land much more scarce. Beginning in the mid-1980s, successive governments in Khartoum inflamed matters by supporting and arming the Arab tribes . . . Africans in turn formed self-defense groups, members of which eventually became the first Darfur insurgents to appear in 2003.[34]

While there is nothing particularly inaccurate about this description, there are several problems with it. For example, there is no real explanation of what the distinctions between "African" and "Arab" consist of, if they are "not always neat" and cannot necessarily be pinned to agrarian and pastoral lifestyles[35] or physical appearance. The general sense of this narrative is that although the lines are blurry and the divisions between African and Arab largely false, "the cleavage is real" anyway; but it does not offer explanations of *how* this cleavage is rendered real for those who know and experience it.

By contrast, in more broad-based consumer media narratives – including that all-important source of popular knowledge, *Wikipedia* – the divisions are more clear-cut. Arab nomads are portrayed as thug-like racial supremacists who have a longstanding hatred of the African population of Darfur.[36] As a co-founder of the Enough Project told CNN,

> The Janjaweed are like a grotesque mixture of the mafia and the Ku Klux Klan . . . These guys have a racist ideology that sees the Arab population as the supreme population . . . They're criminal racketeers that have been supported very directly by the government to wage the war against the people of Darfur.[37]

While in one sense this outcry is understandable, in another sense it is loaded with assumptions about race and ideology that may work in a Western context, but simply do not translate in Darfur. The biggest problem, perhaps, is that the statement conceptually "cleanses" Arab Darfuris from their homes; unacknowledged is that these Arab herders *are* people of Darfur. This exclusion is a byproduct of a larger Western narrative that understands Arabs in Sudan as migrants and Africans as indigenous within the context of a "single history of Arabs and 'Arabization' in Sudan."[38] But the reality is not so simple, and the Arab proxy militias, popularly referred to as the *Janjaweed*, are probably the least studied and least understood of all the parties to the Darfur conflict.[39]

Thus the narrative of the Darfur conflict in the popular and scholarly Western imagination became one in which Arab militias supported by the government were committing race-based genocide against African groups competing for increasingly scarce land and natural resources. If this is the case, it should lead us to ask certain questions about the nature of race in this region of Africa. How is race constructed in Sudan? Are racial divisions defined in similar or different ways than in the United States and Europe? What was the nature of social interaction between these groups in the years and generations before violence erupted? Can those mechanisms be reconstructed, or does genocidal intent preclude any possibility of compromise?

RACIAL CONSTRUCTIONS AND SOCIAL PATTERNS IN DARFUR

One challenge in doing purely scholarly research on Darfur is the dearth of ethnological studies of the region. The historical record, both written and oral, is also spotty.[40] In a review of the literature released on Darfur after the most recent crisis erupted, Darfur historian R.S. O'Fahey mentions three important volumes edited by Sudanese scholars, including Darfuris and some social anthropologists. He points out that as such, they possess an "authority, and not least detail, that studies from the outside cannot match."[41]

Unfortunately, two of these volumes are available only in Arabic. However, the third, edited by Ahmed and Manger, is a valuable resource. I will also draw substantially on the detailed report recommended by O'Fahey, which offers many ethnological observations embedded in a detailed account of the contemporary political history of Darfur: Julie Flint and Alex De Waal's *Darfur: A New History of a Long War*. Where they are available, I also draw on academic works available in English by Sudanese scholars, such as Musa Adam Abdul-Jalil, and historical sources that may offer clues, such as M.W. Daly's *Darfur's Sorrow* and Mahmood Mamdani's *Saviors and Survivors*.

The Arab–African dichotomy in Darfur is not non-existent. Rather, the problem lies in assumptions that many Western scholars and activists make about race, including the assumption that "Arab" and "African" refer to "race" at all in Sudan. So what do the categories "Arab" and "African" mean in the local context, and how have these groups interacted over time? Has the Arab/African distinction been consistent in the way it is understood, or is it in flux? This section attempts to provide a more nuanced picture of the Arab–African dichotomy used in the West to frame the conflict.

Abdul-Jalil notes that the Western media have also managed to bring the nomadic–sedentary dichotomy to the forefront, generally identifying the former as Arab and the latter as African. In this representation, the two lifestyles are diametrically opposed, making them naturally hostile as they compete over access to land and other resources. But he demonstrates that this is an oversimplification, and that while the balance is a fragile one, groups that differ in terms of self-identification and lifestyle also rely on each other and have established mechanisms for resolving conflicts before they spiral out of control.[42]

Mamdani delineates important regional distinctions between Arab groups, and points out that there are multiple histories of Arabism in Sudan. While Arab identity in the north came to be characterized by political power, in Darfur it became associated with disenfranchisement: "If Darfur was marginal in Sudan, the Arabs of Darfur were marginal in Darfur."[43] The northern Arab political elite is sedentary, while most Arab groups in Darfur and southwestern Sudan are nomadic and semi-nomadic and live alongside "African" nomads. Failing to differentiate these groups is incorrectly to conflate the powerful and the marginalized.[44]

In northern Darfur, where the climate is drier, nomadic camel-herding Arabs are known as Abbala, and in the more fertile south the Baggara Arabs tend cattle.[45] Between these two regions lies the lush area of the Jebel Marra massif, just west of El Fasher, where cultivators have their orchards and agricultural schemes. These differentiated regions in fact are home to interdependent and symbiotic production systems that require cooperation between pastoralists and farmers.[46] Thus it becomes apparent that there are three main distinctions among those considered "Arab" in Sudan: enormously powerful sedentary Arabs in the north, privileged during Turkiyah rule and favored by the British, and retaining control of the central government in Khartoum after independence; Baggara Arabs in the south with some political power, at least locally; and the Abbala Arabs of northern Darfur, historically rich in culture and wealth, but over time becoming more and more marginalized, both with respect to the center of political power in Khartoum and within Darfur.

So what does it mean to be "Arab" in Darfur? Some Darfurians look to oral histories to determine whether one is Arab; some look to language.[47] Some argue that "Arab" is a cultural determination,[48] that one who "speaks Arabic and partakes in 'Arab' cultural practices is an Arab – regardless of ethnic origin." Darfuri anthropologist Sharif Harir has argued that Arab culture is a facet of all Sudanese identities, Arab and non-Arab, and that the distinction is racial. Mamdani, however, contends that the distinction is political, and that claimed genealogies do not represent reliable historical accounts so much as contemporary political associations. In other words, genealogies do not necessarily determine political associations; rather, political associations determine claimed genealogies.[49]

Ethnic identity had long been socially flexible in Darfur. In the days of the sultanate, Islam was adopted as the state religion, and Islamic legal procedures were adapted to the substantive law and cultural modes of regulating social, ritual, and political relationships of the Fur (Darfur's largest ethnic group).[50] Arabic and Fur were both used in official capacities and in the legal system; "Darfurians – like most Africans – were comfortable with multiple identities."[51]

The Ottoman Turkiyah regime, which lasted until 1884, congealed around an "Arab" identity inclusive of the sedentary groups in the north, but excluding the Arab pastoral groups in the west and south who lay beyond the sphere of political power. In southern Sudan, the response to this forceful Arabist identity was to assert an opposing "African" identity, in reaction to the northern elite's domination of the state and the heavy slave-raiding taking place in the decentralized communities of the south.[52] The sultanate of Dar Fur also played a role in the slave trade – slaves were one of its largest exports.[53]

The Arab–African dichotomy did not emerge to solidify identity in any kind of comparable way in Darfur.[54] Throughout the history of the sultanate, many Darfurians chose to self-identify as Arab, and their numbers increased dramatically at the height of the slave trade as a way of avoiding capture.[55] In the course of migration from West Africa to Darfur, many West Africans "became" Arab. Southern slaves that ended up in Darfur rapidly transformed their identities as well, becoming either Fur or Arab.[56] Over the centuries, Arabs and Africans also intermarried extensively. Identity was flexible through marriage – not because of changes in physical appearance, but through the social function of marriage, which created familial bonds and obligations between families (and different ethnic groups) and necessitated group acceptance of members of other groups.[57] Some historical accounts indicate that both men and women could change their ethnicity by marrying into another group.[58]

Ethnicity was, furthermore, flexible according to economic standing. For example, a Fur whose store of livestock grew large enough, and who adapted a pastoral lifestyle in order to care for them, might consider self-identifying as Zaghawa (a pastoral "African" group) or Arab. Even these identity changes were not always fixed. The same individual might self-identify as, say, Zaghawa in some circumstances and Arab in others, depending on the situation. Conversely, circumstances could also determine how ethnicity was defined. In some cases, language might be the determinant factor; in others, economic status would predominate.[59]

Within the nomadic Baggara and Abbala Arab groups, there are a number of family- and clan-based "tribal" groupings. The Ta'aisha, Beni Halba, Habbaniya, and southern Rizeigat are Baggara Arab groups. These are the four Arab chieftaincies in the south that were granted *hakura* (land grants) under the sultanate that later became recognized as *dars* (homelands), as will be discussed below. The southern Rizeigat are headed by the Madibu family, and are the most powerful Arab group in Darfur. The northern Rizeigat, with no real political ties to the southern Rizeigat, are Abbala, and are divided into the Mahariya, Mahamid, and Eteifat sections.

Historically, the northern Rizeigat were powerful and wealthy as a result of their expertise in cross-desert expeditions, hauling freight with their camels,[60] but they grew marginalized over time. Unlike the Arab Beni Hussein of northern Darfur, the Rizeigat never obtained their own *dar*.[61] The Zaghawa are generally considered an "African" group, although they are mostly camel-herders in the north and have historically enjoyed greater representation and influence than other groups in the central government, including higher echelons like the Security Services. The Meidob are also "African" camel-herding pastoralists.[62]

The marginalization of the Abbala has its roots in precolonial history. Under the Dar Fur sultanate in the middle of the eighteenth century, the authority of the four main Baggara chiefs in the south was recognized through administrative land grants known as *hakura*.[63] Under the *hakura* estate holders were local *shartai* (senior chiefs), who exercised a measure of local autonomy. The *hakura* divisions were not initially based on ethnicity,[64] but rather were administrative estates set up to facilitate tax collection.[65]

However, the estate holders were usually tribal leaders and their claim eventually became recognized as a *dar*, or homeland. Not all land was allocated under *hakura* grants, and so they coexisted with the system of communal land ownership; in this context, groups began to operate under the assumption that their customary rights were as good as *hakura* (and thus, eventually, a *dar*). As Abdul-Jalil describes it, "This development introduced [a] new function to the land other than its economic potential; it became a symbol of group identity."[66] In the northern areas of the sultanate, no *hakura* were granted to the Abbala Rizeigat, who were thus continually compelled to live under the jurisdiction of others.[67] To this day, many Abbala Arabs "explain their involvement in the current conflict in terms of this 250-year-old search for land, granted to the Baggara but denied to them."[68]

In such a diverse region, where porous borders and flexible ethnic identities were realities of everyday life, efficient ways of managing conflict were required.[69] Under the sultanate, most disputes would have been dealt with at the community, family, clan, or tribe level through customary procedures rather than going to district authorities.[70] Customary law and procedure were thus key in containing violence between and within groups, and these included cultural institutions and practices such as blood compensation and conflict mediation by councils of elders. These mechanisms sought to resolve problems without involving the central administration in El Fasher under the sultanate and, later, the British.[71] This fitted neatly with the British aim of administering Darfur at the lowest possible cost. Traditional authorities were left to rule as long as they maintained their loyalty to the British and legitimacy with their people.[72]

After the Sultan of Dar Fur fell out with the British and was ambushed and killed by British forces in 1916,[73] the British began to administer Darfur as part of Sudan.[74] Along with this political and administrative consolidation came, at least theoretically, the process of "becoming Sudanese."[75] During this process, Darfurians "assimilated, almost entirely peacefully and voluntarily, to a Sudanese political, economic and cultural entity based on the River Nile." This peaceful assimilation of Darfuris reflects their comfort with fluid and flexible ethnopolitical identities. It was not only African Darfuris that underwent this transformation, but Arabs as well; "becoming Sudanese" included alterations in the Bedouin lifestyle of these groups, at least in principle, to harmonize with the imposed conventions that came with being ruled by a sedentary political elite from Khartoum.[76]

As with most of their colonies, in the 1920s, the British established a Native Administration, appointed their own "chiefs," and pursued a system of indirect rule.[77] In keeping with the desire to keep the area under control as cheaply as possible, most of the administration of the sultanate, where officials were willing to cooperate, was simply left in place.[78] At the same time, the organization of this system compelled the British to create rigidly defined and largely imaginary "tribal" groupings in an effort to categorize and simplify the complex and ambiguous ethnic identities and politics of Darfur. British colonialism also advocated the idea of "Arab" racial supremacy, based on European understandings of what it meant to be Arab. This referred in particular to ethnic groups in the north. In Darfur they established six paramount chieftaincies headed by Arab *nazirs* (paramount chiefs), none of which went to the Abbala Rizeigat.[79] The identity-based homelands that emerged under the sultanate's *hakura* system were formalized under the British; under both the sultanate and British rule, the Abbala Rizeigat never obtained their own *dar*.[80]

Until the 1980s, in northern Darfur, camel-herders would spend the rainy season and subsequent three months in the desert, where grazing land was shared among the Abbala, Zaghawa, and Meidob. In January, they would move to the south and southwest to water their camels, all herders sharing the same migration routes.[81] People with camels who did not migrate with them traditionally entrusted their animals to the Abbala and Zaghawa herders for the northern migration. "Settled" people also moved seasonally, leaving farmland behind them for nomads to graze their animals, or for semi-sedentary groups to come in and assume residence and management of the land.[82]

The Abbala of northern Darfur would typically live on a *damra* – a piece of land on another group's *dar*, usually Fur or Tunjur, on which they were permitted to reside temporarily as guests.[83] Special arrangements would be made between pastoral and sedentary groups for use of and passage through cultivated land. These groups in fact relied on one another, as nomads depended on sedentary communities for access to land, and sedentary groups relied on nomads to periodically care for their animals.

Problems that arose between pastoralists and farmers would typically be resolved by the Native Administration through reconciliation conferences, with the participation of tribal councils of elders and supported by provincial government authorities. The government would act as mediator during the talks, and then become the guarantor of the agreements that were made at these conferences.[84] This system persisted in large part because the government officials usually hailed from another part of the country, meaning that they had no personal interest in a given conflict and were thus able to act as effective neutral arbiters.[85]

Alongside the *hakura* system and *dars,* the pre-*hakura* communal land tenure system continued to exist as well.[86] Most of the land in rural Darfur was unregistered, so even in the 1970s and 1980s the *hakura/dar* system coexisted with communal ownership. When pastoralists moved south, some would decide to stay. Communal space within a *dar* allowed for their accommodation, even though in theory the *hakura* holder reserved the right to exact taxes from such settlers. It worked in reverse, as well, for cultivators that became pastoral. The result of this was cultural and lingual assimilation, as settlers were permitted to stay so long as they abided by local custom – with Fur becoming Arab or Arab becoming Fur, for example. Thus, ownership of land by a particular group never became an issue.[87]

Until the 1980s, the Native Administration and traditional conflict resolution mechanisms were sufficient to contain violence and mediate conflicts.[88] A leading factor in the deterioration of the ability of the Native Administration to manage conflicts, in addition to the sheer scale of conflicts that began to emerge, was the extreme polarization and *racialization* of divisions that had until that point been largely *social and political*: namely, the division between "African" and "Arab." As Atta El-Battahani put it, "ethnic dichotomies appear to be a consequence of violent conflicts rather than a cause of them."[89]

THE ONSET OF WAR, THE COLLAPSE OF THE SOCIAL ORDER, AND NATIVE ADMINISTRATION

A number of factors surfaced in the 1970s and 1980s that converged to set the stage for conflict. Ecological changes put enormous pressure on the social structures within which different groups shared land and resources, leading to more intense and frequent conflicts. The abolition of the Native Administration and the introduction of ill-conceived land-use laws by the government further reduced the chances of these conflicts being mediated locally. Furthermore, political reforms curtailed the ability of the government to act as a neutral arbiter. At the same time, exogenous ideological propaganda from Libya began to racialize socio-economic identities in new ways, and the appeal to Arab identity resonated with the destitute Abbala of northern Darfur. Finally, factors such as the return of exiled Islamist militants, the increased availability of arms, and Chadian Arab migration influenced the dynamics of these ecological and political changes.

By the 1970s, it was apparent that trouble was looming when some researchers began to notice an "ecological tragedy" in the making.[90] The growing pressure of human and livestock populations on the environment intensified problems such as short- and long-term desertification, as well as decreases in soil quality and land productivity.[91] Accelerated desertification in the 1970s added to the centuries-long desiccation of the Sahara, and resulted in the gradual shifting of the migration routes of Zaghawa, Rizeigat, and other herders southward to include more fertile areas in the Jebel Marra massif.[92] Lack of rainfall in the 1980s led to further ecological stress.[93]

As a result, pastoral groups began to move in larger numbers into areas where cultivators had sophisticated agricultural systems and were accustomed to hosting smaller numbers of guests; "trespassing animals became a constant problem."[94] It should be noted that although the Zaghawa are an "African" group, the conflicts that erupted between Zaghawa pastoralists and Fur farmers in the 1980s were no less intense than those that emerged between Abbala groups and Fur farmers.[95] The eventual categorization of the Zaghawa as African, in the 1990s and beyond, and their eventual alliance with the Fur despite mounting tensions with them, was probably partly due to the Zaghawa–Arab dichotomy in Chad that spilled over into Darfur, and partly due to government attempts to play on Arab insecurities by suggesting that the Zaghawa "had a grand plan to push Arabs from Darfur."[96]

Normally, these problems would be resolved through reconciliation conferences.[97] With new interactions, such as the new movements generated by the ecological stresses of the 1970s and 1980s, would come negotiations between the Native Administration leadership of both or all concerned parties and agreements as to how land could be efficiently shared.[98] The official abolition of the Native Administration in 1971, and the promulgation of land laws by the central government that ignored traditional land-use conventions,[99] meant that traditional mediation mechanisms were weakened and conflicting land tenure systems existed in the same territories.[100]

The drop in land productivity, coupled with population growth, meant that cultivators were compelled to use larger portions of their land, and thus grew less flexible in what they were willing and able to share.[101] Over-farming and over-grazing led to depletion of soil quality and land exhaustion.[102] The increased use of land for cultivation also resulted in the frequent denial of nomads' access to water for their animals and blocking of nomadic migration routes.[103] This meant that pastoralists had to go further afield in their migration routes to avoid cultivated land, making the operation of the pastoral enterprise substantially more expensive.[104] Nomads also increasingly began seeking more autonomous residence on other *dars,* which was a new and unusual development.[105] Normally if a group of pastoralists chose to stay permanently, "they were assimilated in the local political and social systems . . . However, the influx of ethnic groups into the Fur homeland in the 1970s and 1980s was of a completely different character."[106]

The 1970 Unregistered Land Act complicated matters by declaring that all land in Sudan not officially registered with the government would now be public property; and thus was, in a sense, legally up for grabs. The *dar*-less Abbala, inching southward, saw this as an opportunity to lay claim to some of these areas. "Such claims would have been unthinkable in the past when newcomers were expected to remain as 'guests' of the host tribe and abide by its customary rules."[107] Many Zaghawa also came into conflict with cultivator communities because they rejected the authority of the group on whose land they began to encroach.[108] The increased southward migration, furthermore, did not reverse as it normally would.[109] This defiance of customary land tenure systems and the reaction it elicited from cultivating groups led to escalated ethnic violence.[110]

The regional politics of the Sahara played a pivotal role in how events were to unfold in the face of ecological disaster and increased pressures on the Native Administration.

By the early 1970s, Colonel Muammar Al Gaddafi of Libya was on a mission, and that mission was essentially to create a greater pan-Arab/Islamist zone of influence in Africa. This was driven primarily by Gaddafi's perception that African groups were tools of Western imperialists, while Arab groups were the embodiment of Islamic revolution.[111] His aims were framed by the racialization of Arab and African into rigid categories, in ways that were new to the political landscape and cosmos of Darfur.[112] After coming to power, Gaddafi almost immediately began financing and supporting Chadian rebel groups with this ideological aim in mind.[113]

Predictably, within the context of their own Cold War opposition to Gaddafi,[114] Washington and Paris played their parts in these games by supporting Nimeiry (see p. 234) in Sudan and the African leadership in Chad.[115] In 1982, Khartoum-backed Hissène Habré came to power in Chad with the support of the United States and France.[116] Habré's regime was virulently anti-Arab. Arabs were terrorized by the random violence of Zaghawa camel-raiders who apparently operated with impunity, and tens of thousands of Chadian Arabs fled to Darfur, adding to those that had migrated in the 1970s. In fact, the term *Janjaweed* was initially used in reference to Chadian bandits that crossed the border into Darfur, and the Rizeigat who came to help populate government proxy militias generally reject this term as applying to them.[117]

The Chadian Arab presence in Darfur posed an enormous challenge. The refugees brought their animals with them; intrusions into fields led to crop destruction, which was swiftly followed by a steady stream of retaliations and counter-retaliations, including theft of livestock and burning of pasture. Cultivators began blocking Abbala access to grazing land. In addition to the refugees and their livestock, there were the Chadian rebels chased into Darfur by Chadian army and paramilitary forces. Chadian counter-insurgency forces rustled the herds of both Sudanese and Chadian refugee pastoralists.[118]

In 1985, with the overthrow of Nimeiry and the coming to power of the pro-Libya regime of Sadiq Al Mahdi,[119] exiled Islamist militants returned from Libya.[120] The instability and confusion generated during this transition, particularly the government's refusal to manage humanitarian aid distribution during the 1984–1985 drought and its attendant famine, presented Gaddafi with the perfect opportunity effectively to occupy Darfur; Tripoli sent convoys of troops loaded with humanitarian relief and guns to the region.[121]

The post-Nimeiry government became more aggressive in its war against the SPLA, mobilizing the Baggara to fight for the counterinsurgency[122] and arming them with the help of Libya.[123] This was a way to fight the counterinsurgency on the cheap; Khartoum armed the Arab Missiriya and southern Rizeigat and, at first, non-Arab groups as well.[124] These proxy militias were not paid or given salaries, but were permitted to keep whatever they looted from the suspected SPLA sympathizers they attacked – which in practice meant terrorizing villages, rustling cattle, and kidnapping.[125] Libya was seen as a critical partner in the effort to defeat the SPLA.[126]

As the French pursued Libyan-backed Chadian insurgents, the latter moved deeper into Darfur. The insurgents had partnered with the Mahamid section of the Abbala Rizeigat, and in 1988 they collaborated in an attack on Jebel Marra, sparking the first "Arab–Fur" war. While the Mahamid secured arms from Chadian rebels, the Fur sought their own military support from the Habré government. They also began "attacking the Arabs where they were most vulnerable – their animals."[127] The Fur organized their own militias and took to burning pasture land.[128] In response to Chadian Zaghawa camel-raiders, Mahamid leader Musa Hilal and the Abbala he claimed to represent fought back indiscriminately, attacking Zaghawa civilians in Darfur.[129] The conflicts of the 1980s and 1990s led to the establishment of self-defense groups among the Zaghawa, Fur, and Masalit "African" groups. The first Darfuri rebel movements – the Sudan Liberation Army (SLA) and the Justice and Equality Movement (JEM) – would arise out of these self-defense groups.

In the meantime, Darfuris were still trying to use the Native Administration and traditional conflict resolution mechanisms to resolve the increasing number of disputes. In 1989, the Fur governor called a reconciliation conference, which was to be mediated by the Sultan of Dar Masalit. Arab and African groups were in attendance and the leadership on both sides largely stuck to local problems. The resulting reconciliation agreement dealt with issues such as Chadian migration, disarmament, resource management, and a number of other matters.[130] But the agreement was never enforced. To the inability of the local government to act as neutral arbiter and guarantor of the agreement was added, a week after the reconciliation conference, the 1989 NIF coup that brought President Al Bashir to power, in which Khartoum fortified its alliance with Tripoli. This new government had no interest in maintaining peace through the Native Administration.[131]

A few months after the NIF came to power, the government established the Popular Defence Forces (PDF). The PDF streamlined existing Baggara militias into formal paramilitaries to fight the SPLA-led rebellion in the south, and later came to be the vehicle for mobilization of paramilitary forces in Darfur in the western part of the country. Other quasi-formal units included the Popular Police, Nomadic Police, and Border Guards; the latter of which is structured like a regular military and commanded by members of the Sudanese Armed Forces.[132]

This is the heart of Khartoum's counterinsurgency. Outside this sphere are other armed groups that may or may not be driven by ideology, but are certainly driven by the prospect of material gain, along with bandits and common criminals. This latter group represents the traditional understanding of the word *Janjaweed* in Darfur,[133] but it is easy to see how raids by the Nomadic Police in which villages are burned and women raped would, locally, earn the counterinsurgents this title as well. In Western sources, however, it is often unclear which of these groups – government proxy militias, or more informal militias, or common criminals, or all of the above – qualifies as *Janjaweed*.

While the violence suffered by those identified as African cultivators has been widely publicized, violence suffered by Arab groups has hardly been acknowledged. Few attempts have been made to look at atrocities perpetrated against Arabs or what motivated Arabs to become involved with the government's counterinsurgency.[134] In order to rally their support, the government tried to convince Arab traditional leaders that the rebel movements were not anti-government, but anti-Arab. Attacks on Arab nomadic routes and settlements, camel rustling, and attacks on Arab villages did little to allay these intentionally provoked fears.[135]

Despite this, identity remained localized, and even the leaders of some Arab groups that had been attacked by rebels were highly reluctant to mobilize their people for the counterinsurgency. The *nazir* of the Mahariya rejected the government's offer of arms and maintained the neutrality of the group, even in the face of "abusive behaviour of SLA rebels."[136] Many Baggara, by the time the conflict in Darfur began to heat up, were embittered by their experiences as proxy militias for the government in their war with the south. They had not received recognition or compensation for the role they played in fighting the SPLA. The *nazir* of the Beni Halba refused to allow his people to be used in such a way again, and the leadership of the southern Rizeigat cautioned their northern brethren that they "would regret their role in the war."[137]

But in fact, the *dar*-less northern Rizeigat became some of the most willing conscripts, and this was hardly a coincidence. Nearly all Arabs recruited into the counterinsurgency came from groups without *dars*.[138] The Arab groups with *dars,* north and south, "all attempted to remain neutral and most of their tribal leaders refused to participate in the counterinsurgency." Even in northern Darfur, Arab elders were concerned at what appeared to them to be the government's arming of what they perceived as bands of outlaws under their own jurisdictions.[139]

For those mobilized, the motivation appears to be a combination of fear (that the rebel movements aimed to push Arabs out of Darfur) and incentives promised implicitly and explicitly by the government. Such incentives included cash or salaries, land (and by extension, political power), loot (including livestock), vengeance, and personal power.[140] It is unlikely that ideology played any kind of serious role in their motivations to accept the government story of the rebellion and attendant offer of arms.[141]

With new ways of framing race and ethnicity that were more rigidly defined and inherently incompatible, and with the ethnic character that regional politics assumed after decentralization reforms,[142] conflicts between groups grew larger and more explosive. Groups whose identity was primarily locally situated suddenly had to identify themselves as Arab or African in this new, fabricated set of racial-political categories.[143]

For the government, covertly arming ethnic proxy militias began as a matter of expediency, but it became more than that. It enabled the government to shrug off the violence, at the international level, as "tribal fighting" that it was trying to contain, rather than all-out war that it was actively stoking.[144] The manipulation of Arab identity and Arab fears in order to fight the insurgency, however, blew up in the government's face. Once it became clear to international media that the government was arming ethnic militias – Arab militias fighting African rebels – a counterinsurgency with collateral damage suddenly looked a great deal like what activists in the West call genocide.

In large part as a result, the Darfur Peace Agreement (DPA) was pushed forward under enormous international pressure, mostly by the United States, and signed on May 5, 2006 – a rigid deadline that was not extended when JEM and the Abdel-Wahid faction of the SLA voiced serious and warranted objections to certain aspects of the agreement. This unusual inflexibility, particularly in a set of negotiations that lasted only a few months,[145] resulted in the refusal of these two rebel movements to sign the DPA. Rather than spur a new round of negotiations, the deadline was allowed to come and go, and the DPA came into effect as scheduled. Both signatories – the government of Sudan and the Minni Minawi faction of the SLA – are unsupportive of Native Administration authority (reinstated in 1994). Flint and De Waal portray Minawi as being driven primarily by the prospect of political power in the central government. His forces have bullied, imprisoned, and murdered Native Administration chiefs, and generally terrorized anyone opposed to the DPA,[146] under the implementation of which Minawi was appointed as senior advisor to the President.[147]

The government, the proxy militias, and the rebel movements have failed to recognize the importance of traditional leadership in conflict management and reconciliation.[148] Past experience also shows there is a danger of the government manipulating Native Administration leadership for its own ends to create a semblance of local legitimacy.[149] Local leadership and traditional administrations were largely left out of the peace negotiations that led to the DPA, and this has been particularly problematic with regard to Arab Darfuris, who are not represented in the agreement. Many no longer trust the government to represent them.[150] The war devastated not only farming communities, but also pastoral migration routes and nomadic settlements. Yet the DPA dealt with pastoral migration primarily as a security issue, rather than one involving a need for land-use reform and addressing grievances like the lack of social services and development projects. The government's failure to represent Darfuri Arab concerns in the peace negotiations led to a feeling of betrayal among many prominent counterinsurgency commanders.[151]

Many Arab groups also began to recognize that the collapse of the symbiotic relationship between pastoral and agrarian systems was hurting them as much as it was hurting cultivators. Just under a year before the DPA was signed, the Missiriya and the "African" Birgid on whose *dar* they resided came to a reconciliation agreement; the Missiriya leadership then officially withdrew the group from the conflict.[152] Once it became clear that the government was not interested in addressing their grievances, and that they would not be permitted to participate in the peace talks in late 2005, the highest ranks of the counterinsurgency began talking with the rebel movements. This resulted in a number of non-aggression and cooperation pacts, and even a few military alliances.[153] By October 2007, the UN Special Envoy in Sudan declared that the *Janjaweed* "were no longer a discernible group."[154]

CONCLUSION

There are a number of ways in which ethnological investigations such as the one provided here may contribute to genocide studies. A set of more culturally subjective stories about what a given society looks like outside the sphere of violence demonstrates that it is not ancient ethnic hatreds that provide the catalyst for violence. In fact, these narratives often demonstrate that different groups are apt to develop co-dependent or at least cooperative social systems that encourage peaceful coexistence. The stories also reveal ways in which scholars in the West may better understand social dynamics and cultural factors of societies in other regions of the world, such that more effective mechanisms for genocide or conflict prevention, cessation, and recovery can be established. Anthropologists can play a crucial role as cultural interpreters of these processes.

Anthropologists and ethnographers in the field, for example, may establish or be part of early-warning systems.[155] Their expertise in understanding and interpreting local knowledge and metaphors may enable them to flag sentiments and events of concern that might otherwise go undetected. Once prevention measures are being pursued, this same interpretive capacity can be used to help design culturally sensitive interventions that "stress intergroup ties, promote local mechanisms of conflict resolution, and rehumanize potential victim groups."[156]

If Arab and African in the context of Darfur are not racial categories but political ones, as Mamdani argues, is what happened in Darfur really genocide? The distinction matters because political groups are not victim groups under the Genocide Convention. Was the racialization of these categories in the 1970s and 1980s enough to negate local understandings of what it meant to be Arab or African? As Mamdani points out, while the political violence of a counterinsurgency is seen as being part of the "normal" violence of a sovereign state, even if it involves mass violence against civilians, genocide is popularly seen as requiring international intervention to stop it: "Labeling . . . isolates and demonizes the perpetrators of one kind of mass violence and at the same time confers impunity on perpetrators of other mass violence."[157] Sudan itself provides an illustration in that the war with the south – more devastating than Darfur in terms of attacks on civilians,[158] and arguably less ambiguously genocidal – is still referred to as a civil war and not genocide.

Ethnohistorical analysis can contribute to more informed and effective responses to mass violence. Although initially drawing international attention to atrocities taking place, the condemnation of the violence in Darfur as genocide, and the accompanying Western activist movement to stop it, have had a number of worrying consequences. For example, a lack of understanding about the nature of race in Sudan led to a narrative in which Arab supremacists were on a campaign to eliminate Africans from Darfur. In this narrative, the Arabs of Darfur were driven by racial ideology and not genuine grievances. The demonization of Darfuri Arabs in this construction of the conflict was mirrored by a portrayal of the rebel movements as representatives of victims fighting the perpetrators of genocide. The effect of this was not only to entrench the mistaken racialization of these categories, but to obstruct and delay reconciliation.[159] As Flint argues, reconciliation and sustainable peace will not be possible without the participation and inclusion of Darfuri Arabs.[160]

Lack of knowledge can also have seriously detrimental effects on the efforts of the international community to mitigate conflict and help with recovery.[161] Without the qualitative analysis that anthropology can contribute, we run the risk of presenting a "truth" that is not reflective of the experiences of those who have been subject to political violence. Historical and anthropological sources have been used in this chapter primarily to present a picture of how "race" in Sudan is constructed, and to explore how certain mechanisms previously allowed for a measure of peaceful coexistence between groups with competing interests. Such descriptions are important in terms of reconstruction, truth telling, and how narratives of the conflict are constructed in Darfur, in Sudan, and in the West.

The importance of ethnology extends to recovery efforts that deal with economic development, mental health, transitional justice, disarmament, reintegration, and other issues. For example, economic recovery efforts nearly always assume the primacy of cash and employment. But the meaning of economic productivity could be something entirely different in a place like rural Darfur. To take another example, public health interventions that attempt to deal with trauma have to take into account local knowledge of mental illness and expression of symptoms.[162] Systems of exchange that are not cash-based are important to understand when designing disarmament, demobilization, and reintegration (DDR) programs, since these initiatives so often include support packages for disarmed and demobilized ex-combatants.[163] Finally, livestock should not be thought of as being exclusively economically valuable; it should be acknowledged that their social, spiritual, and ritual functions are just as important.[164]

With respect to the case of Darfur presented in this chapter, an ethnohistorical summary of the local understandings of what it means to be Arab or African challenges official narratives of the genocide as told by the international community, the West, and the Sudanese government. In 2005, a meeting of Sudanese academics was held in Addis Ababa in which scholars presented papers and held roundtable discussions on the crisis in Darfur. The papers and documents generated from the discussions were published by the University of Bergen in Norway, with the express purpose of presenting contextual information to fill the knowledge gap on Darfur. The main worry of the authors and participants was that "the tendency to simplify the issues, especially via the international media, may undermine the search for a sustainable solution."[165] Attempting to understand the nature of race and ethnicity, and the ways in which different groups would normally interact and cooperate, is a necessary exercise if we are to determine what kinds of questions we should be asking about this particular context and how potential answers may lead to effective reconstruction and recovery strategies.

NOTES

1 Alexander Laban Hinton, "The Dark Side of Modernity: Toward an Anthropology of Genocide," in Alexander Laban Hinton, ed., *Annihilating Difference: The Anthropology of Genocide* (Berkeley, CA: University of California Press, 2002), p. 2.

2 Abdel Ghaffar M. Ahmed, "The Darfur Crisis: Mapping the Root Causes," in Abdel Ghaffar M. Ahmed and Leif Manger, eds, *Understanding the Crisis in Darfur: Listening to Sudanese Voices* (Bergen: University of Bergen, 2006), p. 11.

3 Although the subject has been growing as a field of academic inquiry, scholars still note the "dearth of literature" on the anthropology of genocide. Kevin Lewis O'Neill and Alexander Laban Hinton, "Genocide, Truth, Memory and Representation: An Introduction," in Alexander Laban Hinton and Kevin Lewis O'Neill, eds, *Genocide: Truth, Memory, and Representation* (Durham, NC: Duke University Press, 2009), p. 9.

4 Hinton, "The Dark Side of Modernity," p. 14.

5 Nils Gilman, *Mandarins of the Future: Modernization Theory in Cold War America* (Baltimore, MD: Johns Hopkins University Press, 2007), p. 27.

6 Matthew E. Falagas, Effie A. Zarkadoulia, and George Samonis, "Arab Science in the Golden Age (750–1258 C.E.) and Today," *The Journal of the Federation of American Societies for Experimental Biology*, 20 (2006), pp. 1581–1586. Also available at: http://www.fasebj.org/cgi/content/full/20/10/1581.

7 Thomas R. Shannon, *An Introduction to the World-System Perspective*, 2nd edn (Boulder, CO: Westview Press, 1996), pp. 3–5.

8 Hinton, "The Dark Side of Modernity," pp. 8–9.

9 Ibid., p. 13; and Alexander Laban Hinton, "Introduction: Genocide and Anthropology," in Alexander Laban Hinton, ed., *Genocide: An Anthropological Reader* (Malden, MA: Blackwell Publishers Ltd., 2002), p. 7.

10 Hinton, "The Dark Side of Modernity," p. 18.

11 Ibid., p. 2.

12 Hinton, "Introduction," p. 8.

13 Universal Declaration of Human Rights, G.A. res. 217A (III), U.N. Doc A/810 at 71 (1948). Available at: http://www1.umn.edu/humanrts/instree/b1udhr.htm.

14 Lori F. Damrosch, Louis Henkin, Richard Crawford Pugh, Oscar Schachter, and Hans Smit, *Basic Documents Supplement to International Law: Cases and Materials*, 4th edn (St. Paul, MN: West Group, 2001), pp. 24–25.

15 Quoted in Hinton, "The Dark Side of Modernity," p. 2.

16 Kenneth Roth, "Foreword," in Alexander Laban Hinton, ed., *Annihilating Difference: The Anthropology of Genocide* (Berkeley, CA: University of California Press, 2002), p. x.

17 See, for example, the landmark Human Rights Watch and Fédération Internationale des Ligues des Droits de L'Homme report by the late Alison Des Forges, *Leave None to Tell the Story: Genocide in Rwanda* (New York: Human Rights Watch, 1999).

18 Roth, "Foreword," p. ix.

19 Hinton, "Introduction," pp. 1–2.

20 Mohamed Suliman, "The Nuba Mountains of Sudan: Resource Access, Violent Conflict, and Identity," in Daniel Buckles, ed., *Cultivating Peace: Conflict and Collaboration in Natural Resource Management* (Ottawa, ON: International Development Research Centre, 1999), p. 205.

21 "Nuba," *African Link,* 4: 1 (1994), p. 13.

22 Jok Madut Jok, *Sudan: Race, Religion, and Violence* (Oxford: Oneworld Publications, 2007), pp. 53–54.

23 M.W. Daly, *Darfur's Sorrow: The Forgotten History of a Humanitarian Disaster* (New York: Cambridge University Press, 2010), pp. 201–202.

24 Jok, *Sudan,* pp. 67–68.

25 Ibid., p. 73.

26 Ibid., pp. 74–76.

27 United States Library of Congress Country Studies, "Sudan," http://lcweb2.loc.gov/frd/cs/.

28 The current President of Sudan.

29 "Darfur–A History," *The New Internationalist,* June 2007, http://www.newint.org/features/2007/06/01/history/.

30 Daly, *Darfur's Sorrow,* p. 14.

31 United Nations Mission in Sudan (UNMIS), "Comprehensive Peace Agreement," http://umis.umissions.org/Portals/UNMIS/Documents/General/cpa-en.pdf.

32 Save Darfur Coalition, "Save Darfur Primer," http://www.savedarfur.org/pages/primer.

33 Julie Flint and Alex De Waal, *Darfur: A New History of a Long War* (New York: Zed Books, 2008), p. 123.

34 Scott Straus, "Darfur and the Genocide Debate," *Foreign Affairs,* 84: 1 (2005), p. 126.

35 This, perhaps, would have been illustrated more forcefully with the example of the Zaghawa, who are primarily camel herders but are considered "African."

36 Wikipedia, "The Darfur Conflict," http://en.wikipedia.org/wiki/War_in_Darfur. The entry is prefaced by the following warnings: "This article needs attention from an expert on the subject . . ." (December 2009), and "This article may need to be rewritten entirely to comply with Wikipedia's quality standards. . ." (January 2010). Subsequently, the level of nuance with which this subject is treated in this article has been significantly improved.

37 John Prendergast, quoted in Rebecca Leung, "Witnessing Genocide in Sudan," CBS News Online, http://www.cbsnews.com/stories/2004/10/08/60minutes/main648277.shtml.

38 Mahmood Mamdani, *Saviors and Survivors: Darfur, Politics, and the War on Terror* (New York: Pantheon Books, 2009), p. 93.

39 Julie Flint, *Beyond 'Janjaweed': Understanding the Militias of Darfur* (Geneva: Small Arms Survey, 2009), p. 15.

40 Daly, *Darfur's Sorrow,* pp. 47–48, and Flint and De Waal, *Darfur,* p. 11.

41 R.S. O'Fahey, "*Umm Kwakiyya* or the Damnation of Darfur," *African Affairs,* 106: 425 (2007), p. 711.

42 Musa Adam Abdul-Jalil, "Nomad-Sedentary Relations and the Question of Land Rights in Darfur: From Complementarity to Conflict," in Richard Rottenburg, ed., *Nomadic-Sedentary Relations and Failing State Institutions in Darfur and Kordofan (Sudan)* (Halle: Orientwissenschaftliches Zentrum, Martin Luther University, 2008), p. 2.

43 Mamdani, *Saviors and Survivors,* pp. 14, 108.

44 Ibid., pp. 103–104.

45 Ibid., pp. 103–104.

46 Mustafa Babiker, "Conflict and Conflict Reduction in Darfur: Some Initial Thoughts," in Abdel Ghaffar M. Ahmed, and Leif Manger, eds, *Understanding the Crisis in Darfur: Listening to Sudanese Voices* (Bergen: University of Bergen, 2006), p. 43.

47 Mamdani, *Saviors and Survivors*, p. 104.

48 Abdul-Jalil, "Land Tenure, Land Use and Inter-Ethnic Conflicts in Darfur," in Ahmed and Manger, eds, *Understanding the Crisis in Darfur*, p. 22.

49 Harir cited in Mamdani, *Saviors and Survivors*, pp. 106–107.

50 R.S. O'Fahey, "Islamic Hegemonies in the Sudan: Sufism, Mahdism and Islamism," in Louis Brenner, ed., *Muslim Identity and Social Change in Sub-Saharan Africa* (Bloomington, IN: Indiana University Press, 1993), p. 24.

51 Flint and De Waal, *Darfur*, p. 2.

52 Alex De Waal, "Who Are the Darfurians? Arab and African Identities, Violence and External Engagement," *African Affairs*, 104 (2005), pp. 185–187.

53 Mamdani, *Saviors and Survivors*, p. 133.

54 De Waal, "Who Are the Darfurians?," pp. 185–187, and O'Fahey, "*Umm Kwakiyya* or the Damnation of Darfur," p. 712.

55 Flint and De Waal, *Darfur*, p. 8.

56 Mamdani, *Saviors and Survivors*, pp. 103–104.

57 Flint and De Waal, *Darfur*, p. 3.

58 Daly, *Darfur's Sorrow*, p. 62.

59 Flint and De Waal, *Darfur*, p. 3.

60 Ibid., p. 8.

61 Flint, *Beyond 'Janjaweed,'* p. 24.

62 Flint and De Waal, *Darfur*, pp. 4, 65.

63 Ibid., p. 8; Abdul-Jalil, "Land Tenure," p. 25.

64 Daly, *Darfur's Sorrow*, pp. 25–26.

65 Less frequently, they were given by the sultanate as personal fiefdoms to certain privileged individuals. Abdul-Jalil, "Land Tenure," pp. 24–25.

66 Ibid., "Land Tenure," pp. 24–25.

67 Flint and De Waal, *Darfur*, p. 8; and Abdul-Jalil, "Land Tenure," p. 25.

68 Flint and De Waal, *Darfur*, p. 8.

69 O'Fahey, "*Umm Kwakiyya* or the Damnation of Darfur," p. 715.

70 Daly, *Darfur's Sorrow*, pp. 105–106.

71 O'Fahey, "*Umm Kwakiyya* or the Damnation of Darfur," p. 715.

72 Daly, *Darfur's Sorrow*, pp. 117–118.

73 Ibid., pp. 96–99 and 109–111; Gérard Prunier, *Darfur: A 21st Century Genocide,* 3rd edn (Ithaca, NY: Cornell University Press, 2008), p. 22; Flint and De Waal, *Darfur*, p. 10.

74 R.S. O'Fahey, "Land, Law and Administration in Darfur," in Marcel Leroy, ed., *Environment and Conflict in Africa: Reflections on Darfur* (Addis Ababa: University for Peace, 1980), p. 253; Flint and De Waal, *Darfur*, p. 10.

75 De Waal, "Who Are the Darfurians?," p. 196. See also Paul Doornbos, "On Becoming Sudanese," in T. Barnett and A. Abdelkarim, eds, *Sudan: State, Capital and Transformation* (London: Croom Helm, 1988), pp. 99–120.

76 Flint and De Waal, *Darfur*, p. 13; De Waal, "Who Are the Darfurians?," p. 196.

77 Flint and De Waal, *Darfur*, p. 11.

78 Daly, *Darfur's Sorrow*, p. 118.

79 Flint and De Waal, *Darfur,* pp. 11, 16–17.

80 Abdul-Jalil, "Land Tenure," p. 25.

81 Flint and De Waal, *Darfur*, pp. 4–5.

82 Ibid., p. 1.

83 Ibid., p. 34.

84 Atta El-Battahani, "Towards a Typology and Periodization Schema of Conflicts in Darfur Region of Sudan," in Ahmed and Manger, eds, *Understanding the Crisis in Darfur*, p. 37.

85 Babiker, "Conflict and Conflict Reduction," p. 45.

86 Abdul-Jalil, "Land Tenure," pp. 25–26.
87 Daly, *Darfur's Sorrow*, p. 215.
88 Ahmed, "The Darfur Crisis," p. 13.
89 El-Battahani, "Towards a Typology," p. 35.
90 O'Fahey, "*Umm Kwakiyya or the Damnation of Dafur*," p. 714; Ahmed, "The Darfur Crisis," p. 11.
91 O'Fahey, "*Umm Kwakiyya or the Damnation of Dafur*," p. 714.
92 Flint and De Waal, *Darfur*, p. 44.
93 Daly, *Darfur's Sorrow*, p. 228.
94 Ahmed, "The Darfur Crisis," p. 15.
95 Ibid., pp. 16–17.
96 Flint, *Beyond 'Janjaweed,'* p. 23.
97 El-Battahani, "Towards a Typology," p. 37.
98 Ahmed, "The Darfur Crisis," pp. 15–16.
99 Ibid., p. 13.
100 Abdul-Jalil, "Land Tenure," p. 26.
101 Ibid., p. 28.
102 Daly, *Darfur's Sorrow,* p. 214.
103 Abdul-Jalil, "Land Tenure," p. 28.
104 Babiker, "Conflict and Conflict Reduction," p. 44.
105 Daly, *Darfur's Sorrow*, p. 215.
106 Babiker, "Conflict and Conflict Reduction," p. 47.
107 Abdul-Jalil, "Land Tenure," p. 26.
108 Ahmed, "The Darfur Crisis," pp. 16–17.
109 Daly, *Darfur's Sorrow*, p. 214.
110 Babiker, "Conflict and Conflict Reduction in Darfur," p. 47.
111 Prunier, *Darfur*, pp. 44–45.
112 Flint and De Waal, *Darfur*, pp. 47–48.
113 Daly, *Darfur's Sorrow*, p. 205.
114 Ibid., p. 219.
115 Flint and De Waal, *Darfur*, p. 48.
116 Alex De Waal, "Chad in the Firing Line," *Index on Censorship*, 35 (2006), pp. 60, 64.
117 Flint and De Waal, *Darfur*, pp. 52–53, 36.
118 Babiker, "Conflict and Conflict Reduction," p. 48.
119 Prunier, *Darfur*, pp. 54–55.
120 Flint and De Waal, *Darfur*, p. 45.
121 Prunier, *Darfur*, p. 55.
122 Flint and De Waal, *Darfur*, p. 23.
123 Prunier, *Darfur*, p. 55.
124 Flint, *Beyond 'Janjaweed,'* p. 23.
125 Ibid., p. 16 and Flint and De Waal, *Darfur*, p. 23.
126 Prunier, *Darfur*, p. 55.
127 Flint and De Waal, *Darfur*, p. 53.
128 Babiker, "Conflict and Conflict Reduction," p. 49.
129 Flint and De Waal, *Darfur*, p. 65.
130 Ibid., p. 55.
131 Ibid., p. 24.
132 Flint, *Beyond 'Janjaweed,'* pp. 16, 22.
133 Ibid., pp. 11, 15.
134 Ibid., p. 14.
135 Ibid., p. 24.
136 Ibid., p. 26.
137 Ibid., pp. 26–27.
138 Abdul-Jalil, "Land Tenure," p. 30.

139 Flint, *Beyond 'Janjaweed,'* pp. 17, 24.
140 Ibid., pp. 15, 21, 24.
141 Ibid., p. 21; Flint and De Waal, *Darfur*, p. 47.
142 Daly, *Darfur's Sorrow*, p. 224.
143 Prunier, *Darfur*, p. 46.
144 Flint and De Waal, *Darfur*, p. 56.
145 This can be compared with two years of negotiations in the civil war in Mozambique and, in Sudan, a peace process with the south that began in 1993, leading to negotiations in 2001 and finally a peace agreement in 2005.
146 According to Flint and De Waal, *Darfur*, p. 234, with regard to Abdel Wahid,

> One of the first things G19 leaders did on driving Minawi's forces out of North Darfur was to mend relations with the Native Administration, consulting with chiefs on the way forward and asking them to reopen the traditional courts Minawi had replaced with 'revolutionary' courts, even for cases involving civilians.

147 Flint, *Beyond 'Janjaweed,'* p. 36.
148 Ahmed, "The Darfur Crisis," p. 17.
149 Babiker, "Conflict and Conflict Reduction," p. 46.
150 Flint, *Beyond 'Janjaweed,'* pp. 11, 30.
151 Ibid., pp. 30–31.
152 Ibid., pp. 29–30.
153 Ibid., pp. 31–32.
154 United Nations Relief Web, "Sudan: Interview – UN Wants Immediate Darfur Ceasefire After Attack," October 3, 2007, http://www.reliefweb.int/rw/RWB.NSF/db900SID/EMAE-77MQBU?OpenDocument.
155 Nancy Scheper-Hughes, "Coming to Our Senses: Anthropology and Genocide," in Hinton, ed., *Annihilating Difference*, p. 348.
156 Hinton, "The Dark Side of Modernity," p. 30.
157 Mamdani, *Saviors and Survivors*, p. 281.
158 Over 2 million civilian deaths resulted from the second phase of civil war with the south, compared to estimates in the hundreds of thousands – usually below 400,000 – in Darfur. United States Department of State, "Background Note: Sudan," June 29, 2010, http://www.state.gov/r/pa/ei/bgn/5424.htm.
159 Mamdani, *Saviors and Survivors*, pp. 7–8.
160 Flint, *Beyond 'Janjaweed,'* p. 13.
161 Ahmed, "The Darfur Crisis," pp. 11–12.
162 See, for example, Judith K. Bass, Paul A. Bolton, and Laura K. Murray, "Do Not Forget Culture When Studying Mental Health," *The Lancet*, 370 (2007), pp. 918–919.
163 See, generally, United Nations, *Integrated Disarmament, Demobilization and Reintegration Standards (IDDRS)*, 2006, http://unddr.org/iddrs/framework.php.
164 See, generally, Sarah E. Hutchinson, *Nuer Dilemmas: Coping with Money, War, and the State* (Berkeley, CA: University of California Press, 1996).
165 Abdel Ghaffar M. Ahmed and Leif Manger, "Short Introduction," in Ahmed and Manger, eds, *Understanding the Crisis in Darfur*, pp. 6–7.

Figure 14.1 Interior of church massacre site at Nyamata, near Kigali, Rwanda.

Source: Courtesy Lydia Hsu.

CHAPTER 14

The Challenge of Social Reconciliation in Rwanda

Identity, justice, and transformation

David J. Simon

> The past is never dead. It's not even past.
> (William Faulkner, *Requiem for a Nun*, 1975)

Faulkner's maxim that the past is not even past bears a particular relevance to civil conflicts, especially genocides. Since the end of the Second World War, 40 percent of terminated conflicts have lapsed back into conflict.[1] Barbara Harff's model for predicting genocide occurrence found "prior genocide" to hold the strongest predictive value of any variable for which she tested.[2]

The key challenge in the wake of a genocide is thus to prevent its recurrence. Authoritarianism and restrictions upon liberty, often the tools of genocide's perpetrators, sometimes gain unexpected legitimacy post-genocide to the extent that they can coax the genocide genie back into the bottle. These are, however, short-term solutions at best. Extended repression may generate alienation and grievances, which in turn may reignite the rhetoric and antipathies of identity politics that underpin new attempts at genocide.

For the longer term, therefore, reconciliation must be the primary objective of post-genocide politics. Reconciliation has two principal forms: a private (or personal) form that refers to the psychology of someone directly involved in a genocide (whether as victim, perpetrator, or bystander); and a public (or social) one that refers to the way in which people relate to one another. While I do not wish to minimize the importance of private reconciliation,[3] I focus here on social reconciliation, as it is in this realm that state policy is most relevant. At a minimum, social reconciliation requires coexistence without a relapse into conflict. More specifically, (social) reconciliation[4] occurs *when individuals and communities formerly associated with opposing sides of a conflict accept as legitimate a shared set of institutions to govern them and guide behavior.* "Institutions" signify formal ones, but also include what North terms "informal constraints and formal rules [and] their enforcement characteristics."[5]

This chapter explores the challenges of social reconciliation in the wake of genocide. In the following section, I discuss some of the reasons why genocide, as opposed to non-genocidal civil conflict, makes reconciliation particularly difficult. I then turn my attention to post-genocide Rwanda, first to offer a case study of the challenges associated with post-genocide reconciliation, and then to examine how two important planks of the Rwandan government's reconciliation platform – the redefinition of identity from "Tutsi" and "Hutu" to "Rwandan" and the advent of *gacaca*, a local and neo-traditional court system – measure up to those challenges.

GENOCIDE AND THE CHALLENGES OF RECONCILIATION

As the statistics on civil war recidivism suggest, post-conflict reconciliation is rarely easy to achieve. Yet the task of reconciliation is most difficult in the wake of genocides such as those we have witnessed in the recent past. Three factors account for this: (1) the scope of killing in a genocide; (2) the geographic integration of targets and groups in whose name perpetrators act; and (3) the importance of the transmission of ideology from elites to non-elites in a genocide.

First, the *de facto* (though not *de jure*) definition of genocide has incorporated an element of mass murder – hundreds of thousands perished in Burundi, Cambodia, and Rwanda. Where conflict has been less deadly, the losses endured in conflict can be easier to overcome. Homesteads can be resettled. Structures can be rebuilt. Family and community members, however, cannot be brought back to life. Recovering from this sort of conflict involves much more than reconstruction. Every death represents a lost world of human relations. Connections to the genocide are direct and personal, and the losses are irreplaceable.

Second, while geographic integration is not a necessary characteristic of genocide, the late twentieth-century genocides in Burundi, Cambodia, and Rwanda – as well as the ethnicized violence in Bosnia, the eastern Democratic Republic of the Congo, and western Sudan – involved populations that were not geographically distinct. In both Burundi and Rwanda, Tutsis and Hutus lived throughout the country. In Cambodia, people of Vietnamese descent may have been concentrated in the southern and eastern portion of the country, but were found throughout, as were the Cham, a mostly Muslim minority group. In neither case was the rate of integration constant across geography, but few if any areas were ethnically homogeneous. This geographic integration makes the task of political integration more difficult in the wake of genocide. Where communities are separated, only institutions that govern cross-boundary matters require mutual respect. Without separation, institutions governing everyday affairs – from dispute resolution to access to resources, and from protections of personal liberty to fora for communal expression – require a commitment from both sides.

Finally, when divisions among elites are transmitted to non-elites, the challenges associated with reconciliation are greater. We have seen just such transmission in recent genocides for two reasons. First, carrying out a genocide is an enormous task that requires the assistance of a substantial portion of the population. In the genocides cited thus far, the number of members of the targeted population was in the hundreds of thousands, if not millions. Neither a state nor a rebel army can muster the weaponry and labor required to complete the task in question without significant mobilization of the non-state (or non-rebel force) population. Even in the Holocaust, where according to Hannah Arendt the machinery of death was channeled through the bureaucracy,[6] many of those executing the Final Solution were not soldiers. Rather, to use Browning's titular phrase, they were "ordinary men."[7] In Rwanda, mobilization turned on the rhetoric of patriotic duty and taxation.[8] Households supplied labor if they could and capital if they could not. The emblematic weapon of choice in Rwanda – the machete – was a staple piece of equipment that almost every household possessed.

Genocide also requires a transfer of the ideology of conflict from elites to non-elites because killers, drawn from society, must overcome norms against killing in order to carry out genocide. In a non-genocidal civil war, soldiers kill one another, which is within the bounds of social expectations. Genocide is different because civilians are necessarily targeted.[9] To induce people – indeed, soldiers and non-soldiers alike – to kill civilians, one needs to create an ideological commitment to do so. The appeals to transcend the norm against killing non-soldiers may invoke logic (if not necessarily the truth), as in the Rwandan use of the phrase *ibyitso* (accomplice) to describe civilian Tutsis. Such appeals may also invoke emotion, as in the Rwandan use of the slur *inyenzi* (cockroach) for Tutsi civilians. In both cases, elites who conceived of a genocidal project created a rhetoric designed to push civilians beyond the normative barriers to killing.

When the ideology of genocide is transferred from elites to non-elites, it becomes difficult to be a bystander (see also Ernesto Verdeja's Chapter 9 in this volume). The rhetoric of genocide implores mass participation in the project. To generate the level of participation necessary to carry out the project, elites seek to remove the possibility of opting out. Bystanders represent labor that remains uncommitted to the project, and may pose a counterweight to the effort to redefine norms. By casting non-participation as unacceptable, the strategy both generates more genocidal inputs and protects the newly constructed norms that render killing acceptable.

The longer-term consequence of these dynamics is that the oppositional ideology becomes a self-fulfilling prophecy. Teach people to hate one another, and the hate becomes self-generating. The perception of adversarial attitudes on the part of the other makes the perceivers adopt adversarial attitudes of their own. In Rwanda, the spiral of opposition itself became part of the rhetoric as the genocidal interim government took flight. It warned Hutu civilians that the ascendant Tutsi-dominated Rwandan Patriotic Front (RPF) was bent on revenge, and that mass exile to Zaire was therefore the only prudent course of action.[10]

Attempts at reconciliation begin, then, with high levels of distrust between groups. Even if "the other" is not viewed in oppositional terms before the genocide, it is afterwards. Constructing institutions (formal and informal) that are mutually acceptable to members of both groups is an intensely difficult task in this environment.

In summary, genocides differ from non-genocides in three respects, all of which make reconciliation more difficult. The irreversible human cost tends to be higher. The opposing sides are often in close proximity to one another. And the execution of the genocide requires popular participation, which is mobilized through the transfer of an ideology of opposition from elites to non-elites. Reconciliation thus cannot be achieved simply by rebuilding what was destroyed. Rather, it requires a social transformation entailing the establishment of many institutions covering a wide range of interactions. In the remainder of the chapter, I turn my attention to Rwanda, both to illustrate the challenges confronting a situation of post-genocide reconciliation and to conceptualize the types of interventions required to address those challenges.

GENOCIDE'S LEGACY IN RWANDA

The challenges of post-genocide reconciliation are particularly acute in contemporary Rwanda. For one thing, the death toll in Rwanda was very high. Although the figure itself is a matter of unfortunate (but probably inevitable) debate,[11] at least half a million people were killed in the genocide of 1994, and perhaps as many as 1.1 million. The precise number is less relevant here than the pervasiveness of the genocide's impact. At least half of the Tutsi population in Rwanda as of 1994 was killed, and subsequent survey research has shown that almost all of the surviving Tutsi population[12] both witnessed a killing and lost at least one family member.[13]

Second, the targets of the genocide (the Tutsi) were geographically interspersed with their executioners (Hutu extremists). While Rwanda included many households of mixed ethnicity and people who did not view themselves in ethnic terms, the essence of the genocide was to pit Hutus against Tutsis as entire ethnic groups. While some areas – like Bugesera, Nyamirambo in Kigali, or Bisesero, for example – featured a higher concentration of Tutsis than other areas (such as Ruhengeri and Gisenyi), there was a mix of Hutus and Tutsis throughout the country. Most importantly, the genocidal campaign penetrated almost every region of the country. In those where it was least virulent, this was due to the timing and geography of the RPF advance, not because of any feature of the ethnic demography.[14] In the wake of the genocide, Tutsi survivors often returned from hiding to their homesteads (or what was left of them), which were surrounded by the abodes and fields of Hutu. The latter may or may not have been active participants in the genocide, but they were certainly exposed to the genocidal propaganda and mobilization efforts. The return of the short-term refugee population from eastern Congo in 1998 added many more Hutus to the environments in which Tutsis had been targeted (and members of the returning population were probably more likely to have participated in the genocide than people still present in Rwanda in August 1994). Finally, with the confessions program and *gacaca* trials, many confessed participants in the genocide – killers among them – are reintegrating into the communities where they once participated in the genocide.[15]

Third, the Rwandan genocide required widespread participation and therefore intense mobilization across the country. The foot-soldiers of the genocide were not the military or the police, but either militia members (such as the notorious *interahamwe*) or civilians without even semi-formal militia membership. At many of the larger massacre sites, such as Murambi and Kibuye, local townspeople formed a human cordon around places where Tutsis had sought refuge.[16] They assisted in *interahamwe*-led attacks on the sites, and formed a deadly rearguard, catching Tutsis who might have evaded the initial assault. In Bugesera, as Jean Hatzfeld memorably recounts,[17] common farmers formed the bulk of the search parties that combed the swamps for Tutsis in hiding, killing on sight those that they found.

Such participation required intense mobilization. The infamous Radio-Télévision Libre des Mille Collines (RTLM) may have been a major medium for doing so, spreading anti-Tutsi propaganda and instructions for its listeners.[18] More direct mobilization occurred along a chain of command originating at the highest levels of the interim government and extending down to local party functionaries. Indeed, Scott Straus argues that such mobilization played a larger role than the radio, noting that the collapse of local resistance to implementation of the genocide in different prefectures throughout the country was correlated with the arrival of Kigali-based authorities – either soldiers or politicians.[19] The case of Jean-Paul Akayesu, the first person convicted of genocide by the International Criminal Tribunal for Rwanda (ICTR) for his leadership role in the commune of Taba, typifies this pattern. Akayesu reportedly offered shelter to Tutsis in communal offices and tried to keep the *interahamwe* at bay before a meeting with the prime minister, the prefect, and other burgomeisters from the prefecture on April 18, 1994, led him to change his approach. He subsequently exhorted a crowd to kill Tutsi residents of the commune (and condoned the rape of Tutsi women by members of the *interahamwe*).[20] In the prefecture of Butare, which generally resisted implementing the genocide for almost two weeks, killing only began once an anti-genocide prefect (who happened to be Tutsi) was disposed of, and a team of outsiders and eager-to-please rivals of the former prefect was installed to implement the genocidal orders.[21]

Importantly for the issue at hand, both forms of mobilization involved a transfer of the ideology of genocide – of the idea that Tutsis were the enemy of the Hutus and had to be killed – from an elite coterie to the (Hutu) public at large. The incentive structure of Rwandan society during the reign of the genocidal regime – from April 6 through to July 3, 1994 – was realigned to reward those who killed, abetted killing, sanctioned killing, and celebrated the idea of killing. Pre-existing institutions which, at least in everyday normal life, had forbidden killing and had demanded that killers be dealt with by the machinery of the state were rendered inoperative. Indeed, the "success" of the genocidal effort – the achievement of such a ghastly death toll – was a joint product of the mobilization of incredibly widespread participation and the rendering passive of any opponent of what would otherwise be activities far outside the bounds of social norms.

If reconciliation occurs, as I have posited above, "when communities formerly associated with opposing sides of a conflict accept as legitimate a shared set of institutions to govern them and guide behavior," these patterns create acute challenges for post-genocide Rwanda. First, in a population where the *communities* in question are nearly all-encompassing (between them, the Tutsi and the Hutu constitute 99 percent of the population),[22] architects of the genocide used ethnicist rhetoric to solidify the once permeable boundaries between the groups. They promoted a conceptualization of a society bifurcated and stratified by the two groups. Their goal was to force all to identify with one group, and only one group, while pitting the two groups against one another.[23] The genocide's masterminds tried to convince *all* Hutus that *all* Tutsis were the enemy. As with any state-directed propaganda effort, they were not entirely successful (although the context of war created an environment that was highly receptive to such propaganda).[24] The propaganda effort also included rhetoric that Hutus who did not buy into the idea were enemies as well. As a result, the death toll of so-called "moderate" Hutu politicians in the first days of the killing may have been on a par with that of Tutsis during that time, and those who resisted genocidal mobilization could themselves become targets. Finally, and perhaps most importantly, the propaganda effort was so pervasive that even those who did not take part in the genocide not only harbored residual suspicions of Tutsis, but feared that any given Tutsi would assume they had taken part. The rhetoric thus created an interpersonal security dilemma. Even if you did not fall for the rhetoric, the prudent course of action was to act as if you did. Even those who deplored the genocide and the ethnicized thinking that engendered it might legitimately worry that everyone else would remain in the spiral of mutual ethnic antipathy.

As noted above, reconciliation efforts post-genocide require first the establishment of *institutions* to mediate group relations. The high level of residential integration among Hutus and Tutsis means that the institutions in question must cover a wide range. Formal institutions must be established to mediate disputes, protect human rights, guarantee property rights, determine the nature of relations between state and society, provide for public goods, and set the rules for allocating private resources.

With respect to each of these institutional tasks, the friction between groups makes institution-building difficult, largely because members of one group will seek assurance that institutional output does not favor other groups. For example, there must be a state-sponsored system of justice to help resolve disputes and provide sanctions for violations of the legal code. (There must also be an institution to create the code in the first place.) Neither side will accept the legitimacy of a court (and police) system if its members believe the system is biased against them. If they reject the legitimacy of the institution, members of the aggrieved group may turn to extra-legal alternatives – first, to the justice institutions themselves; and, second, to the broader institutional framework that established them. In short, they may reject reconciliation itself.

Similarly, institutions that collect and disburse public revenues must also avoid the perception that they are biased in favor of one group or another. Peter Uvin describes pre-genocide Rwanda as one in which the northwestern prefectures most loyal to Juvénal Habyarimana and his MRND party (which happened to be an area in which the Tutsi population was, historically, low) received the highest level of public expenditures (perhaps as much as 60 percent). Uvin surmises that, in the context of widespread poverty and economic insecurity throughout the country, this situation undermined the MRND's legitimacy among Tutsis and non-northwestern Hutus alike.[25] With incomes and poverty levels not yet appreciably different from those of Habyarimana's era,[26] the perception that economic resources are not spread evenly, or that the burden of taxation is not evenly shared, could generate profound disillusionment, and discredit these crucial state institutions.

Second, and perhaps more importantly, reconciliation requires the construction of informal institutions. At best, these should include interpersonal trust and reciprocal good will – the type of social capital that Putnam lionizes.[27] One should bear in mind, however, that "reconciliation," as I have operationally defined it, need not attain so high a standard. At a minimum, the informal institutions required are effectively *negative* norms of interaction, all of which boil down to the simple idea that people from one group should not mistreat people from another. Put differently, "reconciliation" does not mean that Hutus and Tutsis should not harbor ill will toward each other; but rather, that they must not act on it if they do. At the baldest, most minimal level, the requirement turns on the notion of shared *legitimacy*, wherein a norm is mutually observed, if not embraced.

THE EXPERIENCE IN RWANDA

Social reconciliation, according to the definition I have given, entails the construction of mutually accepted institutions. Having described what these institutions entail in general terms, how genocide exacerbates the challenges involved in creating them, and how these challenges apply to Rwanda, I now turn my attention to two prominent elements of the Rwandan approach to reconciliation: the redefinition of ethnicity and identity, and the role of the *gacaca* process. For each, I describe what has transpired, evaluate the results, and consider whether we can expect these features to promote reconciliation. I conclude by considering whether more fundamental structural changes will be necessary for reconciliation to occur.

Reshaping identity

"In Rwanda, there are no 'Hutus' or 'Tutsis'; only 'Rwandans.'"[28] So goes the familiar refrain in contemporary Rwanda. Ending identity politics is perhaps the centerpiece of the current government's approach to reconciliation. The government argues that genocide is at its core about identity politics, and that outlawing identity politics is therefore the first step to ending the possibility of genocide. To erase the possibility of the perception of bias in favor of one group or another, the government calls for the idea of separate "groups" to cease to exist. The first step, welcomed by all, was to eliminate the "ethnicity" designation from Rwandans' identity cards. The redefinition of identity has extended much further, however. Through the implementation of new laws proscribing "division-ism" and "genocidal ideology," the government outlawed public appeals that invoke the labels "Hutu" and "Tutsi." Designed to prevent political entrepreneurs from generating animosity (and mobilizing discriminatory practices and violence) on the basis of ethnic appeals, the measures effectively prevent individuals from recognizing the ethnicity of others in any public setting except genocide commemoration.[29]

In proscribing public ethnic identification, the government is attempting to reshape an informal institution – specifically, the public nature of one's group identity. The "institution" was the norm that one self-identified – and was identified by others – as a "Hutu" or a "Tutsi," and this label was something that others could then use to form an assessment of the individual in question. In short, the labels were used for prejudice, in a value-neutral sense of the word. The government's argument for prohibiting the public use of ethnic identifiers is that value-neutral prejudice too often becomes value-laden – and negative – prejudice. At its extreme, it can become the foundation for genocide.

The policy of eradicating the public use of ethnic identifiers holds promise as an institutional shift. If it were to take hold, the new norm – that Rwandans publicly self-identify and identify other Rwandans strictly as "Rwandan" – would remove the basis of interpersonal prejudice and oppositional mobilization. Publicly, Rwandans-as-Rwandans would view one another as belonging not only to the same country, but to the same destiny. At its farthest reaches, the norm would hold that Rwandans-as-Rwandans are dependent upon one another, thereby engendering social trust.

In this respect, the effort to reframe identities bears some similarity to the wave of nationalism that swept across Africa in the immediate post-independence period (although not in Rwanda, where the foundation of the First Republic lay in an ethnically defined "revolution"). To varying degrees across Africa, nationalism successfully created a new norm of self-identification, such as in Tanzania and Zambia, where national identities that scarcely existed in the early twentieth century are now widely viewed as legitimate (if not always overriding) at the beginning of the twenty-first century.

However, Rwanda features a markedly different context for reshaping identity politics. First, in Tanzania and Zambia, nationalism arose in the course of an anti-colonial struggle. The anti-colonial struggle in Rwanda was itself divided along ethnic lines, and evolved further along them.[30] Second, in both Tanzania and Zambia, the sub-national ethnic categories used for political purposes were those of linguistically and often geographically distinct tribes, with several dozen in each country. In Rwanda, Hutus and Tutsis share a language, are geographically interspersed, and together comprise 99 percent of the population. Thus, whereas in Tanzania and Zambia, a pan-group identity, was necessary to overcome a colonial "enemy" and to create a sense of nation, in Rwanda, neither condition held. The colonial state formed an alliance with an emerging Hutu elite, finding a common "enemy" in the incumbent (and increasingly anti-colonial) Tutsi elite. Identity politics determined how the national pie would be divided up, not whether it could be created (or seized) in the first place. So nationalist identity in Rwanda must now hang on a hook of reconciliation, rather than one of liberation. The catch is that the idea of reconciliation invokes its obvious antecedent – genocide – which is indelibly based upon ethnic distinctions.

In diverging from precedents elsewhere on the continent, the Rwandan effort runs the risk of unintentionally exacerbating the very ethnic divisions it seeks to eliminate. The government's norm-shifting approach to identity politics in public discourse is manifestly at odds with private sentiment. Private attitudes toward identity have inevitably been shaped by the genocide. Hilker finds (and personal experience confirms) that many Rwandans use knowledge about a person's experience during the genocide to reconstruct ideas about others' identities (albeit not entirely accurately).[31] Moreover, the use of what Hilker calls "conceptual" ethnic categories – identities based on stereo-types that were reinforced by genocide-era mobilization – persists, although it might not be publicly expressed. By contrast, "concrete" ethnic categories, which are less prone to stereotyping by virtue of being both more variegated and actually experienced, are not allowed to emerge.[32] In private sentiment, the ethnicity taboo sustains the conceptual at the expense of the concrete. When public information about the "other" is limited, privately held preconceptions remain unchallenged, and the inter-ethnic security dilemma described above could perpetuate itself among individuals. Thus, a Tutsi may regard her Hutu neighbor with suspicion, uncertain what the latter might have done during the genocide. Likewise, a Hutu may view his Tutsi neighbor suspiciously as well, in light of the genocide-era rhetoric that Tutsis will receive favorable treatment compared to Hutus, and will look for evidence of such favoritism.

Moreover, the genocide intimately shapes family narratives. For Tutsis, the genocide shattered family trees. Survivors speak of their families in terms both of those who survived and of those who perished: for example, "X number of my relatives were killed in the genocide." To the inevitable question, "Why?" the most readily available (and usually most accurate) answer is "only because we were Tutsi." Widows, widowers, and orphans represent the case in the extreme. Why is the spouse or parent not with the family? Because s/he was killed and s/he was killed for being Tutsi. Whether tinged with pride, shame, or regret (or some combination of each), a Tutsi survivor's Tutsi-ness cannot help but define who she or he is.

For Hutus as well, the genocide provides a self-definitional point of reference. First, many Hutus were killed during the genocide. Survivors of those killed have as much reason to make reference to the genocide as the reason for the gaps in their family tree as do Tutsi survivors. Second, the genocide disrupted the trajectory of Hutu families as well: some family members fled to Zaire as the genocide came to an end, and most who did stayed there for over two years. Many Hutus – well over 100,000 – were imprisoned for a time, often for several years. While parts of households were absent, individuals left behind may have dealt with hardship (given the loss of labor), or may have made life-changing adjustments, such as remarrying or moving elsewhere. In each case, the genocide is the ultimate reason for the rupture with the pre-1994 status. As before, the quintessential ethnic nature of genocide means that ethnicity is still felt privately, even if expressions of it are forbidden publicly. Furthermore, between 1997 (after the breakup of the Zairean refugee camps) and 2005 (the country-wide onset of *gacaca*), prisons were overcrowded, filled almost exclusively with Hutus accused of genocide-related crimes. There, the ideology of the genocide had a chance to remain intact and perhaps almost as virulent.[33] Although confession was a requirement for release, prisoners were not required to demonstrate remorse or rehabilitation (something that is obviously difficult to assess anyway). As a consequence, ex-prisoners return to their families having been exposed, up close and personally, to some of the worst anti-Tutsi sentiment.

It is worth noting that the government itself is aware of the enduring power of ethnic identification, and has not been reluctant to invoke it. At annual commemorations of the beginning and end of the genocide, regime figures remind Rwandan and foreign audiences of the importance of remembering the genocide. The government's narrative of the genocide does cite the artificiality of ethnic identifiers, suggesting that the opposition between Hutus and Tutsis was a colonial construct, and that genocide would never have happened if Rwanda had been left alone. However, the post-ethnic or pan-ethnic overtones of that narrative are set against a countercurrent of ethnic identification, amounting to an official rebranding of the genocide as "the genocide against the Tutsi."

As a consequence of the vitality of ethnic identity in private, the effort to enforce a non-ethnic version of identity in public must rely on coercion. The state threatens to sanction those who violate the public ban. Politicians must phrase their appeals to the electorate delicately, lest they be barred from running or arrested. This type of enforcement is counterproductive. Punishing public expression is not likely to end the proscribed ideas being held privately. Identity is both intensely personal and valued within a community (especially in a household). A state that seeks to override such notions, that prohibits a person from saying what they feel or believe, is likely to stoke resentment of "the other" as much as reconciliation.

Moreover, the campaign would be disconcerting if it *did* succeed. If notions about identity could be easily changed by state edict in the contemporary political setting, who is to say they could not undergo a similar transformation in a different and more pernicious context? Arguably, the genocide, as well as earlier violent episodes in the 1990s and at the dawn of the independence era (1962), was stoked by state-directed reconceptualizations of identity. In those cases, political entrepreneurs promoted a definition of identity as fundamental to one's destiny, in opposition to other identities. The consequence was identity-based violence – on a local scale in the early instances and on a mass scale in 1994.

Thus, while there is a need for notions of identity to change, the manner in which that change occurs is crucial. Shifts in identity may be less easily reversed when they occur organically – that is, when they begin with the individual, addressing the possibilities and constraints of daily life, and then moving to the public sphere. Redefining identity by fiat may work in the short term, but falls short of an effective long-term fix.

Gacaca and broader transformations

At first glance, judicial institutions offer similar sorts of trade-offs – and therefore similar limits to promoting reconciliation – to those that stem from state efforts to recast identity. In promoting an institution to address post-conflict justice, the state confronts a trade-off between retribution and amnesty. The former pleases surviving victims, while the latter is preferred by those who committed crimes. Because reconciliation depends on both groups, it is difficult to find the common ground necessary to create the shared sense of institutional legitimacy required for reconciliation.

The RPF regime's approach to justice – specifically through the *gacaca* process[34] – illustrates the difficulties involved in forging such a compromise. *Gacaca*, meaning "on the grass"[35] in Kinyarwanda, is an adaptation of the pre-colonial practice of settling disputes in open-air sessions among community elders. The original form involved only adult men, and was employed as a means of resolving (or at least containing) conflicts over land, grazing, intra-household disputes, and contracts.[36] It was not used to adjudicate accusations of murder or rape (nor, as one author notes, theft of cattle).[37] In their contemporary manifestation, *gacaca* tribunals had jurisdiction over "the offences constituting the crime of genocide or crimes against humanity committed between October 1, 1990 and December 31, 1994."[38] An elected panel of judges – *inyangamugayo*, or persons of integrity – presided, and all adults over the age of 18 were required to attend. The assemblies met once a week, and operated in two phases. The first involved open testimony to catalog all allegations of genocide-related crimes in a given cell. This phase produced a case file (or "*dossier*") for each allegation; except in cases of alleged leadership roles, these dossiers were then the basis for community trials in the second phase.[39]

The *gacaca* law also incorporated procedures for submitting confessions.[40] In what amounts to a standardized plea bargain, accused persons who confessed and expressed contrition[41] – either to a *gacaca* assembly in the first phase, or to a public prosecutor – received reduced or commuted sentences, provided that members of the *gacaca* assembly accepted the confession as complete. A standardized schedule of penalties obviated the need for an additional sentencing phase, with the length of the mandated sentence varying only according to the type of crime and whether a confession had been entered and accepted. The conjunction of mandated sentence reductions for those who confessed and a program to convert prison time into community service meant that a functional result of *gacaca* was the release of tens of thousands of admitted genocide offenders back into their community.

If *gacaca* were to contribute directly to the reconciliation process, one might expect it to represent the sort of compromise that generates legitimacy by holding firm to a middle ground acceptable to all sides. In theory, one might hope that those seeking a strong retributive response would appreciate the sentence reductions as a necessary cost of reducing the potential for future conflict, while those seeking more extensive amnesty would likewise appreciate the fundamental insistence on individual responsibility.

In practice, however, *gacaca* seems to have inspired as much disappointment as legitimacy. Philip Gourevitch reports that he "never [met] a survivor who spoke well of gacaca," with most bristling at what they viewed as lies, obfuscation, and incomplete truths offered by perpetrators, as well as decrying the commuted sentences perpetrators effectively received.[42] Buckley-Zistel cites dissatisfaction among both "sides":

> while survivors are more concerned with being eliminated as witnesses, Hutus fear being accused and imprisoned unjustly for social and economic reasons: denouncing, rightly or wrongly, a genocide perpetrator has become a convenient way of getting rid of personal enemies and competitors.[43]

These results speak to the depth of the sentiments held by Rwandese of all stripes. For many – perhaps most – surviving victims, security in post-genocide Rwanda is paramount and non-negotiable. A program that effectively releases felons convicted of genocide-related crimes back into the community is unacceptable. Conversely, a program that insists on extracting a full confession, holding individuals responsible for acts committed within a specific context, is rejected by many Hutus. These positions, moreover, are impervious to compromise. There *is* no middle-ground formula that will please all concerned parties.

If *gacaca* is severely compromised as a vehicle, whether for retributive justice or for reconciliation alone, should we conclude that the exercise has been a failure, or perhaps yet another travesty that the people of Rwanda must overcome? I contend that such a conclusion is not warranted, for it neglects the discursive value of the exercise. As Clark observes, "critics have ignored *gacaca*'s capacity to facilitate restorative justice via meaningful engagement between parties previously in conflict, in the form of communal dialogue and cooperation."[44]

Reconciliation cannot begin without people coming together, and *gacaca* brings them together. Although the narratives that *gacaca* produces support ethnic presuppositions, they provide a starting point for further discourse. Indeed, for ten years prior to *gacaca*, there were few fora in which Tutsis and Hutus could talk to one another, in part because few wanted to. *Gacaca* is important because it created a forum for dialogue – not because there was a demand for one, but because there was a need for one. As Clark reports, once started, some participants in the *gacaca* assemblies began to express appreciation of the forum they offered:

> Many Rwandans discuss at length the importance of public dialogue during *gacaca* hearings and the need for all members of the community to openly discuss their experiences and concerns. A *gacaca* judge in Buhoma district of Ruhengeri province argued, "*Gacaca* is important because it brings everyone together, to talk together. When we come together, we find unity . . . sometimes there is even too much talking and I have to slow people down."[45]

As Clark himself acknowledges, the experience in many – if not most – locales was probably not as positive as the one observed by the judge in Buhoma.[46] Molenaar finds that in two of the *gacaca* jurisdictions he surveyed, what transpired was less a dialogue than repeated articulations of incompatible narratives that failed to engage with one another,[47] leading to "mutual anger about the behavior of the other group."[48] Even in these instances, however, Molenaar acknowledges that "*gacaca* indeed offers a great opportunity for survivors to expose their version of the truth . . . [and] to tell their stories."[49]

In the short run, it is not necessary to establish which narrative or counter-narrative is most authoritative (although the government's approach appears often to make the mistake of trying to do so). The first order of business is to move narratives from the private sphere to the public one, where they can be contested. Part of *gacaca*'s value is that it provided a forum to do precisely that.

Retrospective evaluations of *gacaca* may miss some of these positive features, in part because the cost of the exercise required that it be finite. Although *gacaca* was cheap in international terms,[50] the weekly imposition on Rwandans' freedom and labor allocation bore an economic and civic cost. The discourse I have lauded above would probably have increased in quantity and value over time, although probably not before another shared narrative – of resentment toward the government for making people sit together on the grass for long stretches every week – would have emerged. No one should harbor any illusions that the reconciliation process is coterminous with that of *gacaca*, however. Instead, reconciliation is a process that will extend for decades and span generations. If anything, *gacaca* provides a basis for reconciliation, more than it does a direct contribution to it.

To be sure, if civic empowerment were the sole objective of *gacaca*, one would wish many elements of the process to have been different. In particular, the structurally created ethnicized elements – which effectively prevented Hutus from obtaining justice for acts of violence committed against them – created uneven empowerment. If some *gacaca* participants – most likely Hutu, but possibly Tutsi in some areas – concluded that their participation in *gacaca* was devalued for the benefit of others, the future might portend a more toxic form of public participation in which the public sphere is used to undermine other participants, rather than pursue civic objectives.

CONCLUSION

Gacaca occurred in the context of a society whose history has essentially rendered politics, justice, and peaceful coexistence – that is, the goal of a process of reconciliation – impossible. The challenge, then, for post-genocide Rwanda, and for institutions like *gacaca*, is to make politics possible in a world where it has not been since the genocide, and even before it. *Gacaca* did not complete that task, but it began it. More broadly, genocide reflects a cycle of violence – structural, rhetorical, and ultimately physical – that cannot be broken by simple political trade-offs, or some static notion of "Pareto optimality." If reconciliation includes, as a matter of definition, broadly legitimate institutions, then post-genocide reconciliation most likely requires the creation of new ones.

Forward-looking studies of the Rwandan genocide, its aftermath, and possibilities for reconciliation among Rwandans must therefore address the question of where new institutions will originate, and how they can be constructed effectively. This challenge is far from straightforward. The study of how such institutions arise, although a field unto itself,[51] continues to torment social scientists – as much as it did when scholars of economic and political development crafted modernization theory half a century ago. Scholars of post-genocide reconciliation need to focus attention on where the transformative potential lies to create new institutions, as well as on which interventions are likely to reinforce, perhaps unwittingly, the old ones.

The contrast between state-mandated reconfiguration of identity and state-mandated discourse production is by no means a comprehensive treatment of the question, but it is nonetheless instructive. Efforts to obviate ethnic identifiers in favor of a national one are unlikely to succeed, although not simply because strategies supposedly aimed at implementing that goal may be misused for political purposes. They are unlikely to succeed because they represent an overreach of the state's powers. People know what they think, and government decrees are ill-suited to change their mindsets. On the other hand, *gacaca* represented a more realistic extension of state authority. Although it cannot be counted on to produce local reconciliation right away, it could potentially serve to break down barriers to a larger transformation.

The most important such barrier is the absence of civic citizenship. *Gacaca* lays a foundation for transformation in several respects: by creating a shared experience, providing a forum for discourse, creating an opening for social reintegration, and generating a record of what happened. Each of these provides a particular benefit, either to a specific group or to civil society as a whole, that helps to make civic citizenship possible. Importantly, each does so without sacrificing a core principle – that in order to break the "cycle of impunity" that has bedeviled Rwanda for decades, justice must ascribe individual responsibility for actions taken during the genocide.

Meanwhile, in making a truly civic public sphere more fathomable, the *gacaca* experience complemented another prominent program of Rwanda's post-genocide government: the aggressive effort to bring about an economic transformation. In the short term, *gacaca* has disposed of the backlog of legal cases and helped to reduce the population of previously overcrowded prisons. It thereby freed up labor for production – at a minimum, to help Rwanda feed itself. The commutation of sentences to community service is also a potential economic boon. Though not without administrative costs, the community service program (known as *Travail d'Intérêt Général*, or TIG) provides low-cost labor for small-scale infrastructure projects and service delivery throughout the country.

But it is the longer-term effects that matter most. In mandating participation in the public sphere, *gacaca* presented an opportunity to empower citizens (especially women).[52] While state authority is still largely hegemonic on matters of policy, *gacaca* provided a precedent for self-representation of one's interests, and for accepting the public sphere as a valid one for making claims on one's own behalf. There is thus a subtle parallel between the civic empowerment inherent in *gacaca* and plans to promote economic empowerment by providing a cow to every rural household within the next eight years. In essence, *gacaca* helped to establish the basis of a middle class. It may thus come to be seen as essential for the establishment of *homo civicus* and *homo economicus*

– both of whom may self-identify as Rwandans for organic reasons more firmly rooted than anything mandated by the state.

NOTES

1   William Faulkner, *Requiem for a Nun*, 1975; Virginia Page Fortna, "Does Peacekeeping Keep Peace? International Intervention and the Duration of Peace after Civil War," *International Studies Quarterly*, 48: 2 (2004), p. 272.
2   Barbara Harff, "No Lessons Learned from the Holocaust? Assessing Risks of Genocide and Political Mass Murder since 1955," *American Political Science Review*, 97: 1 (2003), p. 68.
3   For an extensive discussion of the challenges of private reconciliation in Rwanda, see Ervin Staub, "Reconciliation after Genocide, Mass Killing, or Intractable Conflict: Understanding the Roots of Violence, Psychological Recovery, and Steps toward a General Theory," *Political Psychology*, 27: 6 (2006), pp. 867–894.
4   Throughout, for the sake of simplicity, I use the term "reconciliation" to imply "social reconciliation," unless stated otherwise.
5   Douglass C. North, "Institutions and their Consequences for Economic Performance," in Karen Schweers Cook and Margaret Levi, eds, *The Limits of Rationality* (Chicago, IL: University of Chicago Press, 1990), p. 384.
6   See Hannah Arendt, *Eichmann in Jerusalem: A Report on the Banality of Evil* (New York: Penguin Group, 1963).
7   Christopher R. Browning, *Ordinary Men: Reserve Police Battalion 101 and the Final Solution in Poland* (New York: Harper Perennial, 1993).
8   According to Charles Mironko, local officials coerced participation in mobs by invoking patriotic duty and simultaneously threatening immediate penalties if they failed to join in (Charles Mironko, "*Igitero*: Means and Motive in the Rwandan Genocide," *Journal of Genocide Research*, 6: 1 (2004), p. 54.
9   Civilians may be targeted in a non-genocidal civil war as well, but this is not necessarily so. When civilians are targeted, with or without genocidal intent, the challenge of reconciliation is sharpened.
10 According to Human Rights Watch, tens of thousands of revenge killings did apparently take place. If accurate, this would represent a staggeringly high toll, although nothing on the scale that the fleeing genocidal regime alleged. See Human Rights Watch, *Leave None to Tell the Story: Genocide in Rwanda* (New York: Human Rights Watch, 1999), pp. 16, 734.
11 See Human Rights Watch, *Leave None to Tell the Story*, pp. 15–16; Scott Straus, *The Order of Genocide: Race, Power, and War in Rwanda* (Ithaca, NY: Cornell University Press, 2006), p. 51; Helen Hintjens, "Post-Genocide Identity Politics in Rwanda," *Ethnicities*, 8: 1 (2008), p. 23.
12 A parallel figure for the Hutu population is not available, but is likely lower.
13 See Atle Dyregrov, Leila Gupta, Rolf Gjestad, and Eugenie Mukanoheli, "Trauma Exposure and Psychological Reactions to Genocide among Rwandan Children," *Journal of Traumatic Stress*, 13: 1 (2000), p. 6; Susanne Schaal and Thomas Elbert, "Ten Years After the Genocide: Trauma Confrontation and Posttraumatic Stress in Rwandan Adolescents," *Journal of Traumatic Stress*, 19: 1 (2006), p. 99.
14 See Straus, *The Order of Genocide*, p. 85, particularly in reference to the commune of Giti.
15 For a series of personal accounts of reintegration, see Jean Hatzfeld, *The Antelope's Strategy: Living in Rwanda after the Genocide* (New York: Farrar, Straus and Giroux, 2009). See also Phil Clark, "When the Killers Go Home," *Dissent*, 52: 3 (2005), pp. 14–21.
16 African Rights, *"Go. If You Die, Perhaps I Will Live": A Collective Account of Genocide and Survival in Murambi, Gikongoro, April–July 1994* (London: African Rights, 2005).
17 Jean Hatzfeld, *Machete Season: The Killers in Rwanda Speak* (New York: Farrar, Straus and Giroux, 2007).

18 Human Rights Watch, *Leave None to Tell the Story*, pp. 65–71; Alison Des Forges, "Call to Genocide: Radio in Rwanda, 1994," in Allan Thompson, ed., *The Media and the Rwanda Genocide* (London: Pluto Press, 2007), pp. 41–54; African Rights, *"Go,"* pp. 72–79.

19 Straus, *The Order of Genocide*, p. 88.

20 Judgment, *Prosecutor v. Jean-Paul Akayesu*, Case No. ICTR-96-4-T, paras. 186–187, http://www.ictr.org/ENGLISH/cases/Akayesu/judgement/akay001.htm#5, especially paras. 361 and 452.

21 See Human Rights Watch, *Leave None to Tell the Story*, pp. 439–462.

22 Here I must acknowledge that I am committing the (unfortunately standard) sin of neglecting the Batwa population. For the present purposes, it should be acknowledged that the Batwa suffered at the hands of both Hutus and Tutsis, among whom racist attitudes were rampant, with each tending to suspect the Batwa of aiding the other.

23 For more complete descriptions of group-based mobilization, see Helen Hintjens, "When Identity Becomes a Knife: Reflecting on the Genocide in Rwanda," *Ethnicities*, 1: 1 (2001), pp. 25–55; Human Rights Watch, *Leave None to Tell the Story*, pp. 201–204.

24 Straus, *The Order of Genocide*, p. 150.

25 Peter Uvin, *Aiding Violence: The Development Enterprise in Rwanda* (West Hartford, CT: Kumarian Press, 1998), p. 124.

26 See Humberto Lopez and Quentin Wodon, "The Economic Impact of Armed Conflict in Rwanda," *Review of African Economies*, 143: 14 (2005), pp. 586–602.

27 Robert D. Putnam, *Making Democracy Work: Civic Traditions in Modern Italy* (Princeton, NJ: Princeton University Press, 1993), p. 167.

28 See, for example, "The Road Out of Hell – Rwanda since the Genocide," *Economist*, March 27, 2004. For descriptions of the effort to redefine ethnicity, see Hintjens, "When Identity"; Hintjens, "Post-Genocide Identity"; Eugenia Zorbas, "Reconciliation in Post-Genocide Rwanda," *African Legal Studies*, 1: 1 (2004), p. 43; Lars Waldorf, "Revisiting Hotel Rwanda: Genocide Ideology, Reconciliation, and Rescuers," *Journal of Genocide Research*, 11: 1 (2009), p. 104.

29 Indeed, according to Waldorf, "Since 2008, the government has reemphasized ethnicity in describing the 1994 genocide" ("Revisiting Hotel Rwanda," p. 104). Ethnicity can also be invoked in condemning it.

30 This is well chronicled in Mahmoud Mamdani, *When Victims Become Killers: Colonialism, Nativism, and the Genocide in Rwanda* (Princeton, NJ: Princeton University Press, 2001), pp. 114–131.

31 Lyndsay McLean Hilker, "Everyday Ethnicities: Identity and Reconciliation among Rwandan Youth," *Journal of Genocide Research*, 11: 1 (2009), p. 90.

32 Ibid., p. 96.

33 For examples, see Hatzfeld, *The Antelope's Strategy*, pp. 95–96; Carina Tertsakian, *Le Chateau: The Lives of Prisoners in Rwanda* (London: Arves Books, 2008), Chapter 14.

34 I do not examine the formal Rwandan court system or the International Criminal Tribunal for Rwanda (ICTR), which comprise the other two planks of the judicial response to the genocide, in this chapter.

35 Actually, *umugaca* is a particular type of vegetation – a sort of mossy grass on which it is reasonably comfortable to sit. See Arthur Molenaar, *Gacaca: Grassroots Justice after Genocide* (Leiden: African Studies Center, 2005), p. 11.

36 Ibid., p. 25.

37 Noted by several authors, including Waldorf in "Revisiting Hotel Rwanda," p. 59.

38 Organic Law per the *gacaca* website, http://inkiko-*gacaca*.gov.rw/pdf/newlaw.pdf, p. 3.

39 Officially, the processing of case files comprised a phase unto itself, so the trial phase was sometimes referred to as the "third phase."

40 By the end of 2010, the *gacaca* courts had nearly – but not completely – finished their caseload. I nonetheless employ the past tense in this chapter, when referencing the process, as the vast majority of the undertaking had been completed.

41 This provision was added in 2004, after criticism that confessions were being provided without remorse for the act being confessed. See Waldorf, "Revisiting Hotel Rwanda."

42   Philip Gourevitch, "The Life After," *The New Yorker*, 85: 12 (May 4, 2009), pp. 36–49.

43   Susan Buckley-Zistel, "We Are Pretending Peace: Local Memory and the Absence of Social Transformation and Reconciliation in Rwanda," in Phil Clark and Zachary D. Kaufman, eds, *After Genocide: Transitional Justice, Post-Conflict Reconstruction and Reconciliation in Rwanda and Beyond* (New York: Columbia University Press, 2009), p. 137.

44   Phil Clark, "The Rules (and Politics) of Engagement: The Gacaca Courts and Post-Genocide Justice, Healing and Reconciliation in Rwanda," in Clark and Kaufman, eds, *After Genocide*, pp. 297–320. There are some exceptions to the neglect of the prospective value of discourse. See George Packer, "Justice on a Hill," *Dissent*, 49: 1 (2002), pp. 59–72, as well as Molenaar, *Gacaca*.

45   Clark, ibid., p. 312.

46   Ibid., p. 313: "local factors vary greatly among and within different communities"; and p. 314: "engagement is not an inherently positive dynamic."

47   Molenaar, *Gacaca*, pp. 131–134.

48   Ibid., p. 136.

49   Ibid., p. 145.

50   That is, compared to the greater-than-$1 billion bill associated with the ICTR. Hirondelle News Agency, "Cost of ICTR to Reach $1 Billion by End of 2007," May 12, 2006.

51   For some recent examples, see Avner Greif, *Institutions and the Path to the Modern Economy* (New York: Cambridge University Press, 2006); Douglass C. North, John Jacob Wallis, and Barry R. Weingast, *Violence and Social Orders: A Conceptual Framework for Interpreting Recorded Human History* (New York: Cambridge University Press, 2009); and Kathleen Thelen, *Explaining Institutional Change: Ambiguity, Agency, and Power* (New York: Cambridge University Press, 2009).

52   See Clark, "The Rules (and Politics) of Engagement," p. 324.

Selected bibliography

Ahmed, Abdel Ghaffar M., and Manger, Leif (eds), *Understanding the Crisis in Darfur: Listening to Sudanese Voices*. Bergen: University of Bergen, 2006.

Amnesty International, *Democratic Republic of Congo: Mass Rape – Time for Remedies*. London: Amnesty International, 2004, http://www.amnesty.org/en/library/asset/AFR62/018/2004/en/dom-AFR620182004en.html.

Arendt, Hannah, *Eichmann in Jerusalem: A Report on the Banality of Evil*. New York: Penguin Books, 1963.

—— *Eichmann in Jerusalem: A Report on the Banality of Evil*. Revised and enlarged edn. New York: Penguin Books, 1994.

—— *Eichmann in Jerusalem: A Report on the Banality of Evil*. New York: Penguin Books, 2006.

Bakaršić, Kemal, "The Libraries of Sarajevo and the Book that Saved Our Lives." *The New Combat*, Autumn 1994, http://www.newcombat.net/article_thelibraries.html.

Barnett, Victoria, *Bystanders: Conscience and Complicity during the Holocaust*. Westport, CT: Greenwood Press, 1999.

Bauman, Zygmunt, *Modernity and the Holocaust*. Cambridge: Polity Press, 1989.

—— *Modernity and the Holocaust*. Ithaca, NY: Cornell University Press, 1991.

Bledsoe, A.J., *History of Del Norte County, California with a Business Directory and Traveler's Guide*. Eureka, CA: Wyman & Co., 1881.

Bloxham, Donald, and Dirk Moses, A. (eds), *The Oxford Handbook of Genocide Studies*. Oxford: Oxford University Press, 2010.

Carpenter, R. Charli, "Recognizing Gender-Based Violence against Civilian Men and Boys in Conflict Situations." *Security Dialogue*, 37: 1 (2006), pp. 83–103.

Churchill, Ward S., *A Little Matter of Genocide: Holocaust and Denial in the Americas, 1492 to the Present*. San Francisco, CA: City Lights, 1998.

Clark, Phil, and D. Kaufman, Zachary (eds), *After Genocide: Transitional Justice, Post-Conflict Reconstruction and Reconciliation in Rwanda and Beyond*. New York: Columbia University Press, 2009.

Collins, James, *Understanding Tolowa Histories: Western Hegemonies and Native American Responses*. New York: Routledge, 1998.

Corradi, Juan, Weiss Fagen, Patricia, and Garretón, Manuel Antonio, *Fear at the Edge: State Terror and Resistance in Latin America*. Berkeley, CA: University of California Press, 1992.

de Silva, Kingsley M., *A History of Sri Lanka*. Colombo: Vijitha Yapa Publications, 1981.

di Giovanni, Janine, "The Cleanser." *The Guardian*, March 1, 1997.

Donia, Robert J., *Sarajevo: A Biography*. Ann Arbor, MI: The University of Michigan Press, 2006.

Drucker, Philip, "The Tolowa and Their Southwest Oregon Kin." *University of California Publications in American Archaeology and Ethnology*, 36: 4 (1937), pp. 221–300.

Dudink, Stefan, Hagemann, Karen, and Tosh, John (eds), *Masculinities in Politics and War: Gendering Modern History*. Manchester: Manchester University Press, 2004.

Durkheim, Émile, *The Rules of Sociological Method and Selected Texts on Sociology and Its Method*. New York: The Free Press, 1982.

Ehrenreich, Robert, and Cole, Tim, "The Perpetrator-Bystander-Victim Constellation: Rethinking Genocidal Relationships." *Human Organization*, 64: 3 (2005), pp. 213–224.

Feierstein, Daniel, *El genocidio como práctica social. Entre el nazismo y la experiencia argentina*. Buenos Aires: Fondo de Cultura Económica, 2007.

—— "The Dilemma of Wittenberg: Reflections on Tactics and Ethics." *Shofar: Journal of Jewish Studies*, 20: 2 (Winter 2002), pp. 61–68.

Feitlowitz, Marguerite, *A Lexicon of Terror: Argentina and the Legacies of Torture*. New York: Oxford University Press, 1998.

Field, Mark G., "The Health and Demographic Crisis in Post-Soviet Russia: A Two-Phase Development." In Mark G. Field and Judyth L. Twigg (eds), *Russia's Torn Safety Nets: Health and Social Welfare during the Transition*. New York: St. Martin's Press, 2000, pp. 11–42.

Flint, Julie, *Beyond 'Janjaweed': Understanding the Militias of Darfur*. Geneva: Small Arms Survey, 2009.

—— and De Waal, Alex, *Darfur: A Short History of a Long War*. New York: Zed Books, 2005.

—— and De Waal, Alex, *Darfur: A New History of a Long War*. New York: Zed Books, 2008.

Foucault, Michel, *Society Must Be Defended: Lectures at the Collège de France, 1975–1976*. London: Penguin, 2004.

Galtung, Johan, "Violence, Peace, and Peace Research." In Johan Galtung, *Peace: Research – Education – Action*. Copenhagen: Christian Ejlers, 1975.

Geras, Norman, *The Contract of Mutual Indifference: Political Philosophy after the Holocaust*. London: Verso, 1999.

Gerlach, Christian, *Extremely Violent Societies: Mass Violence in the Twentieth-Century World*. Cambridge: Cambridge University Press, 2010.

Gingeras, Ryan, *Sorrowful Shores: Violence, Ethnicity, and the End of the Ottoman Empire, 1912–1923*. Oxford: Oxford University Press, 2009.

Göçek, Fatma Müge, Naimark, Norman, and Suny, Ronald Grigor (eds), *A Question of Genocide: Armenians and Turks at the End of the Ottoman Empire*. New York: Oxford University Press, 2011.

Gould, Richard, "Tolowa." In Robert Heizer (ed.), *Handbook of North American Indians, Vol. VIII*. Washington, DC: Smithsonian, 1978.

Gourevitch, Philip, "The Life After: Fifteen Years after the Genocide in Rwanda, the Reconciliation Defies Expectations." *The New Yorker*, 85: 12 (May 4, 2009).

Hatzfeld, Jean, *The Antelope's Strategy: Living in Rwanda after the Genocide*. New York: Farrar, Straus and Giroux, 2009.

Hintjens, Helen, "Post-Genocide Identity Politics in Rwanda." *Ethnicities*, 8: 1 (2008), pp. 5–41.

Hinton, Alexander Laban, (ed.), *Annihilating Difference: The Anthropology of Genocide*. Berkeley, CA: University of California Press, 2002.

—— *Why Did They Kill? Cambodia in the Shadow of Genocide*. Berkeley, CA: University of California Press, 2005.

Human Rights Watch, *Seeking Justice: The Prosecution of Sexual Violence in the Congo War*. New York: Human Rights Watch, 2005, http://www.hrw.org/en/reports/2005/03/06/seeking-justice.

Jaspers, Karl, *The Question of German Guilt*. Westport, CT: Greenwood Press, 1947.

Jones, Adam (ed.), *Gendercide and Genocide*. Nashville, TN: Vanderbilt University Press, 2004.

—— *Genocide: A Comprehensive Introduction* (2nd edn). London: Routledge, 2010.

Kévorkian, Raymond H., *The Armenian Genocide: A Complete History*. London: I.B. Tauris, 2010.

Koonz, Claudia, *The Nazi Conscience*. Cambridge, MA: Belknap Press, 2003.

La Capra, Dominick, *Representing the Holocaust: History, Theory, Trauma*. Ithaca, NY: Cornell University Press, 1994.

—— *History and Memory after Auschwitz*. Ithaca, NY: Cornell University Press, 1998.

Lemkin, Raphael, *Axis Rule in Occupied Europe: Laws of Occupation, Analysis of Government, Proposals for Redress*. Washington DC: Carnegie Endowment for International Peace, 1944.

—— *Axis Rule in Occupied Europe: Laws of Occupation, Analysis of Government, Proposals for Redress*. Clark, NJ: The Lawbook Exchange, Ltd., 2005.

—— *Axis Rule in Occupied Europe: Laws of Occupation, Analysis of Government, Proposals for Redress*. New York: The Lawbook Exchange, Ltd., 2008.

Levene, Mark, *Genocide in the Age of the Nation State, Vol. 1: The Meaning of Genocide*. London: I.B. Tauris, 2005.

—— *Genocide in the Age of the Nation State, Vol. 2: The Rise of the West and the Coming of Genocide*. London: I.B. Tauris, 2005.

Levinas, Emmanuel, *De otro modo que ser, o más allá de la esencia*. Salamanca: Sígueme, 1987.

Lieberman, Benjamin, *Terrible Fate: Ethnic Cleansing in the Making of Modern Europe*. Chicago, IL: Ivan R. Dee, 2006.

Lindqvist, Sven, *"Exterminate All the Brutes": One Man's Odyssey into the Heart of Darkness and the Origins of European Genocide*. New York: The New Press, 1996.

Mamdani, Mahmood, *Saviors and Survivors: Darfur, Politics, and the War on Terror*. New York: Pantheon Books, 2009.

May, Larry, *Sharing Responsibility*. Chicago, IL: University of Chicago Press, 1992.

Molenaar, Arthur, *Gacaca: Grassroots Justice after Genocide*. Leiden: African Studies Center, 2005.

Muggah, Robert, *Relocation Failures in Sri Lanka: A Short History of Internal Displacement and Resettlement*. London: Zed Books, 2008.

O'Brien, Mary, *The Politics of Reproduction*. Boston, MA: Routledge and Kegan Paul, 1981.

O'Fahey, R.S., *"Umm Kwakiyya or the Damnation of Darfur." African Affairs*, 106: 425 (2007), pp. 709–717.

O'Toole, Laura L., Schiffman, Jessica R., and Kiter Edwards, Margie L. (eds), *Gender Violence: Interdisciplinary Perspectives* (2nd edn). New York: New York University Press, 2007.

Prontzos, Peter, "Collateral Damage: The Human Cost of Structural Violence." In Adam Jones (ed.), *Genocide, War Crimes and the West: History and Complicity*. London: Zed Books, 2004, pp. 299–324.

Reed, Annette, *"Neeyu Nn'ee min' Nngheeyilh Naach'aaghitlhni: Lha't'i Deeni Tr'vmdan' Natlhsri* – Rooted in the Land of our Ancestors, We Are Strong: A Tolowa History". Ph.D. dissertation, University of California at Berkeley, 1999.

Reynolds, Michael, *Shattering Empires: The Clash and Collapse of the Ottoman and Russian Empires 1908–1918*. Princeton, NJ: Princeton University Press, 2011.

Riedlmayer, András, "From the Ashes: The Past and Future of Bosnia's Cultural Heritage." In Maya Shatzmiller (ed.), *Islam and Bosnia: Conflict Resolution and Foreign Policy in Multi-Ethnic States*. Montreal: McGill-Queen's University Press, 2002, pp. 98–135.

Robins, Nicholas A., and Jones, Adam (eds), *Genocides by the Oppressed: Subaltern Genocide in Theory and Practice*. Bloomington, IN: Indiana University Press, 2009.